THE DOWNWAVE

Surviving the Second Great Depression

THE DOWNWAVE
Surviving the Second Great Depression

ROBERT C. BECKMAN

E. P. DUTTON, INC. | NEW YORK

Published in the United States by
E. P. Dutton, Inc., 2 Park Avenue, New York, N.Y. 10016

Library of Congress Catalog Card Number: 83-72664

ISBN: 0-525-24216-3

Published simultaneously in Canada by
Fitzhenry & Whiteside Limited, Toronto

Designed by Nancy Etheredge

10 9 8 7 6 5 4 3 2 1

COBE

First Edition

*This book is dedicated
to those persons whose actions are deflected
by thought along with the few remaining people
of intelligence who are still able to read
and who do sometimes purchase books.
From this nucleus will come the harbingers of
the glorious twenty-first century.*

Contents

Illustrations

Acknowledgments

Although my name appears as the author, a work of this nature could never be undertaken by one individual. There are many sources of toil and inspiration. In the area of toil, my thanks go to John Percival, Anthea Clift, Betty Stabler, Nils Taube, Peter Carvell, Ian Hassett, Nicholas Pine and Ed Victor. The sources of inspiration are many. To name a few, I must cite Dr. Edmund Goldberger, Dr. R. Opie, Professor F. A. Hayek, Ludwig von Mises, Herman Kahn, James Bellini, and the great Jimmy Dines.

—R. C. BECKMAN

Introduction

Pavlov, in his experiments with animals, demonstrated that one of the most certain methods of breaking down the stability of a dog is to give a trained but anxious animal a random series of positive and negative conditioned stimuli. The result initially will produce uncontrollable neurotic excitement which ultimately led to hysterical and submissive behavior.

"'You will, of course, have heard of Pavlov, the Russian medical psychologist?'" asks one of the KGB agents of the hero in Alistair Mac-Lean's espionage novel *The Secret Ways*. The agent then pauses pensively before the prisoners from whom he intends to obtain classified information, then adds: "'With the combination of the very advanced developments we have made in Pavlov's physiological techniques and certain psychological processes that will become apparent to you in the course of time, we can achieve quite incredible results. We can break any human being who has ever lived . . . and break him so that never a scar shows. With the exception of the incurably insane, who are already broken, there are no exceptions. Your stiff-upper-lipped Englishman of fiction . . . and, for all I know, fact . . . will break eventually like everyone else; the efforts of the Americans to train their servicemen to resist what the world so crudely calls brainwashing . . . let us call it rather a reintegration of personality . . . are as pathetic as they are hopeless. We broke Cardinal Mindszenty in eighty-four hours: we can break anyone.'"

Several years ago, around the time of the U-2 episode which was the basis of an international incident between the Soviet Union and the United States, Dr. William Sargent, of the Department of Psychological Medicine at St. Thomas's Hospital, accused the Communists of using Pavlovian tactics as part of a "psychological warfare scheme." In the rantings and utterances of Nikita Khrushchev at the time of the Paris Summit Conference, Dr. Sargent claims that signals were applied to the free-world citizenry with such skill and subtlety "that some of the British and American press and public alike became temporarily just as suggestible as did Pavlov's dogs." In MacLean's spy tale, the purpose of heightening the intended victim's suggestibility is made clear. The subject is reduced to a soporific state where the extraction of information is facilitated . . . and, as MacLean's KGB devil states, " 'We will add what we please to your minds, and that, for you, will also be the truth.' "

Perhaps, unknowingly, it would appear that politicians and spokesmen of American industry were exposing the free-world citizenry to a similar phenomenon during the years 1979–1983, as a result of the strenuous attempts that were made to produce "forecast-feedback" among businessmen and the electorate in the United States at about that time. Attempting to achieve forecast-feedback is the technique by which vested interest organizations will produce a positive forecast in the hope that if enough people believe in the forecast, the forecast will come true.

In other words, if an economic recovery is forecast, the intention is that in preparing for and anticipating this recovery the recovery will be induced.

The global economy entered a recession during the fourth quarter of 1979. The consensus forecast was that the recession would be short and shallow leading to a recovery during the second half of 1980. Businessmen began increasing their inventories in anticipation of the recovery while members of the public assumed they would be able to coast right through the recession without dismay. The recovery never took place. Inventories remained on the shelf. Businessmen began going bankrupt. The fourth quarter of 1980 saw the recession biting deeper.

At the beginning of 1981 the consensus forecast agreed the recession had lasted longer and caused more destruction than originally anticipated but it was unanimously accepted that the recessionary forces had just about spent their force and an economic recovery was likely to be underway by the spring of 1981. Once again, businessmen began increasing their borrowings, boosting their inventories and generally making preparations compatible with the upsurge in demand that was promised. The fourth quarter of 1981 arrived and once again the high hopes were shattered. The economic recovery which all had agreed upon for 1981 had proved to be just as elusive as it had in 1980. The number of corporate bankruptcies mounted. The number of businessmen and individuals who were willing to believe an economic recovery was around the corner shrank.

You can fool all of the people some of the time and some of the people all of the time. The future of many political appointments rests upon this credo. I'm not saying that politicians all get together and say to each other, "What cock-and-bull story can we make up to convince people an economic recovery is on the way?" I feel their motives are far less sinister and are, indeed, well meaning in most cases. Since 1979, the authorities have wanted very badly to convince themselves that an economic recovery is on the way. They succeeded in doing just that . . . convincing themselves very badly. In early 1982, the self-delusions began anew. The consensus forecast called for an economic recovery during the spring of 1982.

We are now about to enter the fourth quarter of 1983. During the course of the year there have been pockets of strength in a few of the economic aggregates of the U.S. economy but nothing which is commensurate with the type of economic activity that we saw during the recovery phases of the 1950s, 1960s and 1970s. There is also strong evidence to suggest the modicum of economic improvement that has developed will soon peter out. In the meantime, the world's capital markets have been behaving like an elevator with a lunatic at the controls, implying that the participants have now reached the state of "hysterical and submissive behavior" observed in Pavlov's dog. Are we to presume from the evidence that the authorities or their behind-the-scenes manipulators are dallying in markets in order to make capitalistic hay of the findings of Dr. Pavlov? The possibility most certainly cannot be ignored. The Swiss banks, through which the international bankers are in the habit of buying their Italian suits, are not obliged to report their activities in Western markets. In recent memory, a group of expatriates from the United Arab Emirates is rumored to have attempted to manipulate gold markets. A supply of Russian gold is believed to have thwarted the attempt, achieving a coup de grace more efficiently than guns and bombs could ever have done. Attempting to manipulate markets in an effort to convince a skeptical electorate that all is well is certainly not a new trick. Richard Witney, president of the New York Stock Exchange, tried it in 1929 when he confidently strolled across the floor of the New York Stock Exchange buying stocks in an effort to convince the madding crowd there was no need for alarm. The point to be made is that the exercise may have allayed the fears of a few over the shorter term but was ultimately futile over the longer term, as has been the case for similar manipulative endeavors throughout history. The inexorable economic forces that permeate the world economy are far too great for any man or group of men to effectively manipulate for any appreciable period. These seemingly invisible forces dominate not only your investment environment but also the social and cultural fiber of society with unfailing rhythmic regularity, in spite of the efforts of individuals, governments and cartels.

The forces that shape our destiny involve change. Yet, in spite of the certainty of change, most individuals are essentially conservative and fear change more than anything else. Most of us spend our lives in a futile effort to halt the passage of time. Most people expect and wish to continue to plod on, clinging to the paths that are familiar to them. It would not be unreasonable to assume that in a bustling and dynamic society such as the United States, people would prefer change. Yet, this is not so. Most changes are generally regarded as regrettable.

Any sane man must truly reconcile himself to the undeniable fact: change is inevitable. The problem is, there is no consensus as to the direction of change. Few people feel any competency in deciding the direction that change will take. We are told that history will repeat itself, that the changes that have gone before will happen again. George Santayana tells us that if we cannot learn from history we are condemned to repeat it. The only thing we can really learn from history is that nobody really ever learns anything from history. The lessons of the past are often denied.

We resort to planning our lives as if the future involved nothing more than a straight line projection of the past until death do us part. We demand higher salaries because we think prices will continue to go up. We have been brainwashed by successive governments into believing that a steadily increasing standard of living is our inalienable right. So we continue to seek higher wages to pay for higher prices which we think will go on rising forever, because they have gone up for as long as we can remember.

Along with this inalienable right to a steady increase in our living standards, we also believe we are entitled to our own homes. It is part of the system. Maybe the best part. Over the past couple of years we've seen the rise in house prices slow and actually fall in some places. We assume this is temporary, because we have been programmed to believe that house prices will always rise. It might be a tighter pinch nowadays to meet those higher mortgage repayments, but buying a house has always been a good investment. There is really no reason to doubt that it wouldn't always be a good investment. We are undeterred by the recent sluggishness of prices. We will buy a house as soon as we can, or move into a bigger and better one.

As businessmen, we have learned to live with inflation. By and large, inflation has been our friend. Interest rates may be high, but as long as we have inflation we will also be able to pass those borrowing costs on to our customers in next year's price increase. If we borrow now to expand, the money we pay back will be worth less than the money we are borrowing. Inflation is not really such a bad deal. The last thing a businessman wants is empty shelves when his customers come into the shop to buy. He will keep those shelves full, no matter what the cost of borrowing. Inflation will always be around to bail him out. After all, it always has been . . . hasn't it?

As consumers, we are determined to live within our means even if we have to borrow to do it. A recent advertising campaign featured the slogan, "Now you can borrow all you need to get completely out of debt." The last thing in the world we want to do is save. We see how inflation has ravaged our life insurance policies. Twenty years ago when we took out a $10,000 endowment policy, we thought $10,000 would see us clear through our retirement. Now we see that $10,000 barely provides the down payment on our vacation home. No, we are certainly not going to get caught in that trap again. We should at least be capable of demonstrating the conditioned response of Pavlov's dog.

Live today, pay tomorrow. Why not? The government will see to it that we don't starve. The unions will protect our jobs. Inflation will protect our businesses. Over the past few years we have learned to keep up with inflation. Some of us have learned how to beat inflation by buying gold, property and other things that have risen in value faster than the rate of inflation. Now that we have learned to handle the problem, the rest of our lives should be serene.

While change is accepted, it is inconceivable that life as we perceive it in the future should be subject to any dramatic change. Our elders spoke of the Great Depression and falling prices. To us, that was just a freak, an on-off social phenomenon that could never happen again. Our programming instructs us that government has learned a great deal since the bad old days. Nothing like that could ever happen in our society. It never has since the dawn of creation . . . which we believe began just after World War II.

Most people are aware that inflation has accelerated at an alarming rate. A frightening rate. But that was only temporary. We now see that inflation is coming down again. It is assumed that the economy will soon return to normal and life will be just the same as it always was. Persistent inflation will disappear along with any other economic discomfort we can conceive. We've had a recession but that recession has enabled the government to bring down the rate of inflation. Large numbers of people have lost their jobs in the process but we still have our jobs; our businesses. The other guy losing his job or going bankrupt is a small price to pay for having our lives returned to the state to which we've become accustomed. All in all, there may be temporary dislocations to our life-style but we are confident that government will be able to solve these problems . . . if not this government, another government. Pavlov lives!

If I were to describe the attitude of the American people during the early 1980s as one of self-satisfied complacency, shared by the majority of the people, I don't think I would be too far off the mark. Adults behave like children and children behave like adults, but this is progress. Government has gone into business while business has gone into government. This is also progress. This is also considered to represent social progress. Uncle Sam has turned the country over to his Big Brother. Everybody loves Ronnie! Anyone who challenges this complacency is coded at best as a radical, at worst a lunatic.

Yet, this complacency must be challenged. The well-being of vast multitudes depends on it. We are now entering a social/political/economic environment of immense and dynamic change. Only a handful of people alive today are able to remotely recollect the nature of such changes. For most of you, the vast changes that are now taking place are totally unrecognized. To many, they will be without precedent. To those whose perspective goes beyond recent history, what is about to happen has happened before.

Changes in our environment which lie beyond the experience of four or five decades are in the course of development. What we are about to relive happens during only two decades in six. Personal life-styles are about to be reversed and the precedents which served us so well during the past few decades will be of no use at all. As I will demonstrate, we are now embarking upon a period where the political, social, cultural and economic structures which we all know so well will be turned upside down. Our personal well-being will rely solely upon adapting to this much-changed social structure. The savers, the cautious, the prudent, the frugal, all who have been penalized during the past four decades, are about to be rewarded. The spenders, the profligates, the borrowers, the gamblers and the speculators, who have been rewarded over the past four decades, could soon be faced with the most horrifying experience of their lives.

Very few people will be prepared for the changes that lie ahead. A large number will be unwilling or unable to accept that such changes could occur. It is a known fact that dynamic changes in our economic and social structure occur because most people never prepare for them, continuing in the future to make the same mistakes they've made in the past. In the following pages, I will try to broaden the horizon of the reader by demonstrating the nature of the likely changes in the life-style of every person on this planet while providing the empirical evidence to support the likelihood of the changes that I foresee. Secondly, I will try to help my readers develop a program and a life-style which is compatible with the alterations that are likely to take place in our social and financial structure.

I am not forecasting either apocalypse or disaster in the years that lie ahead. I am doing nothing more than anticipating change. Those who are unable to adapt to these changes may suffer. Those who are willing and able to make the adjustments will flourish and may find they are about to enter the most rewarding period of their lives.

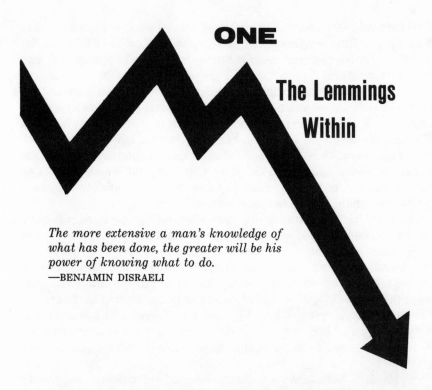

ONE

The Lemmings
Within

*The more extensive a man's knowledge of
what has been done, the greater will be his
power of knowing what to do.*
—BENJAMIN DISRAELI

On they rush, headlong toward the sea. They scramble over one another. They bite and tear, shriek and squeal. Gripped by a seemingly mad compulsion, thousands of lemmings sweep down the countryside, destroying everything in their path, in a wild and frenzied stampede toward the Arctic Ocean in search of food. They cross tundra, rivers, even lakes, at an ever-quickening tempo. Finally they reach the water's edge. Then, something strange happens. The quest for sustenance is abandoned. Their mass migration continues, straight into the sea. Through some mysterious process of natural selection, a few remain on shore. They form the nucleus of the lemming population. And 3.86 years later, they are off again on a ritual of mass suicide.

Theories abound to explain their suicidal behavior. Some say that when food supplies in their natural habitat are exhausted, the lemmings move on, en masse, to new vegetation near the sea. But this does not explain why these furry little creatures self-destruct on arrival. A more definitive theory points to radical hormonal changes. Intense stress induces shifts in their hormone balances. During the cold winter months the circulation system of the lemmings becomes saturated with steroid hormones that act like antifreeze. This allows them to remain active in a climate where most other small animals would hibernate. Overcrowding is believed to be the trigger that releases these steroid hormones into the central nervous system; the hormone level soars to thirty times normal when the lemmings are most numerous. But even this scientifically based theory has flaws. The life cycle of the lemming remains one of the many mysteries of the natural laws governing this planet.

Repetitive patterns of plant and animal behavior are all around us. There is a peak in the population of Canadian snowshoe rabbits averaging about 9.6 years. The life cycle of the lynx, marten, fisher, owl and hawk populations also averages 9.6 years. Each has its own self-correcting, self-destructing life sequence. Thousands of cataloged phenomena in our world occur over and over again with rhythmic regularity for which there is no logical explanation, no known cause. Yet, the knowledge of their existence can be of inestimable value in planning our future.

Knowing what the lemming does and when he's going to do it is quite important . . . especially if you are a farmer tending land in the path of lemming mass migration every 3.86 years.

We humans suffer a major drawback because we have convinced ourselves we are not subject to the same behavior patterns that exist elsewhere in the animal kingdom. Somehow, it seems demeaning that our lives may in some way be preordained by a force or forces still unknown and possibly uncontrollable by human effort. It is anathema to scientists, economists and forecasters to suggest that human life cannot be planned and regulated.

We choose to believe we are the masters of our destiny, and choose leaders who will master this destiny for us. Yet, our chosen leaders, regardless of political persuasion, continue to lead us into war, depression, recession, inflation, conflict and all sorts of economic and social mayhem with unfailing regularity. Inevitably we trail lemminglike behind, albeit unwillingly at times.

Are we so inept at choosing our leaders? The political party that is out of office claims it has the solutions to the problems created by the ruling party. Yet, as soon as it wins power, it too is landed with the same dilemmas, the same lack of solutions as the political party it ousted. Naturally, the dethroned party suddenly acquires the solutions while in opposition.

A gentle flirtation with logic and reason should tell you that if our leaders could prevent high unemployment they would. If they could prevent prices spiraling ever upward or could keep us out of a recession, they would. If they could stamp out social disorder, they would. The idea that government can play a meaningful role in controlling these factors is a politically induced self-delusion.

For centuries, governments the world over have attempted to convince the electorate and themselves that it is possible to produce a social and economic climate devoid of wild gyrations. Their track record speaks for itself. During the last decade we have experienced excruciatingly high unemployment, raging inflation, the dislocation of disinflation, capital market instability across a broad front, and social disorder on an alarming scale, while being faced with global confrontation that could lead to a devastating war.

Whatever a government claims, whatever the sophisticated political and economic tools employed, there remains apparently no answer. We continue to repeat the same mistakes that were made throughout history, failing to learn from our predecessors. Obviously, if governments were able to control the multifarious aspects of our social, political and economic order to the extent claimed, we would never have the type of experiences that are habitually repeated. It should be quite clear that we are not in command of our destiny.

Still, there is no reason to become totally fatalistic. Far from it. There are a great many opportunities for health, wealth and the pursuit of happiness. Most people fail in these pursuits because they are either unable or unwilling to perceive precisely how life on earth actually works. Those who are aware of the lemming tendency can prepare for the problems well in advance.

When Neanderthal man discovered that winter and summer alternated with a degree of regularity, he took a major step forward in adapting to his environment. He was able to anticipate that warm periods were better for hunting, and could store food and fuel for the cold periods to come.

A fur trader, perhaps, should possess a knowledge of the rhythms of the lynx to prepare for the price fluctuations of lynx fur. Then he can maximize his profits.

Anyone with a passion for partridges may find it useful to know that every 22.7 years there is a peak and a trough in the partridge population. By using data accumulated between 1727 and 1909 on an old Bohemian estate in Kramau, Czechoslovakia, partridge hunting can be confined to periods when birds are abundant.

Given the advent of computer technology and the tremendous ability we now have to store and correlate data, we can now make use of other phenomena with regular patterns. In many ways, we plan our lives on the assumption that what has happened before will always happen. Our lifestyle involves working, playing and sleeping, linked to the regular rhythm of a twenty-four-hour day. We purchase a home on a twenty-year mortgage. We are now able to make the repayments on that mortgage. We see little reason why that will not continue. In our twenty-four-hour day, we have many thousands of years of repetition to convince us that night will follow day at reliable and regular intervals. Yet, the data we rely on for our continued ability to repay the mortgage is likely to be far more subjective and far less reliable.

We assume that what has happened for the past five years will happen over the next five years but if we watched the lemming population grow for two years, and assumed the lemming population would always grow, we would be totally unprepared for their mass suicide every 3.86 years.

If we studied the salmon for five years and concluded that since the salmon population had been growing for five years, it would continue to grow forever, we would not be prepared for the peaks and troughs in the salmon population which occur every 9.6 years on average. If our standard of living has been improving for the past fifteen years, it would certainly be wrong to assume it will continue to improve without some evidence to support that assertion. It would be downright dangerous to enter long-term financial commitments by supposing that the future will always follow a straight-line projection of the past without investigating whether it makes sense.

As history has repeatedly demonstrated, the future is certainly not a straight-line projection of the past. Dramatic changes take place at fairly regular intervals. We seem perfectly content to anticipate the future on the basis of an historical repetition of the past. But there is a primary weakness in our ability to anticipate the major changes that are also a part of historical repetition. We seem to resist change.

The economic recession of 1973–1975 was the most severe depression since the 1930s. The recession was believed to be attributable to the oil crisis, and was considered the underlying cause of considerable worldwide dislocation. During the fourth quarter of 1979, the global economy began another recession. In terms of production cutbacks and numbers thrown out of work, this recession has been deeper than that of 1973–1975. But still no one actually believes we could experience a depression on the scale of the 1930s. Guess what? During the 1920s that was exactly how people felt about the depression of the 1880s. During the 1870s they felt the same about the depression of the 1830s. Historical accounts of the 1830s demonstrate conclusively that no one believed that economic dislocation on the same scale as the 1780s could ever happen again.

"Our leaders will save us," "Governments of today know much more than they did in the 1930s and are better equipped to handle the problems," "Economic planning is now far more sophisticated." These are the clichés and platitudes we cling to, to convince ourselves that this time around history will not repeat itself. This time around, we say, we will be spared. We dismiss the repetitions of history as coincidental quirks based on suspect statistics. But what evidence do we have to indicate the situation will be any different this time around? With unfailing regularity, we have had inflations, deflations and depressions, each spread about fifty years apart.

For 200 years and more, our leaders have attempted to smooth the periodic dislocations in our economic lives, and have failed. All the evidence indicates that we are going to continue to fall into the same traps we have fallen into over the past 200 years . . . possibly, thousands of years.

THE LONG WAVES OF ECONOMIC LIFE

There was a depression in the 1780s. There was another in the 1830s. Most of the historical data on these great depressions have faded from memory. Our great-grandfathers could recall the depression of the 1880s during their childhood. Most people alive today need no reminder of the Wall Street crash which precipitated the depression of the 1930s. In the latter part of 1979, one of the most detailed chronicles of that era was published, *The Day the Bubble Burst* by Gordon Thomas and Max Morgan-Witts. It followed J. K. Galbraith's superb account of that time, *The Great Crash, 1929* (1954) and spelled out the horrors of the 1930s. The era will not be forgotten easily . . . at least not until there is another great depression to replace that one. It is likely that the depression of the 1930s will join the historical remnants of the previous depressions when future generations come to reflect on the "Great Depression of the 1980s."

Now, you may have come to the conclusion that what I'm about to deal with is a 1980s replay of the depressions of the 1930s, 1880s, 1830s or 1780s. That we have a depression every fifty years or so and have not had one for the past fifty years may suggest that a depression is now due. But suggestion based on such scant evidence would be of very little interest. This type of oversimplistic treatment of global economic trends has been the nemesis of analysts for decades. The periodic depressions that have occurred since the time of the Industrial Revolution are merely fragments within a much grander design. A depression is just one of the wheels within wheels or circles within spirals that comprise the total framework of socioeconomic life on this planet. There are many, many factors that contribute to our lemminglike pattern of behavior. The sequential repetition of the past offers the vague suggestion that a depression could now be due. A study of our political, social, cultural and economic behavior over the decades takes that value assumption and turns it into conclusions that I believe are inescapable.

Within a time frame of about fifty to sixty years we build a metaphorical beehive and then tear it down again. The building process is a socioeconomic phenomenon that students of long wave economic theory have described as the "upwave." The demolition process is called the "downwave."

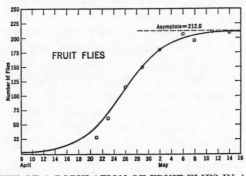

FIGURE 1   GROWTH OF A POPULATION OF FRUIT FLIES IN A BOTTLE

Reprinted from Dewey & Bakin, *Cycles: The Science of Prediction*,
Henry Holt Co.

There are many factors common to the "upwave" that are not common to the "downwave" and vice versa. These factors run the gamut from the number of new inventions in any one year to the length of a woman's skirt. The common denominator that is used for measuring the building process and the tearing down process is raw material prices. Raw material prices are the nucleus of our economic existence and offer the most practical point of departure. During the "upwave" or that period of the long wave cycle when we're building the metaphorical beehive, the prices of wheat, sugar, copper and other raw materials move up at an ever-increasing rate until finally we reach the trend of exponential growth when prices can be seen to be soaring . . . like the growth trend of the lemming population, or the growth of a population of fruit flies in a bottle. Eventually, the point is reached when the rise in prices becomes unsustainable. That point is reached when the limited growth in other aspects of the society leads to a situation where the populace can no longer afford to pay the lofty prices that have been reached, usually as a result of speculative endeavors. What follows is a series of financial crises, a nasty recession and a depression.

When it comes to prices, nothing ever goes up or down in a straight line. Prices fluctuate. There are periods of advance and periods of contraction. During the "upwave" the periods of advance are relatively long and the periods of decline relatively short. The periods of advance are associated with prosperity. The periods of decline are those of recession. During the "upwave," every recession is followed by a much longer and greater recovery. Life continues to get better. Standards of living improve . . . until we reach the point of the "big bang"!

The "big bang" comes when the rate of growth in raw material prices peaks and is then no longer able to rise. The repercussions send shock waves through the economy. The first shock wave takes the form of a recession which is deeper and longer than any experienced during the "upwave." Instead of an ongoing economic recovery following that recession, which people have become accustomed to, there is only an anemic recovery. After the anemic recovery, we then get a financial calamity, like the "Crash of 1929" or the "Panic of 1873." The house of cards comes tumbling down. It's brother-can-you-spare-a-dime time, with the apple sellers appearing on street corners, and often remaining there for possibly a decade.

Essentially, our economic beehive and lemminglike existence takes about fifty to sixty years to rebuild and tear down again. Of that fifty to sixty years, twenty-five to thirty of those years are spent building the beehive. After the beehive is completed we then spend about eight to ten years stagnating. When we finish stagnating we then start tearing the beehive apart so we can start building again . . . fifty to sixty years after we began building in the first place. The building phase is the growth phase. A severe recession is followed by a "secondary recovery." The recession is deeper and longer than any recession that occurred during the growth phase while the "secondary recovery" is shallower than any recovery during the growth phase. When the "secondary recovery" runs its course, a depression ensues. Such is the model of our long wave of economic life.

Figure 2 is an impression of the idealized long wave model. It takes you through the period of rising prices associated with the growth phase along with the minor recessions that take place during that phase. There comes a price peak and a recession worse than anything that happened during the growth phase coinciding with the fall in the growth rate of raw material prices. The recovery phase that follows that deep recession is usually longer than the recovery phases that most had become used to, but it is also much more fragile. At the end of the long, shallow recovery there is a financial catastrophe, unemployment, bankruptcies, general mayhem and depression.

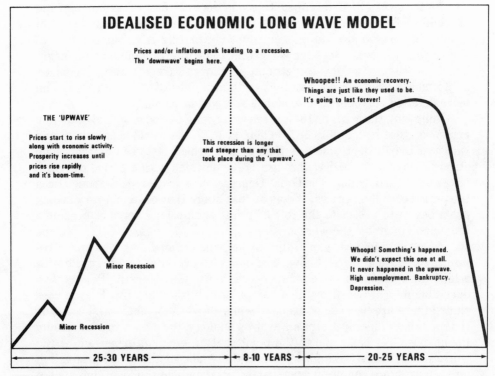

IDEALISED ECONOMIC LONG WAVE MODEL

Prices and/or inflation peak leading to a recession. The 'downwave' begins here.

Whoopee!! An economic recovery. Things are just like they used to be. It's going to last forever!

THE 'UPWAVE'

Prices start to rise slowly along with economic activity. Prosperity increases until prices rise rapidly and it's boom-time.

This recession is longer and steeper than any that took place during the 'upwave'.

Whoops! Something's happened. We didn't expect this one at all. It never happened in the upwave. High unemployment. Bankruptcy. Depression.

Minor Recession

Minor Recession

← 25-30 YEARS → ← 8-10 YEARS → ← 20-25 YEARS →

FIGURE 2

PIONEERS OF THE LONG WAVE

I neither discovered nor invented the long waves of economic life that have just been described. I wish I had. But the discoveries belong to several great economists. Up until the nineteenth century, the existence of a business cycle lasting about three or four years was an accepted phenomenon.

Some economists found business cycles of a longer duration, lasting nine years, each containing segments of shorter business cycles. Joseph Kitchin is associated with the shorter term business cycles, which last from thirty-six to forty months. Clement Juglar is credited with the discovery of the longer term ten- to eleven-year cycle. The first mention of a business cycle of yet longer duration appears in a paper that was published in the *British Railway Register* for 1847. The paper was entitled "Physical Economy" and dealt with the physical laws governing periods of famine and panic. The author was Dr. Hyde Clarke, who claimed the existence of a definable fifty-four-year cycle that began with the crisis of 1793 and ended with the panic of 1847. He saw this period as consisting of five separate Juglar cycles of ten- to eleven-year periods. Each of the Juglar cycles ended with a crisis. There was a crisis in 1804; one in 1815; another in 1826; another in 1837; and finally a megacrisis in 1847.

As far as can be determined, this was the very first observation of the possibility of a long wave sequence of economic behavior. Clarke made no attempt at explaining the phenomenon. He merely felt that the ten- to eleven-year intervals were too consistent to be of a random nature, insisting there must be a "physical economy." Clarke's conjectures were based on nothing more than comparisons of the famines of 1793 and 1847. The more detailed corroborative evidence was yet to come.

Following the crisis of 1847, there was a long period of global economic expansion that lasted until 1873. Then, in 1873, the world became afflicted with the Great Depression of that period, which lasted until 1896. The strong recovery from 1847 through 1873 coincided with a period of rising prices of equal duration. The Great Depression of 1873–1896 coincided with the period of falling prices. It was at that stage that contemporary economists began to associate the role of prices with a long wave of economic life, supplementing the work of Clarke.

According to J. J. van Duijn, in his work, *The Long Wave in Economic Life,* the first well-known economist to correlate the price cycle with a long-term business cycle was Pravus, a Russian Marxist. Pravus produced his long wave theory in a pamphlet published in 1901. Pravus concluded there are periodic occasions "when the development in all areas of the capitalist economy . . . the state of technology, the money market, trade, the colonies . . . has come to the point that an eminent expansion of the world market must take place, lifting the whole of the world production into a new, more comprehensive basis." Pravus held the view that such a period begins with the rejuvenation of capital investment leading to a growth phase. During the growth phase, the normal sequence of shorter business cycles continues. The upswings in the business cycle become progressively stronger while the periods of economic decline are of shorter duration. This process continues until the development potential of the growth phase of the long wave cycle works itself out. Pravus noted that after the growth phase reaches its optimal level of achievement there is an economic crisis which develops into an economic depression. The depression phase is characterized by a slowdown of economic development. The expansionary phases of the cycle, which were strong during the growth phase, suddenly appear much weaker during the depressionary phase. Periods of economic contraction become more prolonged. Levels of output have remained low and have difficulty in recovering. That process continues until the potential for a new growth phase has developed.

Pravus was far less specific than Clarke when it came to the timing of the long wave cycle. He made no reference to cycle turning points other than in the vaguest terms. However, his contribution was significant in terms of developing a path along which other economists could travel. Particularly useful was his outline of the factors which he believed were responsible for the development of the growth phase of economic activity that began in 1896. Pravus cited these factors under three distinct headings: (1) opening up of new markets, (2) increase in gold production and (3) use of electricity.

No doubt the work of Pravus greatly influenced the studies of two Dutch economists, Van Gelderen and De Wolff, who were also Marxists. Van Gelderen was actually the first economist whose work demonstrates the correlation between long periods of price movement and fluctuations in industrial development. Van Gelderen scrutinized price series for a number of Western countries and linked the alteration of long periods of rising and falling prices with fluctuations in general economic activity. Van Gelderen saw a close relationship between the strong upward surge in economic activity of the European and United States economies from 1850 to 1873 and the upswing in wholesale prices. He saw the period of slow economic growth that ended in the early 1890s as characteristic of a period of falling prices. Like Pravus, Van Gelderen considered the year 1896 as the beginning of a new growth phase . . . a new "springtide," as he called it.

Van Gelderen also discovered many more important correlations within the framework of the long wave economic cycle besides the price series. He included production statistics, financial flows, the aggregate level of international trade and statistics involving transport. Van Gelderen decided that for a long wave of expansion to begin, the background must be compatible to a powerful increase in industrial production. He felt that the climate for such a powerful upsurge in production could occur through the opening of new territories or the establishment of new industrial activities which were capable of meeting a need which had hitherto been unsatisfied, such as the invention of the steam engine, electricity or new modes of transportation, like the railroads. As a result of these new markets or new inventions, demand impulses would be propagated through the economy, and growth would begin. Van Gelderen finally decided that the upsurge in production would eventually carry the seeds of its own self-destruction. The rise in prices would lead to increased profitability for businessmen whose inherent greed would lead to final-goods markets being

flooded and overproduction. At the same time, the quest to produce more
and more, faster and faster, leads to raw material shortages which drive
up production costs as the growth phase of the cycle feeds upon itself. It
is not possible for any market in any goods to adapt to price increases in
perpetuity. Eventually, a level in the price cycle is reached which inhibits
demand. The demand for goods decreases. Businessmen who were late in
producing their products and whose production costs are the highest, find
they must adjust prices downward to a level where demand exists, and
often sell at a loss. That means a fall in profitability. The tide turns downward.

Van Gelderen's paper was published in 1913 and was followed by
several other studies on long wave economic behavior. There were three
French works published at just about the same time as Van Gelderen's
paper making reference to long-term price movements, by Aftalion, Lenoir
and Von Tugan-Baranowsky. Lescure published two articles on the long-
term fluctuation of prices. All of these authors supported the findings of
Pravus and Van Gelderen, but none were actually able to offer any explanation for the long wave cycles themselves. The only thing we do know for
certain is that, circa 1913, many eminent economists were beginning to take
the study of long waves of economic behavior very seriously indeed.
Whether or not they envisaged another great depression in twenty years
time is not clear.

De Wolff, a friend of Van Gelderen, approached the study of the long
wave patterns of economic behavior from a slightly different vantage point,
and also came up with the first concrete implications regarding the time
frame of these cycles. Up until the work of De Wolff, most authors were
conspicuously vague on the timing element. De Wolff saw the long wave
economic cycle as subject to an echo effect caused by the reproduction of
obsolescent capital goods. De Wolff's ideas agree with the principles of
Karl Marx, who believed the destruction and replacement of capital goods
was the sole reason for the business cycle, the length of the business cycle
being determined by the average life of machinery and equipment. De
Wolff expanded on the work of Marx by surmising that an even longer term
business cycle existed which was related to the duration of usefulness for
capital goods such as industrial plant, bridges, dams, roads, wharfs, harbors, railroads and the like. De Wolff took the average depreciation rate of
various categories of capital goods and, on the basis of a 2.615 percent
depreciation rate, assumed the average reasonable utility period spanned
thirty-eight years. Eureka! All of the studies up until then unanimously
agreed upon a long wave peak in 1873 and another in 1913. Voila! From
peak to peak, a period of forty years. The trough of the decline that began
in 1873 ended in 1894. The trough of the decline that began in 1913 ended
in 1930. That makes thirty-six years from trough to trough, and an average
of thirty-eight years for the complete cycle. Whoopee! De Wolff had the
answer. Anyone who could master simple arithmetic could now predict the

future. "Therefore, the long wave is determined by the life of the long-living fixed capital," said De Wolff. De Wolff had part of the answer. Not all of it. But we're getting close.

KONDRATIEFF RULES . . . O.K.!

It is the early 1930s. A stooped emaciated figure trudges in chains through the dreary Siberian landscape and disappears into history—one of the hundreds of thousands who die in Stalin's prison camps. His name, Nikolai Dimitryevitch Kondratieff. Occupation: Economist. Crime: Thinking for himself.

Forbes, November 9, 1981

Nikolai Dimitriyevitch Kondratyev—Kondratieff as his pals used to refer to him—was a Russian agricultural economist. He was born in 1892 and became Minister of Food under the provisional government of Alexander Kerensky in May 1917. He also worked with the Agricultural Academy in Moscow. In 1920 he founded the Conjuncture Institute, which he directed until 1928 when he was invited to become a guest of the government at one of the less popular holiday camps in Siberia, which was known for its activities involving salt. The Communists believed his view of the economic developments was heretical and dangerous to the State. His theories were deemed a threat to the Communist regime.

Kondratieff is actually referred to in Solzhenitsyn's *Gulag Archipelago* where the author describes the trial of 200,000 "members" of the Working Peasants Party, which was to have taken place in 1931 but which was canceled by Stalin. From the Working Peasants Party, Stalin separated the more influential spokesmen and simply arrested them. Kondratieff was captured with others and was accused of being the instigator of an illegal "Working Peasants Party." He was then sent to Siberia without a trial where he was sentenced to solitary confinement, became mentally ill and died. No one really knows when he died. The official Soviet *Russian Encyclopedia* refers to Kondratieff's long wave theory in one short sentence. "This theory is wrong and reactionary."

Up until Kondratieff's contribution to the long-term behavior of economic sequences there was a central theme running through the work of the Marxists who were the principal originators of long wave cycle theory. The works of Pravus, Van Gelderen and De Wolff were all inspired by the business cycle of Marx, whose expectation was the total disintegration of the capitalist system. The analysis of Kondratieff implied that a new upswing caused by the dynamics of the capital system was inevitable, and had occurred twice since the beginning of the eighteenth century and was likely to occur again in the 1930s. That's where Kondratieff made his big mistake politically . . . a mistake that cost him his life.

Kondratieff's work began where the studies of the Marxists ended.

While John Maynard Keynes was sipping champagne in well-appointed Edwardian drawing rooms, formulating an economic policy for manipulating the world out of the recession of the 1920s when that recession was coming to an end, Kondratieff was thinking in much grander terms. He was pondering the long sweep of economic history. He questioned the nature of the waves of prosperity and adversity ebbing and flowing in price sequences spanning hundreds of years. These upswings and downswings seemed to persist throughout the period following the Industrial Revolution in all industrialized nations, regardless of political or economic policy. There was even evidence to suggest these long tidal waves of growth and attrition, which appeared with such rhythmic regularity, had been occurring long before the Industrial Revolution. Kondratieff concluded there was a supreme order in our economic affairs, an uncontrollable order involving great tides of economic activity capable of humbling economists and plundering politicians.

Kondratieff based his long wave theory on a study of nineteenth-century price behavior which included interest rates and wages along with raw material prices. He also used a value series comprising the levels of foreign trade, bank deposits and other data which were applicable. These two series were also supplemented by the volume of change in the aggregates. The work of pioneers of long wave behavior before Kondratieff followed set conclusions:

1. A long wave pattern of economic behavior was observable in a relatively fixed time frame.
2. During the second half of the century there could be seen a relationship between the movement of raw material prices and the movement of the economy in general.
3. The long wave of economic behavior was deemed an inherent aspect of the capitalist mode of production, peculiar only to capitalism. Propositions were laid down as to why upswings and downswings took place. One such proposition involved the opening of new trade territories. Another, the effect of new inventions on the production cycle.
4. Compatible with Marxist theory, attempts were made to explain the long wave as an endogenous cyclical process which would ultimately self-destruct and annihilate the capitalist system.

Kondratieff advanced beyond the studies and preconceptions of his predecessors and formulated the most comprehensive long wave economic thesis ever devised. He was convinced that the historical material on the development of economic, social and cultural life on the whole of this planet proved beyond any reasonable doubt that a long-term order of economic behavior did exist and could be used for the purpose of anticipating future economic developments. Kondratieff formulated the following empirical characteristics for the growth phase and the contractionary phase of the long wave patterns of economic behavior he had discovered.

1. During the period of growth, the number of years in which prosperity predominates outnumbers those where contraction is evident by a significant ratio. During the contractionary phase there are far greater numbers of years of decline than years of prosperity.
2. During the years of contraction, agriculture usually suffers a more pronounced stage of depression than other areas of commercial activity.
3. During the years of contraction, there are many new important inventions along with the development of techniques and communication that assist the productive process and ultimately lead to rapid expansion. However, these new innovations are not applied on any meaningful scale until the contractionary phase is complete and the next long-term growth phase begins.
4. At the beginning of the growth phase, gold production usually expands. The world market for goods and services is enlarged by the assimilation of new countries, especially from former protectorates.
5. Wars of major economic significance occur near the end of the contractionary phase of the cycle. Wars of emotive significance usually occur near the end of the growth phase of the cycle.

Kondratieff began developing his long wave hypothesis in the late 1910s and early 1920s. His first published work appeared in 1922 in an article entitled "The World Economy and Its Conditions During and After the War." In 1923, 1924 and 1925 additional papers by Kondratieff appeared, the last of which contained the final results of the Kondratieff hypothesis. A German version of Kondratieff's magnum opus was published in 1926. An abridged version in English later appeared under the title "The Long Wave of Economic Life" in 1935. It was through the English translation of the German paper that Kondratieff's work became known to the Western world. In this paper the rhythmic sequences of economic activity for the previous 130 years appeared for the first time. Kondratieff said:

> The upswing in the first long wave embraces the period from 1789 to 1814, i.e. 25 years; its decline begins in 1814 and ends in 1849, a period of 35 years. The cycle is therefore completed in 60 years. The rise in the second wave begins in 1849 and ends in 1873, lasting 24 years. The decline of the second wave begins in 1873 and ends in 1896, a period of 23 years. The length of the second wave is 47 years. The upward movement of the third wave begins in 1896 and ends in 1920, its duration 24 years. The decline of the wave, according to all data, begins in 1920.

Kondratieff never lived to see the startling conclusion to this third wave. The price cycle actually peaked in 1920. It was followed in due course by a downwave lasting twenty years, involving the Great Depression, and the completion of another long wave lasting forty-four years. Our current position within the long wave cycle is just about where it was when Kondratieff's work was terminated about fifty years ago.

I have applied the idealized long wave economic model to our global

FOUR LONG WAVE CYCLES 1780 - 2000

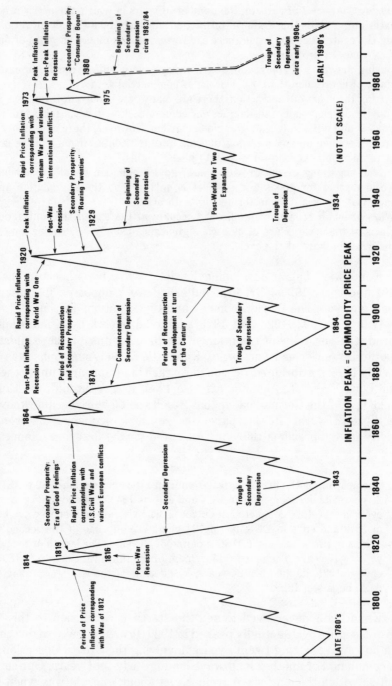

FIGURE 3

experience over the past 200 years. Figure 3 shows three distinct repetitions of the long wave tendency from 1789 to 1940. The horizontal grid on the chart is a time scale. The vertical grid on the chart represents a raw material price scale.

My intention is not to cloud your mind with facts and figures, but to demonstrate the consistency of the long wave economic model. Its shape and the timing of the peaks and troughs correspond to peaks and troughs in the price indices of several countries. This is not peculiar to the United States. The crests and troughs of the waves do not repeat themselves at any precise time. The actual highs and lows of the price level are distorted. There is, however, a marked tendency for periods of extreme strength to follow each other at forty-five to fifty-five year intervals. Such time spans are separated by periods of weakness. Although the precise time relationships may be somewhat obscure, in no way does this undermine the forecasting value of this phenomenon.

THE FIRST CYCLE, 1783–1843

Due to the lack of availability of data and the inconsistency of that data that is available, it is difficult to include the period to the late eighteenth century as part of the long wave economic cycle schema. We do know that the period of 1750–1760 was a time of great economic activity. It was during that phase that the full impact of the Industrial Revolution was being felt in England. There were many rapid changes in life-style and throughout the various branches of industry there was a general tendency to mechanize and substitute machines for human skills. The general growth in economic activity could best be seen in the textile industry. Until the invention of the spinning machine in 1765, the textile industry in England employed hundreds of thousands of cottage workers. The spinning machine meant that productivity was increased by 1000 percent which put an end to manual spinning. At the same time the market was flooded with cheap yarn. Manual spinning limited production. With mechanized spinning production exploded, a typical characteristic of the growth phase of the cycle. Other industries, such as mining, metal work and machine manufacture underwent similar changes. As a result, British coal production increased fivefold. Pig iron production increased tenfold.

Employment was abundant during the middle of the eighteenth century. Wages rose substantially. That particular period might be regarded as something of a "golden age" for labor. An especially favorable period for consumers was from 1730 to 1750, when wheat averaged only $2.80 for a quarter of a ton, less than it had been for 150 years past, and all the staple foods, in normal years, were cheap and plentiful. Meat was half the price of five years earlier. A rabbit could be had for two cents. The quickening pace of industrialization lowered the cost of many manufactured articles such as cotton and soap, then available to the workers in abundance.

While the period preceding the middle of the century held all of the characteristics of the growth phase of the long wave cycle, which I will subsequently refer to as the upwave, the period immediately thereafter contained all of the symptoms that usually lead to the depression within the downwave of the cycle. There was a steady shift of labor and capital from agriculture and non-mechanized crafts to the new mechanized branches of industry that offered the promise of the highest profits. Progress was neither equal nor simultaneous, leading to dislocations within the system involving surpluses in production in some areas and shortages in capacity in other areas. In spite of the great effort to build roads and improve their surfaces, the speed of transportation remained very slow because of the limited power of horses. Many of the manufactured goods were too heavy for land transportation. Heavy goods had to be conveyed by boats via canals and navigable rivers which was a time-consuming process leading to a bottleneck in distribution.

But all good things must end. After a long period of stability, prices began rising from 1750 onward. In 1783 the boom broke in a crisis. Price rises, catastrophic harvests, war, monetary inflation followed by depression ushered in the last decade of the century with poverty and famine for a large number of individuals.

On a global basis, the depression actually began in the 1770s and persisted through the early 1800s. The boom and collapse in England was only one aspect of the international collapse in trade. A factor contributing to the financial catastrophe in England was a speculative orgy which has since become known as "The South Sea Bubble." The bursting of the ill-fated bubble produced a series of economic panics that raged throughout Europe for most of the 1780s. The French also suffered a similar financial panic under the guidance of John Law. John Law was responsible for the introduction of fiat money and the formation of what has now become known as "The Mississippi Bubble." The shares of the Mississippi Company were actually linked to the French currency.

When the upwave of the eighteenth century ended, European economies were severely squeezed and raw material prices fell. Wheat, which was the backbone of the global economy at that time, was especially hard hit. Needless to say, the embryonic American economy felt the full brunt of the international holocaust.

The depression of the 1780s hit bottom in 1783, from which point we begin the first observable upwave. European economies slowly began to pick up. There is little doubt that 1787 was a year of prosperity which went on intensifying itself through 1793. The prosperity was linked to cotton innovation and canal construction. There were also minor features such as the introduction of the steam engine. After the outbreak of war between Britain and France in 1793, the gradual rise in prices turned into an explosive upsurge. A further surge in prices took place between 1798 and 1801 and again after the Napoleonic Wars. By 1814, raw material prices and economic activity approached what could later be seen as an unsustainable peak. There was a minor post-war boom during the period 1815–1816 but that miniboom was never able to reproduce the levels of economic activity of two years prior. In the United States the boom centered on the expansion of the textile industry in the New England states. The rise of the cotton industry in America had all the characteristics that fuel a speculative boom. The boom was global. There was a massive export drive in England reaching a stage where exports to Europe and the United States far exceeded all possibilities of resale. But the boom was only temporary. A depression was lying in wait.

The depression was precipitated by a sharp crisis in the affairs of the second Bank of the United States. The Bank had not fulfilled its intended purpose of checking inflation. In 1818 the Bank management embarked upon a policy of contraction. The resulting pressure brought about the suspension of payments in many areas and by many banks. An outcry against the Bank led to a congressional investigation that turned up mismanagement and dishonesty, leading to a movement to repeal the Bank's charter.

The collapse of this financial facade was merely a signal rather than a cause of what was to follow. The problems of the Bank of the United States were the precursor to a change in attitudes from confidence to fear and the rapidly spreading distress that is so characteristic of depression. Business bankruptcies multiplied; prices fell; unemployment rose. In 1819 there was a sharp fall in the price of wheat. Cotton sales collapsed and so did land sales. By 1825, the depression was a global affair. The value of stock and bond investment in canals collapsed along with that of South American government bonds and mines. In 1830 there was a period of speculative mania in railroads. But railroad speculators had ill-timed their investment. By late 1830, the economy was heading into a tail spin. Except for the brief period between 1815 and 1819, there was an extraordinary series of financial panics between 1814 and 1843. So severe was the downwave of the first cycle that prices fell a startling 59 percent.

THE SECOND CYCLE, 1843–1896

A new wave began in 1843, sixty years after the trough of the depression of 1783. The "lemmings" that were left on shore and survived the worldwide depression of the 1830s and 1840s began to build anew. As they began rebuilding the economic beehive, sections of the world's economy could be seen to recover, one by one. Industrial production picked up, exports between nations increased. The volume of world trade expanded. The price of wheat took a large jump. Between 1852 and 1854, the surge in raw material prices mirrored what happened in 1798–1801. Inflation was on the move again for the second time, just when people were getting used to falling prices as a permanent part of their existence. Consumer prices

jumped by 33 percent. Just as the Napoleonic Wars produced an upsurge
in prices, so did the American Civil War. Just as the crisis of 1809–1810
gave the initial warning that all was not well within the economic beehive,
the Panic of 1857 shouted that the situation was getting out of hand before
the final peak in economic activity in 1864. A crash is a financial shout for
the hard of hearing.

On August 26, 1857, just two days after the New York branch of the
Ohio Life Insurance and Trust Company suspended payments, the *New
York Herald Tribune* predicted that the financial difficulties then beginning were certain to acquire the proportions of a great crisis. As early as
1854, when the speculative boom in railroad stocks was halted by a sharp
decline in prices, the *Herald Tribune* predicted the imminent approach of
a crisis, one that would mark the end of the then current "Fitful Spasmodic
System" of American business. During the winter of 1854–1855, business
stagnated, unemployment increased greatly and there was considerable
distress and popular unrest.

The recession of 1854–1855 never actually took on the calamitous
proportions of a depression, in part because the South was less affected. It
was the approaching Civil War that was to finally bring the far-reaching
economic and social consequences of inflation and subsequent raw material
price collapse leading to deflation and depression for the entire country.

The first stage that often marks the transition from expansion and
boom to one of contraction and depression, these being the characteristics
of the downwave of the long wave cycle, is a panic. Panics figured prominently in the America of the nineteenth century. It was an age of individual
and virtually unregulated enterprise. There was little by way of means for
stabilization and prevention through advance, concerted and united action.
During the second cycle, the panic came in the middle of 1884. Prices
tumbled rapidly in both commodity and stock markets, accentuating the
shift from speculation to an orgy of selling. Banks then joined in the panic
by contracting their loans and withdrawing funds from the very volatile
call market. Money shortages developed, causing recourse to many substitute devices and adding to the psychological uncertainty of the time. Accompanying the panic phase there was the progressive decline in prices of
most goods and services and the deflation of values. All forms of property
were affected although precise measurement in statistical terms is not
available for most of the nineteenth century. Distress, hunger and depriva-
tion were widespread in the drab working quarters of the nineteenth-
century cities and towns from New York City downward and outward.

Elsewhere, the global system appeared unable to sustain itself for
quite some time. A series of financial panics began in Germany in 1873 and
spread to England just a few months later. Economic activity on a global
basis contracted steadily throughout the 1880s and 1890s. A depression
that engulfed all of Europe commenced at the end of 1890. Prices fell and
hardships mounted. For the third time since the late eighteenth century,

the world was once again plunged into a deep depression whose only parallel was in the depression of the 1840s . . . and the 1780s, which most people believed could never happen again.

A second long wave cycle that began in 1843 was completed in 1896, just under fifty-four years. A coincidence? A freak? Two repetitions . . . maybe. But three? Most unlikely!

THE THIRD CYCLE, 1896–1940

While railroad developments in the 1840s, particularly in England, are the chief reason for citing the commencement of the second cycle along with the trough of the 1840s depression, the feature of the third cycle was the introduction of electricity, which was simultaneous with the unmistakable complexion of business in 1896 which, at the time, emerged from what has come down to posterity as the Great Depression of that era. The proprieties of the social pattern, as revealed by the foreign, social and financial policies of the great nations, confirm that 1897 was the year that can be taken as being the pivotal year that marked the end of one era and the beginning of another. The first decades of the twentieth century saw tremendous innovations from the production of electricity and from the expanding American automobile industry. Cars and trucks began to replace horses and coaches. The mass production of cheap passenger cars called for a complete reorganization of the industry and led to advances such as the creation of assembly lines and the standardization of parts. The growth in the auto industry also stimulated related industries such as steel, glass, rubber and synthetics, petroleum exploration and the production of cement and asphalt, all of which were necessary for the newly required construction of roads and bridges. A modern economy was emerging in the United States, which has become the leading industrial nation of the world.

All seemed to be going quite well but suddenly an ugly monster reared its head. The monster who had appeared so many times before was a war: World War I. Prices of raw materials had been inching up steadily since the 1890s. But, after World War I, raw material prices took off like a display of Independence Day rockets, and kept on rising right through until 1920. What had happened three times before during the preceding 150 years was happening again during the second decade of the twentieth century. The lemmings were still at work, getting ready to begin tearing down the economic beehive.

From the end of World War I until 1920 there was an uninterrupted rise in raw material prices and also in consumer prices. It was a traditional post-war boom involving affluence for all. Then, suddenly, in 1920, raw material prices crashed. The crash in prices was devastating. Professional operators were brought to ruin. The phenomenon was worldwide. In Britain, hundreds of small investors went bankrupt, speculating in Argentinian companies of dubious merit. The crash in commodity markets was a

U.S. Economic Statistics Marking the Peak and Subsequent Trough of Each Cycle

Kondratieff Cycle Trough / Peak / Trough	Wholesale Prices (1967 = 100)		Consumer Prices (1967 = 100)		High-Grade Bond Yields	Common Stock Prices
#1						
1780s — 1814	59 (1814)		38 (1814)		7.7% (1816)	25 (1835)
1843	24 (1843)		18 (1843)		4.3% (1821) } Double	6 (1842) }
					4.0% (1852) } Trough	Decline = 76%
#2						
1843 — 1864	67 (1864)		47 (1865)		6.7% (1861)	22 (1853)
1896	25 (1897)		26 (1895)		3.2% (1899)	8 (1856)
						Decline = 64%
#3						
1896 — 1920	76 (1920)		59 (1920)		5.2% (1920)	390 (1929)
1940	34 (1933)		39 (1933)		2.5% (1945)	41 (1932)
						Decline = 89%
#4	Index	% Change	Index	% Change		
1940 — 1973	1973=134.7	+15.4%	1973=133.1	+8.8%	9.1% (1974)	???
	1974=160.1	+20.9%	1974=147.7	+12.2%		
	1975=174.9	+4.2%	1975=161.2	+7.0%		
	1976=183.0	+4.6%	1976=170.5	+4.8%		
	1977=194.2	+6.1%	1977=181.5	+6.4%		
1990s (?)					Trough = ?	

*Obtained by splicing several indexes together, with all related to Dow Jones Industrials for index uniformity. SRC Bicentennial Chart of Investment and Economic History; Securities Research Co., Boston, Massachusetts, 1976.

FIGURE 4

precursor to the 1920–1922 recession. That recession was relatively short and sharp in the United States, but far more serious elsewhere. In Germany, in a different monetary context, the economic collapse took the horror of the hyperinflation of 1923. Although prices exploded in Germany, the result fell far short of any semblance of prosperity. Whether a loaf of bread costs a dollar or a penny, the only thing that counts is whether you have the dollar or the penny. In Germany, a loaf of bread cost 30 billion marks. Very few people had 30 billion marks in 1923.

In England, unemployment soared from 15 percent in 1920 to 25 percent in 1922. It was not until 1929 that the British economy actually began to recover from the recession of 1920–1922, and that recovery was very short lived . . . for the worst of the global financial disaster was yet to come.

Following the recession of 1922 there was just enough strength left in the system to provide a reasonable recovery. Enter the Roaring Twenties. But no matter how loud the twenties roared, they proved to be nothing more than a final fling at economic expansion which was to be brought to its knees by the inexorable economic forces that had predominated throughout history. The Great Crash of 1929 and what followed needs little elaboration. The depression of the 1930s didn't reach a meaningful trough until the United States entered World War II. For the fourth time since the 1780s, the world was plunged into deep depression. You know what comes next!

THE FOURTH CYCLE, 1940–1994?

Without a doubt, the most important economic sequence of the past 200 years is the one that is now taking place. We are aware that prices of consumer goods have been rising throughout the post-World War II period in America and elsewhere. Less obvious is the strong evidence which suggests that we have now passed a price peak of a similar nature to that of 1920, 1864 and 1814, such prices peaks signifying the end of the growth phase and the beginning of economic conditions that were to lead to severe global depression.

While prices have continued to rise in absolute terms for most goods and services, in addition to raw materials, the year-over-year percentage change of consumer prices on a global basis peaked and then collapsed in 1974. The Wholesale Price Index growth rate peaked in early 1974 a few months before the Consumer Price Index. The *Economist* Dollar All Item Commodity Index actually peaked in late 1973. After reaching an astronomical inflation rate of close to 88 percent, the growth in commodity prices plunged and prices were falling throughout most of 1975. The engine for price rises is monetary growth. World domestic credit expansion also peaked in 1973 as did the growth in world money supply.

Clearly, 1973 was a watershed year. Western industrialized countries embarked upon the worst recession since the 1930s at that time. It is generally accepted that the cause of the severe 1973–1975 recession was the quadrupling of the oil price. But it was certainly not the rise in the oil price that brought an end to the great post-war prosperity. It would be far too simple to blame the recession and slow growth of the 1970s on the oil crisis, just as it would be a gross oversimplification to argue that the Great Depression of the 1930s was caused by the crash in the stock market in 1929. Economic research on the impact of the oil crisis suggests that the annual GNP growth rate of OECD countries during the period of 1973–1979 was reduced by a mere 0.15 percent as a result of the oil price increases. It is also estimated that the global rate of inflation rose by no more than 0.6 percent from the rise in the price of oil; the fall in the productivity growth rate was no more than 0.14 percent and the rate of growth in real income per workers in OECD countries slowed by no more than 0.41 percent. Statistically, the effects of the rise in the price of oil must be considered of limited significance. The quadrupling of oil prices cannot explain the deep structural changes that have occurred in the world's economy since 1973, nor does it explain the retardation of growth or the considerable drop in productivity growth. Far more sinister forces were at work than the rise in oil prices . . . forces that have persisted for 200 years . . . and more.

Once a price peak has been reached, the long wave pattern of economic behavior involves a recession deeper than any that had occurred since the trough of the previous depression. After the deep recession there comes a period of slow growth or "secondary prosperity" that culminates with a major depression. A period of "secondary depression" began in 1975 with a renewed upsurge in commodity prices and inflation. Both have now peaked again, well below the peaks of 1974. During most of 1980, commodity prices were falling. Gold collapsed and so did silver. Prices of many finished products from the factory gate have also experienced widespread falls. And the price of oil, which many believed would never fall again and would continue to rise and rise again, has also fallen. So have property prices. During the early part of this year, prices were rising again but such rises are merely tertiary movements within a long-term inexorable secular downwave.

The complete cycle from the trough of one depression to the trough of the next takes fifty to sixty years. The period from the peak of the price cycle to the peak of the next is somewhat more consistent, involving approximately fifty-four years. In 1920, commodity prices peaked. In 1974, the growth in commodity prices peaked again, fifty-four years from the previous top. As we have seen, the peak in commodity prices in both instances, and in examples that go all the way back to the eighteenth century, is followed by a deep recession. The trigger that aggravates the recession and seems to coincide with the peak in the price cycle is some form of financial panic. In the current cycle this financial panic came as real estate and banking crises in the United States and the collapse of the second-line banking empire of England, hot-on-the-heels of a global prices peak. The bell was rung, and the warning signal was given, just as in the past.

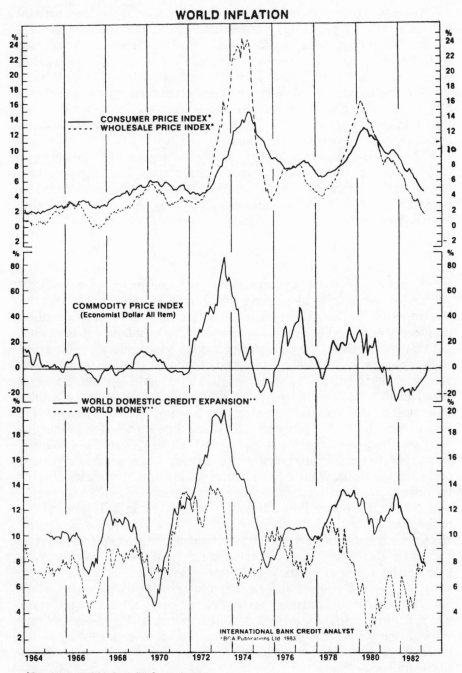

WORLD INFLATION

CONSUMER PRICE INDEX*
WHOLESALE PRICE INDEX*

COMMODITY PRICE INDEX
(Economist Dollar All Item)

WORLD DOMESTIC CREDIT EXPANSION**
WORLD MONEY**

INTERNATIONAL BANK CREDIT ANALYST
BCA Publications Ltd 1983

* The weighted sum of U.S.A., Canada, U.K., Germany, Japan,
  France and Italy.
* * The weighted sum of U.S.A., Canada, U.K. Germany and Japan

FIGURE 5   From *The International Bank Credit Analyst*, May 1983.

The long wave model calls for a declining plateau of economic activity following the deep recession. The economic upturn that followed the real estate and banking crises of 1974 lasted until 1979. It was more buoyant in the United States than elsewhere but growth in national income masked a progressive decay in many traditional industries such as autos, construction and engineering. The late phases were characterized by a speculative fling in housing, precious metals and collectibles of all kinds. This was typical in every respect of the "secondary prosperity" expansions which have ushered in previous depressions.

The period of deep recession, recovery and a gradually declining plateau, according to the model, lasts about a decade. The deep recession began in 1973. The model calls for a plateau that would be completed some time during 1983. When the "secondary recovery" is over, a depression begins. You are there!

THE 1930s REVISITED

This cycle of upwaves and downwaves has been going on for about 200 years. You would think by now we would have enough sense to prepare, but we never do. Rollicking and frolicking during the Roaring Twenties, people may have had a vague recollection of the depression of the 1870s, but that was far from the mind's eye amid the bootleg booze, short skirts and sexy flappers. Prices were falling in the early 1920s and unemployment was rising, but a man with a steady job had little to worry about. He might have had little chance of a raise in wages, but the fall in the prices of food, housing and clothing meant his purchasing power was rising. Prices always rose in war, then fell in peace as the war machine switched to production for peace and consumption. It had been that way since the Industrial Revolution. There was no reason why the average man should expect any change in the 1920s. What did he know about history? History was for the historians.

The Industrial Revolution demonstrated many things. It brought one of the most dramatic and dynamic changes in life-style and the family unit since the beginning of Christianity. The Industrial Revolution was built on improving the means of production, using fewer people to produce a greater abundance of goods and services. The fewer the people and the more the goods, the lower the prices and the greater the spread of goods and services for all, provided society remained in relative equilibrium, which it never does. As the effect of the Industrial Revolution worked through the global economic system from the eighteenth century to the twentieth century, there were periods of disequilibrium, temporary dislocations and hardship.

Immediately following World War I there was such a time. At the start of the 1920s unemployment was high. For a while, people felt totally disillusioned. Soldiers returned from the front to discover they had no jobs to go to. But peacetime output began to grow, and so did demand for goods and services. The number of jobs grew, and the number of unemployed fell.

Throughout the industrialized world, the 1920s was a decade of prosperity, powered by the commercial application of the internal combustion engine and the electric motor. The average man believed that prosperity would last forever. His dad may have been alive in the Great Depression of the 1870s, but only as a youth. Our twentieth-century Neanderthal knew that the prosperous days of the 1920s were quite different from all the other prosperous times that had collapsed before. Governments and economists were so much wiser in the 1920s than ever before . . . *ça va?*

As we now know, that proved drastically wrong. Remember what happens in the economic beehive? Prices reach an unsustainable peak and then decline. After that, we get a recession. After the recession, there is economic recovery. Then everyone thinks everything is just as it used to be . . . but it is not. The beehive is being destroyed. It has already reached its optimal level of growth.

The calamity of the 1870s was repeated following the Crash of '29. The secondary prosperity of the 1920s went up in smoke, and a multitude of businesses were wiped out. It is highly probable there would have been no depression if the assumptions about continued prosperity had not been so widespread. There might have been no World War II, if fewer people had assumed it could not happen again.

The prospect of depression perhaps only a few months away may be frightening. But it need not be. During the 1930s, 25 percent of the workforce may have been unemployed. But that meant 75 percent of the workforce was employed. Falling prices brought an effective wage rise with every fall in price.

There were several boom industries during the 1930s depression. The film industry was at its height. The Stork Club and the Copacabana were packed every night. Many of the get-rich-quick millionaires of the "swinging sixties" are now defunct. Those who began making their fortunes during the 1930s still have their millions, and many more to boot. More self-made millionaires came from the ruins of the 1930s than from any other time over the past fifty years.

If the long wave cycle of economic life repeats itself, those who are unprepared will suffer hardship. So will anyone who is unable to prepare for the crunch. But anyone who can anticipate what lies ahead, and plans accordingly, could gain the opportunity of a lifetime.

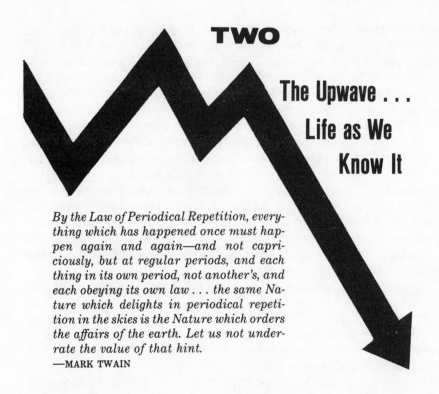

TWO

The Upwave . . .
Life as We
Know It

By the Law of Periodical Repetition, every-
thing which has happened once must hap-
pen again and again—and not capri-
ciously, but at regular periods, and each
thing in its own period, not another's, and
each obeying its own law . . . the same Na-
ture which delights in periodical repeti-
tion in the skies is the Nature which orders
the affairs of the earth. Let us not under-
rate the value of that hint.
—MARK TWAIN

Modern economic theorists revel in the trivia and minutia of contemporary history. They treat any economic event before World War II as if it were prehistoric. To understand and use the patterns in the long wave, you do not need an IBM 1264 with 2,000 megabytes and a daisy-wheel printer or to understand alphas, betas, sigmas and differential calculus. The principle is simple enough. It is based on the idea that there is a strong interaction between political and social developments, wars and the long-term economic cycle, all of which come to a peak at fifty- to sixty-year intervals. The complete economic sequence involves four basic components: first an up-wave, then a recession. Then there is secondary prosperity, and finally, secondary depression. The cycle then starts all over again.

THE COMPONENTS OF THE UPWAVE

Recently I have been giving a series of lectures entitled "Personal Survival in a World Turned Upside Down," so-called because all of the things people have been doing correctly during the upwave, everything that currently seems normal and natural, will soon have potentially disastrous consequences. We are now heading downward in the long-term economic scheme. Social, economic and investment worlds for the past thirty years are being turned upside down.

An understanding of the four components I have mentioned will not only help you shift your emphasis and life-style in the future. It will also demonstrate conclusively that the upwave which began in 1939 has come to an end.

The long wave pattern of economic life is based on a model of prices, the foundation of economic behavior in the capitalist and pseudocapitalist system. The price model carries with it some definitive and seemingly unalterable implications. They will affect your finances and your way of living in tomorrow's world. The price of money, or interest rates, is an important element during the expansion phase of the long wave. When you negotiate a mortgage of, say, 6 percent in one part of the upwave, and 15 percent at another, you will feel the effects at firsthand. These long waves of economic behavior may at first glance seem rather esoteric. But if you were among the unemployed or were made bankrupt between 1930 and 1940, your plight would have been more than just a passing interest. All the more so, because your plight could have been predicted fairly accurately several years before it happened. What lies ahead during the next two decades is no less predictable.

INFLATION DURING THE UPWAVE

We have lived through nearly four decades of inflation, and many people think inflation is a permanent part of our existence. They believe that prices will rise because prices have always risen. History shows that

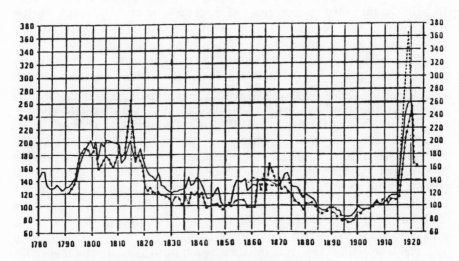

Index Numbers of Commodity Prices
(1901-10 = 100)

United States ----- England ----- France

FIGURE 6   THE LONG WAVE OF COMMODITY PRICES

this is not true, but preconceptions die hard. Inflation is now considered "Public Enemy Number One" by most governments. Politicians love to promise to control inflation. Americans thought an inflation rate of 10 percent astronomical, but in the mid-1970s, Britain was cited as a nation on the brink of becoming a "banana republic," with inflation up to 28 percent. Now it is thought that inflation must be conquered at all costs. This fear that something horrible will happen if inflation is not conquered and obliterated leads us into the same trap as other governments in other countries during periods of high inflation.

If there is one thing to be learned from studying these long waves of economic life, it is that rising prices are certainly not a permanent part of the economic system. Wheat prices from 1295 to 1980 show that clearly. Long waves of economic life ebbed and flowed well before the first observable wave began in 1798. French price indices beginning in the 1850s verify this. So do English and American prices back to the close of the eighteenth century, and British prices back to the thirteenth century. It seems the British have a penchant for keeping records.

The upswing in the first long period of rising prices, or inflation, went from 1789 to 1814. In those twenty-five years, prices advanced, slowly at first, building in momentum with the increase in business activity. After the war between Britain and France began, the gradual increase became an explosion. At the time, the Gayer Index of Domestic and Imported Prices was the standard inflation index for Britain, similar to the modern Consumer Price Index. From a prewar trough of 88.0 in 1792, the Gayer Index reached 107.9 in six years. In the following three years to 1801, the price increased was much more spectacular, leaping from 107.9 to 155.7. It reached a peak of 168.9 in 1813.

According to the Gayer Index, prices soared by 92 percent from 1783 to 1813. In just three years, from 1798, they shot up 44 percent. Such a massive gain over a comparatively short period is not unusual. History shows that it is characteristic of practically all inflations.

Prices did not go straight up from 1783 to 1813. There were peak years in commodity prices in 1799, 1805, 1810 and 1814. There was no dramatic fall in prices between those years, merely an easing back. But, after 1814, the downward trend had begun, the turning point had been reached.

The second upwave began in 1849, and lasted twenty-four years. Inflation again returned after an absence of thirty-five years. Prices began rising slowly at first, duplicating the pattern of the upwave of five decades earlier, then suddenly surged. From 1862 to 1867, U.S. prices increased 60 percent, quite something for people accustomed to falling prices for thirty-five years. This price rise was almost identical to the huge jump between 1798 and 1807. Over 90 percent of the price rises during the 1849–1873 inflation took place in two years (1852–1854).

The world was free from inflation again until 1896. In the mid-1890s prices drifted upward, as they had during the 1780s and 1850s. And just

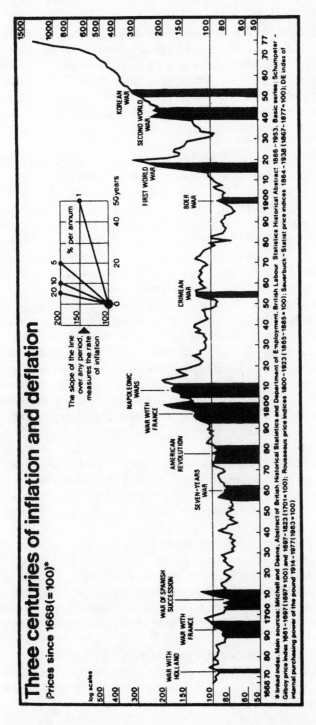

FIGURE 7

Source: *The Economist* (June 1978)

Reprinted from Sheila Hopkins and E. H. Phelps Brown,
Three Centuries of Inflation and Deflation.

as there had been big price rises over relatively short periods before, (1798–1801 and 1852–1854), the steady increase from 1893 to 1918 saw a similar pattern. The bulk of the increase came in the last three years.

History repeated itself elsewhere. Inflation during 1893–1920 was largely the result of gold-mining, war and cyclical expansion. The same combination was responsible for the inflation of 1849–1873. It was not until the crisis of 1920, another turning point in the upwave, that prices stopped rising.

About nineteen years passed between the end of inflation in 1920 and the beginning of the fourth upwave. Once more, prices rose gently at first. Then World War II broke out, and produced another price convulsion. The Korean War played its part. So did the war in Southeast Asia. But the Middle East war sparked off the biggest price explosion. Oil prices quadrupled, and inflation produced the same kind of phenomenon as in other upwaves—an explosion in prices over a relatively short period. It may seem absurd, insensitive even, to compare the Middle East war with the great world wars. But in our context it is the economic significance of wars that is relevant. And it would be by no means absurd to suggest that the economic dislocations caused by the oil crisis—seen as a direct consequence of the Israeli war—were comparable to those of World War I.

The mind often plays tricks on people, and the most recent difficult experiences often appear to be the most painful and intractable. The inflation of 1939–1974 was, of course, the historical legacy of the previous depression. During the 1920s, inflation was perceived as the common enemy; an excruciatingly painful enemy as demonstrated by the horrifying German hyperinflation of the early 1920s. The depression of the 1930s left a lasting impression with the policymakers of the time. But, by the end of the decade, the problems of inflation were all but forgotten. Nothing could ever again be as painful as the depression the world had been forced to live through. High unemployment and queues of people on breadlines seemed a far greater evil than anything ever produced during the inflationary times.

So the policymakers embarked on measures to curb unemployment and provide sustenance for the unemployed. They thus sowed the seeds for the inflation of the 1939–1974 era, in precisely the same manner as the economic policymakers in the wake of previous depressions. The measures of the late 1930s, 1940s and 1950s may have differed in detail, but the objectives were still the same. What had happened in the previous 150 years meant nothing.

The economic theories of John Maynard Keynes provided the foundations upon which the inflation of the past four decades was built. If it had not been Keynes, somebody else would have provided the philosophy which appealed to policymakers who were totally preoccupied with averting another depression, and blind to the inexorable forces within the social and economic fibers of a nation. Keynes's theory said that economic recovery

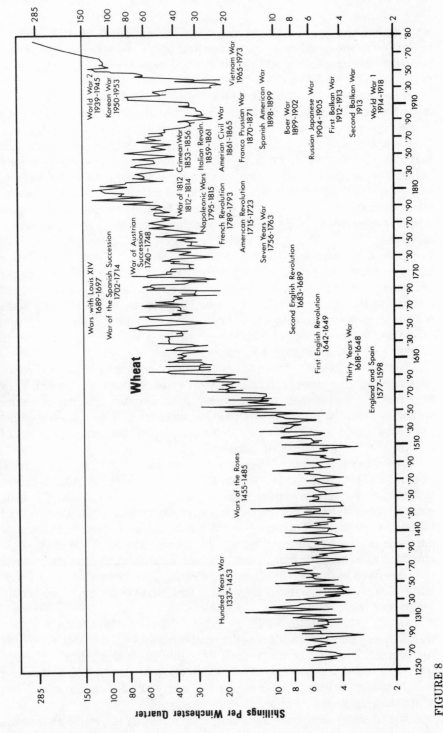

The Price of Wheat in England: 1259-1975

FIGURE 8

could be induced by government spending. During periods of slack demand, the government could create new demand by its own social expenditure program. In turn, this would result in an overall increase in demand for goods and services throughout the entire economy.

President Roosevelt's "New Deal" was based on the Keynesian doctrine. So were the policies of the British administration during the tail end of the depression of the 1930s. Keynes, of course, recognized the dangers. He knew his principles could cause high inflation and was quite emphatic that if high inflation, and deficits, were to be avoided from government-induced economic stimuli during bad times, governments would have to make every effort to maintain budget surpluses during boom times. In other words, recessions could be prevented from deepening through government stimulation. But since the government was likely to be paying out more than it was taking in, a deficit would result. Deficits, the result of living beyond our means, are inflationary. Keynes believed the inflation could be mitigated, provided the government cut social spending once the economy picked up again. What Keynes did not foresee, or perhaps turned a blind eye to, was that once politicians commit themselves to buying votes with promises of a "chicken in every pot," a "car in every garage," and "Giacometti on every public building," there is no turning back. Social spending grows, and keeps on growing.

Governments always tend to underestimate inflationary forces, preferring to accept the more optimistic of any two estimates put forward. They fear that otherwise they will be replaced by another government more willing to feed the public with a political plethora of pusillanimous piffle. Political considerations allowed policies designed to ease the depression of the 1930s to fuel the fires of inflation.

The depression of the 1930s, the depression of the 1880s, the depression of the 1830s and the depression of the 1780s shared another common denominator: countries imposed high trade tariffs to protect their domestic markets once demand contracted. Soon, currencies became debased, and inflation was fueled. Soon high trade tariffs failed to protect vulnerable domestic markets. Major industrialized nations had to abandon the gold standard as a basis for fixing currency relationships. The next step was to abandon fixed parity and float exchange rates. That inevitably led to instability. History has repeatedly shown that floating exchange rates gain only temporary relief.

In the 1940s, floating exchange rates achieved little success. So, postwar planners put their heads together and came up with the Bretton Woods Agreement. This worked magic during the late 1940s and 1950s, and world trade expanded considerably. But it also allowed the United States and Britain to live far beyond their means for nearly two decades, and, in doing so, pushed up world inflation.

For twenty years after the war, great chunks of the world underwent a dramatic rebuilding program: first Europe, then Japan and West Germany. Since the United States was never devastated by the war, there was nothing to rebuild. But it certainly profited by selling the tools that others needed to rebuild their countries.

The 1950s and 1960s also saw the victors of World War II surrendering control over Third World countries. Britain gave independence to India and several other colonies. France was ousted from Indochina. Holland severed its relationship with Indonesia. These were the kind of empire liquidations witnessed during the early 1800s and the 1860s. These emerging nations were in no position to cut the financial umbilical cord with their mother countries. This meant that poor people in rich countries were taxed for the benefit of rich people in poor countries. Huge debts began piling up among Third World countries. The outcome? You guessed it . . . more inflation.

The list of factors contributing to the inflationary upwave of 1930–1974 is virtually endless. But all that is important now is to recognize the nature of inflation and its relationship with previous periods in the long waves of economic behavior.

Inflation is a common enemy, just as it was in the past. But it is an enemy few people actually understand. At first glance, having no inflation might seem ideal. Yet the inflationary forces seemed to improve the quality of life, except in recent years when it appeared to be out of control. Compare this with Switzerland, one of the few countries with virtually no inflation for most of the current upwave. Price stability has made very little impact in *improving* the material quality of Swiss life—high though it is.

Today, a lot of people are reexamining their material goals. "Is it worth it?" they ask. The answer is "yes," provided that inflation and its incumbent problems can be avoided. These people would be quite content to dispense with growth. No growth is suddenly becoming desirable and acceptable in many quarters. Inflation is a monster; anything must be better than inflation.

This attitude is a fallacy. The upwave and its inflationary counterparts have provided prosperity that otherwise would never have occurred. More people own their own homes in America than ever before. The standard of living worldwide is higher than ever. Most people in industrialized societies today demand an improved standard of living. Labor unions preach that an increasing standard of living is their inalienable right, regardless of the quantity they produce. Most people would strongly resist any measure to halt the long economic upwave if they were aware of it.

The problems associated with inflation are not characteristic of inflation itself, but are a product of the type of inflation experienced as we near the end of the upwave.

Like the lemming population, whose growth exceeds the supply of vegetation for its sustenance, the demands made of the industrialized economy near the end of the upwave are too much for the economy to bear, so it self-destructs. The rise in prices reaches a point where inflation is no longer an asset, but a severe penalty; one which is likely to lead to an economic holocaust, perhaps even worse than any we have known before.

The battle against inflation begins in earnest when that massive bulge occurs during the latter stages of the upwave. It came in 1920 and 1974 with peaks in commodity prices, followed by peaks in growth of wholesale prices, and then in retail prices. This final price bulge usually occurs when a fully extended economy is forced to battle it out with an event such as an energy crisis, a banking crisis, a war, or a combination of them all.

The economy will start to falter, unemployment will start to rise. The government is then forced to spend massive amounts while unemployment is rising and production is falling. Shortages caused by falling production, combined with expansive monetary growth, force prices to skyrocket. This, in turn, puts pressure on workers. They demand bigger wage increases to maintain the standard of living they have been virtually guaranteed by government. This is obviously frightening and confusing to people who misunderstand the root cause of inflation.

Contrary to popular belief, prices do not rise because of increases in subordinate areas such as labor. Labor is used often as a political scapegoat. During the final stages of expansion, prices rise because of the imbalance between supply and demand for goods and services. Demand continues to increase, while supply contracts.

The combination of rising prices, sizable industrial overcapacity and a labor force which cannot be used, is formidable. It certainly cannot go on for an indefinite period. We have simply passed the end of the upwave.

One important way of spotting the final inflationary spurt is to note when it happens during the upwave. The majority of price increases occur within a relatively short period. During the first upwave, the price index rose 92 percent from 88.0 to 168.9 between 1792 and 1813. From 1798 to 1801, prices rose from 107.9 to 155.7, a gain of 44 percent. Nearly half of those price gains over twenty-one years were achieved in just three years. During the second upwave cycle, there was a similar pattern. Between 1852 and 1854 prices rose by 33 percent. That was more than 90 percent of the total gain from 1843 to 1864. In the third upwave, the big jump in prices took place during and after World War I. During the current wave, inflation did not really become chronic until the 1970s. Most of the price rises occurred between 1973 and 1980, although high rates persisted. This is further evidence of an inflationary spiral that has spent its force.

In the case of the United States, the inflation rate, after subsiding from the 1975 peak, accelerated to a new record in 1980. But for the rest of the developed countries the inflation peak fell short, far short in some cases, like Japan and Britain. Taken as a whole, inflation in the industrialized world has been in a declining trend since 1975, after a forty-year buildup. And the very low rate in the United States since early 1982 points to the same conclusion. Prices may still appear to be rising because of an "echo" effect that reflects monetary excesses of previous years working through the economy. These monetary excesses were originally generated by the energy crisis, and supplemented by the burden of social benefits during a recent period of lackluster economic activity. When the echo dies, there will be no other big noise to replace it. The mutually exclusive conditions of recession and inflation of recent years will disappear. The effect of falling prices will be more pronounced, and will bring far more devastating consequences than inflation ever could produce. Deflation is much more difficult to control than inflation.

TECHNOLOGY ... FURTHER FUEL FOR THE UPWAVE

The "star" of the upwave is inflation, but several other characters play extremely important supporting roles. Inflation is certainly not confined to raw material, wholesale and retail prices. It includes interest rates, wages, foreign trade, music, fashion and the production of industrial bellwether resources like coal, pig iron, steel and lead. All of these appear to be related to, or dominated by, overriding natural economic forces within the long waves of economic and social life in industrialized societies. Dynamic phases of technological achievement seem inexorably linked to the behavior pattern of the long wave cycle. These long waves are characterized by sharp gains in economic activity whose peaks are separated by long valleys of stagnation. Prices and inflation follow this path and the same seems to be true of technological development and achievement—but involving a time lag. The latter part of the downwave sees outstanding innovations but these are not fully exploited, nor do they act as a spur to economic activity, until the upwave begins and capital investment starts to expand—which may be years later.

The first period of major technological achievement took place during the early part of the nineteenth century, soon after the first observable upwave began in our long wave scheme. A new form of society was built on the invention of the steam engine and the spinning wheel during the Industrial Revolution. At the beginning of the nineteenth century, British trade, as that of other countries, was dominated by the cotton industry. Steam was the new source of power. The spinning wheel was the revolutionary tool. Both significantly boosted production. Both brought boom times for cotton. They also fueled the upwave that began in the 1780s. And when technological momentum in cotton waned, so did economic activity.

The second major technological advancement came in the early 1840s, coinciding with the beginning of an upwave. Railway transport began in Britain, and opened a new era of expanding British coal exports. The train was a powerful catalyst during the second upwave. Railways lowered transport costs, brought new areas and supplies into national and international markets and helped to generate export earnings. They, in turn, permitted the whole process of expansion to move faster.

Railways also accelerated new technologies in coal, iron and engineering. Their expansion altered and modernized the institutions of capital formation during the middle to late nineteenth century. This new transport system also accelerated the pace of urbanization. It has been estimated that the railway alone lifted national income in Britain by more than 10 percent.

Almost a quarter of the growth in Britain between 1840 and 1865 can be attributed to the train.

During the third upwave, many new technologies made their debut. The third wave gave us the automobile, propellor-driven aircraft and the radio. New methods of steel production were introduced in 1902. Over the next three years, alloy steels, such as stainless steel and nonferrous alloys, and new methods of aluminum production came into being. The electric furnace technique was introduced between 1903 and 1906. Modern methods of tin-canning came in between 1905 and 1918. Diesel engines for large ships appeared in 1912. Many new products and processes completely transformed the distributive trades.

The fourth period of technological innovation started just after the Great Depression of the 1930s, before World War II. It was about forty-five years after the beginning of the third period of major innovation and the third upwave. The fourth upwave provided a host of new products and processes—television, penicillin, synthetic rubber, radar, DDT, nuclear power, jet aircraft, antibiotics, agricultural chemicals, microcircuitry with transistors, "the chip" and electronic computers.

While many marvel at the wonders of the silicon chip, genetic engineering and biotechnology, none of the recent developments actually involves new technologies; they merely extend existing ones. Over the past ten years, technological innovation has virtually come to a halt with the end of the upwave. Global markets are no longer expanding fast enough to encourage the investment or to absorb new technologies.

Between 1930 and 1950, however, there were great strides in new technology. We now have artificial satellites and missiles. There have been commercial spinoffs from jet aircraft development and fuel technology. We have word processors, a spinoff from the microcircuitry developed during wartime. Whatever product you can imagine, investigation will show it to be merely an extension of what has already been achieved, rather than a new area of development.

At the beginning of the upwave, we find dynamic technological achievement and new innovation. This continues throughout a large portion of the upwave. When we embark on transferring and using existing technologies, instead of coming up with something new, we know the upwave has ended. It is unlikely we will see a new era of technological innovation much before the 1990s.

THE PATTERNS OF WAR DURING THE UPWAVE

Every upwave has produced two major wars, one at the beginning and one at the end.

War at the beginning of an upwave lands on an economy with unused resources, deflated prices, reduced debts and reasonably low interest rates. The increased production and new demand for war goods assists the subsequent business recovery of the upwave.

War at the end of the upwave has a negative impact. Inflated debt, high prices, high interest rates, undercapacity and full employment tend to accentuate the inbuilt distortions of an expansion which has run out of control. War at the end of the upwave adds to the underlying forces which terminate the upwave.

War is not the cause of variations or extensions in the economic scenario. It is the effect of a series of negative forces caused by many other deep-rooted factors, most of which have psychological origins. War is a symptom of social and economic pressures that build up in the system, at the beginning and at the end of the upwave. Wars at the end of the upwave are due in part to the same social tensions associated with hyperactivity during high inflation, generating exceptionally strong emotions. Wars at the early stages of the upwave are far less popular and are more or less accepted as faits accomplis by the electorate.

The war at the end of the first upwave was the Napoleonic War, which generated strong emotions on a global basis. It was a period of unusually excessive social tension. Not only was there a major international war, but civil wars were being waged the world over. Rebellions against the Napoleonic regime broke out, along with a series of revolutions to free Latin America.

At the peak of the second upwave, two major wars were fought, the Civil War in the United States and the Crimean War. They took place against a background of strong public feeling. The Civil War in the United States was a direct result of President Lincoln's refusal to allow the southern states of the Union to secede peacefully. Strong emotions were aroused between black and white Americans. In July 1863, there were bloody riots in New York City by objectors to conscription. There were race riots. It was reported that as many as 50,000 people had been roaming the city streets without stopping for four days, burning, looting and killing Negroes. Lincoln's move to free the slaves was a central issue of the war, arousing racial tensions and prejudices in a society already burdened with problems associated with the end of an upwave.

World War I occurred at the end of the third upwave. The emotive element for America was the supposed violation of the rules of war by Germany. It was claimed that illegal German submarine warfare was responsible for killing Americans at sea. Germany had shown herself the major aggressor with her attack on Russia and the invasion of neutral Belgium. The spirit of the Allies was particularly easy to arouse.

Like other wars at the tail end of long prosperity, World War I began as a crusade for America. But the public soon became disillusioned, and mass rioting followed. There were frenzied May Day riots in 1919, and a series of terrorist bombings in the financial district of New York.

The typical tensions, frustrations and excitement following a long period of rising prices and social unrest resulted in the cluster of wars at the end of the most recent upwave. The Korean War, the Vietnam war, and the Middle East war combined to produce the same conditions that were

Sociopolitical Events

Cycle	Previous Trough War	Peak War	OTHER PARALLELS
#1 1780s to 1843	War of Independence 1775-81	War of 1812 1812-15	1. Federalist Party accused of treason for protesting War of 1812; dies in election of 1816. U.S. has only one party for next term. 2. Westward expansion (1791-1819) culminating in overspeculation in Western land. 3. First secondary schools for women (1820s).
#2 1843 to 1896	Mexican War 1846-48	Civil War 1861-65	1. Johnson impeachment attempt (1868); no scandals. 2. Railroad overexpansion (1865-75). 3. Women's suffrage in Wyoming (1869).
#3 1896 to 1940	Spanish-American War 1898 (Phillipine Intervention, 1899-1902)	World War I 1914-18 (Mexican Intervention, 1914-17)	1. Teapot Dome scandal (1921-1923): Harding died in office before prosecution. 2. Real estate construction boom (1920s) & Florida land boom (1925). 3. National Women's Suffrage (1920).
#4 1940 to 1990 (?)	World War II 1939-45 (Korean War 1951-53)	Vietnam War 1964-72	1. Watergate scandal: Nixon forced out of office (1974). 2. Real estate boom (1970s). 3. Equal Rights Amendment passed by Senate and sent out for ratification (1972).

FIGURE 9

prevalent at the time of World War I, the U.S. Civil War, and the Napoleonic Wars. The three wars of the upwave that ended in 1974 overlapped. The Vietnam war, instigated to stem the spread of communist aggression, produced student rioting and demonstrations as people became disillusioned when the objectives were not being achieved. In the Middle East war, Europe was outraged by the transfer of wealth from the West to the East, bringing a blow to Western pride. The conflicts of the 1970s ultimately brought bitter disillusionment, and the feeling that people had been put to great expense with very little gained. Essentially, the wars near the peak of the upwave reflect the emotional climate created by the two decades of increasing prosperity. It seems people are no longer able to cope with the mounting complications of their lives. They lose their stamina and their ability to keep up with the accelerating rate of change.

The Napoleonic Wars, the U.S. Civil War, the Vietnam war, and the Middle East war, all lost public support as they became larger, more protracted, increasingly difficult to manage, and progressively more costly to win. The three wars of the fourth upwave led to the economic troubles which normally occur when an economy has become grossly overextended. They also generated the kind of public discontent and disorder typical of the emotional state at the end of the long wave pattern of social and economic life. Resistance to wars or the political system responsible for them is common at the end of an upwave.

Wars at the beginning of the long upwave are totally different. Then people are still relatively calm, waiting for the wounds of the downwave to heal. Following the long austere years of the downwave, a war at the beginning of an upwave falls on a people who are primarily concerned with their own well-being, and less interested in international affairs and military crusades.

The world was at war in the 1780s and 1790s when the first upwave is seen. Except for the French Revolution in 1789, there was little national spirit behind global conflicts at the time. England was at war with Spain. There was conflict between England and Holland. Russia invaded Turkey. Sporadic battles were breaking out all over the world.

Similarly, the Mexican War, at the beginning of the second upwave, and the Spanish-American War, at the beginning of the third upwave, both failed to generate public excitability equal to that in wars at the end of the upwaves.

World War II was horrendous and brought severe hardship. Yet, the character of the war and the people's response fit the type of war that follows a depression rather than prosperity. At the end of a war following prosperity, there is disillusionment and resentment, public disorder and rioting. At the end of World War II, there was peace and rejoicing. The secondary depression at the end of the downwave is long and tedious, involving painful upsets for most people. The initial response to the first glimmer of light at the beginning of the upwave is cautious relief. The depression appears less intense. Few recognize that a major recovery lies ahead or that a permanent change has taken place.

Historical evidence suggesting there will be no return to the secondary depression for at least four decades is not obvious to many when the upwave begins. Problems associated with depression may ease, but most people continue to believe that the depression will be part of their lives forever. War at the early stages of the upwave diverts attention from the problems at hand, temporarily. This does not last. People remain preoccupied with keeping their jobs and staying above the poverty line. They live in fear of another depression.

World War II began soon after the last upwave started. It was not a war of public issue or national pride. It was forced upon a people who had no choice. As the upwave that began in the late 1930s approached a peak, there was a steady increase in the number of military conflicts associated with a period of mass excitability fought over matters of public issue. This was the case with the Korean War, the Vietnam war, the Middle East war, and even the Falkland Islands crisis early in 1982. Polls then show the British people screaming for blood and battle.

The timing of war as evidence to support the completion of an upwave and beginning of a downwave is overwhelming. It adds further confirmation that the upwave was completed in 1973–1974, at the commodity price peak, duplicating the sequence for the fourth time in 200 years.

There is little evidence of major international conflict during the downwave, according to the social pattern of the long wave. There need be no fear of a nuclear war or any other type of major conflict, at least until the downwave is over. War is usually the last of several attempts to reverse the deflationary cycle that follows five to ten years after the trough of the secondary depression, punctuating the transitional phase from downwave to upwave.

There appears to be a move away from wars involving open combat and mass death and destruction. Recent conflicts have been far more localized, not unlike those of the eighteenth and nineteenth centuries. The combination of wars near the terminal phase of the most recent upwave resulted in the same type of financial problems associated with the 1914–1918 war, but were limited to localized conflicts. While another major war can be expected during the 1990s, after the beginning of the next upwave, that war is likely to be localized, probably in the East. The damage will be mainly financial, not physical with the destruction of people, goods and property.

Aside from offering clues to the possibility of international conflict and mass destruction, the long wave tendencies governing warlike attitudes also help to establish our current place in the economic sequence. Wars in recent years appear after a period of prosperity. The response of the population to recent military conflict is further evidence to support the long wave thesis. We have passed the final phase of the upwave.

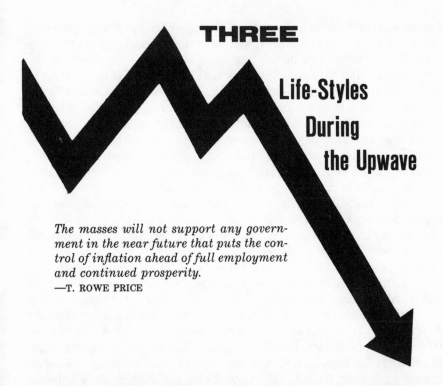

THREE

Life-Styles
During
the Upwave

The masses will not support any govern-
ment in the near future that puts the con-
trol of inflation ahead of full employment
and continued prosperity.
—T. ROWE PRICE

The economic life of the Western world, and your personal future, hangs by a single international thread. That thread is monetary policy. I have treated the period of rising prices and inflationary prosperity as the "up-wave." Rising prices are not the cause of the upwave. They are the effect of underlying forces which can be traced to the actions of politicians; they, in turn, reflect the demands of the electorate.

Take a hard look at inflation. What is inflation, precisely? The root of inflation is, of course, "inflate" . . . the way you would inflate a balloon. When it comes to the inflation we know so well, the supply of currency is being inflated. Who controls the currency we have in circulation? You guessed it . . . the government! And the government benefits handsomely from inflation through substantially increased revenues which provide the illusion of prosperity.

To understand why prices rise, you must grasp the concept that rising prices, mistakenly referred to as inflation, are simply caused by more money chasing fewer goods, or the same amount of money chasing goods. In the classic quantity of money theory, there is a balance between the amount of money in circulation, the amount of goods and services available for consumption and the price of those goods and services. The govern-ment creates money through various means. When the amount of money in circulation is increased, but the quantity of goods does not increase

proportionately, the further injection of money is used to bid up the existing prices of goods and services. That is what happens during an upwave,
and that is why prices rise during the upwave.

There is another fundamental cause for rising prices. If the amount of
money in circulation stays the same, but falling production creates fewer
goods and services, then we have a smaller number of goods and services,
competing for the same amount of money. Again the result is rising prices.

Government can reduce the money in circulation with the same ease
as it can be expanded. During the early stages of the upwave, money tends
to increase faster than the volume of goods and services, until severe
shortages occur, and people begin hoarding, sending prices rocketing. During the latter stages of the upwave, production begins to fall, but the
money in circulation continues to rise.

The power of various cartels and self-interest organizations increases
with the upwave. As the upwave develops, people tend to group together
like the lemmings. Labor is a powerful cartel. If labor cartels exert their
muscle for higher wages "to keep up with inflation," the result is inevitable.
Unless there is a corresponding increase in productivity, the money to pay
the wages will have to come from the money creation pool within the
banking system. Higher prices will result. Rising wages are believed to be
a further cause of inflation. But they are the effect of rising inflation, since
wage demands "to keep up with inflation" would not occur if there were no
inflation to start with. Rising prices cause rising wage demands, which lead
to further price rises, leading to further wage demands, ad infinitum.

At the early stages of the period of prosperity, increased money in
circulation leads to a reduction in unemployment, and full employment in
the middle of the upwave. As the upwave becomes more mature, the only
way to break spiraling wage and price increases, and to reduce labor costs,
is for employers to start economizing on labor, increasing unemployment.

A fall in demand for goods and services follows, once again leading to
higher prices and higher unemployment . . . a self-feeding spiral down and
down. At the end of the expansion phase, a severe recession becomes
unavoidable. Prosperity and full employment raise the expectations of the
electorate so that a recession becomes intolerable. The resultant mounting
confusion cannot be solved in a democracy. When peak prices combine with
a lull in business activity, and higher wage demands are rejected and met
by higher unemployment, an untenable disillusionment occurs. Uncertainty
and confusion become unbearable. The government is blamed for mismanagement. It is voted out of power, and political instability, uncertainty and
rapid changes in government peculiar to the final stage of a prosperity all
follow.

POLITICAL TRENDS DURING THE UPWAVE

The first major sociopolitical shock during the early stages of the
upwave is the outbreak of war. This starts the adrenaline flowing again.

There is a rapid pickup in economic activity and employment as the economy moves into wartime production. Expectations begin to rise as the economy becomes more prosperous, and then even more prosperous when there is a conversion to peacetime economic activity. During the transition phase at the end of the war, there are fears of a slump. To keep the economy moving and to avoid a post-war slump, the government will usually launch a peacetime spending program to maintain wartime demand levels by encouraging consumption. This sows the seeds of the ultimate inflation. Social spending increases. Welfare payments increase. The government prints more and more money, and the balance of payments moves steadily into deficit. As the upwave progresses, expectations are heightened. The common enemy is believed to be recession, as the depression remains fresh in the minds of the electorate. Booms during the upwave create excesses. Recessions reduce excesses. Government policy prevents the elimination of excesses throughout the upwave, leading to an overextended economy ultimately doomed to extinction.

There is a distinct interaction between political trends and the long wave pattern of economic behavior. At the beginning of the upwave there is usually a shift from right wing to left wing politics. At the end of the upwave, there is a shift back to the right, before a period of political disarray and uncertainty. This has led to the demolition of the democratic processes in some societies during the downwave.

During the upwave, the correlations between political preferences and prices appear unreliable. During the latter stages of the upwave, there is a distinct tendency toward left-wing politics. At the end of the upwave, the left is ousted and a right-wing government usually takes over.

The upwave begins following a long period of austerity. The depression; lack of business opportunity; the absence of war for several years, all tend to leave the nation in a rather tranquil, subdued state, with little taste for politics. A major shift in political parties is likely to have taken place toward the end of the downwave. The political party in power at the time would have been held responsible for the depression. As living conditions begin to improve in the early stages of the upwave, people are primarily concerned with their day-to-day existence.

As the upwave progresses, it becomes fashionable for the "haves" to make demands on behalf of the "have nots." Union membership and power increase. The government is lobbied by more self-interest cartels whose demands must be met if they are to retain office. The political strategy is to placate the electorate. Whether the economy can meet the demands made of it is of little importance.

As the upwave continues, consumers are encouraged to consume. The more they are encouraged, the more they want. Consumers are not economists. The more the government promises, the more people will expect. When government rhetoric encourages people to believe that a steady increase in the standard of living is an inalienable right, they will demand that right.

| Major Sociopolitical Changes In the Phases of Each Cycle | | | | |
Cycle	Growth Phase Excluding Last Decade	Last Decade of Growth Phase & Primary Depression	Plateau Phase	Stagnant Phase
#1 1780s to 1843	1788-1804 -Bill of Rights (1791) -Alien & Sedition acts (1798)	1805-15 -Banned importation of slaves (1807)	1816-19 -First protective tariffs (1816)	1819-43 -Land Act of 1820 -Jacksonian Democracy (1828-42) (equal suffrage for males) -Tariff of Abominations (1824) (increase) -Anti-Slavery issues (1820) -Modern Democratic Party formed (1825)
#2 1843 to 1896	1843-55 -Free vs. slave states issues -Modern Republican Party formed (1854) -Tariff reduction of 1846	1856-65 -Homestead Act (1862) -College Land Act (1862) -National Banking System (1863) -Emancipation Proclamation (1863) -Tariff of 1857 (reduced) -Tariff of 1861 (increased)	1867-73 -Knights of Labor formed (1869) -Voting rights to blacks (1870) -Women's suffrage in Wyoming (1869)	1873-96 -Silver Purchase Act (1878) -Civil Rights Act (blacks) (1875) -Interstate Commerce Act (1887) -Sherman Anti-Trust Act (1890) -First Civil Service Law (1883) -McKinley Tariff Act (1890) -Silver Purchase Act (1890) -AFL formed (1881) -Wilson Tariff Act (1894) (reduced) -Immigration restricted (1882 & 85)
#3 1896 to 1940	1896-1910 -Dingley Tariff Act (1897) (increased) -Payne-Aldrich Tariff (1909) (reduced) -Currency Act (Free Silver) (1900) -Federal Railroad Regulation (1903) -FDA created (1906) -Dept. of Commerce & Labor created (1903)	1911-21 -Workmen's Compensation Act (1916) -Break up of Standard Oil (1911) -Federal Reserve Act (1913) -Income Tax enacted (1913) -Prohibition enacted (1919) -Women's Suffrage (1920) -Immigration limited (1921) -Clayton Anti-Trust Act (1914) -FTC created (1914) -Federal Farm Loan Act (1916) -Child Labor Law (1916) -Major tariff reduction & reform (1913)	1922-29 -Immigration limited (1924) -Fortney-McCumber Tariffs (1922) (big increase)	1929-40 -CCC (1933) - WPA (1935) -Prohibition repealed (1933) -Smoot-Hawley Tariff (1930) (big increase) -FDIC created (1933) -TVA created (1934) -Nat'l Industrial Recovery Act (1933) -Social Security enacted (1935) -Nat'l Labor Relations Act (1935) -Fair Labor Standards Act (1938) -Public Housing Act (1938) -SEC formed (1934) -FHA formed (1934) -Reconstruction Finance Corp. (1932) -Norris-LaGuardia Pro-Union Act (1932)
#4 1940 to ?	1940-63 -Full Employment Act (1946) -Taft-Hartley Act (1947) (restricted unions) -Civil Rights sit-ins begin (1960) -Trade Expansion Act (1962) (to reduce tariffs) -Dept. of HEW created (1953)	1964-75 -Federal Aid to Education (1965) -Medicare enacted (1965) -Voting Rights Act (1965) -Civil Rights Act (1964) -Voting Rights to 18-year-olds (1971) -Major race riots (1965 & 67) -Equal Rights Amendment passed by Senate (1972) -Pension Reform Act (ERISA) (1974) -Dept. of HUD created (1965) -Environmental Protection Agency formed (1970) -Occupational Safety & Health Act (1972) -Nat'l Rail Passenger System (1971)	1976-? -Dept. of Energy created (1977)	
TOTAL ITEMS IN COLUMN	16	32	7	30
ITEMS PER YEAR	0.23	0.71	0.35	0.49

Note: Names of acts were revised as needed to be more descriptive. Foreign policy issues are not included.

FIGURE 10

The upwave is a period of more . . . more . . . more . . . more, more, more, more. Any political party promising more than the party in power will gain popularity. Toward the end of the upwave, no political party can satisfy the heightened expectations of the masses. The electorate is not prepared to accept the slightest sacrifice or inconvenience. At the first sign of economic trouble at the end of the upwave, the government is ousted, having failed to provide the unprovidable. Complete political disarray follows, with changes in party, sometimes leading to a coalition government or a dictatorship.

Long-term political trends show several converging factors at the end of the upwave coinciding with a shift in the political cycle and leading to turmoil, economic deterioration and the kind of instability seen all over the world during the past five years or so. The breaking down of political parties into separate factions is a warning of the political disarray to come. Instead of the normal two-party system, with the winner having a majority, in Britain, France, Italy and West Germany, we see a three-, four- and sometimes twenty-party system.

Political disunity, and a break-up of the party system, merge with economic factors which also have political implications, at the end of the upwave. Productivity falls against seemingly intractable inflation. Government finds it difficult to collect taxes. There is an explosion in the subterranean economy. The amount of goods and services produced by workers steadily falls. All of these factors have been operating in America for quite some time, and the electorate has been unwilling to acknowledge the root cause of the problem, preferring instead to blame government.

If we superimpose the political cycle onto the long wave patterns of economic behavior, we find a period of relative stability during the early stages of the upwave. The party in office tends to hold office for relatively long periods. There is a tendency toward left-wing politics as the upwave matures. In the later stages of the upwave, the strong move to left-wing politics remains, but the promises of politicians are insufficient to meet the demands of the electorate. At the beginning of the downwave, the left-wing party is ousted, leading to political turbulence for about a decade. The turbulence often involves several changes in government, or political philosophy. The mid-decade covering recession and secondary prosperity brings the greatest number of shifts in political preferences. Then many new parties emerge, all with proposals for solving the problems of the mid-decade.

Downwave politics move to the right until the secondary depression gets underway. At the end of the secondary depression there is a shift back to the left and democracy is most vulnerable. Whatever party was in office during the secondary depression is naturally booted out. The incoming party usually has left-wing leanings but sometimes the result has been a dictator.

Three factors must be considered when relating the political trends to the long wave. The first is the public support for right-wing or left-wing politics at various stages of the long wave model. The second is the general level of interest in politics. The third is the "overlap" between political parties.

U.S. presidents in office at the end of the upwaves reveal a distinct link between politics and the long wave economic pattern. There is additional evidence to suggest that an upwave has recently ended. Without exception, every U.S. president in office approaching the long wave peak, or immediately thereafter, favored "left-wing" politics. Each of those presidents was ousted from office immediately prior to or slightly after the end of the upwave.

At the peak of the first upwave in 1814, James Madison was president. He was elected in 1808, reelected in 1812, and voted out in 1816, two years after the peak of the first upwave. James Madison was a liberal or "left-wing" politician by today's definition. James Monroe, who succeeded him, would have been described as right-wing.

At the peak of the second upwave in 1864, Abraham Lincoln was president. He could have been called left-of-center. In 1868, Ulysses S. Grant took office, four years after the peak of the second upwave. President Grant was a right-wing politician.

President Woodrow Wilson, another public administrator with liberal leanings (or left-wing politics in the metaphoric sense), was in office during the peak of the upwave in 1920. He was succeeded by President Harding, a right-wing conservative, in that year.

Jimmy Carter was elected president as the upwave was in its final throes in 1976. Carter was an advocate of public spending and liberal monetary growth, and was probably the most left-wing Democratic president America has ever had. In traditional fashion, as the downwave ensued, inflation and profligate spending became politically unacceptable, and Ronald Reagan, an exceptionally conservative right-wing politician, was elected to preside over a more stringent monetary policy in November 1980.

Are there any parallels today with such political shifts that have been observed through history? Maybe, maybe . . . In the early stages of the depression, Herbert Hoover was a very popular president. Even as late as 1931, by which time unemployment had doubled to 8 million, Herbert Hoover still held the peoples' hearts. It was firmly believed in Washington and Wall Street that if only confidence could be restored, the banks would lend money again, factories would reopen, workers would be hired and life would return to normal.

If economic growth could have been restored by exhortation it certainly would have been. Hoover and his aides were constantly predicting recovery just around the corner. "The economy is fundamentally sound," the president kept reminding the people. The Depression was just a "passing incident in our national life," he kept saying. Repeatedly, he predicted a recovery by a given date or month, only to have his prediction turn sour.

Secretary Mellon was an equally indefatigable and equally erring prophet. "I see nothing in the present situation that is either menacing or warrants pessimism," he said as the Depression dragged to the end of its second year. Myron C. Taylor, chairman of the U.S. Steel Corporation, told a gathering in New York in October 1932 that the general industrial situation was "more promising" than at any time in the previous two years and that the recovery was "definite and progressive." Do you see any parallels with the exhortations of Ronald Reagan and Donald Regan in the past two years?

President Hoover had been trapped by the conventional wisdom of the day. The system as people had known it was simply incapable of adjusting automatically to the mountainous stresses that had been piled on it since 1929. The adjustment required in the early 1930s was unlike the cyclical adjustments of the past—the post-war recession of 1920–1921 or the money panic of 1907. The dawning of this bitter truth in mid-1932 as the presidential election campaign got underway left Hoover saddened, dismayed and helpless. The outcome of the elections, however, was hardly in any doubt at the time. Herbert Hoover believed that a couple of major speeches were all that was needed on his part to ensure reelection—so soundly had the Democrats been trounced in the election of 1928.

It is difficult to determine precisely when President Hoover began to lose the support of the American people. It could have been on the very same day that Franklin D. Roosevelt received the presidential nomination at the Democratic National Convention. Roosevelt, a cripple, was considered almost a left-wing extremist.

The rest, in any case, is history. Roosevelt won by a landslide and the Democrats returned a large majority to Congress. It was time for the New Deal. Will it be time for a New Deal in November 1984?

PERSONAL VALUES DURING THE UPWAVE

The government we get is the government we deserve, because it is the government we ask for. That has become a cliché. Nevertheless, there is a distinct relationship between the change in personal values and our choice of leaders during the sequences of economic life in industrialized societies.

Economic hardship will produce an emotive response. When people experience pain or hardship they often become subdued; they retrench and seek some type of solace to avoid further discomfort. When people see their friends and relatives suffer a depression, and see the world as a risky place to live, they feel helpless. Individuals lose faith in their own powers. Most people believe they are in complete control of their own destinies, but during periods of severe economic dislocation, this belief is openly challenged. People become cautious, introspective and unwilling to accept risk. They attempt to shelter themselves from uncertainty wherever possible. Their feelings run counter to the principles of individualistic capitalism where the risk-taker reaps the greatest rewards. The upwave begins under such a psychological atmosphere.

As the upwave progresses, and signs of prosperity appear, people become more willing to assume risk. They become more outgoing and gregarious. The pleasure principle takes over, and people become more prone to hedonistic behavior, seeking fun and excitement. They indulge in their quest for pleasure and leisure. There is a move to abolish any form of censorship imposing intellectual or physical restraint. People want to stand on their own as individuals, and express themselves freely.

During a long period of prosperity, people will favor a government whose policies allow maximum permissiveness, self-indulgence with minimal restrictions. They see the world as relatively risk-free. When people become carefree and begin to assume the prosperity of previous years will go on forever, they once again feel they control their own destiny. They no longer need the strength of "big brother" trade unions behind them. They start businesses, borrow money to increase their living standards, begin playing the stock market and engaging in speculative ventures. There is greater interest in politics, as people feel that they have the power not only to solve their own problems, but also the problems of society at large. Endless prosperity is taken for granted. Capitalism and laissez-faire economics reign supreme during the final stages of the upwave. There is increasing competition and a move toward freeing all markets, and reducing trade barriers. This behavior appears during each upwave of the long-term economic pattern—including those of the eighteenth century.

The peak of the last upwave in 1974 brought the "Age of Aquarius." From the mid-1960s to the mid-1970s, there was a tidal wave of social and economic legislation the world over. World leaders promised to cure all the miseries of the human condition at the stroke of a pen. It was supposed to be the dawn of a new era, when people would be less concerned about achieving success, their inalienable right.

New-found values meant people should be more intent on having fun, "doing their own thing." Women's skirts became shorter and shorter until "hot pants" turned hemlines into crotchlines. The female form was emancipated. Promiscuity was fashionable. Women could take the "Pill," and enjoy the sexual freedom long enjoyed by men. Sex was fun, not filth. Millions were made in the pornography industry. *The Happy Hooker*, the story of an illustrious prostitute, became a best-seller. *Deep Throat*, the adventures of a fellatio expert, was a notoriously successful film. It was fashionable for single people to live like married people, and for married people to live like single people.

The final stages of the upwave promised a period when the human spirit would liberate itself from the discipline and authority of repressive social and political institutions. Instant gratification was the primary objective. Liberation meant glue-sniffing, acid rock, mind expanding drugs, hippie communes, group sex, wife-swapping, abortion and an alarming deterioration in the family unit. During the 1960s and 1970s, the divorce rate soared. Following a cluster of inflationary wars that led to public resentment, the tranquility of the 1940s and 1950s came to an abrupt end as black ghettos in the United States and Britain erupted. Extreme political groups sent shivers down the spines of the middle classes. Bombings, hijackings, kidnappings, and terrorism throughout the world became almost routine.

As inflation moved up and public morality went down, many felt they were entering a period of civilization without precedent. Of course, this was untrue. During the early 1900s, a new upwave began, characterized by the same type of public attitudes, peace and tranquility, as were prevalent during the emerging prosperity of the 1950s. But, like the 1960s and 1970s with the peak inflation wars, the period surrounding World War I bears a strikingly close resemblance.

The third upwave began shortly before the death of Queen Victoria in 1901, and marked the beginning of changes that were felt with broadening impact all through the early twentieth century. There was a swing away from Victorianism. As the economic improvement gained momentum, and prosperity began to be taken for granted, the same type of idealistic hopes prevailed as in the late 1960s. Following World War I, a new era was believed to be underway. Fifteen years of prosperity convinced people that a depression on the scale of the 1890s could never happen again. It was generally assumed that people were again in control of their destiny, and it would always be that way.

A social revolution began in the period after World War I. People began adopting attitudes totally different from anything at the turn of the century. The period from 1919 to 1929 was a time of abundance. A taste for the good things of life: home ownership, motoring, foreign travel, previously the preserves of the rich, came within the purchasing power of the lower-middle- and upper-working-classes. The $2,000-a-year man could afford a holiday in Europe. The latter stages of the third and fourth upwaves shared a curious blend of soft-option idealism on public issues with a desire to evade private responsibilities.

The post-World War I younger generation was as rebellious as the generation of the 1950s and 1960s, for much the same reasons. Affluence and irresponsibility bred a hell-raising revolt against discipline and parental authority. They wanted fun, thrills and living for the moment. The end of the war ushered in the "Jazz Age," hip-flasks, flappers and the Charleston. It was a time of alcoholic abuse and a decline in moral values. Hedonism blossomed, as it did in the 1960s.

During the fourth upwave, women got the Pill. During the third upwave women got the vote. What followed was a form of women's liberation that took the world by storm. Women took off their corsets. They smoked and drank alcohol in public. They bared their knees, their backs and bosoms, and began painting themselves with lipstick and rouge. Woman's place in the world was being discussed as never before.

The upwave leaves its mark on many areas of industrialized society. In addition to the economic, political and social aspects, there are also decided trends in fashion, music, literature and religion.

CULTURAL TRENDS DURING THE UPWAVE

The central cultural characteristic of the final stages of the upwave is the consumer mentality. During the upwave of the eighteenth and nineteenth centuries, the West rejected two kinds of authority: the authority of the king to tell us what to do, and the authority of the church to tell us how to think. Freedom came to be understood as the absence of external constraint. In the 1920s, the Freudian gospel appeared, interpreted to mean that repression was harmful to the individual. Not only external constraints, but also internal constraints with their inherent moral codes, were seen as illicit restrictions upon personal freedom.

At the latter stages of the upwave, society becomes so preoccupied with consumption that even religion becomes a commodity to be ruled by the whims of shoppers in a religious marketplace. Alternative religions spring up like weeds, since the repressive status of the traditional religions, which can cope with the social mores of the early stages of the upwave, are incompatible with the freedoms required during the later stages of the upwave.

Fashion, music, literature, theater and dance all fall under the influence of the upwave. The years of rising excitement can be heard clearly in the increasing excitability of the music. The 1950s and 1960s gave birth to rock music. It grew, slowly at first, but ultimately captured the entire "pop" idiom. Rock became progressively more frenetic, reaching the epitome of musical discord with "punk rock" in the late 1970s. Rock symbolized the mood of the final stages of the upwave in the 1970s, just as jazz symbolized the period of increasing affluence prior to World War I, and continued into the secondary prosperity of the 1920s. The pre-World War I jazz and the 1950s rock were joyful, a unique release from the traditions of the early stages of the upwave. But they were totally inappropriate for the heightened excitability later in the upwave. Action music is a product of the final stages of prosperity, relieving the tensions generated at a time of mass excitability in many areas.

Action dances are invented to accompany action music. During the 1940s and 1950s dancing was a peaceful romantic experience to be shared by a man and a woman. They held each other gently, their bodies touching, swaying to the rhythm of the sweet lilting strains of an orchestra. Just as the Charleston and Blackbottom were the action dances of the third upwave, our recent upwave produced the Madison, the Mashed Potato, the Twist, the Frug. Ultimately they led to free-style narcissism, where young girls and middle-aged women jerk their bodies at mirrored discotheques, oblivious to the problems of their sometimes less than loose-limbed male companions who often take on the unfortunate appearance of spastics.

The 1970s was the fashion age of the male peacock. Middle-aged men wore tight trousers with navel-level waistbands and see-through paisley shirts. Jackets were thrust aside. Jeans and open-necked shirts became acceptable at establishments previously only open to those wearing a jacket and tie. During the final stages of the upwave, clothing followed the mood of the young . . . excited, rebellious, defiant. Whatever the style was previously, it had to be changed. The change had to be noticeable, exaggerated. Above all, clothes served as a uniform of identification, signifying that the wearer was "with it," a member of the new movement. His clothes told others he was "letting it all hang out." He was "together." The attire of the young was a statement of open rebellion against the constraints imposed by parents. But the adult population also became ensnared by the excited tempo of steadily increasing prosperity. And, as adults began adopting the fashions of the younger generation, rebellious youth had to adopt even more outlandish styles to remain at arms-length from the adult world.

Women's fashions are linked to the upwaves and downwaves with even greater clarity. The amount of feminine charms on display during periods of growth as opposed to periods of contraction is especially striking. According to James Laver, of the Victoria and Albert Museum in London, there was no such thing as fashion in ancient Greece or the Roman Empire; fashion didn't exist until the middle of the fourteenth century. From the fifteenth century onward, fashion trends can be seen quite clearly as inextricably linked to economic conditions. As armament in the fierce battle for masculine attention, the woman of the court during the fourteenth century adopted some of the most effective weapons known, even today, displaying various amounts of decolletage combined with tightly-laced corsets and elaborate hairstyles. During the fifteenth century, necklines were high, corsets loosely tied, and the feminine form well-covered.

The following century brought a complete change in the fortunes of nations, and a change in women's fashions. Bosoms were exposed by low-cut bodices, and derrieres were thrust outward through tight-pinched wasp-waisted corsets. During early Tudor times the wealthy nations declined. Bosoms were covered again, corsets were loosened and the feminine form was removed from display. Then came Elizabethan times and prosperity, and out came the bosoms and bottoms. The same pattern could be seen in seventeenth-century America, as fashion shifted from the modest Puritan styles to the lively, exposed style of the Restoration.

During the upwave that followed the French Revolution, women's fashions were light and near-transparent. Legs came into diffused view, sometimes suggested under dresses of such diaphanousness that pink tights had to be worn beneath the skirt. From 1814 to 1843, legs and bosoms vanished again.

In fashion, there is the thesis of "erotic capital," by which the effectiveness of women's fashion depends on its newness to men. When concentration is on the legs for a considerable period, fashion will then shift to bosoms and bottoms. Following the display of legs during the upwave that began in the late 1780s and ended in 1814, it was not until the upwave of the 1840s to 1860s that bosoms and bottoms appeared once again. Early Victorian styles permitted horizontal lines of decolletage, revealing not only breasts, but shoulders, a new zone of erotic capital.

The downwave of the nineteenth century sent necklines back up to the neck. Hemlines fell so low that skirts had to be lifted when a lady walked.

During the prosperity of the upwave beginning at the turn of the twentieth century, erotic capital achieved its grandest exploitation in history by revealing the feminine form. Necklines opened up into a long *V*. Hemlines moved up until knees appeared. The female back emerged with evening dresses, and some daytime clothing, open in the back down to the waist.

During the downwave of the 1930s, ladies covered up again. Hemlines dropped to the ankle, bosom lines rose to the neck and backs were covered.

It would appear that by the time of the fourth upwave, there was nothing new to display. But never underestimate the ingenuity of fashion designers. Our recent prosperity brought the hemline up to the crotch, the neckline down to the waistline. Bras were discarded, and nipple erections were outlined under outergarments. Some young women were having their pubic hair tinted and permed for purposes best left to the imagination.

Trends in women's fashions and their link with economic activity have been so consistent that an investment analyst devised the "Hemline Indicator," supposedly to help predict the course of the stock market. If skirts went higher, the stock market would go higher. If hemlines fell, shares would fall.

The increasing desire to shed social mores and rid ourselves of constraint as the upwave progresses also has its influence on literature and theater. *Oh Calcutta!* and *Hair*, with full frontal nudity on stage, were the hit shows of the 1960s. During the 1940s and 1950s, movies could not show a man and a woman in bed together, even fully clothed. During the 1970s, filmgoers were treated to a varied diet of male and female copulation on the screen involving couples together in bed, unclothed. The film *Caligula*, released in late 1979, featured homosexuality, sodomy, fellatio, cunnilingus, rape (the male and female variety) and a scene where the mother of the Roman emperor was having a sperm bath while a group of centurions masturbated into the bathing vessel to keep it topped up.

This was an action replay of the terminal stages of the previous upwave during the 1920s. The Roaring Twenties was also a time of sexual permissiveness. Outlandish behavior was accepted and tolerated. There was a proliferation of sex magazines. Lewd pantomime and lascivious sitcoms kept the burlesque houses packed. Men and women ogled at spinning tassels that whirled clockwise, then counter-clockwise, around pendulous bare breasts. The five-foot giant penis strapped to the buttocks of a clown was a standard prop which assured a good laugh.

The movement toward sexual liberation—and female liberation—during the twenties was not, of course, confined to America. Berlin and

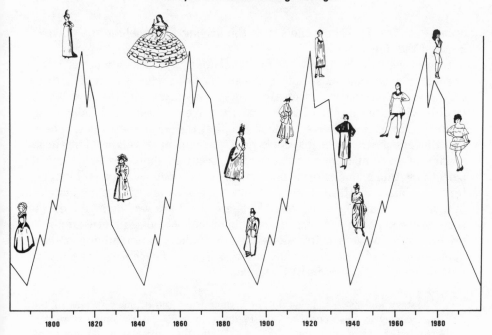

The Cycle of Fashion through the ages

1800   1820   1840   1860   1880   1900   1920   1940   1960   1980

FIGURE 11   THE HEMLINE INDICATOR

Paris were the great fun centers of Europe. Here is how Walter Laqueur's book *Weimar* describes the Berlin scene in the latter part of the decade. "According to the new *Zeitgeist*, sex, like justice, had to be seen to be done. The new sex wave ranged from the establishment of scientific (or pseudo-scientific) research institutes to nude shows and hard core pornography. Periodicals called *Free Love, The Grass Widow, Woman without Man*, tried to imitate their counterparts in Paris, while a couple of theaters did the same with the Folies Bergères and the Casino de Paris."

The spirit of liberation grew more open as the roaring of the twenties grew louder. They had started prudish. The doings of a movie colony in California were portrayed in a play called *The Demi-Virgin* in 1921. Its English playwright was actually jailed on a charge of "promoting an immoral, impure play with intentional appeal for box-office profit to lustful, licentious, morbidly erotic, vulgar and disorderly minds." Five years later, portrayal of the antics of Hollywood would have produced yawns.

If the 1960s and 1970s were the era of a new morality, it was most certainly not an invention of the period. The term was invented in 1922. The handbook to the New Morality was a book called *Hypatia* by Mrs. Bertrand Russell. The counterpart of *The Joy of Sex* in the 1920s was a book on birth control by Dr. Marie Stopes which was a record best-seller.

The nature of the upwave permeates practically every conceivable

area of society. Public psychology is the driving force behind the upwave
. . . and the downwave.

Opponents of the long wave theory claim that it lacks a motive. Many
say a long wave may exist but, in the absence of evidence to demonstrate
why, deep suspicions have been aroused. It is my firm belief that the causes
lie deep within the psyche of the human race. We can look at inflation, wars,
political trends, speculative manias, etc., but these are not causes. These
are the effects of mass psychological phenomena involving long-term
swings of pessimism and optimism that occur in short-term rhythmical
patterns within a longer-term rhythmical pattern and within a still longer-
term rhythmical pattern thereafter, like wheels within wheels, and circles
in a spiral. According to L. Peter Coogan, there are well-defined correlations between patterns of pessimism and optimism and sequences of share
prices, major business contractions, business indicators and other economic
phenomena. In his extensive work on the subject, *The Rhythmic Cycles of
Optimism and Pessimism*, Coogan states:

> Monetary and fiscal policies do not appear to be the primary causes of the
> business cycle, but appear to modify the amplitude and, to some extent, the
> timing for better or worse, depending upon the correctness, liquidity and
> ingenuity of lenders, borrowers, and spenders. It would appear that 1929–1932
> would have been a major turning point regardless of who had been President.
> Despite the importance of the military and political decisions upon the econ-
> omy, the business cycle and the private sector persists.

The upwave spans a period of psychological desolation to a period of
excessive optimism, covering the full spectrum of people's greed and fear.

FOUR

When
the Bubble
Bursts

*Financial genius is a short memory in a
rising trend*
—J. K. GALBRAITH

In the beginning God made morons. He did that for practice. Then He got down to the serious task of making total imbeciles. And on the dawn of creation, He placed a group of people upon this planet who shared the profound belief that wealth could be created in a vacuum, and who went forth among the populace, entrusted with the task of such wealth creation.

The king's alchemists, many centuries ago, tried to create wealth by attempting to manufacture gold by combining horse manure with goat urine. They failed, of course. The job was turned over to the king's chancellors. They invented counterfeiting.

If the kingdom had 1,000 gold coins and one gold coin was required to purchase one bushel of wheat, then only one thousand bushels could be bought—unless more gold could be found to make more coins. As long as 1,000 bushels of wheat were sufficient, there was no problem. If the peasants suddenly became greedy and demanded more wheat, then more gold had to be found to buy it. The king ran the risk of an uprising, or possibly exile, if he did not produce the goods. Normally the way to get more gold was to make goods in the kingdom and sell them outside at a profit. But if the peasants wanted more wheat and did not want to exert themselves by producing more goods, the chances of accumulating more gold were slim. That was when the king turned to his alchemists. When they failed, he turned to the chancellors. They advised the king that if the edges of the gold coins were shaved off, just a little, more gold coins could be made from the shavings. The chancellors believed no one would notice the gold coins were just that little bit smaller.

Coin-clipping led to a little dilution with base metals, which led to a major dilution. Gold value became a silver value. Silver value became a paper value. Paper money acted as a certificate entitling the holder to claim its value in gold, then in silver, then in the paper of a different country, known as foreign reserves. This process evolved because of the ease with which paper wealth could be created compared to real wealth. It is far easier to clip coins, dilute gold with base metals, and print paper money than it is to produce goods. And that brings us to the massive expansion of currency in circulation during the 1970s.

In the year 1974 the American economic and financial system suffered a severe jolt. It survived well enough, but the jolt was a warning of worse things to come in the 1980s. Borrowing was to blame; borrowing and speculation. The same old story.

During the 1960s, the expansion of the U.S. money supply fell broadly within the range of 2 to 8 percent. In 1971, there was a sudden explosion up to 14 percent and it stayed in a range of 14 to 8 percent throughout the decade.

The early 1970s were marked by the most massive increase in bank lending in U.S. history. Bank loans ran way ahead of deposit funds. In 1973, the ratio of total loans to deposits of all U.S. commercial banks actually exceeded the previous recorded peak of 77 percent which was—guess when —in 1929. This was the time when U.S. bankers began scouring the world to lend money to anyone who wanted it. And the bigger the sums the better. For about the same effort, a loan of $100 million at 0.25 percent can seem a much more attractive proposition than a loan of $1 million at 1 percent. Twenty-five times more attractive. This was the beginning, just the beginning of course, of the mighty growth of the Eurodollar market—that is, dollars lent outside America. It was the infancy of what was practically a twentieth-century invention, international wholesale banking: you fixed up your loan to North Korea at 0.25 margin and then you borrowed the money from the banks who had missed out on the deal. If Citibank was doing it so should Chemical Bank and if they were doing it so should the First Bank of Peoria. There was no risk. Supertanker owners and developing countries were favorite targets. Of course in time it turned out that they were not such good risks after all.

At home, real estate was all the fashion. The stock market was booming in 1973, and so was the market for rented accommodation. Put the two together and you came up with the real estate investment trust (REIT). At its peak, bank lending to REITs totted up to $21 billion, which when added to a futher $10 billion of direct loans on REIT properties was equivalent to a cool 2.5 percent of national income.

Throughout history such speculative booms have always ended in a bust. In the event, the oil crisis was the trigger. The slump on the stock market, when it came, was the most severe for thirty-five years, since the early 1930s. The Dow Jones Industrial index plunged from over 1000 to under 600. Loans secured on supertankers were practically valueless: nobody needed all the hulls that were still coming out of the shipyards. Besides, when the Suez Canal opened after the second Egypt/Israel war, supertankers were too big to pass through it. Meanwhile all those apartments, offices and shopping malls that had looked half-full in the days of optimism, looked half-empty when fear took its place. With no rent coming, you can't pay your interest bills. There were many mortgage foreclosures. The banks were left with a tally of nonperforming loans that in some cases had not been exceeded even after the round of South American defaults in 1982.

Yet, New York in the winter of 1974 was a beer garden compared to the City of London. In those dark days the British stock market suffered its worst decline in recorded history, with a fall of 78 percent in the leading stock index from peak to trough. The trouble lay in the buildup of debt and the speculative vehicle to which all the borrowing was devoted—commercial real estate. The bust in London was a full-scale financial panic on a par with the very worst in British history. It deserves a chapter all to itself: it is dealt with in Chapter Seven.

But once again, the real estate bubble in Britain was a symptom. The underlying sickness lay in the attitudes of the time—particularly attitudes to money. The British government in 1972 undertook an experiment in reflation by money which was far more drastic than its U.S. counterpart; it was more reminiscent of the Weimar government. In mid-1972, the U.K. money supply was growing at 31 percent. And none of this money was finding its way into productive investment. Manufacturing investment was down 10 percent on the previous year at the time of this peak in money growth, while financial assets grew 42 percent.

The financial crisis in London did provide such a shock that certain bad habits (like the more speculative real estate developments) were abandoned indefinitely. It even paved the way, perhaps, for the return to conservative finances and the Thatcher government's attack on budget deficits that drew some applause from the incoming administration in Washington. But that is jumping the gun. For the period between 1974 and 1979 saw the wildest money explosion in peacetime America.

America reacted to the oil crisis in the fall of 1973 with a tightening of the money horns: the economy had been overheating and the prospect of double digit rather frightened a nation unused to it. The result of the tightening was to exacerbate the deterioration in the economy, and by mid-1974, the cause for alarm was the steepest plunge in the economy since the war. So it was that America (and most other nations) reflated out of the 1974 slump by printing money. Figure 4 tells the story. It was during the next few years that the term "inflation hedge" gained currency.

The smart guys with the slide rules had seen earlier on at the start of the 1970s the way things were headed—especially if they kept tabs on what happened in South America or talked to people in Europe. But the great American public was relatively slow to see that when prices were rising fast money bought less goods: so the first step was to exchange all your money for goods. If that was right, then it was even more right to go short of money, that is, borrow, and borrow all you could. Uncle Sam made it easy by making interest tax deductible.

This is fairly obvious with hindsight. It was less clear at the start of the 1970s. In 1976 people still remembered the 1974 slump and inflation was falling fast. It was falling again in 1977 and some thought that maybe the post-oil-crisis inflation really was an on-off affair. But in 1978 the money machine took off again ahead of the presidential elections the next year. By 1979 few could be in doubt about the wisdom of exchanging money for things. Also the money machine was keeping interest rates low at the end of the 1970s, so there was a further incentive to maximize borrowing. People borrowed to buy precious metals, coins, antiques and even junk. Above all they borrowed to buy homes, but that story, the story of the greatest public speculation in history, is for Chapter Seven.

The gold price peaked in January 1980. The silver bubble collapsed soon after. The point about the gold boom was the extent to which it involved members of the public who had never hitherto had any interest in the metal. The point about the silver bubble was the mentality that allowed it to happen. Oh, and the borrowing, that meant that Bunker Hunt was in hock for over $1 billion when the crash came. We just never learn, never.

ANATOMY OF A SPECULATIVE ORGY

When the upwave comes to an end, when prices peak and the final burst of economic activity in the upwave takes place, the speculative bubble bursts and sets the downwave in motion. During the early 1970s, this happened in the stock market and in real estate, and brought a banking crisis. It was an exact repetition of what has occurred after very long period of prosperity throughout history. The force propelling the speculative mania at the end of the upwave is growing optimism, born out of long periods of prosperity.

Increasing numbers of businessmen and individuals adopt the view that business contractions will be minimal, and that prosperity will continue indefinitely. This leads to overconfidence and a willingness to assume ever-increasing risks. According to economist Hyman Minsky, the events which lead up to the end of a speculative boom and subsequent financial crisis begin with some sort of "displacement," an exogenous event which acts as a shock to the macroeconomic system. The exact nature of the displacement has varied from one speculative boom to another in different countries at different times. It could be the ending of a war, a bumper harvest, a new invention which boosts economic development, an improvement in production methods or transport, a sudden financial success by an individual or group of individuals. That displacement could be a dramatic change in the political arena sparked off by war, revolution or a major shift in public attitudes. All of these factors have served as the vehicles for speculative orgies in the past. Any event or series of events potent enough to alter the perception of profit opportunities within a nation's economy could set the speculative ball rolling.

Without exception, every boom throughout history has been fed by an expansion of credit. It is endemic to every upwave. Easy money enables people who would normally never have participated to join in the boom. Easy money also encourages many to speculate well beyond their means. The credit conditions preceding the Wall Street crash of 1929 were cited as the major reason for the collapse. Then it was possible to buy securities for a mere 10 percent of their market value. Many borrowed to obtain that 10 percent. Some held many thousands of dollars worth of securities, all on borrowed money. But, of course, the money had to be paid back.

As the long period of prosperity continues and risk seems to diminish, the desire to make a quick profit grows in diametric proportion. The displacement is the harbinger of newly perceived investment opportunities which astute businessmen attempt to exploit at the incipient stages of the upwave. The urge to speculate gets stronger, and the upwave continues.

Eventually, alarming numbers of individuals are speculating without any real understanding. The rational profit potential of investments which attracted more astute investors is exhausted. Speculation for profit, and profit only, leads people away from the normal investment criteria prominent in the early stages of the upwave. Marginal ventures emerge, along with imitations of ventures that were previously profitable. Frauds and swindles proliferate. What has been described as "mania" and "bubble" is the final result. Says Minsky, "the word mania emphasizes the irrationality . . . bubble foreshadows bursting."

Obviously those who fall prey to mania in the later stages of speculation euphoria pay the highest prices. They also incur the highest financing costs, since there is a much greater demand for credit at that time. So, late participants are the most vulnerable when the bubble bursts. Two-thirds of the participants in a speculative orgy are drawn into the stampede in the final stages. And the price of the speculative vehicle usually loses about 80 percent of its gains, made during the previous upswing, when the bubble bursts.

ANATOMY OF A BUST

In the past thirty years of my investment career, I have never been the victim of a speculative orgy. I have a perverse nature: I become an enthusiastic buyer after a severe price decline, then become extremely anxious

after a long period of rising prices and rampant speculative activity. I
attribute that to my early career as a Wall Street stockbroker, where I was
guided by astute and successful operators. One event I recollect took place
during the 1960s stock market boom in America. For several years I shared
a desk with Charlie Meyer, one of Wall Street's old-timers. He had been
around during the Wall Street crash, and had witnessed the events leading
up to it. Charlie was an instinctive stock market operator. He would gauge
the investment climate by the tempo of speculative activity. Without balance sheets and other popular investment aids, he managed to acquire
several million dollars just by watching the prices as they traveled across
the New York Stock Exchange ticker tape, and by monitoring the expres-
sions of greed and fear on the faces of his fellow investors.

One day, Charlie spun around in his chair, slapped me on the back and
said, "Beckman! Too many dummies are getting rich. I'm getting the hell
out!" Charlie telephoned the firm's floor broker on the New York Exchange, and sold every investment he had within the hour. That was two
days before shares peaked and began tumbling. Charlie reckoned the stock
market craze had turned to insanity, and that share prices had reached a
level beyond any realistic measure of value.

Toward the end of every speculative boom, the more astute investors,
who got in on the ground floor, take their profits and sell out. When the
speculative bubble reaches a peak, prices hesitate as new gamblers to the
speculative mania are balanced by the smart money crowd who are then
heading for the exits. When the speculative mania's slowing tempo
becomes more obvious, latecomers are more reluctant to participate. Existing players increasingly decide to turn paper profits into cash. And so the
gradual move out of the speculative counters accelerates into a race to
secure the best prices before they fall further. The rush to turn paper into
cash becomes a stampede. Many who borrowed heavily are late in turning
paper into cash; others are forced to cash in their paper by worried lenders.
The steep decline in values is self-feeding. Proceeds fall below the amount
borrowed, and an entirely new set of problems is created.

BUBBLES AND PANICS OF PERIODS PAST

The trigger which turns a speculative orgy into a financial crisis can
take as many forms as the initial displacement which starts it. It could be
the failure of a bank heavily committed to financing speculative activities,
such as Penn Square financing the speculative oil boom. It could be the
failure of a large company in the industry which attracted the most speculation. Sometimes it has been the unfolding of massive swindles, one sufficient to reverse speculative mania. An early example was the South Sea
Bubble, which forced England's entire financial system to its knees. During
the early 1700s, wild speculation in the South Sea Company sent the shares
rocketing. A number of satellite companies which were imitations also

crashed in. In one scheme, promoters sold one million pounds worth of shares to the greedy and gullible in a company to produce a wheel for perpetual motion.

Speculation was so rife that other promoters did not even bother to inform prospective investors what the funds would actually be used for. A typical financial prospectus might simply have announced the formation of a company whose purpose was to "carry on an undertaking of great advantage." One such prospectus added, "Every investor who deposits £2 per share is to be entitled to £100 per annum." Within five hours, that absurd prospectus had attracted £2,000. In the sixth hour, the director absconded with the investors' funds, no doubt headed for the South Seas.

It has been estimated that £300 million was ploughed into various speculative investments during this eighteenth-century mania. It reached such a dangerous level that the so-called "Bubble Act" was passed in 1720, making it illegal for companies to raise funds without a royal charter. All too quickly, the act proved counterproductive. No one really knew which of the bubble companies were legal or illegal. When the bubble burst, every company became suspect, and a potential victim of a selling stampede. The torrent of forced liquidations and distress selling affected the South Sea Company itself. It went bankrupt in 1720. Many banking institutions were heavily committed to financing the company, and many individuals had pledged the shares as security. Company ofter company went into bankruptcy, leaving all who had financed or invested in them in a total financial disarray. Before the bubble burst credit was easy to come by. After the bubble burst, the English credit system was taken to the brink of collapse; commercial ventures lay strewn in the financial wreckage throughout London, testimony to the ravages of post-speculative mania.

1720 was quite a memorable year for the speculative bubbles and attendant financial panics. The Mississippi Company had a trade monopoly on French possessions in North America. It was in a unique financial position, thanks to the wizardry of John Law. He was among the first who would be described as a monetarist today, introducing our current concepts of credit. In one paper he submitted to the French government, Law wrote, "The workings of trade revolve wholly about money . . . the more you have the more people you can keep employed. Credit will take the place of money and will have the same results." The creation of money by government decree was born.

In 1716, John Law formed the General Bank in France, which became the Royal Bank in 1718. The sole shareholder was the French government. The Royal Bank was permitted to issue paper currency. It was not backed by gold or silver, or any other tangible with a fixed price. Instead, the Royal Bank's—and France's—currency was backed by shares in the Mississippi Company. As long as the company's shares were strong, so would the currency be. The converse applied when shares in the Mississippi Company were weak.

The Mississippi "Bubble" caught on, and spread like wildfire. People pledged their homes, jewelry, livestock, whatever they had. The demand for credit reached explosive levels. As in England, bankers scrambled to satisfy the demand for credit which appeared to be well-secured. After all, the Mississippi scheme was apparently being promoted under the auspices of the French government itself.

A nation's currency cannot possibly be linked to shares whose value can fluctuate violently. The Mississippi Company crashed in 1720. With it the entire credit and banking system of France was swept away. People were staggered: after all, the French government had been party to the scheme; the French regent had patronized it. Members of the French government had grown rich on the scheme.

The average French investor did not fare quite so well. Over one million families in France held bank notes issued by the Royal Bank. They were investors in the Mississippi Company without actually wishing to participate in the speculative orgy. When the company crashed, those bank notes became valueless. The desire for the French to hold gold is a hangover from those earlier years.

The South Sea Company and the Mississippi Company both had totally different objectives, and were sold to greedy investors for entirely different reasons. Both were spurred by an overextension of credit which produced an unreal property, an illusion, a "bubble" where expectations went beyond the wildest dreams of avarice. When the normal laws of economics came back into play, these "bubbles" burst.

The upwave which lasted through 1760 was accompanied in its final stages by heavy speculation in commodities, especially sugar. In Holland, heavy speculation in sugar was being financed by Wisselruitiji in Amsterdam, involving a chain of accommodation bills. In addition, there was a speculative mania involving the East India Company, fueled by credit advanced by the Bank of Amsterdam. In England, there was a speculative boom in housing, turnpikes and canals. A lot of the money to support the boom in England was provided by the Ayr Bank, and a number of independent provincial banks. The speculative orgy reached a crescendo in the early part of 1763. Sugar prices peaked, wobbled, then fell. The same thing happened to wheat. The East India Company collapsed. A host of English companies heavily involved in the Dutch East India Company tumbled after it.

When a speculative bubble bursts, the fallout soon extends across international boundaries. The collapse of commodity markets and the East India Company in Amsterdam brought the collapse of the speculative boom in construction, housing, turnpikes and canals in England. The Ayr Bank also collapsed, taking with it a host of smaller provincial banks. Thousands of investors in England and Europe lost their savings. The end of the upwave around 1763 led to an extremely severe recession and the beginning of the new downwave lasting until the late 1780s.

The secondary depression of the 1780s followed a financial collapse around 1772. After that, the first observable upwave in the long wave economic pattern began. In the early 1800s, England was enjoying robust trade with Brazil and Scandinavia. Credit was again extended by various provincial bankers in unregulated fashion. The usual formula nurtured the boom which eventually collapsed, leading to financial panic. Greedy British businessmen sold more goods than they could possibly produce or acquire to Brazil and Scandinavia, who were importing at record levels on the back of rapidly growing economies.

While the British were selling goods from production facilities which had been mortgaged for years in advance, the Brazilians and Scandinavians were purchasing them with credit facilities they had little hope of repaying. The entire affair produced a totally false prosperity. The boom came to an abrupt end when British exporters were cut off from their Baltic outlets by a naval blockade set up by Napoleon. Many exporters went bankrupt.

A delay in payment means default. As exporters began to default, many of the financing banks failed in their obligations, leading to a chain-reaction default called the "domino effect." The crisis in England reverberated, spreading to Hamburg and New York, where banking institutions were also financing British export trade. The domino effect soon became an international phenomenon. A global recession followed the Panic of 1814. It was deeper and more severe than anything from the beginning of the upwave in the late 1780s. The bursting of a speculative bubble, financial panic and a deep recession, confirmed existing evidence that the first observable downwave had emerged in the long-term economic pattern.

The speculative mania which snowballed in the early 1850s was halted by the Commercial Crisis of 1857–1858. It marked the end of the second observable upwave, and set the stage for a series of worldwide panics. The upwave in the price structure did not actually end until 1864, when the series of financial crises which began some seven years before reached epidemic proportions worldwide.

The 1850s brought the railroad bonanza, new gold discoveries, speculation in wheat and other commodities. Once again it was a period of runaway credit inflation. In spite of the series of financial crises around the 1850s, the upwave was carried on by the Crimean War and the Civil War in America. Speculative bubbles were popping one by one before the end of both wars. After the Civil War, the entire international financial structure seemed to break apart at the seams. In August 1857, there was a panic in America. Two months later it had spread to England. The following year it hit Europe. By 1863, France had become the major victim of financial panic. In May 1866, the Overend Gurney Company collapsed, triggering the stock market crash in London. America, England, France, Italy, Germany and Austria were all in an international financial panic and banking collapse of horrendous proportions between 1864 and 1866. It would appear that each financial crisis in the final stages of an upwave contains deep roots

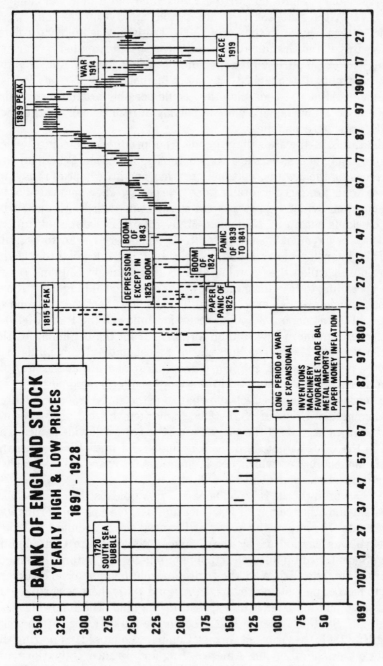

FIGURE 12

Reprinted courtesy Forbes, Inc., successor to B. C. Forbes Company, from *Stock Market Theory and Practice* by Schabacker, published 1930, page 703.

which extend throughout the entire international financial structure. Charles P. Kindleberger, in his book *Manias, Panics and Crashes* (1978), reflects upon the experience of one Parisian banker:

Alfred Andre, a Parisian banker with major interests in Egypt, spent an "exhausting week" in London looking after the interests of his firm at the time of the Overend Gurney crisis. He returned to Paris on May 17, having con-

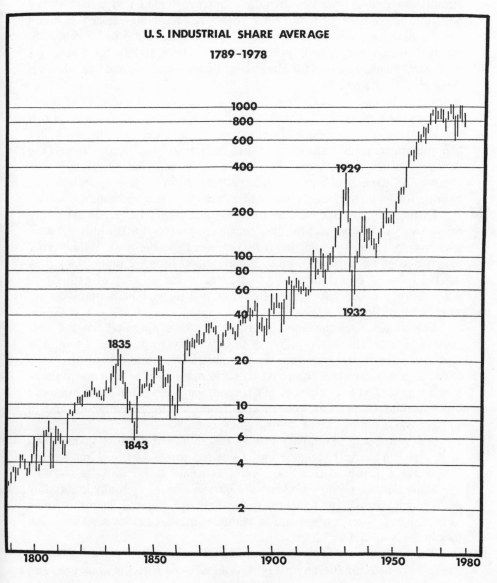

FIGURE 13

cluded that the finance companies were ruined and that business was paralysed in Italy, Prussia, Austria and Russia, with France standing up pretty well, but only momentarily. The speculative mania that led up to the series of financial crises involved heavy speculation in cotton and shipping companies in France, England and Italy.

In 1864, another sequence was completed. What followed was a period of panic, collapse and deep recession, brought about by excessive credit stimulation and speculation. Another upwave ended and a downwave began. In September 1873, the New York Stock Exchange closed its doors for the first and only time in history. On best available estimates, U.S. national income declined 32 percent between 1873 and 1878, to start off what came to be known as the Great Depression—the original one—lasting through into the mid-1890s.

After the end of World War I, the inbuilt monetary excesses of financing a war were combined with financing the monetary expansion common to a long period of prosperity. The prosperity which began in the late 1890s had minor hiccups, but always managed to bounce back. By the turn of the decade of 1920, most were thoroughly convinced that prosperity was forever. As usual, such an attitude culminated in intense speculation in various forms of business, commodities and the stock exchange.

During the post-World War I boom, most people believed that rising prices were no less permanent than continued prosperity. The only variable was how fast prices would rise from one month to the next. Wild buying took place in all sorts of items. Businessmen ordered more than they needed from several different sources, hoping for delivery of at least as much as they needed. As prices escalated in 1918 and 1919, many orders were left unfulfilled.

Consumers were the worst hoarders of all, fighting and clawing over goods in shops. There was a frenzy to buy everything and anything. The higher prices rose the more consumers wanted. In Britain, when sugar rose to 1s. 2d. a pound in 1920, there was a nationwide shortage. In many shops sugar was limited to one pound per person. Shoppers often left a standing order for one pound a day. Others went from shop to shop buying as much as they could before prices went higher again.

A surefire way to increase profits was to buy or produce goods, then delay sales. That way, traders could get top prices as prices moved up. There was a continual thirst for credit as prices spiraled. Sales were so profitable that the credit-worthiness of borrowers was virtually ignored by lenders, who were booming as the cost of money escalated. There was also heavy lending to businesses and individuals outside of Britain who wanted to join the speculative binge.

The suggestion that the boom could ever end was inconceivable. Everyone tried to beat inflation by using it. Comparisons with previous eras and price declines were thrust aside. Britain and the world were embarking on a new era of prosperity, according to most commentators. It was believed that the American banking system, the Bank of England, and the other central banks would ensure that panics and financial crises would never occur again. Very few actually realized that the banking system itself ensured future panics were possible. Why? Because of one major weakness. Bankers are *Homo sapiens*, just like those responsible for previous booms and panics.

Another popular notion around 1920 was that workers would never be willing to work for low wages again, that they would insist on a continually rising standard of living. It was argued that a steady rise in wages would mean that consumer demand would always be buoyant, and that prices would continue to rise. What seemed to have escaped detection was that prices at which goods can be sold, not the demands of organized labor, determine whether or not workers are employed.

Workers produced a multitude of reasons why wages would rise; employers retaliated with as many reasons why costs would continue to rise. And bankers explained why interest rates would go on rising. Their combined explanations produced an irrefutable equation: there would be no foreseeable end to the boom.

The bubble burst in May 1920. Commodity prices were the first to plummet. When prices began to fall in one area, businessmen were quick to explain why it was impossible for them to cut other prices. They insisted early falls were only temporary. All were confounded as prices fell faster and faster. As the falls accelerated, goods could not be sold at any price. In May 1920, the widely followed global commodity index stood at 260. In fifteen months, it fell to 115. It was a half-price sale for practically all goods and services the world over. In America, no such drop in prices had been experienced since the American Revolution in 1776.

The long period of economic expansion that began in the late 1930s brought the most sustained growth of any upwave as far as can be told from available records. Certainly it brought a level of prosperity to the general run of mankind that was a quantum jump from anything known before. Has the world moved onto a permanently high plateau of growing prosperity from which there can be no backsliding? Well, so far the pattern has been remarkably like all previous patterns of expansion—which ended in contraction.

The initial crack in the expansion came just where it was to be expected, in 1974, in terms both of time (fifty-four years from 1920) and of the maturity cycles of industry, technology and the human psyche. After the crack that marks the end of the upwave, there has invariably been a period of prosperity, enlivened by a wave of speculation but faulted at its heart. We had it, between 1975 and 1979: the speculation as never before, in housing and collectibles and the faulty heart. For all the while unemployment had been growing and corporate profits falling in real terms. Behind the growing service sector, chunk after chunk has broken off the traditional industries. Those now in decay include automobiles, construction, farm equipment, steel, bulk chemicals, airlines, shipbuilding . . . why go on?

The world recession since 1979 has been deeper than that of 1973–1975 —the first descending trough since the expansion started. Yet at the first signs of recovery, the talk has been of a steady but unusually prolonged business upturn ahead. Certainly no one is paying more than lip service to the greater lessons of economic history. Yet to complete a practically model wave pattern all the way from 1860 and probably from 1780, just one item is missing—the crisis, the crash that can be expected to hasten the downwave. Its form is already discernible.

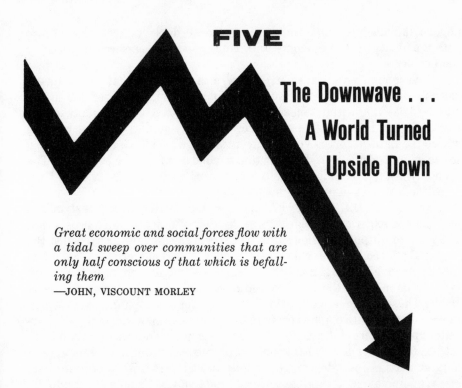

FIVE

The Downwave . . . A World Turned Upside Down

Great economic and social forces flow with a tidal sweep over communities that are only half conscious of that which is befalling them
—JOHN, VISCOUNT MORLEY

Snow White was absolutely fascinated by the constant silence of Dopey, one of the seven dwarfs. When Snow White asked the other dwarfs whether or not Dopey actually could speak, she was told that neither Dopey nor anyone else really knew if he could talk or not because he never tried. Snow White might also ask if our life-style might be more stable if government were to cease meddling in the economy, acquiescing to the demands of an electorate that seeks prosperity in perpetuity. It is likely that such a question would evoke a reply no more satisfactory than that pertaining to Dopey.

No government has actually permitted the natural economic forces in our society to take their own course for any period of time. For thousands of years, so as to avoid the inconvenience associated with even the slightest economic tremor in economic activity, our chosen leaders have piled excess upon excess until the economy could no longer support the burden of such excesses. Through the control of the monetary aggregates, governments have been clipping coins, debasing currencies and printing fiat money in an attempt to deflect the economies' self-adjusting mechanisms. During good times, and bad, through the use of the same monetary mechanism, government has supported redundant incompetent business and fueled speculation, while encouraging people to assume debt burdens which they ultimately are unable to honor. The result has been to push economic activity beyond the level of achievement that would ordinarily be commensurate with the ability of that economy to produce goods and services required by the people.

Government encourages us to convince ourselves that the economy can meet objectives which are not possible, involving an ever increasing standard of living without meaningful interruption, which is equally impossible. We continue to blind ourselves to reality until a point is reached where the natural forces within the economy, which have been supressed for so long, become overwhelming and beyond any measure of control. The economy is then no longer able to provide us with the life-style we have demanded of it. A depression ensues.

By the early 1970s, America, along with other Western industrialized nations, had experienced nearly three decades of uninterrupted prosperity. The level of output experienced by the world's economy far exceeded the potential offered by the technological innovations that were the locomotive for the upwave that began in the 1940s. Deep structural changes took place in the economies of the Western industrialized societies during the early 1970s. These changes were also shared by the developing countries and those countries with planned economies. None were immune. When a thirty-year expansion crumbles and a bubble bursts, panic follows: financial institutions fail, companies go bankrupt, corporate profits decline, losses appear in large sections of industry, commodity prices start falling, output plummets, unemployment escalates, world trade slows. Confidence gradually gives way to fear. And, as we continue to stumble into the agonizing 1980s, a variety of patterns are emerging.

The downwave is likely to span two decades or so, according to the historical pattern. Economic life as we have known it during the upwave will be turned upside down. The best personal and financial strategies in the upwave will become inappropriate for the downwave. Prudent actions during the upwave will be tossed to the winds, becoming imprudent and irresponsible in the downwave.

Most people were afraid to borrow money during the early 1930s and 1940s. They remembered how their homes were lost when mortgages were called, and how families were bankrupted when the debts of a failing business wiped out everything they had. They remembered the burden of installment purchases, and the repossession of goods when monthly payments could not be met. But time eases painful memories. All too soon people forget. By the 1970s, people were eager to borrow, many taking as much as they could lay their hands on. In the 1980s, fear of borrowing has been all but obliterated. We live in a society geared to consumers. It is all too easy to consume today, and pay tomorrow.

During the upwave, people on fixed incomes watched helplessly as the value of their cash was eaten away by rising prices. Those who refused to save, who borrowed dear money and purchased lots of goods which were eventually paid for with cheap money, were rewarded. Savers and lenders were penalized throughout the upwave, while borrowers and profligate spenders benefited.

In the early 1950s, you could get a home mortgage at an interest rate of 4–5 percent. A rate of over 6 percent was considered usurious. On the other hand, if you wanted to rent a property you would have to pay anything from 15–20 percent and still never own it. Any fool could see that buying a property was better than renting. The arithmetic was simple. If you bought a home for $25,000 over, say, twenty years, on an 80 percent mortgage, it would cost under $1,000 in interest payments plus $1,000 in capital repayments. After twenty years the home was yours with nothing else to pay. If you rented the same home at 15 percent per annum rental, you would be paying $3,750 a year. At the end of twenty years, you would have paid out $75,000 and still have nothing. You didn't need a degree from the Harvard Business School to see which was far the better deal.

The 1980s are a far cry from the 1950s. The world of residential housing has been turned upside down. Rents are no longer 15–20 percent of capital value. They are closer to 10 percent. In 1981 the conventional home mortgage rate soared to 18 percent. It has been estimated that at that rate, less than one-tenth of American families can afford the mortgage payments on a medium-priced new home. An industry that prices 90 percent of its customers out of the market is a disaster. When that industry normally accounts for a 4 percent slice of the nation's economy, it's a catastrophe. Obviously, residential property no longer has the attraction it used to have in the 1950s, 1960s and 1970s. Homes are no longer a good investment. Buying a home during the downwave may turn out to be one of the most costly and dangerous commitments anyone can undertake.

Employment is another area to go topsy-turvy. During the upwave, job hopping was popular. Workers rented their time and skills to the highest bidder. Strikes have been an epidemic of the upwave, and workers usually triumphed, largely because labor was in high demand. When the downwave comes, those who demand the highest wages are among the first to go. Job competition is fierce. Workers lower their sights just to get a job . . . any job.

During the upwave, businessmen expanded inventories and increased prices as speedily as they could. During the downwave, the businessman who postpones expansion plans and harbors cash is in the strongest position. The businessman who builds a factory, or opens another shop, in the early stages of the downwave finds himself at a disadvantage. If he postpones expansion plans, he will eventually find that costs have come down and he is at an advantage over those who expanded earlier. The financing mechanism is reversed during the downwave. In the upwave, businessmen attempt to borrow dear money and pay back in cheap money. During the downwave, this approach can be catastrophic. The borrower will end up borrowing apparently cheaply and paying back in dearer money. Sir Freddie Laker discovered this when he borrowed $30 million on the cheap and had to pay back with far more expensive dollars in 1982; Laker Airways collapsed.

During the upwave, the price of money rises, but its value falls faster. For example, if interest rates are 10 percent but prices rise 15 percent, it costs 10 percent to borrow money which will buy 15 percent fewer goods. The money you borrow is, therefore, progressively less valuable and usually easy to come by. During the downwave, the equation is reversed. The price of money may fall, but its value is likely to increase faster. If interest rates are 8 percent, but prices rise at only 3 percent, the money you borrow becomes progressively more valuable. It is also likely to be more difficult to obtain. When money has been losing its value, there is a flight from money into "things." When money appreciates in value, people hang on to it and are less prone to reckless spending.

The prudent and cautious investor of the 1930s and 1940s bought government bonds and triple A corporate securities. During 1945–1946, the yields on high grade tax-exempt municipal bonds actually fell to 1 percent. Yet many investors were willing to accept this low return in favor of the safety that appeared to be offered. During the downwave, having experienced the calamitous effects when a speculative bubble bursts, people are willing to pay a high premium for safety and security.

During the upwave, prices rise. People begin to see that rising prices erode their savings while the purchasing power of money is continually squeezed. Investors who insist on playing it safe with low-risk holdings that offer little more than repayment of capital are penalized. The U.S. bond market began a decline in 1945 which lasted for over thirty-five years. Those who locked money away in "safe" bonds, insurance policies or savings accounts found that in early 1980, their savings were ravaged.

The final stages of the upwave were devastating to savers. Naturally people tried to protect themselves. Many have now convinced themselves they are able to beat inflation by using it. They have shunned fixed interest holdings and savings accounts and switched to "tangibles." During the 1970s there was a progressive scramble into gold and other precious metals, gems, paintings and antiques of all sorts, stamps and all kinds of bric-a-brac. But, as always, just when people finally thought they had learned the rules of the new inflation game, the whistle blew and the game was over. One after another, the tangibles crashed in value. There will be revivals, for such painfully acquired new habits die hard. But those who try to revive the inflation game of the upwave when it is all over may lose most of their savings. The downwave has begun—with all its awesome implications.

For the first time in five decades, the world will have to come to grips again with *deflation*. The threat will be *falling* prices, not rising prices and it will be a far bigger worry. In due course, government policy will have to shift to fight deflation rather than inflation. Speculators and manipulators who thrived on inflation will be wiped out during the downwave. The primary beneficiaries will be the prudent and the cautious—the winners back in the 1920s and 1930s—and the rewards of prudence and caution will be far higher than anyone expects. Cash will be king as the downwave gains momentum.

Life-styles too will change markedly. Fashions will change. Attitudes will change. Old social mores will be resurrected. Existing social attitudes will be buried. A sharper division between the "haves" and "have nots" is likely to develop. There will be fewer "haves" and more "have nots."

Women will cast aside their banners of equal rights, put on their bras and return to the home. People will turn increasingly to friendship, and the comfort of the home for security. Alternative religions will fade. Alternative medicines will be discarded in favor of the bedside manner of the old family doctor. These dramatic changes in values, morality, fashion and culture will exert a dynamic influence on the economic background during the downwave.

THE NATURE OF THE BUSINESS CYCLE

The nature of the business cycle is such that, at one point, businessmen become overpessimistic. The goods and services produced fall well short of the nation's needs. Businessmen and entrepreneurs with foresight then reverse their strategies. Manufacturers begin producing more goods to compensate for society's demands. Those businessmen who spot the improvement in the early stages of the upwave begin their re-expansion programs at the lowest costs for the goods, services, labor and money needed to increase production.

As business activity begins to turn upward, profits soar for those who acted early. This restores confidence in the business community as a whole. Soon everyone is leaping onto the bandwagon of boosting production. And the effects spill over to the consumer.

Manufacturers begin rehiring. Unemployment levels fall. More people have more money. Consumer demand improves. This leads to further drops in unemployment. Increasing numbers of workers go on overtime. Bigger and fatter paychecks result. People increase their spending. They borrow more and consume more as the tempo of activity spurs businessmen to even greater expansion.

As the nation prospers, and as confidence grows, more people are prepared to take risks. Those willing to gamble include individuals who simply live beyond their means, leaving little room for savings. No one believes this prosperity will ever end. This optimism is so strong that entrepreneurs steadily increase expansion plans, and ultimately take on commitments that once would have been considered irresponsible. Many new, inexperienced entrepreneurs jump on the bandwagon. Those who remain employed borrow on the assumption that next year's income will be greater than this year's, and the income for the year after that will be greater still.

The inevitable occurs. Everyone becomes recklessly overconfident.

When too many people demand goods they cannot pay for, when too many are producing too many foods that cannot be paid for, the system becomes exceedingly unstable and collapses under its own weight. The downwave begins.

As the end of the period of expansion approaches, the price of money and the cost of labor have moved up substantially, bringing higher risks and lower profit margins. The growing demand for labor, especially nonproductive labor, has cut productivity, amplifying risks. Businessmen who were late to expand become vulnerable to the slightest ripple. Some businesses begin to lose money; retrenchment becomes the order of the day; confidence is shaken.

When trade becomes sluggish, businessmen cut back purchases of goods and services for retail distribution, while manufacturers cut production. These reductions cut consumption, less labor is required and businessmen lay off workers.

In an effort to reduce unsold stocks eating up interest on borrowed money, businesses cut prices. When demand drops off, prices fall, the need for more labor disappears and the cost of labor is reduced as employees accept lower salaries to remain employed. Attempts to cut out labor-intensive areas and cut costs only exacerabate unemployment. Productivity therefore increases during the downwave, but is of little overall benefit since demand is likely to be falling faster than productivity is increasing. The increase in productivity, in effect, serves to push prices down and unemployment up. What was a self-feeding spiral of expansion during the upwave becomes a self-feeding spiral of attrition in the downwave.

THE DEADLY DECENNIAL

The downwave begins following the interaction of several unsustainable phenomena:

> *the effect of war*
> *a surge in prices*
> *a speculative bubble*
> *overexpansion by industry*
> *profligate monetary policy.*

All of these are superimposed on a community with abnormally high demands and expectations. Within a relatively short period, at the end of the upwave, there is a massive, bursting climax.

The upwave involves continuing prosperity, interspersed by minor contractions. But the downwave is more complex. Each downwave is characterized by two important financial panics. The first in the early stages of the downwave is accompanied by an abnormally destructive recession. Then a second financial panic totally collapses the system.

The bursting of the speculative bubble at the end of the upwave does not bring on the depression. It is only a warning of far worse to come. There is still considerable resilience at the end of the upwave, which results in a short period of recovery. When the second speculative bubble bursts at the end of the recovery phase, a 1930s-style depression starts. The time between the bursting of the first speculative bubble, the recession, and the subsequent recovery leading to the bursting of the second speculative bubble, is about ten years. Two of those years are in recession, eight in secondary prosperity.

When studying the speculative boom in the 1760s it can be seen that the initial plunge in commodity prices circa 1763 was not the collapse that led to depression. There was a serious recession following the plunge in markets . . . but not a depression. After several years of speculation in housing, turnpikes and canals in Britain and heavy speculation in Amsterdam in the East India Company, another panic seized financial markets that was described as one of the fiercest financial storms of the century. This was the panic of 1772. It was that panic that ushered in the depression of the 1780s, nine years after the initial plunge in commodity markets. There was enough resilience in the system to allow for a secondary prosperity following the crash of 1763. By the time of the panic of 1772 the system had been so weakened that a depression was inevitable.

Once again we see the pattern repeating itself in the nineteenth century. U.S. wholesale prices peaked in 1814 after the War of 1812 and declined by as much as a third the following year. This severe deflation was mirrored in a steep fall in bank deposits. Currency held in Massachusetts banks, for example, slumped from $7.3 million in 1814 to $1.3 million in 1816. Although the financial crisis of 1816 was greater than any since the 1780s, there was sufficient strength in the global system to allow for a fairly rapid recovery, that was characterized by violent speculation in commodities on both sides of the Atlantic. But the wounds of the earlier crisis never fully healed. The international crisis of 1818 was sparked off in America by the collapse of the Second Bank of the United States and the slump that followed was even more severe than the recession of 1814–1816. The international crisis that snowballed in 1819 fell on a system where speculation had been rekindled and the initial crisis had not been fully resolved. In 1818 and 1819 there were financial panics on both sides of the Atlantic. The collapse in commodity markets sparked off a crisis in Britain in 1819. According to one contemporary estimate, unemployment had swollen from nothing in 1818 to half a million in August 1820 as bankruptcies escalated. There were "enormous numbers of persons utterly ruined; multitudes in distress." In case that number of half a million unemployed seems small, half a million was about one-sixth of the American workforce at that time.

The decade that followed the panic of 1818 was in fact curiously calm for the stripling American economy. Speculation had been discouraged.

Prices stagnated. Life went back to normal. Not so in Europe, or England in particular. There, a further round of speculation in Latin American bonds, mines and cotton led to a crash in 1825. According to one of the chronicles of the time, "a panic seized upon the public such as had never been witnessed before." The panic of 1825 was a precursor to the depression of the 1830s. Of 624 companies publicly floated in 1824–1825 only 127 survived in 1827. Although commodity prices continued declining until 1847, the worst of the depression was over by the early 1830s. Once again roughly ten years had elapsed between the panic that terminated the upwave and the panic that started the depression.

The period of 1864 to 1866 saw a series of financial panics. Heavy speculation in cotton and shipping companies led to a financial crisis in 1864 which originated in France, spread to Italy and then to Britain. One of the worst financial panics on record in Britain was associated with the collapse of the Overend Gurney Company in May 1866. A fairly severe recession followed. Recovery came after the deep recession, and calm was restored. There were further extensions of credit and a new wave of speculation.

The system had not fully recovered from the first panic of 1864 which ended the upwave when a second crisis occurred. In the five years from 1868 to 1873, bank deposits in the United States increased by $43 million, but bank loans rose by a colossal $283 million. Debts rose 50 percent, while circulating capital rose a mere 7.5 percent. By 1871, the cracks were beginning to show. During that year, 2,915 businesses failed. In the following year there were 4,069 failures involving debts of $121 million. In the early part of 1873, financial commentators were warning of the risk of crisis from the perilous debt structure in the U.S. banking system. Most of the problems were due to financing speculation in American railroads and homesteading. The big crunch came in 1873, when the New York Warehouse Company failed. Five days later, Kenyon Cox and Company failed. Rumors spread quickly that several other large companies were in dire straits. On September 17, 1873, the U.S. stock market collapsed and there was pandemonium on the New York Stock Exchange. The year ended with over 5,000 business failures, with liabilities a staggering $228,500,000.

America plunged into deep depression, and took the rest of the world with her. Losses from heavy speculation in American railroads were shared by the Germans. A crisis erupted first in Austria, where banking was more vulnerable than in Germany. When several Austrian banks failed, several moratoriums in weaker German banks followed. Italian banks heavily involved with German banks failed. Dutch banks financing both German and Italian banks collapsed. Dutch banks had borrowed heavily from Belgian banks. They too failed. The sequence was completed. The second collapse was essentially a crisis of confidence which was sufficient to topple the system in 1874. There were roughly ten years between the first panic and the second—just about the time it takes for people to forget painful lessons they should have learned about financial panics in general.

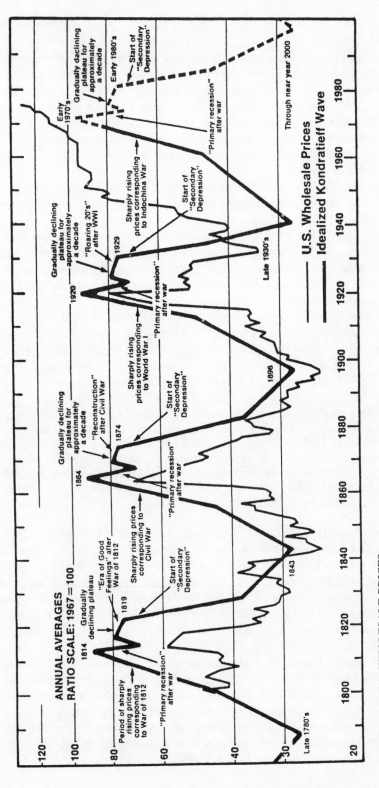

FIGURE 14 U.S. WHOLESALE PRICES

The next two decades seem to illustrate the inexorable pressure of the prevailing downwave. Despite the enormous forces for prosperity in America at the time, an economic recovery from about 1878 was cut short by the slump of 1882. By 1885, business failures were running at twice the rate for 1873. A survey by Bradstreets in October 1884 put unemployment at 13 percent for twenty-two northeastern states. The British statistician Sir Robert Giffen noted in 1885 the popular view that "the present depression is the worst on record."

Panic again on Wall Street in May 1893 was followed by a depression lasting through 1897. According to six major economic series which serve as a guide to overall business activity, there was a fall of 25 percent over the period. A professor at Cornell University writing in 1897 saw the whole period from 1873 to that day as a continuous depression "in great waves covering a score or more years and bearing the panic fluctuations on its surface like mere ripples." No wonder the period was later referred to as the Great Depression.

The crisis that followed the commodity price peak of 1920 was reminiscent of the slump of 1874. As usual, the business community had no inkling of the troubles ahead. Christmas trade was "enormous" with supplies of merchandise "inadequate to the call from consumers." Alexander D. Noyes recounts in *The War Period of American Finance*:

> In a carefully selected symposium of financial forecasts for 1920, published at the end of 1919 and including the views of four well-known economists, three high experts in financial branches of government service and fifteen presidents of banking institutions, a substantial majority expressed belief in continued American prosperity throughout the New Year, while eight predictions of falling commodity markets were opposed by nine judgments in favor of sustained higher prices.

The optimists were not right for long. Commodity prices rose till May. Then confidence was shaken by two unexpected events. The first came from the Far East, in reports of a sensational collapse in Japan. Without warning the failure of a Tokyo bank toppled a crazy stock-market boom and brought it tumbling down. The panic that followed closed every financial and commercial exchange in Japan. All trade was brought to a halt, and prices of goods plunged under forced sale of overloaded inventories. In less than six weeks, Japanese commodity prices fell 35 percent.

The second was a bizarre development in America—the "consumer strikes." In resentment at the way prices had carried right on rising in the post-war years of 1919 and 1920, Americans across the nation grouped to withhold purchases of goods and services until prices were lowered. The groups were known as "Overall Clubs" or "Old Clothes Clubs." Members would pledge to buy no new clothes until prices came down. There were spectacular demonstrations. In April 1920 there was an Economy Parade

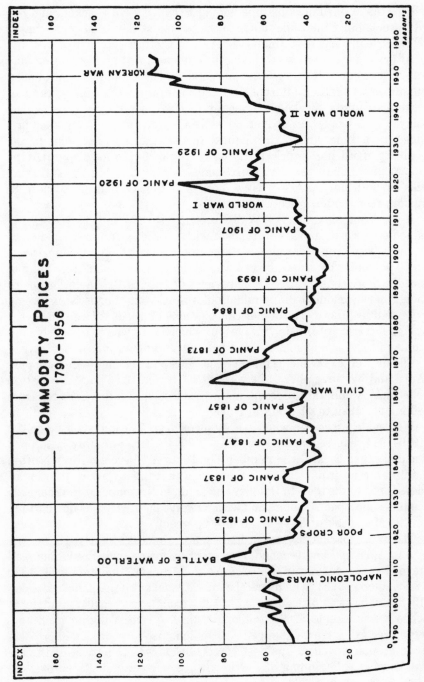

Commodity Prices
1790–1956

INDEX

160	
140	
120	
100	
80	
60	
40	
20	
0	

KOREAN WAR

WORLD WAR II

PANIC OF 1929

PANIC OF 1920

WORLD WAR I

PANIC OF 1907

PANIC OF 1893

PANIC OF 1884

PANIC OF 1873

CIVIL WAR

PANIC OF 1857

PANIC OF 1847

PANIC OF 1837

PANIC OF 1825

POOR CROPS

BATTLE OF WATERLOO

NAPOLEONIC WARS

BABSON'S

FIGURE 15

in New York. Consumers marched along Broadway with pickets and pla-
cards, proclaiming their allegiance to the buying strike. In May the mayor
of New Orleans declared a holiday for "Old Clothes Day."

At first the retailers were just a little uneasy. But an incident on May
3 was to give cause for more than uneasiness. The announcement of John
Wanamaker was rather different from the run-of-the-mill spring or summer
sales notice of the typical department store, clearing out old stocks. Widely
displayed in a heavy newspaper advertising campaign, Wanamaker proclaimed: at a time when "the highest financial authorities point to the
probability of still higher prices" the store would "put to the disposal of the
public $20,000,000 of the best merchandise . . . by offering the full retail
stocks of both our stores in New York and Philadelphia at 20 percent
reduction from actual prices."

It was Wanamaker day on Wall Street, and in the Windy City stock and
commodity prices tumbled—in tandem with a series of announcements of
consumer price reductions across the nation running to 10, 25, sometimes
even 50 percent. The dreaded word was soon out in the open. According to
one of the more conservative trade reviews of May 1920, "Deflation seems
to be gathering momentum; liquidation of stocks and bonds is extending
to commodities; there are further cancellations of goods." *Deflation*—the
first characteristic of the downwave—of which there was to be much more
to come in the ensuing months and years, was now visibly underway.

The first cracks came in farm prices. Sheep prices had begun slipping
in April and by November 1921 were down from $10.66 to $3.84. Cotton
cracked in May and fell 75 percent in the next twelve months. Corn fell from
$1.86 in July 1920 to 41 cents in November 1921.

Wholesale prices as a whole were slower to go. The index, based on 100
in 1910–1914, had reached 244 in May 1920. In June and July it stopped
rising and edged back. By September it had slipped 7 percent. But it is often
the autumn that brings crises, for it is then that the inventory position of
traders is put to the test. In October and again in November, the Wholesale
Price Index slumped 16 points and within twelve months it was down to 141
from the May peak of 244—a fall of 42 percent.

The stock market, as usual, had seen the red light early. Its decline
began in April and had reached 33 percent by year's end. Production had
gone to pieces. Steel output, for example, fell from 42.1 million tons in 1920
to 19.8 million in 1921, which was the lowest level since the panic recession
of 1908. Business failures doubled in 1921 from a year earlier. Bad debts
reached a remarkable $269.5 million, or three-quarters higher than any-
thing on record. Exports slumped $3.7 billion, also a record. In short, this
was no ordinary cyclical business correction. It was the crack of the upwave. It was the beginning of the downwave, correctly identified by Kondratieff in the early 1920s.

It was normal for prices to fall after the inflation of a major war. What
was abnormal this time was that prices had carried on up after the war and

had built up inflationary expectations and bloated debt levels, not just in America but throughout Europe and Japan. Between May 1920 and February 1922, average prices in France fell by 47 percent; in England by 49 percent. The slump in industry came with frightening speed and took on appalling dimensions. By March 1921 unemployment had risen to 1.35 million in England. By December it had raced to over 2 million or nearly 18 percent of the workforce. It was indeed a bleak Christmas in 1921 in Britain. Business was at a standstill. Unemployed ex-servicemen, showing their war decorations, were to be seen rattling collection boxes in London's theater district. To historians of the 1920s this was "the slump." Throughout Europe, unemployment was the highest for a hundred years of records. Yet, strangely, there was no money panic. That particular phenomenon was down the road a few years and would bring a global Armageddon that made the slump of 1920–1921 look like a Sunday school picnic.

Once again, the system was cracked, but not broken, and in 1922, on cue, a secondary prosperity began which, in America at least, was to become legendary. But its origins were suspect. They followed the usual route of credit creation, in the absence of a corresponding increase in wealth. At no time in history has the creation of credit been able to alter the direction of market forces for any meaningful period. Market forces always win.

However, for a while, it worked. Iron production, which had slumped by three-quarters in the recession, recovered and passed its previous peak of 109 million tons. In mid-1923 it was up to 125 million. Check clearings through the country's banks, which had declined by a third from the 1919 peak to $83.7 billion, had risen again through the $100-billion mark in the final quarter of 1922. But flaws began to show in the expansion by 1925. Housing starts peaked in that year at 937,000 before dropping to 849,000 in 1926. Automobile sales hit a record in 1925 at 3.6 million but then fell away. They touched that record again in 1928, only to sink again the year after.

But for those who had ears to hear it, it was the Florida land boom, busting in 1926, which sounded the death knell of the expansion and signaled the terrible depression to come. The story is told in Chapter Seven. The Florida land boom was a symbol of the speculative mania that was to seize the American people and cost them so dear. As J. K. Galbraith put it in *The Great Crash*:

> One thing in the twenties should have been visible even to Coolidge. It concerned the American people of whose character he had spoken so well. Along with the sterling qualities he praised, they were also displaying an inordinate desire to get rich quickly with a minimum of physical effort.

That was indeed the story of the secondary prosperity of the 1920s. It was euphoria that pulled the United States out of the incipient recession of 1925–1926. The fallout from Florida, and others' sensing a new and even more exciting play, turned people's attention to the stock market. Here was to be the high drama, the most famous stock market boom in history—still in living memory—that accompanied the second leg of the tiring economic expansion of the 1920s. As economic expansions go, it was long and relatively sustained, not unlike the expansion of 1974–1979, which extended into 1981 after a relapse in 1980.

As the final hours of the Roaring Twenties approached, it was generally believed that the old rules were dead. Anyone who wasn't convinced that prosperity would last forever was thought a fool or dismissed as a Cassandra. But the forces of darkness would not be denied. Interest rates had been rising for some time. Early in 1928, the rise heated up, and by the end of the year they seemed excruciatingly high. Commodity prices were falling along with consumer prices. The high level of interest rates became more and more painful. The cost of borrowing could not be passed on in consumer prices since final demand was soggy.

Conditions deteriorated early in 1929. Some businesses went into decline while others increased profits quarter after quarter. Suddenly, during the fourth quarter of 1929, prices on the New York Stock Exchange went into reverse and there was a panic. The collapse in the stock market came without warning and sent shock waves through the global community.

Some historians claim the pin that pricked the bubble came from Britain. Just before the stock market crash in New York, the Clarence Hatry empire collapsed. The Hatry group was a ragbag of British companies involved in everything from grain to pinball machines. Clients of Hatry, banks and businesses, came under severe pressure. Losses from the Hatry collapse were prodigious, and forced sizable sales of American securities, which may have been the catalyst that sent the spiraling crash of the American stock market into motion.

Such stock speculation as there had been in Europe was mild compared with that on Wall Street. Substantial funds had in fact been drawn from Europe to the United States, and this had caused bitterness among European bankers. England had been unable to hold her gold in the face of the high interest rates ruling in America at the time. The British government was forced to raise the discount rate from 5.5 percent to 6.5 percent in September 1929: domestic credit lines were being exhausted to finance speculation in U.S. stocks. Bankers grew impatient and withdrew credit facilities, eventually strangling international money markets. When credit is withdrawn, the boom ends.

Whether the source of the collapse in 1929 was the failure of the Hatry empire or not is irrelevant. Whatever the trigger mechanism, the destructive forces unleashed in tandem with the stock market crash were followed by one of the worst depressions the world has ever known. Commodity prices collapsed along with stocks. The U.S. commodity price index slid from 141 in August 1929 to 93, in due course, in June 1932.

G. F. Warren and F. A. Pearson in *The Prices Series* commented on the dislocations that followed:

> Economic changes, drastic in character, occurred with such rapidity that it was difficult for the human mind to foresee them or even to grasp the significance of the changes after they occurred.

Practically every financial or international institutional change that occurred between the wars seems to find its roots in the depression— including even World War II. But the historical view is deceptive, because it seems to collapse events up together in such a way that it appears they all followed automatically from each other. That was not the way it happened at the time. Nobody *knew* in 1929 how it was going to turn out.

Each successive wave of collapse in the New York stock market was viewed, as it would be today, as a "reaction" offering the chance for bargain buys. Each bank default or corporate bankruptcy offered the hope that the excesses had at last been cleared out of the system and had left the way open for a healthy recovery—"just around the corner," as Hoover used to say. The ultimate horror of the depression simply could not be conceived until it had happened, just as people today think of an international banking crisis as the kind of thing that only happens in bad dreams, or maybe in history books.

Speculative fever doesn't develop until the latter stages of the upwave. During the three decades of prosperity that followed World War II, there were the usual bouts of speculative activity in the stock market and elsewhere, but nothing that could be called intense speculation—at least not until the early 1970s. The early 1970s seemed to offer an action replay of the Florida land boom of the mid-1920s, but on a global scale. What the Florida land boom was to the U.S. economy in the 1920s, the real estate market was to the world in the 1970s. In 1974 the property bubble was only punctured, just as the collapse of the Florida land boom only punctured the spirit of speculation of the day. In 1974, the Dow Jones Industrial Averages had their worst fall since the 1930s, but they ran a poor second. Many real estate investment trusts went into default, but the banks picked up the tab. There was a memorable banking crisis in England, but it was confined to the minor banks, who were bailed out by the larger banks under cover of the "lifeboat" operation launched by the Bank of England. The worst recession since the war was turned round by easy money policies on a global basis—the same as had happened in 1922. The system, though much weakened, was capable of a further fling. Once again, a powerful secondary prosperity was born in 1975. Bank lending, across international borders particularly, had a new lease on life and the speculative mania—in real estate and other tangible assets—began anew. Two hundred years of history have foreshadowed the path ahead, but they haven't prepared men for the direction the path will take nor of the incline . . . down, savagely.

Our contemporary secondary prosperity has ended. This has been recognized. Now all eyes are focused on the possibility of a recovery from what is perceived as having been an unusually deep recession. Each weekly up-tick in the economic aggregates offers new hope that a new recovery is on the way. These hopes will be denied. Two hundred years of history, marked with strategic points which are yet to be violated, suggest a financial holocaust is due during 1983 or 1984. This will represent the second financial collapse in the downwave that began in 1973. The international system will not be able to absorb the crisis without moving into depression.

"SECONDARY PROSPERITY" . . . HAPPY DAYS ARE HERE FOREVER

The reason that recessions, depressions and panics occur with such persistence is that few people ever prepare for them. If everyone took precautions to protect himself as soon as there were signs of overheating in the economy, there would never be any collapses. The business cycle would merely look like a horizontal line across the page, as would our long wave patterns of economic life. The most treacherous part of the early downwave comes with a false sense of security from the secondary recovery which follows the first major move into the downwave.

During the recession there is a marked change in social, cultural, political and economic attitudes. An unsuspecting public invariably assumes the recession will be similar to the recessions in the upwave. Those are relatively shallow and brief. The first recession in the downwave is long and deep. When they end and secondary prosperity finally takes hold, most people believe that conditions will be exactly the same as they were before the severe recession. During the secondary recovery, which lasts six to eight years, almost the entire range of cultural and social change which took place in the upwave is compressed into this much smaller time frame.

During the recession, people become frightened, and thus more prudent. There is a change in dress. Styles become more conservative. Music is quieter, more subdued. Church attendance increases. Speculative activity drops sharply.

In the secondary recovery, hemlines start rising again. Music becomes more frenetic. Morals lapse. Labor disputes resurface. Speculative activity is rekindled. People start buying houses again.

It is not uncommon for the final stages of secondary prosperity to resemble on the surface an extreme version of the end of the upwave. But, beneath the surface, there are very marked differences. Inflation at the end of the secondary prosperity is much lower than at the end of the upwave. Business activity is appreciably slower. Monetary expansion is strong, but nowhere near as strong as in the latter stages of the upwave. The speculative bubble which bursts at the end of the secondary prosperity involves extremely high numbers of people. They are the principal victims. Members of the public are more easily seduced by the secondary prosperity than the business community. Most individuals become even more reckless and spendthrift during the secondary prosperity than they were during the upwave.

Many fortunes are made in business and in speculation during the upwave. But they tend to make only the rich richer. The secondary prosperity of the downwave offers something for everyone. Prices rise far more slowly than in the final stages of the upwave. There is a plateau between the peak of rapidly rising prices and the abyss of their rapid fall. Often referred to as the plateau period, the secondary prosperity phase represents a kind of disinflation, or no-flation.

The decade embracing the secondary prosperity has been one in which the national budget has balanced more often than in any other decade in the five-decade wave pattern. The three decades which follow inflationary peaks have, over the past 200 years, provided surpluses twenty-three times and deficits only seven times.

There are indications that it has been easier for governments to cut borrowing requirements and run a surplus while inflation is declining. In general, the attitude of the electorate following an inflationary phase has always been one of complete resolve to eliminate the swollen debt. High public sector borrowing is blamed for inflation. But, as the secondary prosperity continues and demands increase, memories fade. Hostility toward public spending also fades; determination to mop up the debt fades, and tax cuts begin. Eventually, screams for reflation are heard at the first sign of discomfort when the secondary prosperity nears its end.

Through four long wave sequences since the 1790s, tax cuts have appeared with rhythmic regularity during the secondary prosperity. Each time, they seemed to have the magical effect of increasing revenues when expenditure is falling and commodity prices are easing. The result is stimulation of the economy which deflates it at the same time. During secondary prosperity, tax cuts work because the economy had previously been overtaxed during the upwave, and the level of deficit financing in the inflationary spiral had been high. When the secondary prosperity begins following deep recession, pent-up domestic demands are met by turning economic output toward the consumer.

Tax money is returned to the consumer to spend. The tax cuts in America and Britain in 1980, in France in 1981 and in West Germany in 1982, could all have been forecast many years in advance, so consistent were they in the secondary prosperity phase of the downwave.

As the period of secondary prosperity gains wider public recognition, the atmosphere steadily improves. During the early years, most people are highly skeptical. After a year or so, skepticism turns to optimism. Wages increase faster than prices during the latter stages of secondary prosper-

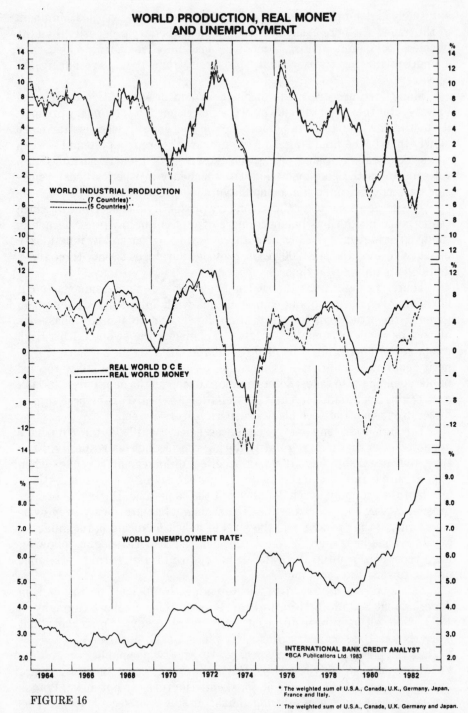

WORLD PRODUCTION, REAL MONEY AND UNEMPLOYMENT

WORLD INDUSTRIAL PRODUCTION
——— (7 Countries)*
- - - - (5 Countries)**

REAL WORLD D C E
- - - REAL WORLD MONEY

WORLD UNEMPLOYMENT RATE*

INTERNATIONAL BANK CREDIT ANALYST
*BCA Publications Ltd. 1983

FIGURE 16

* The weighted sum of U.S.A., Canada, U.K., Germany, Japan, France and Italy.

** The weighted sum of U.S.A., Canada, U.K. Germany and Japan.

From *The International Bank Credit Analyst,* April 1983.

ity. The consumer feels a tremendous sense of well-being. Money is plentiful. Industrial output improves. Unemployment remains high. But those
who are employed never had it so good.

Secondary prosperity brings a change in the entire psychology of a
nation. The crisis industry goes into a slump, and journalists begin to think
positively again. They totally ignore cracks in the prosperity. They are
oblivious to the vast differences between normal prosperity and secondary
prosperity. The secondary prosperity is a time when the nation psychologi-
cally returns home to business, back to personal lives and careers which
were disrupted by the previous recession. People turn away from labor
strife, political unrest, soaring inflation and personal crusades.

The peak inflation around the world in 1974 also represented an emotional peak. Pent-up repressions gushed out in a kind of global catharsis.
By the time the secondary prosperity was into its second year in 1976,
public feeling had changed considerably. Nations had rid themselves of
considerable aggression and were returning to a state of equilibrium. Unfortunately, such a situation cannot last. The economy can never remain
stable. It constantly fluctuates, as it has to.

During early 1975, it was generally felt that there was little possibility
of an economic recovery getting underway. Forecasts ranged from an
oncoming depression to a period of hyperinflation. Stagflation became a
byword. Some economists claimed the world was experiencing a recessionary depression. The term "inflession" was invented to denote inflationary
recession. In all actuality a normal phenomenon was taking place. The
Federal Reserve began to expand the monetary aggregates in early 1975.
Since the recessionary forces had run their course for the time being, the
effect of an expanding money supply was a renewed bout of credit creation.
Inflationary pressures persisted since the excesses had not been fully elimi-
nated from the economy. America thus embarked upon a somewhat anemic
secondary prosperity along with the rest of the world.

Industrial production began to rise in early 1975 and continued to rise
strongly through 1977. Consumer trends usually lag behind industrial
trends. There was a mild pickup in retail sales between 1975 and 1976 which
aborted in early 1977. Then, in 1978, there was an explosion in retail buying
which sent the Consumer Price Index soaring to a post-war peak. Consumer prices in America rose at an average rate of only 3.4 percent per
annum during the first two years of the decade. During the last stages of
secondary prosperity, in the final two years of the decade, consumer prices
were soaring at a rate of 11.2 percent. Just before it was finally curtailed
by a sudden business downturn in the spring of 1980, the inflation rate had
reached 17 percent.

At the same time, government and private borrowing were racing
ahead. Mortgage lending was at record levels, along with all other forms
of consumer credit. By 1980 the new era of economic recovery was plainly
visible to one and all, and there was a stampede of eager participants. What

most did not know was that 1980 marked the beginning of the end of an era . . . of secondary prosperity such as we had witnessed so many times before.

Mass psychology takes an epicurean turn during times of plenty. The year 1978 was such a period. It ran parallel to the late 1960s and early 1970s, when public interest centered on consumption, sexual liberation and drugs. Attention turned from convention and the work ethic much more dramatically this time. There was a greater proliferation of X-rated movies and sex shops, topless barmaids and waitresses, wife-swapping and group sex. Alternative religions were making the headlines. In Britain, there was a move to ban the Scientology sect. Parents of teenagers attracted by alternative religions were hiring psychological exorcists to effect debriefing and debrainwashing. Divorce had reached record levels.

Waves of sensual excesses marked the peak in the Roman, Greek and French civilizations. The downwave in the Roaring Twenties (the secondary prosperity) ushered in the speakeasy, bootlegging, university hi-jinks, and . . . as a mark of new sexual freedom demanded by the suffragettes . . . the rising hemline. It is no coincidence that, as we approach the final stages of the secondary prosperity that began in 1975, we see a repetition of the social, cultural and moral patterns that foreshadowed the decline of these great civilizations.

The laxity in self-discipline reflected itself in government. There was an absolute lack of any form of discipline. Whereas the period of secondary prosperity usually involves periods of government surplus, throughout the 1970s the U.S. Treasury never managed to close one single year with a surplus. By the start of 1980, the Treasury debt load had become so heavy that interest payments alone accounted for well over 10 percent of total outlays.

The most damning aspect for the government when Carter ran for reelection in 1980 was that, for the first time in decades, the inflation rate exceeded the rate of personal income growth. Carter was ousted from office because his government could no longer be relied upon to provide optimum prosperity with minimum inconvenience. There was a swing to the right, as usually occurs during the end of a secondary prosperity. The Republican Party, led by Ronald Reagan, offered the promise of a new form of prosperity in tax cuts and the like. The election of Reagan followed the election of a right-wing government in Britain the previous year, led by Margaret Thatcher, considered to be a neo-monetarist.

Business continued to turn downward during late 1979 and 1980, and neither the Thatcher government, with its monetarist policies, nor the program of "Reaganomics" was able to provide what the people had expected of it. Initially, the electorate was promised a short, shallow recession followed by recovery, but that never happened. The recession just bit deeper and deeper. Unemployment rose and rose and rose. Since 1980, each time the government forecast signs of recovery, those signs proved abort-

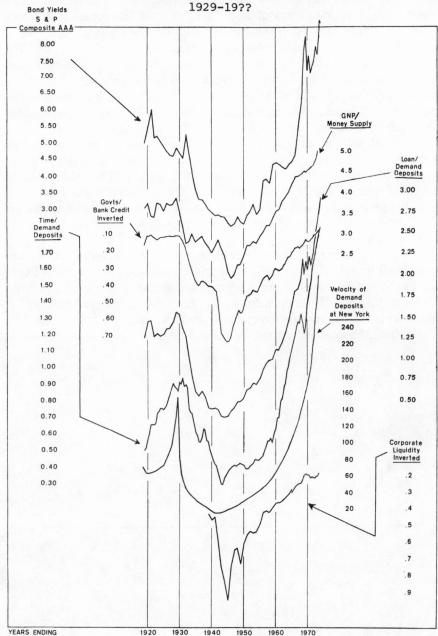

FIGURE 17

From *The Prices Series* by G. F. Warren and F. A. Pearson.
Reprinted by permission of Chapman and Hall, Ltd.

ive. The fourth quarter of 1979 produced the first stages of a recession that has, to date, been long and stubborn. In my opinion, this recession will lead into a secondary depression of severe magnitude. The economic upturn that began in early 1983, like the minor upturns before it, in 1980, 1981 and 1982, is doomed to extinction. By the time you read this, that upturn may have already become extinct. As the recessionary forces reappear, prices will tip downward; deflation will once again gain momentum. The business community will become demoralized as a result of what will appear as yet another false dawn; crisis and depression will be the inescapable result.

Almost without exception, the end of any secondary prosperity has been followed by one of the worst economic declines in history. These depressions have always been the most unexpected. When the phase of secondary prosperity is finally over, and the impact hits the consumer-oriented sectors, the economic aggregates do not simply move gradually from good to bad; they move rapidly from what was clearly an idyllic state to total disaster.

When one considers the debt structure of individual economies and of the global industrialized society as a whole, combined with the debt burdens of lesser developed countries, recognizing the debt mountain will not go away, we have the formula for a nightmare. When the gradually declining plateau turns into a secondary depression, with its incumbent debt liquidation, the financial Armageddon will be devastating.

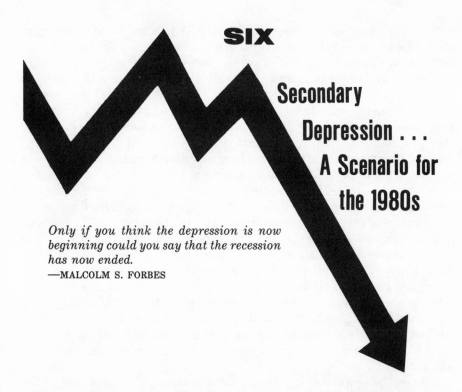

SIX

Secondary Depression . . . A Scenario for the 1980s

Only if you think the depression is now beginning could you say that the recession has now ended.
—MALCOLM S. FORBES

Fish gotta swim and birds gotta fly and we gotta find scapegoats for everything that goes wrong until the day that we die. When Adam and Eve blew it in the Garden of Eden, we blamed it on the filthy old snake with his disgusting pomegranate. If a trumpet player hits a sour note he quickly pulls the horn away from his face, stares menacingly at the mouthpiece, starts pumping the valves up and down or begins fiddling with his spittle cock. If your favorite team loses a game the immediate response is to blame the umpire or fire the manager. If the world moves into recession we blame it on the government or OPEC.

Having made a complete and total mess of diagnosing the cause of our problems we then proceed to compound the error by adopting an equally dangerous and correspondingly simple-minded prescription. The prescription usually involves relying on government to get us out of the mess we like to believe someone or something has gotten us into. Of course, government is more than willing to oblige. That's how it gets elected: by telling people it is able to solve the problems that people can't solve for themselves. This is, without a doubt, mankind's greatest self-deception.

Although snakes and evil pomegranates come from heaven, sour notes, bad ball players and economic depressions are not of extraterrestrial origin. They're manufactured here on earth. We make them for each other through our incessant overreaction to events and circumstances coupled with an allegiance to the forces of unreality. We abdicate responsibility to our leaders who we believe are capable of motivating and determining the behavior of four and half billion people, which, of course, is a somewhat prodigious and unrealistic task. Yet, this seems preferable to assuming responsibility for our own actions.

Fortunately, America and a large part of the rest of the world remains a capitalistic society. As long as we remain in such a society, it will be free market forces that determine recessions, depressions and the demand for goods and services. There is also a strong indication that free market forces determine the demand for goods and services in the planned economies as well. When the 1973–1975 recession took its toll, its effect on the planned economies was not markedly different from that of the industrialized economies. Free market forces are determined by the behavior and demands of those individuals who are operating in those markets. In other words, free markets represent the demands and dictates, directly and indirectly, of all those who populate this planet. No group of people, no government, no cartel, has ever been established or ever will be established that is able to determine and manipulate the actions of those four and a half billion people who populate this planet. As a result, the market *always* wins. The sequential behavior of free markets over several hundred years of history indicates we are now due for a great depression. The free market is about to win again!

When the upwave ended, the downwave began. The beginning of the downwave was marked by the recession of 1973–1975. When the secondary prosperity that began in 1975 ends, the depressionary phase of the downwave will begin. As the 1973–1975 recession took hold, almost anyone could have seen that something had gone awry and the world was building up to some drastic adjustment. At the time, many economists attributed the deep recession to the oil crisis. Some still believe the oil crisis was the cause of the recession. This idea is utter nonsense, just another example of the manner in which our leaders and their soothsayers attempt to abdicate responsibility. The oil crisis was a symptom of underlying malaise. The oil crisis was the result of a system that was under severe strain rather than a cause. Free market forces *permitted* the price of oil to rise. The cause of the underlying crisis could be traced to several decades of affluence when the world as a whole insisted on living beyond its means. The oil crisis was merely one of many voices that shouted, "It's time to pay the piper, kiddo!"

THE OIL CRISIS . . . FACT AND FALLACY

Very few were prepared for the depth of the 1973–1975 recession although the long wave pattern of economic life had been issuing warnings of the likelihood of a severe dislocation for years. The supposedly oil-induced slump was far more severe than the most pessimistic expectations while the extent of damage which was actually inflicted by the rise in the oil price is far less than is envisaged.

The damage for which the explosion in oil prices is cited as the cause is impressive. During 1974 and 1975, all major industrial nations, with the exception of West Germany, suffered inflation in double figures. There were deep structural changes in the global economy. Compared with the quarter of a century or so ending in the early 1970s, the rate of advance of total world output and output per capita showed a marked deceleration in the subsequent ten years or so, dropping by about one-third to 3.4 percent per annum as regards total production and 2.0 percent per annum as regards per capita production. The slowing down in output was shared by all countries . . . the mature industrial countries, the low-income countries and the rich capital-surplus oil-exporting countries.

The current accounts of the industrialized countries deteriorated markedly. As a group, the current accounts of these countries turned downward in 1974 and remained negative for the rest of the decade with the exception of 1978 when there was a relatively insignificant surplus. Countries which had for decades maintained a strong trade balance suddenly found a surge in imports. The increase in imports represented some 1 to 3 percent of GNP of individual countries.

The downturn in the business cycle in 1973 roughly coincided with the Middle East war which ultimately led to the upward spiral in oil prices. By 1974, the price of oil was four times that of its level prior to October 1973. The recession that was already underway continued and developed into the worst recession since the 1930s, the same type of recession that separates the downwave from the upwave. The recession was followed by a weak recovery that lasted from 1975 to 1979, the same type of economic recovery that has been associated with the secondary prosperity phase that usually

Growth of GDP and GDP per capita since World War II, (% per annum compound)

	GDP		GDP per capita	
	1950 to 1973	1973 to 1980	1950 to 1973	1973 to 1980
Industrial countries	4.8	2.4	3.4	1.9
Developing countries (inc. China)	5.8	4.9	3.5	2.7
Planned economies	5.0	3.2	3.9	2.3
Capital surplus oil-exporters	12.0	8.2	7.3	4.2
Total world	5.0	3.2	3.4	2.0

Notes
(1) These figures, because of numerous reservations and qualifications attaching to them, must be treated with caution and regarded as no more than indicators of orders of magnitude.
(2) Developing countries are countries with per capita income of less than $2,000 and include China. Capital surplus oil exporting countries comprise the Gulf States and Libya.

FIGURE 18

follows the peak-inflation-recession of the downwave. In 1979, there was another business downturn and another rise in the price of oil. Between 1979 and 1980 the price more than doubled. At the end of 1980 the price of oil was $34.00 a barrel. Early in 1970 the price was $2.00 a barrel. In September 1973, the price was $3.00 a barrel.

The 1973–1974 oil price explosion was met with an expansion of the money supply to absorb the shock. Price rises came through rapidly and the growth in world money led to accelerating inflation and a new wage-price spiral in most nations. When there was a further oil price explosion during 1979–1980, government policies were more restrictive, aimed at lowering inflation. Since that time, oil prices have been under severe pressure, falling back to as low as $26.00 a barrel. The evidence suggests that if monetary policy had been more restrictive during 1973–1975, OPEC's then-attempt at quadrupling the oil price might have been self-defeating.

In June 1977, an OECD team headed by Paul McCracken, chairman of the Council of Economic Advisers under President Nixon, concluded that the "most important feature of the severe problems of 1971–1975 was an unusual bunching of unfortunate disturbances unlikely to be repeated on the same scale, the impact of which was compounded by some avoidable errors in economic policy. We see nothing on the supply side to prevent potential output in the OECD area from growing almost as fast in the next five to ten years as it did in the 1960s."

In the spring of 1970, one of Europe's most prestigious forecasting bodies, the Organization of Economic Cooperation and Development, made its predictions for economic growth over the next decade for the major industrial nations. It was forecast that Japan's national output would grow on average at a rate of 10.2 percent per annum for the rest of the decade. For other countries the predictions were a bit less robust. For France, the projected growth in output was set at 6.3 percent, Italy 5.9 percent, the United States 5.1 percent, West Germany 5.0 percent and the United Kingdom 3.6 percent. When McCracken was giving his dissertation in 1977, no doubt it was his view that the OECD economists were finally going to get it right after being so wrong for so long. Here we are six years later and none of the countries have achieved more than 50 percent of the targets that were set. In the case of Japan, the increase in national output was only one-third of that which was originally expected.

So, how much of the 1973–1975 recession, the poor economic performance during 1975–1979 and the recession that began in 1979 was actually attributable to the oil crisis? According to several learned studies, not a great deal. Nordhaus, in an exhaustive document on the impact of the oil crisis published in 1980, claims that the annual GNP growth rate of the major industrialized nations was reduced by a mere 0.15 percent as a result of the oil price increases. He also concludes that the annual rate of inflation rose by no more than an extra 0.6 percent as a result of the oil price rises. Furthermore, the maximum drop in productivity growth was estimated at

0.14 percent and the rate of growth in real income per worker among the major industrialized countries slowed by no more than 4.41 percent. In another authoritative document on the macroeconomic consequences of the oil shock, Tobin argues that "the 1973–1975 recession and the low recovery path of 1975–1978 cannot be attributed to the unavailability of oil."

CONVENTIONAL WISDOM VS. UNCONVENTIONAL LOGIC

It is no more logical to blame the 1973–1975 recession, along with the depression we are now entering, on the oil crisis than it would be to blame the Great Depression of the 1930s on the stock market crash. In both instances, the resulting phenomena were the products of deep-rooted deterioration that had been taking place for decades. Conventional wisdom says that supply-side shocks caused "the Great Recession of 1973–1975." According to popular myth, the combination of quadrupling of oil prices and serious crop failures drove up the prices of manufactured goods and food, fueling inflationary expectations. The consequence was high inflation in spite of a low level of aggregate demand. This oversimplistic dogma is totally unsatisfactory. It does not explain how newly industrialized countries have managed to combine rapid growth with persistently high inflation, nor does this conclusion explain the retardation of growth that has occurred since 1973. Conventional wisdom also fails to explain the reason for the considerable drop in productivity growth or the most recent recession, which is deeper than the 1973–1975 recession while the rise in the price of oil has been significantly smaller.

The oil-induced recession argument doesn't hold up at all. A recession was underway before OPEC raised the price of oil. The beginning of the recession, according to the National Bureau of Economic Research, was in November 1973. Inflation was also a problem long before OPEC raised the price of oil. The first significant increase was in 1965–1966. By 1970, inflation was considered a major problem in most countries. Profits in industry were slowing long before the oil crisis. The growth in industrial production began to slow before 1973. Structural unemployment has been increasing since the mid-1960s. The quantifiable effects of the oil price rise on the world's economy over the past decade have been seen as minimal. Far more sinister forces have been at work, not the forces of OPEC but natural economic forces of a free market economy that has been producing upwaves, downwaves, inflations, recessions and depressions for 200 years, probably longer.

For some unfathomable reason, economists, journalists and commentators continue to assess the economic background as if the dawn of creation were after World War II, treating documentary activity prior to the war as being of little consequence. Econometric models have been constructed on the basis of post-war experience. Since we've seen deep structural changes in the world's economy over the past decade, there are no precedents to which these econometric models based on post-war data can be related. For those with a knowledge of history, the 1973–1975 recession was certainly not without precedent. The global economic community had experienced similar recessions many times before . . . on several occasions . . . just after the long upwave of prosperity spent its force.

The 1973–1975 recession was indeed destructive. Banks failed. Companies went bankrupt. Unemployment soared. The stock market plunged. The financial media, it is true, recalled memories of the 1930s depression. But that was inappropriate. Conditions were in no way comparable. To start with there was nothing like the same degree of speculation in the early 1970s as there was in the late 1920s, at least not in the United States.

In Britain and elsewhere it is true that the year 1974 will rank among the classic crises of financial history. The British suffered one of the most severe banking debacles in their history known as the "secondary banking crisis." Small fringe banks, along with a host of eager entrepreneurs . . . both big and small . . . got caught up in a seemingly endless bonanza in the commercial real estate markets. Like bubbles of days gone by, the commercial real estate bubble of the early 1970s burst in 1974. When the house of cards came tumbling down and the bankruptcies started rolling in, some of the small banks who financed the boom found the size of defaults running into nine figures in several cases. The fringe banking system collapsed. In order to protect some of the depositors, the commercial banks staged a rescue operation and floated what was termed a "lifeboat." But the level of bankruptcies had grown so massive that the commercial banks could no longer shoulder the burden and the Bank of England was called in to help, leading to one of the biggest bailouts in history. The support operation of the Bank of England cost taxpayers in Britain nearly $6 billion. Most was used to protect depositors from the banks that failed. Only a handful of the banks that were "rescued" actually survived.

In the United States, there was no such speculative real estate boom in the early 1970s. Speculative fever never reached the heights that it reached elsewhere. The 1973–1975 recession did, however, leave its mark when the Real Estate Investment Trust went belly-up. To those investing in the stock market, 1973–1975 was certainly no joke. The Dow Jones Industrial Averages dropped 45 percent, from over 1,000 in 1973 to under 600 in 1974. True to form, we once again see earmarks of the end of an era . . . the end of an upwave. The fall in the Dow-Jones Industrial Averages between 1973 and 1975 was the worst since the depression of the 1930s. Many believe the stock market is a barometer capable of predicting future economic trends. That fall in the Dow Jones Industrial Averages was obviously predicting a recession that would be worse than anything seen since the 1930s . . . and so it was. During the recession of the early 1970s, output fell sharply, unemployment rose dramatically, bankruptcies increased, commodity markets slumped and stock markets plunged, but the calamity was certainly nothing like that experienced during the 1930s. That is yet to come.

Several long-term macroeconomic theorists continue to relate the recession of 1973–1975 to the terminal depression of the 1930s and, as a result, assume sufficient excesses were washed from the system to generate a sustainable recovery now. This interpretation is totally incorrect. There were striking contrasts between the recession of the early 1970s and the depression of the 1930s. Probably the most dramatic contrast of all was in prices and wages. Between 1929 and 1931 wages fell by 39 percent in the United States and wholesale prices fell by 33 percent. The early 1970s recession had prices and wages still rising. In 1932, one-half of the total productive capital in America was idle and 14 million people were unemployed. The depression of the 1930s was truly a business collapse of stupendous proportions. While the 1973–1975 recession was the worst anybody had seen during the thirty-year-long period of expansion, the depression of the 1930s made that recession seem like a garden tea party.

To those who know their history, the most appropriate comparison for the 1973–1975 recession was not with the depression of the 1930s, but with the shock recession of 1920–1921 that followed the peak in the Wholesale Price Index of that time. The 1973–1975 recession, like that of the recession of 1920–1921, was the kind of recession that ensues from the buildup of structural strains creeping into the economic system following a long period of expansion. Like the period preceding the 1970s, the expansion that was a precursor to the 1920–1921 recession brought record prosperity and indeed the feeling that prosperity would be a permanent part of our lives. Economic growth during the two decades that followed the turn of the century, and the two decades following World War II, was taken for granted. Both periods witnessed the mass-produced availability of consumer durables . . . the spread of electric light, radio, telephone, the refrigerator and the automobile in the United States of the 1920s; television, home computers, laser discs, hi-fi equipment, electronic games and citizen band radios in the United States of the 1970s. While the proliferation of consumer goods mounted, manufacturing industry was placed on the sacrificial altar of consumption while structural problems mounted. Overexpansion developed in a number of basic industries, notably the primary industries of agriculture, the extractive industries, shipbuilding and subsequently the automobile industry during the 1920s in America. During the 1970s, we saw overexpansion in the secondary industries of basic chemicals, oil refining, shipbuilding, steel and also the automobile industry. Both the recession that began in 1920 and the one that began in 1972 were preceded by a downturn in the Kuznets building cycle. In both periods, significant merger waves took place signaling attempts to acquire new product lines and accompanying profitability through horizontal and vertical corporate integration as opposed to expanding profitability through research and technological innovations. The seeds of the upwave are sown in technological innovation. When diversification replaces technological innovation, we have the marks of an expansion which is about to end. The late 1960s and early 1970s were the age of the conglomerate . . . the end of an era.

The recession of 1920–1922 and that of 1973–1975 were typically the kind that follows a long wave of prosperity. That kind of recession reveals the cracks in the system but the recessionary forces are not yet developed sufficiently to shatter the system. This is not an academic issue. Nor are the observations made by hindsight. For, it was my knowledge of past waves of expansion and contraction within the context of the long-term pattern of economic behavior that allowed me to gainsay the prophets of doom.

In August 1974, the following forecast appeared in my publication, *Investors Bulletin:*

> Projecting this phenomenon into the future, assuming that commodity prices have peaked this year, we would expect a trough in the stock market cycle between late 1974 and mid-1975 leading to a secondary recovery, which will ultimately lead to another great depression, likely to begin in the early 1980s . . . *but not likely to materialize this decade.*

I wrote that nine years ago. As expected, the trough in the Dow Jones Industrial Averages came in late 1974 and as I had anticipated the world embarked upon a secondary recovery which no one else expected at the time. I was certain the 1973–1975 recession was one that would leave sufficient resilience in the system for that last phase of secondary prosperity. In fact, that recovery was to involve four years of persistent output growth in the United States at least . . . but it was achieved at a cost which only became apparent to most in our current decade.

On a global basis, during the 1973–1975 recession, unemployment became a critical issue. In early 1975 governments the world over began increasing their deficits to prevent demand from falling too far, acting to contain the rise in unemployment and to limit the fall in output. The same medicine was used effectively in 1922, and seemingly it worked again in early 1975. That good old Keynesian formula. Nobody bothered to find out where the money expansion of the 1920s ultimately led to. The priority was to pull the world out of recession at any cost in early 1975.

The Democratic Party, under the leadership of Jimmy Carter, known for its somewhat profligate spending habits, began to pump money into the economy as never before in peacetime. The budget deficit rose to $75 billion from $11 billion the previous year. At that level, it amounted to a horrifying 5 percent of the nation's income, which was twice the post-war peak level of 1971. But there was far worse to come. In total, the amount the U.S. government borrowed between 1975 and 1979 was greater than the entire

growth in national income measured in 1975 dollars, a strategy which led
to the current deficit of $200 billion. In the meantime, money supply bal-
looned into a double-figure growth rate. As a result, by the turn of the
decade, inflation in the United States was making post-war records.
Whereas other major industrialized nations managed to hold inflation
below the peaks reached in 1974–1975, the U.S. rate of inflation exceeded
the 10 percent peak of 1974–1975 and proceeded to push upward to 13
percent by 1980.

By late 1975, recovery could clearly be seen in the United States and
in the rest of the world. Many people believed a return to normal was taking
place. The good old days of the 1950s and 1960s had returned at last
... or had they? To the astute observer, there was something very wrong
about the recovery that began in 1975. It was certainly not like any of the
business upturns that were characteristic of the expansionary period of the
1940s, 1950s and 1960s. The 1970s upturn had a peculiar flavor to it. It was
a reluctant expansion. Overcapacity could be seen to be affecting not just
the old industries like shipping but actually great swatches of industry.
While service industries were buoyant and consumers bought color television sets until their eyes were beginning to look square with rounded
corners, there remained a deep malady in practically all areas of transport,
auto, rail and air; the whole bulk chemical industry; steel; metal transfor-
mation; construction.

On the surface, America seemed to fare well during the recovery of
the 1970s. Manufacturing growth in the period 1973–1979 at 2.8 percent per
annum may have been a far cry from the prerecession years, but with the
exception of Japan it was still the highest of the industrialized countries.
Beneath the surface, the trouble with the expansion was its foundation. It
was an expansion in the United States and everywhere else that was being
bulldozed forward by credit creation, explosive money supply growth and
ballooning federal deficits. It was the story of the 1922–1929 expansion all
over again, only more so. The real progress in the economy was being
disguised by the inflationary trends and was far lower than the economic
numbers indicated. Productivity per head was growing at a mere 1.14
percent during the expansion of the 1970s as against 2.44 percent in the
preceding decade. Labor grabbed an increasing slice of the national income
cake, grabbing 75 percent as opposed to 70 percent during the 1960s. The
result of organized labor's avarice was to leave much less for corporate
profits which are the lifeblood of any healthy economy. Corporate profits
represented a 14 percent share of national income in 1965. By 1982 that
share had fallen to 8 percent.

As the decade went on, America wanted more and more for less and
less effort. They wanted welfare but they didn't want to pay for it in taxes.
That was one of the problems that led to the difficulties in New York City
circa 1975 and later, in Cleveland. The Steiger amendment was a striking
example of the attitude of the nation at the time. President Carter had

proposed an *increase* in capital gains tax: he ended up by signing for a cut in taxes. Proposition 13 in California was another similar case in point demonstrating a national attitude which was totally incompatible with the ethics of an expanding economy. Real estate taxes were ultimately limited to 1 percent of house values as a result of public pressure. The end result was that municipalities had to borrow more and overextended themselves to meet existing expenses.

As the lopsided recovery proceeded into the second half of the decade of the seventies, household borrowings saw an absolutely astounding increase. From 1975 to 1978 the rate of borrowing soared from $35 billion to $180 billion . . . a fourfold increase. As people's homes rose in value, the need to save seemed to lose its importance. In fact, the need to save became obsolete. But there was also a disarming contrast. Gary Shilling & Co. Inc. estimated that 50.2 percent of the population was dependent on some form of social welfare by the end of the decade of the 1970s. In 1960, the figure stood at 37 percent. The recovery of the 1970s was indeed a strange one. High inflation, instability, social disorder, continued disruption in labor markets and shortages were the price that had to be paid for this secondary prosperity which differs markedly from an economic recovery. Recovery is synonymous with a return to good health. There was never a return to good health in the American economy of the 1970s.

During the period of secondary prosperity a nation actually runs the psychological gamut of the previous thirty years, compressed into a period of four or five years. During the secondary prosperity of the 1970s, the American people felt their economic environment was returning to the way it used to be during the 1950s, 1960s and early 1970s. In many respects it was, even down to the labor disruption, shortages, lack of inventiveness, social conflicts and inner strife that have characterized the end of every prosperity for the past 200 years. The cycle of consumer trends shows that the consumer does not achieve the maximum benefits of an economic prosperity until the final stages of that prosperity. The long wave of prosperity that began after World War II did not really provide consumer benefits until the 1950s and 1960s. Similarly, the secondary prosperity that began in 1975 and which served to compress the experiences of the previous decades into four years, did not provide consumers with the life-style they would like to become accustomed to until the maturity stage was reached at the turn of the decade.

Bitter labor disputes, combined with rising unemployment and consumer affluence, are characteristic of the final stages of a long wave of prosperity, and of the final stages of a secondary prosperity. Bells warning the end of the secondary prosperity began to ring in late 1979. At that time, America was looking for the odd man out among the major nations, as an uncontrolled money supply sent inflation to record levels for peacetime. The Fed acted to tighten credit. Carter approved. But the economy was too weak to withstand even the slightest constraint and it became readily apparent that the Carter move had sent the economy into a kamikaze dive. This was only months before the presidential election of 1980. Carter quickly shifted gears and went from reverse to a turbo-charged overdrive. The exhausted and limping economy was goaded into a final staggering burst in late 1980 but the change in tactics and the temporary appearance of economic strength during the November 1980 election was not enough to change sentiment in Carter's favor. Carter was accused of gross mismanagement of the economy during his term in office, and considered an incompetent peanut farmer. He was returned to the peanut farm, leaving Ronald Reagan entrusted with the task of determining the lives of 200 million Americans.

Before Reagan had a chance to finish polishing the mahogany swivel chair behind the desk in the Oval Office, the economy dropped, panting and exhausted, the fiscal steroid having accomplished all it was capable of producing by the mid-1980s. Since then, the Reagan administration has had to live with an even deeper recession than that of 1973–1975—a recession that can only end with a 1930s depression.

To all intents and purposes, 1975–1979 was a period of global recovery. But it was not the type of recovery normally associated with the interruptions that take place during a long wave of prosperity, when recessions are brief and shallow and recovery periods take the economy to new heights. At no time during the 1975–1979 recovery did the U.S. economy achieve the real growth levels comparable to the low-inflation growth of the 1960s or at the turn of the decade. Although the U.S. economy was deemed to be recovering from 1975 through 1978, for the first time in decades the inflation rate of the late 1970s exceeded the rate of personal income growth. Even though the gross domestic product increased sharply in current dollars (and moderately in constant dollars), the real spendable income of the average worker actually began to fall in 1977. The decline in purchasing power in a nonrecessionary period was something altogether new in the post-war era. It was the experience of a different era, one that most economists chose to ignore.

Another disquieting aspect of the period of secondary prosperity was the loss of jobs in the manufacturing industry. By the end of the 1970s, manufacturing industry was providing work for only one American in five. The shrinkage would have been even more pronounced had there not been a heavy emphasis on finding work for almost 20 million young Americans who were the product of the baby bulge of the 1950s and who swelled the U.S. labor force by no less than 20 percent. One million jobs in the American manufacturing industry disappeared during the 1973–1975 recession. The recovery that followed failed to rekindle the number of jobs lost. By the autumn of 1980, there were over 2 million unemployed in heavy industry and engineering, and a further 1.25 million plus out of work in construction, transport and the utilities. The country's jobless blue collar workers numbered 4 million, or half of the total unemployed. In Detroit, a quarter of the automobile industry's workforce was laid off in a brutal wave of firings that revived memories of the 1930s, and the city's mayor, Coleman Young, warned that the Detroit industry's survival also meant the survival of a further 16 million jobs elsewhere in the U.S. . . . almost a sixth of the entire workforce. The fundamental cause for the disjointed trends of the 1970s was the major slowdown in the growth of demand and the rate at which industrial production was growing. The phenomenon was not just peculiar to Britain. It was worldwide in this period of secondary prosperity. In a growing economy, companies must have new capital to augment their working capital and to finance new expansion programs. The pattern during three decades of expansion showed that most firms were able to meet all or most of their needs by putting profits back into business. In other words, companies would strive to generate cash internally in order to minimize borrowings. These were the growth companies of the era. During the 1970s, internally generated cash flows became progressively more inadequate due to rapidly rising costs. In addition, companies also liberalized their dividend policies which further reduced the amount of capital available for reinvestment in business. Finally, rapid inflation sharply increased the replacement costs of both inventories and capital plants which led to a situation where the profits of most U.S. corporations tended to be overstated, thus perpetuating the myth of recovery, which Jim Dines refers to as "the indivisible crash."

THE END OF THE ROAD

At the beginning of every year I prepare a program of guidelines based on what I believe will be the likely nature of business activity in the year ahead. In early 1979 I presented my program for the year to listeners of my daily radio broadcast and to readers of my publication, *Investors Bulletin.* For the most part, 1979 looked a reasonably promising year for those sectors of the American economy with the most resilience, essentially the consumer sector. There appeared to be ample scope for further gains in the housing market. The stock market appeared capable of moving higher in the United States and elsewhere, particularly in Britain, if there would be a general election and a Conservative government victory. Commodity prices looked like they were all set for another rise, along with the rate of inflation. Consumer spending was rising steadily and it looked as if the U.S. consumer was ready to embark upon another spending spree in 1979 even though the manufacturing industry in America was languishing. Most of the economic forecasts for 1979 were glowing. Consumer spending was seen to be the driving force.

The consensus of forecasters felt that 1979 was going to be a good year. So did I . . . until the fourth quarter. It was forecast that in the fourth quarter of 1979 a worldwide recession would begin. It was my belief that the recession would bring a final end to the consumer boom and ultimately an end to the stock market boom, an end to the housing boom and a fall in U.S. living standards. In other words an end to the secondary prosperity of the 1970s. Time had run out.

It was clear that government in the mid-1970s had no idea whatever of how to restore equilibrium to a system with a colossal debt structure, floating currencies, contracting markets and inflation that kept going up, and up and up. Throughout the 1970s, the global economy remained sluggish while the international monetary system remained out of control with planners powerless in the face of natural economic forces that raged beneath the surface of the world's economic system. Beneath the surface of what appeared as a reasonably healthy economy in early 1979, the cracks and fissures were beginning to open up again. This time around, they were likely to turn into yawning caverns, irreparable by fiscal and monetary stimuli.

The economic downturn of 1979 started in Europe, principally in the West German zone countries, where concern with inflation was uppermost. It then spread to Britain, whose industrial output had been the lowest of any industrialized nation through the secondary prosperity of the 1970s. In 1979, Britain's industrial output resumed its precipitous decline, falling a staggering 13.8 percent between 1979 and 1980. By mid-1980, the global recession had spread to the United States. As the year passed, warning indicators (new housing starts, the stock market, the number of bankruptcies and the average hourly work week) were all showing deterioration. There was brief celebration on the stock market in November 1979 following the Reagan victory, but the economy was in the course of deteriorating. A change in government was certainly not sufficient to alter the inexorable economic tide.

The recession in the industrialized world since 1979 has been the worst since World War II: far worse than the slump of 1973–1975, at least when measured in terms of manufacturing output, capacity utilization and unemployment. Eight years on and manufacturing output in much of the industrialized world is below the trough levels of the recession of 1975. Shortly after the downturn of 1979 economists' predictions of resumed growth have been confounded. In 1980 the consensus economic forecast was one indicating a short shallow recession followed by an upturn in early 1981. The recession was neither short nor shallow nor was there an upturn in early 1981. Revised forecasts in mid-1982 stated that the economic decline was deeper than expected but an upturn could be expected during the second half of 1981. There was no upturn. At the end of 1981 the economists generally agreed that the recession would be over by the spring of 1982 and that business would show a brisk second-half recovery. As late as July 1982, the consensus of "blue chip" forecasters assembled by Eggert Economic Enterprises Inc. was for a tidy growth of nearly 4 percent in both the third and fourth quarters. Growth in the second half of 1982 evidently turned out to be zero. The recession that began in 1979 will probably go down as the worst in post-war history.

Throughout 1982, recovery was being constantly predicted, first, as early as the first quarter, but it did not come. It was forecast again for mid-year. Again it did not show. Nor did it show the third quarter or the fourth. Why has the track record of the traditional economists been so appalling over the past four years? Some say the 1982 forecasts were off the mark because the economists underestimated the devastating impact of the Fed's attempt to adhere to specific monetary targets. Reaganomics and his experiment with supply side economics have also been blamed. The truth is less discernible and not readily acceptable. It suggests economic life is preordained and economists are a useless species. The true cause of the poor performance of gurus over the past four years lies in their inability to accept and recognize the forces of the underlying long wave. The econometric models, which assume the dawn of economic creation was after World War II, have been wrongly programmed. We have the GIGO factor as applied to econometric models at work: garbage input–garbage output. The assumptions of most econometric models are based on rules of economic behavior that may have been valid during the post-war period, until the 1970s, but deep structural changes in the world's economy have taken place since then. These rules are no longer valid.

For example, the economics textbooks say that interest rates decline in a recession. Well, in the deepening recession of 1981, U.S. interest rates rose and rose and for all anyone knew they would have carried on rising forever had their rise not been interrupted by a mighty shift to easy money by the Fed. What went wrong? It has become clear this decade that the traditional formulas for managing economies, Keynesian or monetarist, have turned into a whole series of vicious spirals. The normal forces for reflation have lost their power.

The vicious spirals embrace budget deficits, unemployment, interest rates, inflation, investment and inventory levels—and a whole lot more. Higher budget deficits increase inflation and interest rates. Higher interest rates lower investment and inventory levels, and hence raise unemployment. More unemployment raises budget deficits. And so on.

Have previous long waves of expansion produced similar vicious spirals? Yes and no. Without a doubt, the peculiar characteristic of the post-war expansion has been inflation. To judge by records from England which go back many centuries, there has been no inflation like the post-war inflation since the sixteenth century—and even that was a feeble effort by comparison.

The feature of the post-war economy has in every industrialized nation in the free world been the same. Wages have grown faster than the economy. They have taken more than their share. And they have taken it from the corporate sector and the government. Without exception, every government has allowed this to happen and indeed encouraged it (they need votes) by printing money and running deficits.

Well, now the corporate sector and the government have reached the end of the road. They cannot go deeper into debt without giving the vicious spirals another twist, which would mean yet higher interest rates, yet more bankruptcies and unemployment, with no exit. Fifty years ago, men could not foresee all this—at least very few could—whether the cause is laid at the door of a humanitarian desire for equality or inexorable cyclical forces which would have produced a comparable situation by any other route.

What the economists now expect for 1983 is much the same as what they expected for 1980, 1981 and 1982. From the rubble of record business bankruptcies, shuttered plants, double-digit unemployment and depressive capital spending, the signs of an incipient economic upturn were visible during the early part of 1983. What has been described as a fragile recovery by the majority of economists has given way to a futile dialogue. Will the recovery be strong . . . or feeble and short-lived? Is it actually a recovery, or just a temporary upturn? Sides are taken according to the temperament of the observer. There is even a growing agreement that the pace of recovery from previous recessions may not serve as a reliable guideline in this case. Yet, it could not matter less whether the recovery resembles a bird, a plane or Superman, or whether the recovery will be strong or weak, if its subsequent course will be to plumb deeper levels of recession than it sounded in 1982. It would be wise to question the basis upon which assumptions of a normal expansion will resume in the years ahead. These assumptions are based on nothing more than an unquestioning acceptance of the validity of the post-war econometric models which have produced disastrous results for the past decade.

THE MESSAGE FROM COMMODITY MARKETS

The recession that began in 1979, and has since continued, is certainly not peculiar to the United States. Its effects are global. The roots of the worldwide recession can be traced to world commodity prices. The fall in commodity prices sounded the early warnings of global economic difficulties first in 1973. The same warnings were given by commodity markets in late 1979 as the rate of change teetered and then slumped.

Commodity markets are the nearest to reality in terms of response to economic conditions. At the beginning of the economic process, commodity prices give advance warnings of changing trends elsewhere. Copper and tin are important indicators of future construction and manufacturing activity. Cotton shows the direction of consumer spending and retail sales, well in advance of any pickup in consumer durable items. Silver and gold reflect inflationary expectations and the possibility of approaching chaos, like raging inflation, the debasement of currencies and international disruption. Gold and silver are the world's frightened money. Corn and wheat prices tell us something about the future prospects for the price of goods in the grocery store as well as the prospective future rate of inflation.

The economist, or anyone interested in attempting to anticipate the future trend of economic conditions, would be wise to take a lead from the commodity technicians' notebook. There is a seemingly unshakable perception that economic trends move in straight lines without interruption and the behavior of the various economic aggregates respond similarly. If there is an upturn in economic activity, it is deemed that the upturn will continue indefinitely. If there is a downturn in economic activity it is deemed that the downturn will continue for the foreseeable future. There seems to be very little effort made in attempting to determine terminal junctures of these trends and even less effort in attempting to segregate the random fluctuations from the overriding major impulses. As every student of capital markets is fully aware, there are major long-term cycles, secondary cycles and tertiary movements, all three of which move together simultaneously. During the course of a long-term upward movement that may last four or five years, you may have intermediate changes in the price structure that are diametrically opposed to the upward movement. In turn, you may have shorter movements that last anything from a day to a week that are moving in the opposite direction to the longer-term movement. This is true of commodity markets and stock markets. As we know, during the course of a long-term economic expansion, such as was experienced from the 1940s through the 1970s, there have been several minor recessions that moved counter to the prevailing trend that lasted thirty years. The short-term movements that ran counter to that trend lasted anything from nine months to two years.

Several years ago I wrote a book called *Supertiming*. The book concentrated on a somewhat esoteric form of capital market analysis called the Elliott Wave Principle. The principle involved the categorization of capital market cycles and subcycles, defining the movements in the main trends as impulse movements which occur whether the prevailing trend is upward or downward. The trends were classified according to duration. The grand super cycle was the longest of all, then the super cycle, cycles, etc. Think of that long upward movement from the 1940s to the 1970s as a super cycle: the recession that happened in between as movements of the lower degree which would be categorized as cycles, moving counter to the super cycle.

Based on the principle that for every action there is a reaction, when a super cycle reaches its optimal level of achievement, it then becomes subject to a correction. If we consider the long-term expansion from the 1890s until the 1920s as a super cycle, the downturn that followed served to correct the expansion. A supercyclical expansion led to a supercyclical correction. Within the expansion phase there were cycle movements of a lesser degree which were the recessionary phases. Within the super cycle correction, there were also cycle movements of a lesser degree which were brief economic upturns within the long-term prevailing downturn. The

major difference between the phase of expansion and the downward corrective phase is that during the phase of expansion, upward impulse movements are long and extended while the downward corrective movements
are short and contracted. However, during the down super cycle corrective
phase, downward impulse movements are long and protracted while the
upward cycle movements are short and condensed. In other words, during
the phase of expansion we can expect economic recoveries to last from
three to five years and periods of economic contraction to be brief, lasting
from nine months to two years. During the downward phase that tendency
is turned upside down. Periods of economic expansion last nine months to
two years while periods of economic contraction last from three to five
years.

Now let's turn to the real world of capital markets. The trends in
commodity prices lead stock market trends. The stock market is merely an
anticipatory device which tells you about the expectations of future economic activity by stock market participants. The stock market fluctuates
to reflect changing expectations and changes in economic activity. It therefore stands to reason that the economy is likely to fluctuate also and is also
subject to the same major trends and subtrends. It's easier to see these
trends in the stock market because there is an index such as the Dow Jones
Industrial Averages that fluctuates daily. It is not as easy to see the same
type of fluctuations in economic activity.

Now let's apply the principles that govern capital markets to those of
the future prospects for the economy. After a long-term period of growth
that began in the 1940s, the long-term growth trend in commodity prices
began a supercyclical decline in 1973. By 1975, the growing trend in non-oil
commodity prices was falling sharply. From 1975 through 1977, there was
a resumption of the growth trend in commodity prices which reflected the
phase of secondary prosperity that was taking place at the time. The upward phase in the growth of commodity prices peaked in 1977, never reaching the levels that were achieved in 1973. Here we have a strong indication
that the prevailing trend is downward and that the peak in 1973 represented a major terminal juncture in the supercyclical growth phase that
began in the 1940s.

In 1977, the growth rate of non-oil commodity prices began to decline
again. There was a minor recovery from 1978 through 1980 but early in
1980 the secular downtrend in the growth of commodity prices was again
resumed. The 1980 peak in growth not only failed to rise above the 1973
peak but also failed to rise above the 1977 peak. It can also be seen that
those periods when the growth rates were falling lasted far longer than
those periods when the growth rate was rising. This adds further evidence
to the assumption that the major upward phase of growth ended in 1973
and since then the major secular trend has been downward and is likely to
continue downward until the excesses of thirty years of expansion are fully
corrected. A corrective trend usually lasts from one-third to two-thirds as

long as the trend that it is correcting and retraces a corresponding amplitude. Thirty years of growth is likely to take from ten to twenty years to correct.

During the second quarter of 1982, commodity prices appeared to be at the incipient stages of collapse. Gold and silver were plunging to new lows for the cycle. Tin had lost nearly a third of its value between early 1980 and mid-1982. In the summer of 1982, in a desperate attempt to ward off the cumulative problems of mounting bankruptcies, falling commodity prices, sluggish economies and an international banking crisis that was rearing its ugly head, the Fed began an expansive monetary policy and pushed interest rates downward, a move that was soon repeated in one international center after the other. Commodity prices were among the first of the economic series that started to rise and, as of mid-1983, were still rising. Attempting to produce an economic recovery with fiat money is like pushing on a string. It sows the seeds of its own self-destruction. The prevailing trend is downward. The recent upswing in commodity prices, which has been translated into improving economic activity, is counter to the overriding supercyclical downtrend. Commodity prices are soon likely to resume their downtrends. These will soon after be reflected in economic trends. Businessmen were promised an economic recovery in 1981. It never took place. Businessmen were then promised an economic recovery in 1982. There was no recovery. In 1983, businessmen were promised an economic recovery again. This time around the rhetoric was so powerful and so convincing that more people were convinced by the story than at any other time since the world recession began in 1979. When it becomes obvious that the meager improvement in economic activity has been aborted and the economy is turning downward again, there will be total demoralization in the business community leading to a crisis in confidence of unimaginable dimensions. The early warning signal will come when commodity prices start tipping downward again. Watch for it!

Non-Oil commodity prices

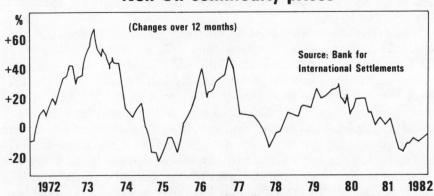

FIGURE 19

A new phase in the long wave pattern of economic life has now begun. The upwave was completed in 1973. The recession that followed the upwave was completed in classic fashion in early 1975. The recession was typical of the type that comes at the end of a long period of expansion in the same manner as had occurred at the end of each upwave for the past 200 years. In 1975, a secondary prosperity began. In 1979 the secondary prosperity was completed on a global basis leading to a "gradually declining plateau" of economic activity. This has been called a recession, but I believe it will lead to the depression of the 1980s, the second great depression of the twentieth century. During the second half of 1983, the evidence suggests we will begin that phase of depression that leads to panic and distress. The world remains on the brink of monetary collapse and Western industrialized society is faced with the prospect of the worst depression since the beginning of the Industrial Revolution. That means . . . breadlines, soup kitchens, capital losses, bank failures, a collapse in the housing market, ruin, worry, joblessness, hunger . . . where 60 percent of the country's population will be affected, possibly more.

THE TIMING OF THE SECONDARY DEPRESSION

A recession or a depression does not happen all at once. It is not a matter of going to sleep one night feeling prosperous, and waking next morning to discover you are in a depression. A depression begins slowly in vulnerable areas and gradually spreads. It does not reach everything, even at its nadir. Many businesses will go bankrupt. Many banks will fail. Many individuals will suffer severe hardships, but not all. Neither the United States nor the rest of the industrialized West will disappear into oblivion, never to recover.

As the long wave pattern of economic life takes us into the 1980s, it is certainly not a matter of whether a depression will occur; it is a matter of how far and how fast the depression will spread. In many areas of Europe, there has been a depression for some time. Unemployment in Ireland is equivalent to that in the Great Depression of the 1930s. In Britain, several towns have become ghost towns, because there is no work available. The inhabitants of Corby know that Britain is in a depression. So do the people in Port Talbot. The steel industry used to supply employment for the citizens of Corby and Port Talbot but the steel plants were closed during the period of secondary prosperity.

The red light that flashes oncoming depression is often signaled in the stock market. In 1920, stock market prices rose to a peak and then crashed, signaling the 1920–1922 recession. Share prices recovered during the secondary prosperity of 1922–1929, and then crashed again. A depression followed. Some people actually believe the crash was the cause of the 1930s depression. The idea is naïve. The stock market crash was only one of many elements revealing an economy due for collapse.

The recession at the end of the upwave, combined with the period of secondary prosperity, lasts for about ten years. In 1973, the Dow Jones Industrial Averages peaked and then fell sharply, signaling the worst recession since the 1930s. The decennial pattern indicates another peak in the stock market cycle some time during 1983. The collapse in stock prices that will follow is likely to resemble the type of collapse that usually occurs at the end of a secondary prosperity . . . a 1930s-type collapse.

I do not place much stock in these oversimplistic attempts at judging the future by fixed periodicity cycles from the past. Although they serve as guidelines, they can be dangerously inaccurate, particularly when dealing with a pattern of economic life over fifty to sixty years. Timing could be off by five to ten years. Far more important are the economic markers that form the long wave pattern, and their course of development. They make a far more convincing case for the approach of a secondary depression.

Obviously, if we can determine whether we are facing a period of prolonged prosperity or merely a secondary prosperity, we can plan accordingly. It is vital to recognize the difference between a period of inflation and one of deflation. When that final stage of secondary prosperity ends, and depression, danger, crisis and acute panic threaten, it is vital to be able to make the correct economic moves. This can be done by placing emphasis on the shorter waves of economic behavior within the fifty- to sixty-year framework.

The most serious work on business cycle synergy was carried out by Professor Joseph Schumpeter at Harvard University. Schumpeter combined the findings of three cyclical economists, Kitchin, Juglar and Kondratieff. The Kitchin cycle involves a period of approximately forty months. The Juglar business cycle runs for eight to ten years, and the Kondratieff cycle approximately fifty-four years. In terms of the overall rhythm, there are three Kitchin cycles in a Juglar cycle, six Juglar cycles in a Kondratieff cycle, and eighteen Kitchin cycles in a Kondratieff cycle, involving a distinct interaction. Of greatest interest are those periods when all three cycles moved in tandem.

To determine the type of environment immediately ahead, the Juglar cycle is most useful. Juglar, like Kondratieff, finds one primary cause for his nine-year rhythm: the fluctuation in commodity prices. According to Juglar, the prosperity that precedes a crisis always brings high commodity prices. As prices rise, exports become more difficult, the balance of payments becomes less favorable. Gold and then foreign exchange flow out of the country, weakening the internal financial position. The unique cause of the crisis, according to Juglar, is the ending of the price rise. In Schumpeter's magnum opus, entitled *Business Cycles* (1939), he refers to Juglar, stating:

> His great merit is that he pushed the crisis into the background and that he discovered below it another, much more fundamental, phenomenon. . . . Henceforth, although it took decades for his new view to prevail, the wave ousted

the crisis from the role of the protagonist in the play. . . . The problem has changed its complexion. It is no longer a problem of the wave. It is the problem of identifying and, if possible, isolating the many waves and studying their interference with each other.

Schumpeter discovered these Juglar cycles in the economic life of West Germany, England and the United States. The Bartels test of probability suggests that the recurrence of the nine-year business cycle (which is in effect a 9.2-year business cycle) could not occur by chance more than once in 5,000 historical repetitions.

Combined with the fifty-four-year rhythm, the nine-year rhythm of Juglar can often signal important events in the economic flow. The 1919 peak in the nine-year rhythm came when the longer term fifty-four-year rhythm was also reaching its final peak at the end of the long prosperity. In the late 1920s, so long as the nine-year rhythm continued to rise, the momentum of the stock market was maintained. When this nine-year rhythm peaked again in 1928, and then turned down, after the fifty-four-year rhythm had been falling for almost eight years, the beginning of the great collapse in stock markets, commodity markets and the global economy was at hand.

Juglar divides the cycle into three periods: (1) prosperity, (2) crisis and (3) liquidation. He emphasized the influence of bank credit on the development of crisis. After studying the accounts of the Bank of England, the Bank of France, and the leading American banks, Juglar deduced that there was a law of crisis and a recurrent periodicity. Juglar felt that wars, droughts, abuse of credit, excessive issue of bank notes and even events such as the oil crisis, would not be sufficient to provoke an industrial crisis if the general economic situation did not warrant it. These events may hasten a crisis, but only when the economic factors make it inevitable.

According to Edward Dewey in his marvelous book, *Cycles—The Science of Prediction* (1947):

> Inversely, it was after this rhythm had reached a trough in 1923–1924 that the economy started rising expansively to the peak reached in 1928. And it was after its trough in 1932–1933 that recovery began from the 1928 fall in commodity prices and from the subsequent 1929 crash in share prices. The well-known peak in 1937 followed. The next peak of the ideal wave was in mid-1946.

In 1867 there was a massive peak in commodity prices. It preceded the depression of 1873–1878. Approximately fifty-four years later, in 1920, there was a further peak in commodity prices, confirming the continued presence of the long wave cycle which ultimately involved the Great Depression of 1929–1932. On both occasions, the peak of the nine-year cycle was close to the peak of the fifty-four-year cycle.

The trough in the stock market cycle occurred on schedule in late 1974

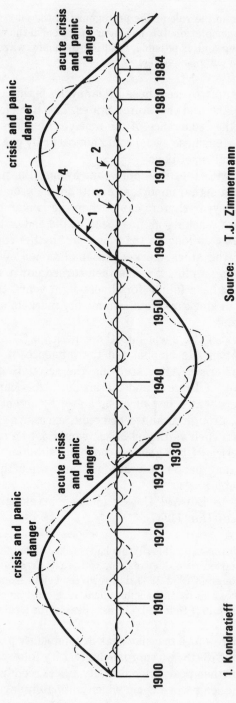

THE 20th CENTURY BUSINESS CYCLE
AND CRISIS POINTS
(Calculated Path)

crisis and panic danger

acute crisis and panic danger

crisis and panic danger

acute crisis and panic danger

1900 1910 1920 1929 1930 1940 1950 1960 1970 1980 1984

4

1 3

2

Source: T.J. Zimmermann
          Geschichte der theoretischen
          Volkswirtschafts-lehrs
          –Dr. P.E. Erdman - unpublished paper

1. Kondratieff
2. Juglar
3. Kitchin
4. Composite of 1, 2, & 3

FIGURE 20

when the Dow Jones Industrial Averages dipped below 600 and then rebounded. The ensuing stock market boom has since taken the Dow Jones Industrial Averages to above 1,200. The recovery in the economy and the stock market upsurge took place precisely as I had forecast six months before the event. The tremendous stock market rise over the past seven years more than vindicated the use of the nine-year rhythm. Here we are "in the early 1980s." I have little doubt that the nine-year rhythm discovered by Juglar will prove no less valuable to those who heed its warnings.

Another major contribution to the work of Professor Schumpeter was made by Joseph Kitchin, with a business cycle lasting approximately forty months. The cycle had manifested itself in industrial ordinary share prices since 1871, and was first discovered by a group of American investors in 1912. The original formula for the forty-month business cycle is attributable to the banker Rothschild, who reputedly had analyzed British Consols and dissected the price fluctuations into a series of repeating curves, combing these curves and using them as a forecasting device. Some ten years after the Rothschild discovery, Professor W. L. Crumm of Harvard University noted a cycle of "39, 40 or 41 months" in the length of monthly commercial paper rates quoted in New York from 1866 to 1922. Professor Crumm reported on this in the *Review of Economic Statistics* for January 1923.

At about the same time as Crumm's discovery, Professor Kitchin, also of Harvard University, discovered a business cycle which he claimed ran for approximately forty months and involved six economic time series: bank clearings, commodity prices and interest rates, for both the United States and Great Britain. The continued repetition of the rhythm was noted throughout the period 1890–1922. Professor Kitchin reported his findings in the same issue of *Review of Economic Statistics*.

Charles Hoskins, totally unaware of the previous work on the forty-month cycle, concluded early in 1935, as a result of a time-chart analysis of pig iron production and many other economic series, that a cycle of approximately 40.5 months seemed to be operating over a considerable period. The forty-month rhythm first attributed to pig iron production is also duplicated in scores, if not hundreds, of other economic phenomena. These include bank debits, industrial production, commodity prices and share prices. George Armstrong, a research analyst for the Bell Telephone Company in the United States, determined that the length of general business conditions in America since 1885 was approximately forty months.

Professor Schumpeter liked to refer to this forty-month cycle as the Kitchin cycle. Schumpeter noted that the long wave economic cycle should contain six individual Juglar cycles, and that each Juglar cycle would comprise three Kitchin cycles. However, Schumpeter clearly stated that expectation from the theory would be much less regular.

The work of these four great economists can be applied to the real world of the 1980s. Dewey, who has probably done more research into business cycle development than any man alive, claims that all cycles of the same length tend to turn at the same time. In other words, they act in synchrony. From this, there might be some clue as to the probable emergence of a financial crisis along with an international battle, because both cycles of crisis in Britain are 9.6 years. Dewey states:

> I suspended my personal judgement in regard to cycles for many years. It was only after we discovered that cycles persisted over hundreds and even thousands of years, and after we were able to make comparative cycle studies that showed that substantially all the cycles of any given length turn at about the same time, that I became convinced without any lingering doubts as to the significance of at least some of these behaviors.
>
> It is simply inconceivable that all the observed coincidences should have come about as a result of random forces.

Applying the synchrony of Schumpeter's three-cycle schemes involving the long wave Kondratieff cycle, the nine-year Juglar cycle and the forty-month Kitchin cycle, we find that the initial crisis, panic and danger occur when these three cycles turn down simultaneously. This occurred circa 1973–1974, with the fall in the stock market and the oil crisis. The only time these three cycles turn down simultaneously during the upwave is in the very last stages of that upwave. When these three cycles are falling simultaneously during the downwave, then acute crisis, panic and danger develop, leading to depression. If we now apply the nine-year cycle, projecting forward from the 1973–1975 crisis, then a period of acute crisis, panic and danger is due for 1982–1983. If we attempt to pinpoint the timing by using the forty-month cycle, it is likely to begin in June 1983 with a renewed collapse in commodity prices then.

The period of "acute crisis, panic and danger" begins with a crisis in confidence when many suddenly get the idea that a decisive change for the worse is happening. In a relatively short space of time, a feeling of insecurity turns into expectations of possible catastrophe. The crisis begins after a psychological climax. During the second half of 1983, such a psychological climax could develop from one of a number of sources. We may have a resumption of banking problems in the autumn of 1983. Such a psychological climax could be the result. By the autumn of 1983 we may find ourselves in the midst of yet another oil crisis with even more far-reaching implications than the last one. This could trigger a crisis in confidence. At the moment, many banks and U.S. companies are teetering on the edge of bankruptcy. The bankruptcy of a bank or major corporation could be the straw that breaks the camel's back of confidence. The world is currently in such a precarious state that it is difficult to pinpoint which calamitous event is the most likely. Whichever it is, it's likely to come like a bolt from the blue on an unsuspecting public following a period of temporary euphoria. The megacrisis will then feed on itself until it turns into a megapanic sometime during 1984.

Panics develop purely out of human emotion. With a bang, the herd begins to stampede, dashing madly in all directions at once, fearing everything from left to right. Panics are, by definition, irrational. Instead of attempting to develop rational ways to deal with the oncoming depression, most people simply try to escape the future by running. People dump investments unmercifully, leave their homes and seek solace wherever they can find it. The nadir of the crisis, the panic, cannot be anticipated by any statistical systematic fashion. To a large degree, it is psychological. It can happen at any time during a crisis. The crisis period was entered in 1983. The evidence to support the high probability of an oncoming panic and depression, in my opinion, is overwhelming. Thus far, the evidence I have presented is of a statistical and cyclical nature. There is more evidence, much more.

WHAT MAKES A RECESSION TURN INTO A DEPRESSION?

Jokers have said that when your friend loses his job, that is a business contraction. When you lose your job, that is a recession. When your wife loses her job, it is a depression.

The first use of the term "depression" can be traced to Henry Vansittart. He used it to describe the slowdown in business during 1793. In more recent years, Professor John Kenneth Galbraith told us that "depression" was resurrected as a substitute for "panic." Karl Marx preferred "crisis" for "panic." Herbert Hoover, who presided over the chaos of the 1930s, adopted what he believed to be a much softer term, resuscitating "depression" so as not to panic the crisis-prone.

When it was suggested to President Franklin D. Roosevelt that America was likely to remain in a depression for a considerable period, the president waggled a menacing finger and warned his opponents never to speak of rope in the house of a man who was about to be hanged. Since then, hard times have been euphemized as "business contractions," "periods of stagflation," "inflession," "rolling adjustments" and "extended seasonal slumps."

The difference between a recession and a depression seems to be a matter of degree. A severe recession may be termed a depression, and a mild depression might be called a recession. The National Bureau of Economic Research in the United States defined a recession as a "recurring period of decline in total output, income, employment and trade, usually lasting six months to a year and marked by widespread contractions of the economy." This definition was ultimately reduced simply to a decline in GNP for two consecutive quarters.

This definition has now received international acceptance. Obviously, there is a big difference between recession as it has come to be accepted and the panic, crisis, paralysis and unemployment from 1929 to 1933. Economist Alan Greenspan defines a depression as "either a 12% unemployment rate for nine months or more, or a 15% unemployment rate for three to nine months." Richard Rahn, another U.S. economist, says, "I would consider the country to be in a depression if there were a sustained, major drop in GNP for more than one year, combined with unemployment well into the double-digit range for an extended period of time."

The level of unemployment appears to be the agreed common element in a depression and a recession. Any doubts that the Western industrialized economies of the 1980s are heading for a depression on the scale of the 1930s should largely be removed by serious consideration of the current unemployment problems.

As we continue into the 1980s, we are confronted with a double-edged sword. High technology offers the possibility of producing more goods at lower prices, while escalating unemployment means the market for these cheaper, more abundant goods is steadily diminishing. Since the late 1960s, the global economic environment has been experiencing a shift in emphasis which is no less dramatic than the Industrial Revolution, when an agrarian society became an industrialized society. In 1800, 95 percent of the British working population was employed in the fields. By 1980, the number had fallen to 2.5 percent. High technology food processing and great strides in agricultural production mean that 2.5 percent of the population in 1980 can do as much as 95 percent of the population in 1800. Food production per man-hour of labor has increased prodigiously, while the Industrial Revolution opened new areas of employment to absorb the labors of former farm workers.

Over the past decade, we have seen the introduction of a vast array of labor-efficient devices. We have robotics, where one machine can perform the work of ten men and more, untiringly and without overtime pay, holiday pay, redundancy payments and without strikes. Microtechnology in business equipment is allowing the number employed in offices to be cut by as much as 50 percent. The cost of equipment has been falling rapidly, while the efficiency of new equipment is racing ahead. Today we have a pocket calculator that costs about $5.00 doing the work of a similar calculator costing $200 less than ten years ago. We have desk-top microcomputers with a storage capacity and output capability that would have required housing in a small ballroom fifteen years ago. Machines are becoming far cheaper to employ than men and women, at a time of peak labor surplus, with jobs being lost in the manufacturing industry at an alarming rate, never to be replaced. Unlike the transition from agrarian to industrialized society, where the industrial base grew as the agricultural base declined, this time around the United States and others have yet to provide a post-industrial base capable of absorbing the surplus labor which comes from labor-efficient technology and a global recession.

Coupled with the increasing number of people employed by government, a vast new class of service workers is being created in America, instead of workers skilled in mass production. Service jobs are just that, service to the manufacturing industry. They depend on both the value and the volume of the goods being churned out by the factories. As there are really very few "new" goods being invented, merely new machines for making old goods or spinoffs of old technologies, industrial countries are now being forced to think very carefully about the potential demand for the increase in production facilities for the goods they are making.

Worldwatch of Washington has estimated that by the year 2000 we will need a billion extra jobs to give work to the world's population. Put another way, the United States, along with the other industrialized countries, is confronted with a massive oversupply of labor. If we just single out the rich industrial countries, forgetting about the lesser developed countries for the time being, we find that unemployment in early 1983 was fast approaching 20 million. In the developing world, the unemployment level is many times greater. People who are unemployed are not a particularly potent source of savings or demand. Industry requires savings to provide the capital needed for production . . . demand to absorb that which is produced. Both are shrinking fast.

Most American experts agree that the whittling away of the manufacturing sector's importance as a source of jobs is inescapable. Eli Ginzberg, a Columbia University economist, considered the Grand Old Man in the business of analyzing unemployment trends, reckons that by 1995 only 15 percent of all jobs will be in manufacturing. Peter Drucker, a well-known management expert, sees the deterioration in the number of jobs available in the manufacturing industry contracting even further. Drucker believes that manufacturing work in America by the end of the twentieth century will occupy no more than 7 to 12 million people. He linked the future of U.S. industry to the recent experience in American agriculture. Employment in agriculture dropped from 30 percent of the entire labor force to just 5 percent since World War II.

As the service class is expanding, the number of workers employed in factories where goods are produced is rapidly decreasing. The catastrophic aspect of this equation is that jobs that are being created in the service industries and that are likely to be created in the service industries in the future only represent a small fraction of the number of jobs being lost in manufacturing industry. The closure of these factories, along with the steady process of deindustrialization, is creating a vast reservoir of human beings who may be permanently unemployed. Britain is a perfect worst case example. From 1964 through 1974, approximately one million jobs in manufacturing industry were lost. In the three years that followed, Britain's industrial force was reduced to a mere 7.5 million people which is less than 15 percent of the total workforce. In Britain, the flight from manufacturing industry is likely to continue at an even faster pace in the years ahead. At the current rate, by the year 2000, a further 2 million jobs are likely to have disappeared, leaving less than one-tenth of the British population to produce goods for 60 million people.

In the United States and elsewhere, industries are collapsing just as the young people from the 1960s baby boom are seeking work. It is estimated that 8 million high school graduates will be hunting for jobs in Common Market countries alone during the first half of the 1980s. One in three currently has prospects of finding employment. Unemployment in Britain could reach 5 million by the mid-1980s. In the Common Market, there are likely to be at least 12 million officially unemployed by 1985. Taking the industrialized countries as a whole, we are already two-thirds of the way toward the 35 million people some expect to be without work at the middle of the decade.

Most governments are deeply uncertain and divided about the job crisis. Their response has been to underemphasize the seriousness of the problem, rather than to confront it. In France, in 1979, key forecasts indicating the growing problem were suppressed by government edict. The manner in which U.S. policymakers have continued to suggest that a recovery was in the offing throughout the continuing recession of 1980, 1981 and 1982, completely refusing to acknowledge any forecast contrary to this prepared doctrine, is testimony to the way governments can deny credibility to those whose warnings are not welcome. Forecast feedback, an attempt to produce an economic recovery by predicting one, was the futile platform of the Hoover administration during the Great Depression of the 1930s. Economic growth by rhetoric is the policy of the 1980s.

Burgeoning unemployment combined with industrial contraction and decay present an inexorable formula for depression. We are at what Professor Gerhard Mensch has termed a "technological stalemate."

We have trancended great cycles of change which are the product of new technology and invention. Minsky describes these as "displacements." Each of the distinct patterns has been marked by a technological revolution —steam power in the 1800s, electricity and the rise of mechanical transport in the 1880s, electronics and plastics in the 1950s. Each cycle of technological innovation ended in a crisis of stagnation. Kondratieff believed that, during the upwave of the long wave pattern, invention resulting in increased productive capacity produced prosperity. But during the downwave, a technological crisis developed as a generation of productive capacity ran into obsolescence, leading to a secondary depression.

Professor Jay W. Forrester sheds considerable light on the technological sequence of the long wave pattern of economic life in an article entitled "Changing Economic Patterns" in *Technology Review*, published by the Massachusetts Institute of Technology. Forrester has developed his "System Dynamics National Model," which is essentially a computerized econometric model of the U.S. economy. Forrester claims his experiments confirm that there is a long wave cyclical pattern with a time frame of forty-five to sixty years. Forrester also asserts that the U.S. economy is nearing another depression.

Forrester's model of the U.S. economy contains fifteen industrial sectors, such as consumer durables, capital equipment, energy, agriculture, housing and building construction. He says, "The Model is a translation into computer language of the knowledge people have about organizational structure and operating policies surrounding their daily activities. Such a model is designed to be a role-playing replica of the real economy. It should behave like the key economy, generating growth, fluctuations, shifts in population between sectors, inflation, unemployment, and other phenomena of the real world."

Forrester's model includes three of the major business cycles, the short-term (three- to seven-year) cycle, the medium-term (fifteen- to twenty-five-year) cycle, and the long-term (forty-five- to sixty-year) cycle. He believes that the longer-term cycle is the most important in explaining economic behavior.

> The long wave manifests itself as a massive expansion of the capital sectors followed by a relatively rapid collapse in their output. It is usually described as a peak of economic activity followed by a 10-year plateau, then a drop into a depression period for about a decade, and a long climb over some 30 years to the next peak. Long wave behavior seems to account for the great depressions of the 1830s, 1880s and 1930s, and it may be of critical importance in explaining our present economic situation. Forces arising from the long wave seem to explain many present economic cross-currents, raising the spectre of another depression period in the 1980s.

Forrester, who developed the computer model used in the famous *The Limits of Growth*, sees the long wave pattern of economic life as a process in which the capital goods sectors grow to a size which cannot be sustained, and ultimately collapse. He traces the dynamics of long wave patterns from the industrial expansion in 1945.

Following the Great Depression and World War II, many industries were ravaged and there was a widespread shortage of capacity. The consumer durables sectors, housing, office buildings, factories, transport systems and schools were also insufficient to meet the growing post-war demand. The need to rebuild the capital stock as quickly as possible meant that the growth in construction rose beyond real long-term requirements. The limits to growth in capital expansion were believed to have been achieved in the middle 1960s, since which time tremendous forces to sustain the process of capital accumulation have persisted. This has left an unbalanced economic system, with too much capital equipment and too much debt. Excess capacity in capital equipment has caused the upward trend to falter, while the need to liquidate debt has meant a dismantling of capital plant. The tendencies in Forrester's model go a long way toward explaining the current state of industrial degeneration in Britain.

Governments would like people to believe that if businessmen would get off their backsides and invest, our problems would be solved, and we would have renewed economic recovery.

Forrester says, "I don't share the widespread expectation that the resumption of business investment will solve existing economic problems. The current slowdown in investment is attributed by many to a lack of confidence. But that lack of confidence is produced by the underlying facts. Return on gross investment has been declining for the past decade and there is no longer a significant risk premium for investment. And, as you look around the economy, there is a strong tendency toward excess capacity; you see it in office buildings, in the steel industry, and in airline seats. New tankers have been coming out of shipyards and going immediately into lay-up. College graduates, who represent investment in human capital, find it increasingly difficult to get jobs."

The economic conditions of the 1980s present amazing parallels to those following the peak of all of the long wave patterns of economic behavior since the eighteenth century. We are witnessing a decline in capital investment, rising unemployment, a leveling out of labor productivity and reduced innovation. Similar conditions existed in the 1920s, 1870s and 1820s, and during the latter part of the eighteenth century, when interest rates rose to historic highs as investment opportunities diminished and heavy debts were incurred.

Forrester sees the U.S. economy poised on the brink of a slump similar to that of the 1930s. Until such a depression takes place, imbalances in the system cannot be removed to pave the way for the new technological era that will follow.

In 1976, Ehud Levy-Pascall, of the International Functional Staff Office of Political Research, Directorate of Intelligence, Central Intelligence Agency, produced a study entitled *An Analysis of the Cyclical Dynamics of Industrialized Countries.* At that time, the study predicted "especially troubled times lie ahead." In 1979, Levy-Pascall suggested that energy problems might serve as the trigger for a downturn. Levy-Pascall believes in the fifty-year Kondratieff cycle. Adding further dimensions to the long wave pattern of economic life, Levy-Pascall's model consists of five basic elements or phases, which together span approximately fifty years.

The first phase involves one or more major technological innovations which usher in new industries. The new innovations bring a dramatic uplift in the economy. From the beginning of the first phase to the end of the second phase, about thirty years elapse. During the third phase, a backwash of economic change revolutionizes the system once again. Major changes occur in life-style, values and the social system generally. These changes first take place among the youth, later among parents, and generally after severe sociopolitical turbulence. During the fourth phase, politicians eventually switch to policies in keeping with the changed technological, economic and social system. A relatively calm period follows. The final phase involves the stagnation of economic, social and political systems, and optimism gives way to pessimism. Politically, there is a shift to right-wing conservatism.

Prior to the election of President Reagan, Levy-Pascall believed the United States was ripe for a change of political leadership. Such a change took place in the United States in 1980, and in Britain in 1979. Levy-Pascall points out, and most economists would agree, that periods of economic expansion and contraction among Western industrialized nations are becoming more closely attuned. The world economies are becoming increasingly synchronized. In 1975, virtually every Western industrialized nation experienced an economic downturn of almost equal severity. Now a depression in the United States, with its $3 trillion economy, will be echoed in every corner of the globe. Levy-Pascall's model is darkly pessimistic. He believes the United States entered its "fifth phase" in the early 1970s, pointing to the end of the upwave. He sees little hope of avoiding disaster.

THE SHAPE OF THINGS TO COME

Writing in *The New York Review of Books* in June 1974, Geoffrey Barraclough implied that the steep plunge into a depression could be expected sometime around 1979. In *The Wall Street Journal* of October 1974, Alfred L. Malabre, Jr., foresaw a deep secondary slump in the early 1980s. Walter W. Rostow, author of *The World Economy*, believed that if the price explosion of 1973 was, in fact, analogous to that of 1919–1920, then we might expect a second crash in 1983. Shuman and Rosenau foresaw a plunge in or about 1981. The work of Schumpeter's three cycles schemes would indicate crisis and panic are due about now.

For quite some time I have been advising listeners to my broadcasts and subscribers to my *Investors Bulletin* that a depression is inevitable. If we use the definitions of Alan Greenspan and Richard Rahn, many countries across the globe are suffering a severe depression. A depression is certainly not a matter of "if" or "when" . . . it's a matter of how wide, how deep and for how long. As far as the individual is concerned, it's a matter of how to cope with the actualities of the future.

The lessons of previous depressions suggest that we are currently only at the incipient stages of a depression. Over the next few years, we can expect to see unemployment increase, inflationary expectations will be shattered and the biggest problem will be for businesses to survive. International tensions are likely to heighten, leading to protectionism and trade wars.

Some governments in Europe now fear that mass unemployment may lead to another major conflict before long. Frank L. Klingberg carried out an examination of U.S. foreign policy dating back to 1776 and discovered what he defined as alternating phases of "introversion" and "extroversion" in U.S. international relationships. According to Klingberg, warlike tendencies are manifest during periods of extroversion. These phases of introversion and extroversion are seen to average about twenty-seven years. Klingberg believes that a fourth phase of extroversion began in 1940 in the United States, extending until 1967. In 1967, Klingberg cites opposition to the Vietnam war as the major politically potent element at the time. It is Klingberg's view that by 1988, when the memory of the Vietnam war has faded from the consciousness of most Americans, there is likely to be an even more vigorous involvement in world affairs which could plunge the United States and her allies into another great war. Quite clearly, the attitude of the electorate dictates whether or not a war is a politically desirable achievement. The popularity afforded Prime Minister Margaret Thatcher in her waging of war against the Argentinians in defense of the Falkland Islands not only demonstrates the electorate finds war politically acceptable . . . but actually desirable, at this time.

In domestic economies, debt has reached unsustainable levels. Many companies have been borrowing to survive, hoping for economic recovery. When lenders and borrowers realize that no such recovery is likely in the immediate future, lenders will become more prudent and borrowers will abandon hopes of survival. A wave of bankruptcies can be expected that will reduce debt burdens, and ultimately restore domestic monetary stability.

We have entered a period of intense global financial instability which will inevitably lead to an international financial crisis before the depression of the 1980s has run its course. Bank failures on a massive scale can be expected over the next few years. A bank holiday similar to that in the 1930s must also be considered. Adding to the current financial chaos has been the stupendous growth of Euro-currency, involving currencies outside the control of individual central bankers. The unregulated Euro-currency market may be where the first clear signs of a major financial collapse appear. Euro-currency bankers have gone furthest in using short-term deposits to finance long-term loans to less than perfectly creditworthy borrowers.

It is my view that the depression of the 1980s will be far worse than that of the 1930s. During previous depressions, a far larger segment of the economy was in agriculture, and was largely self-sufficient in food. People are much farther removed today from the subsistence agriculture which once provided for those who were out of work.

Consumer debt levels have been extended beyond anything ever seen before. As a result, many more people will be affected by the depression of the 1980s. People have been encouraged to live beyond their means for decades. The nature of a self-feeding debt liquidation, which comes with deflation, will mean that these debts will have to be repaid. Personal bankruptcies are likely to reach terrifying proportions.

Socially, the decline in the family unit will intensify the problems for many who will find themselves without a home and without a job. The far more closely knit family of the 1930s and the 1880s provided a cushion for many whose survival was assisted by friends and relatives. During the depression of the 1980s, the more introverted nature of society will mean that fewer friends and relatives can be counted upon to help.

People will turn to the government for help. If government were as powerful as people would like to believe, or as politicians would like us to believe, we would never have inflation, recession or depression. It is likely that government itself will be unable to help much. Ironically, the very heavy pressure to take action will in itself reduce the government's ability to function effectively. Washington could become a major battleground for demonstrators and protestors of every description.

The major turning point in every depression involves the bursting of a speculative bubble. Historically, a speculative boom in the stock market, commodity markets, property markets or anything else, was immediately followed by the "bust," after which the forces of depression become all too obvious. The "bust" phase probably poses the greatest threat to the largest number of people in the 1980s. Due to inflation and taxes, many people have put most of their savings into their homes. The decline in home prices has already begun. An extended decline will leave many with no assets at all. If they lose their jobs and cannot repay their mortgages, they will be homeless and destitute. More people in the United States now own their own homes than ever before. The irresponsible drive to provide credit for housing among lenders leaves the homeowner with a high mortgage excessively vulnerable to a depression and with 60 percent of the homes in the United States owner-occupied the effects could be catastrophic.

Individuals who face the implications and possibilities of the type of depression that I have described will be able to protect themselves from the disorder to come. Some may even profit by it. There are many who refuse to acknowledge the true nature of global economic developments, who will be content to believe what they wish to believe, who will cling to an unshakable faith that a depression of the style of the 1930s can never happen again. Sadly, those individuals whose judgment is governed by complacency and unreason will suffer most, and provide the unpreparedness which is at the root of the self-perpetuating boom-bust cycle.

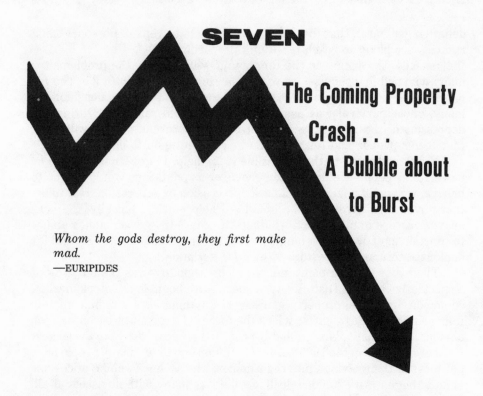

SEVEN

The Coming Property Crash . . . A Bubble about to Burst

Whom the gods destroy, they first make mad.
—EURIPIDES

The lemmings are headed for the sea. They are on a stampede of mad unreason, determined to trample over anything or anyone in their path, intent on repeating the ritual of self-destruction passed down through their psyches over the ages. In Holland, during the seventeenth century, the human lemmings chose tulip bulbs as their vehicle for financial self-annihilation. In the eighteenth century, shares in the South Sea Company, the Mississippi Company and the Dutch East India Company were the self-destruct mechanisms. In the nineteenth century, cotton, wheat and railways carried financial holocaust. In the 1920s, it was stocks. During the 1980s, residential property is likely to be the grim reaper bringing financial genocide.

Nothing is immune from becoming the subject of a speculative bubble. Intense speculation can break out in any country, in virtually anything. Silver, tobacco leaves, tulips, canary seed, peppercorns, salt, seashells, orange juice, railroads, ships, gold, building land, commerical property and residential property have all been the victims of frenzied speculation in the past. And just before they burst, almost all bubbles are accepted as safe and sound.

In retrospect, most people judge speculative booms as bordering on the ridiculous. Can you imagine a Dutchman being foolish enough to pay the equivalent of a hundred acres of land for one tulip bulb? Sounds crazy, doesn't it? But that is hindsight. If you are to be objective in future decision making, you must be acutely aware that when these bubbles were biggest they looked perfectly normal. No less "normal" and "respectable" than gold at $900 an ounce, or buying a home at today's grossly inflated prices.

Few people today would become enamored of tulip bulbs, tobacco leaves or canary seed as a safe place to keep money. Yet most were readily able to justify and consider normal the overextended prices of gold, silver and property not long ago. In early 1980, when gold was heading up to $1,000 an ounce, it was generally accepted that gold was undervalued. There were claims that it should be $2,000 or $3,000 an ounce. Some were predicting $5,000. At the time, it was inconceivable that gold could actually fall.

People soon discovered that its price could go down as well as up. It lost more than 50 percent in a few short months in early 1980. The reasons why this should never happen—why gold was different—were not too hard to find. The financial pages were saturated with them. But gold collapsed, in spite of the multitude of so-called guidance to prove it never could.

Could the same thing happen to residential property? Most people will answer No! They will be no less emphatic than the many property operators who believed that commercial property could never fall in value before the collapse in 1973–1975.

Somehow, residential land and the buildings on it are looked upon as the one sure investment. Most people today have little doubt that their homes will always hold their value. They feel that if there is a price decline, it will only be temporary. It is difficult to find anyone who is not totally convinced his property will protect him against inflation, the deterioration of currencies and any political climate.

On the surface, these assumptions sound reasonable. Unfortunately, history shows that residential property has not always protected its owner against inflation. It has not been able to shelter him against political risk, and for long periods it has been a very poor investment.

There have been times when the value of residential property has collapsed, and some property became unsalable. The same factors that sent property tumbling in the past could easily happen again. You do not have to be a Rasputin of the ready-reckoner to work it out.

After a speculative bubble bursts, there is usually a decline of approximately 80 percent from the peak. It happened when commodity prices crashed in the 1920s. The Wall Street Crash involved a decline of almost 90 percent. When the London Stock Exchange crashed between 1973 and 1975, the *Financial Times* 30 Share Index lost 78 percent.

Residential property during the 1970s and 1980s is far removed from merely being a home for people to live in. Homes have become gambling tokens and residential property has taken on all of the characteristics of a historical speculative bubble. Purchasing a property for its investment potential based on future assumption is speculation. As such, house prices are likely to respond to the same mechanisms as any other medium, once the bubble stage has been reached. A decline of as much as 80 percent of the peak values achieved in certain classes of houses would therefore not be inconceivable in the period that lies ahead.

THE GLOBAL HOUSING ROLLER COASTER

Most people harbor the illusion that the price of their homes can only go up . . . never down. A reporter for the London *Times* says, "House prices always move up, step by step, reaching a plateau, then moving higher." Professor Irving Fischer of Harvard University said the same thing about the American stock market in 1929. The idea is no less fallacious when applied to housing than it is when applied to the stock market. Not only do house prices move up and down quite vigorously, but in the past they have fallen much faster than they have risen. The trends in house prices are less visible than those of the stock markets, commodity markets, gold, silver and the like, because we don't have an index or a daily price monitor to watch. Trends in house prices move slowly and ponderously over long periods of time before the collapse becomes ostentatiously obvious.

A collapse in house prices is certainly not rare, or unusual. Crashes in residential property values have been plundering speculators, property developers and homeowners for centuries. The somewhat elusive trend in house prices seems to have an eighteen-year rhythm involving major peaks at fifty- to sixty-year intervals. Actually, residential property prices move in tandem with the long wave of economic life to a more exacting degree than any other capital market. Severe price declines occur about once in every fifty years in different places around the globe conforming to the peak in the overall price cycle as seen since the late eighteenth century. The subdominant eighteen-year rhythm in real estate activity is linked to corresponding rhythms in new building and the marriage rate which also succumbs to major peaks in activity about every fifty to sixty years, which provides further evidence to justify the validity of the long wave of economic behavior. We may hazard a postulate that man's mating instinct and man's building instinct may be aboriginally associated in his being, just as they extend down the scale to the nesting of birds and the periodic abandonment and rehousing of the hermit crab in his shell.

As far back as the eighteenth century, which is about as far as available statistics on the subject of residential land prices and building construction can be obtained, we can see traces of the recurrent rhythm in real estate activity at work. In 1934 H. A. Shannon published the results of research carried out on the number of bricks produced in England and Wales during the period 1785 through 1849. It was the fact that bricks were taxed at the time and records kept that made the research possible. Warren and Pearson, soon after, then interpolated population data, adjusting brick production per capita during the same period. The result was further vindication of both the sixteen- to nineteen-year rhythm of activity and the

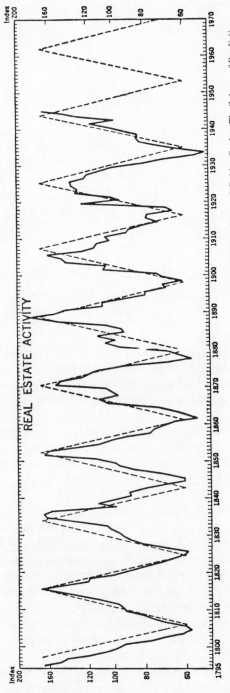

REAL ESTATE ACTIVITY

Reprinted from Dewey & Bakin, *Cycles: The Science of Prediction*, Henry Holt Co.

FIGURE 21

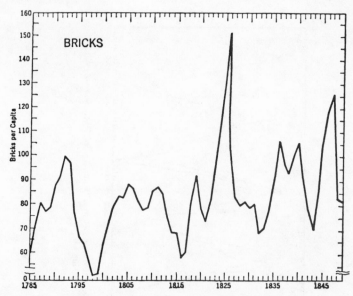

FIGURE 22   BRICKS PRODUCED PER CAPITA IN ENGLAND AND WALES, 1785–1849

From *The Prices Series* by G. F. Warren and F. A. Pearson.
Reprinted by permission of Chapman and Hall, Ltd.

overriding fifty- to sixty-year rhythm revealing the parallel between housing activity and our long waves of economic behavior. The fall in brick
production that terminated in the early 1790s would appear to conform with
the trough of a downwave that occurred at just about that time. The peak
in brick production, per capita, taking place in 1813, is common to the peak
that occurred in the long wave cycle during 1814. The collapse from the
1825 peak is clearly a component of the devastating depression that began
in 1819 and continued until 1843. The sharp rise in brick production that
began in 1844 took place just after the second long wave cycle began in
1843.

If it is assumed that the price of land bears some relationship to the
price of the house that sits on it and that the cost of building that house
also bears some relationship to the price, we can certainly envisage some
wild acrobatics in house prices over the past century, at least in England.
E. A. Vallis, in his paper, "Urban Land and Building Prices," published in
the *Estates Gazette* in 1976, shows that the 1892–1895 price median was
£130 ($205) per acre of residential land. That price rose to almost £900 an
acre during the long wave upswing that began in 1894 and ended in 1920.
By 1922, the price per acre of residential land in England was down to
£250 an acre, from which point residential land prices drifted gently downward through the rest of the 1920s and 1930s. After World War II, England
experienced its biggest boom in home ownership ever. According to the
works of Vallis, who meticulously extracted land prices from thousands of
mortgage deeds, by 1969 the price of residential land in Britain had risen

to £10,600 per acre. That boom rivals any speculative bubble in history. The rise in residential land prices in England after 1969 makes the increase even more astounding in its historical perspective.

A constant fallacy that prevails when discussing the subject of property values is that prices must always go up because the price of bricks, cement and construction costs will always go up. This erroneous belief assumes inflation will rise forever, which is demonstrably untrue. Vallis has demonstrated quite conclusively that land prices are subject to wild fluctuations. He also shows that building costs run in very close parallel to land prices. Between 1905 and 1948, both the price of building land and construction costs were falling, with building prices actually falling faster than land prices. Land prices began turning upward in 1939. Construction costs did not turn upward until 1948, then both rose together in that explosive uptrend which many people now believe will last forever. It won't.

The dangers of residential property investment in England in the 1890s were hinted at in Noreen Branson's historical account of the 1920s, entitled *Britain in the 1920s*:

> The great housing boom of the century has been one of houses built for investment purposes. They had proved an attraction to the smaller investor, such as retiring tradesmen, who had felt their savings would be safer in bricks and mortar than in less tangible stocks and shares. The boom has come to an end because it was said that Lloyd George's People's Budget of 1909–1910 had frightened the small investors away from land and property.

It is a fact that more financial crises have been attributed to land and property investment than to any other area of speculative activity. In Charles P. Kindleberger's book, *Manias, Panics and Crashes*, there appears a stylized outline of financial crises covering the period 1720 through 1722. One of the first major panics in Britain occurred in 1763. Kindleberger traces the cause of the panic to housing. In 1828, there was a financial collapse in France. The reason? Speculation in building land. In 1837, there was a financial catastrophe in the United States which could also be traced to excessive speculative activity in building land. In 1838, there was another financial catastrophe in France. Once again one of the major causes could be seen to be intense speculative activity in building land. Investment in building sites and railroads provided the vehicles for the crashes in Germany and Austria in 1873. Homesteading in the United States was the cause of the American financial debacle during the same year. Although the Roaring Twenties was a time of plenty for most areas of speculation, in America the collapse in land prices in Florida ruined many Americans in 1925. Between 1974 and 1975 another property hiatus nearly annihilated the total savings of those who had invested in Real Estate Investment Trusts.

If we assemble the somewhat fragmented data from various international sources, the records suggest a deep depression in residential property in the United States and elsewhere at around the turn of the century when the terminal juncture of the third downwave was reaching a nadir. It is likely that house prices edged marginally higher during the early part of the twentieth century and then embarked upon a thrilling and explosive rise following World War I, reaching a peak at just about the time of the 1920–1922 recession. From 1920 to 1922, the combination of a sharp fall in construction, land and building material costs resulting from global deflation would certainly have affected the price of residential housing. Building costs in Britain for example, had fallen by 50 percent. In France and Germany, building costs were down 28 percent and 37 percent respectively.

Most individuals believe that residential property prices will always rise because land and construction costs will always rise. This is a fantasy that does not conform to the facts. Only a fool argues with fact. Although a fall in construction costs may seem like an unprecedented occurrence, there have been many wild fluctuations in construction costs in the United States and elsewhere throughout history. Between 1941 and 1944 the construction costs for houses in the United States dropped by 12 percent. Between 1937 and 1939 costs fell by 8.5 percent. The periods 1891, 1895 and 1897–1899 all witnessed notable falls in construction costs. The same holds true for the periods 1901, 1903–1904, 1911 and 1921. There was also a significant fall in construction costs from 1960 to 1962 and during 1970. The most severe drop in construction costs on record took place during the five years from 1929 through 1934. In the United States the cost to build a home plunged by 39 percent during that period.

Land prices also fluctuate with the same degree of volatility. Between 1890 and 1920 the average cost of one acre of residential land in the United States rose from $747 to $1,507. Beginning in 1920, residential land prices began to slide and continued to slide for twenty years, reaching a trough in 1940 at $798 per acre. There was a rise in land prices from 1940 through 1950 when the average price per acre in constant dollars reached $1,061. It is interesting to note that while consumer prices in the United States trebled between 1890 and 1950 and the population of the country grew by two and a half times, land prices only increased slightly.

Another variable in the house-price equation over the years is the relative cost of land to the total cost of the home. In 1890 the cost of the land accounted for nearly 40 percent of the price of a single family home. The cost of construction amounted to 60 percent. By 1953 that figure had changed appreciably. Construction costs amounted to 83 percent of the price of the home. The amount of the cost that was attributable to the price of the land had fallen to a mere 17 percent. It has been demonstrated that both land prices and the cost of construction fluctuate widely over time. Neither can be said to offer the promise of support for house prices in the future. The aspect of land scarcity is certainly not a consideration. There is sufficient land in the United States to provide each citizen with forty acres if it were equally divided. John McMahon of Stanford University says, "On a national basis there is not now, nor has there ever been a physical shortage of land for real estate activities."

The cause for debacles in residential housing and land activity can be traced to the variations in material costs, the cost of construction, the cost of labor and the fluctuations in land prices, all of which are related to the various peaks and troughs in residential building activity. During boom times, more people have more money and there is more credit available. Demand for housing increases as does the cost of materials and the level of building activity. When a crunch comes, demand for housing falls; the level of building activity also falls along with the demand for land and raw materials. During the period of expansion, builders who are late to develop are still able to make a profit on their unit costs since the rise in the price of the house is usually faster than the rise in the cost of materials. However, when there is a contraction in demand and material costs fall, those who begin their developments later in the cycle are able to reduce the cost per unit as a result of lower unit costs of production. Those who were locked into high cost developments find they must then sell at a loss in order to compete with builders whose development costs are lower.

Data have been assembled correlating trends in residential building activity in various countries. What can be seen is a distinct commonality in housing trends among the industrialized nations. While the extent of expansion and contraction differs from one nation to the next, over the past 200 years we can see that peaks and troughs in residential housing activity, which is directly related to price activity, have occurred in sequence without deviation among all of the major countries. More important, according to Dewey, a tendency for major global panics has come within two to four years after the peaks in building activity. There was a peak in building activity in the United States in 1836. There was a major panic in 1837. There was a peak in building activity in several countries simultaneously in 1871. There was a global panic in 1873, two years later. Construction peaked in Hamburg, Germany in 1890. The number of new houses built in London, England, peaked in 1890. Brick production peaked in the city of Glasgow, Scotland, in 1890. Real estate activity in the United States peaked in 1890. In 1893 there was a worldwide depression of immense proportions.

It must be recognized that over the past fifty years there have been significant structural changes in the residential housing market. As such, residential housing is a much more potent capital market than it has been at any time during the past 200 years. Widespread home ownership in the United States and elsewhere is essentially a production of the last three decades just as widespread shared ownership was a product of the 1920s. The wealthy landed gentry in England may have owned the homes they lived in, along with farmers in the United States during the pre-1940 era,

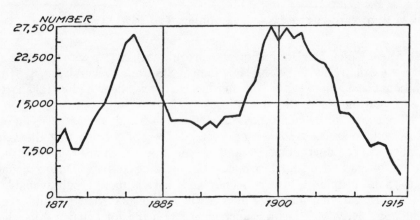

FIGURE 23   NEW HOUSES BUILT IN THE METROPOLITAN POLICE DISTRICT OF
LONDON 1871–1916

From *The Prices Series* by G. F. Warren and F. A. Pearson.
Reprinted by permission of Chapman and Hall, Ltd.

but for most people, home ownership was out of reach. The financial structure of the housing market before the 1930s was such that the average
individual would have to save for years to acquire the 50 percent of the
purchase price he would need to get a mortgage. When he finally did put
together enough money for the 50 percent down payment, the mortgage
he would get would be for a relatively short repayment period, usually five
years, but sometimes as short as one year. This meant monthly repayments
on the mortgage were quite high.

In the nineteenth century, in the United States and elsewhere in western Europe, building and loan associations were formed to hold the savings
of working people who eventually wanted to buy their own homes. In the
interim, those savings were loaned to people who could afford to buy their
own homes at the time. The building and loan associations were more
liberal with regard to down payments that were required but still limited
the repayment period to three to five years. As late as 1920, 60 percent of
all the homes in the United States which were occupied by their owners had
no mortgage on them at all. These were the homes of the wealthier members of society.

The trend in Britain and most of Europe is similar to that in the United
States. In 1914 only one home in ten was occupied by its owner in Britain.
Between 7 and 8 million families rented their house or bits of houses, from
private landlords. There was a revival in house building during the secondary prosperity of the 1920s. Credit available for housing was liberalized to
a degree. The down payment required on the average home was about 25
percent of the purchase price. In Britain during the 1920s, it was still
considered that only an exceptionally highly paid worker could afford to
own his own home. Individual home ownership continued to play a relatively small role in both the American economy and the British economy
during the 1920s. By the time of the Great Depression, less than one in five

homes in Britain were occupied by their owners compared with three out of five in 1980, figures strikingly similar to home ownership in the United States.

It is difficult to ascertain precisely how the Great Depression affected house prices. There is strong evidence to suggest that prices fell sharply but attempts at constructing actual house price indices have been notoriously unreliable. A good deal of the fall in house prices during the Great Depression of the 1930s took place over the relatively short period between 1930 and 1933. Much of the fall can be attributed to cheaper labor and the fall in raw material prices. Records for house prices in the United States are suspect for that period. However, in Britain, we find that a third of the houses built in 1931 cost £600. By 1939 nearly half the houses available cost £600. Secondhand homes cost from £400 to £500 at the time. It is likely that builders and developers had quite a difficult time selling houses during the 1930s, though speculative building in America was rife. Builders began moving down the scale. They negotiated schemes with savings and loan banks which by then were able to provide mortgages over fifteen years involving a deposit of 25 percent, sometimes less. With a struggle, many middle-class and salaried people could manage to buy their own homes, but not the average industrial worker or most clerical workers.

The fall in house prices during the 1930s could not really be described as a collapse even though many people had lost their homes for nonpayment of mortgages. Since there was never really a boom in house prices to start with, there was no exalted plateau from which house prices could fall. The fall was merely that of a normal cyclical decline rather than that which follows a speculative mania. Speculators who borrowed heavily and overextended themselves in residential housing were, of course, devastated by the contraction in housing activity, but not so much as a result of the fall in house prices as the inherent commercial risk in the industry. But this time around the situation is somewhat different. It is not the commercial builder who is assuming the risk of the mania in housing, but the individual.

What a reading of history shows us is that whole nations, like individuals, have their whims and peculiarities, their seasons of excitement and recklessness. What we can also see is that these periods of excitement and recklessness conform to a long-term rhythm of a fifty- to sixty-year periodicity, involving the commingling of many social, economic and cultural phenomena, of which real estate activity is prominent. When peaks of activity are approached within these rhythmic cycles, we have found whole communities will suddenly fix their minds upon one object and go mad in its pursuit; that millions of people become simultaneously impressed with one delusion, and run after it till their attention is caught by some new folly which is more captivating than the first. While the past two decades have brought about a worldwide boom in housing, in the United States we have what can only be described as a housing mania, which involves the same characteristics of the bubbles that have been described throughout history. Financial constraint has been thrown to the winds. Conventional wisdom says that about one-quarter of the family income should be spent on housing. In 1971, 17.6 percent of the average family income was being used to service monthly mortgage repayments. By 1981, 45.6 percent of the median annual family income of the average American was being used to service monthly mortgage repayments. According to the Department of Housing and Urban Development, in 1970, half the families in America were able to afford a medium-priced new house. By 1980, the figure of 50 percent had fallen to 13 percent. By 1981, the figure had fallen to 5 percent. In other words, 95 percent of American families were unable to afford a medium-priced home in 1981. Increasingly, many Americans had to rely on a second income to help meet mortgage repayments. Sometimes that second income would involve not only two people working but one person taking on a second job to meet these mortgage repayments.

In mid-1983, the promise of economic recovery echos throughout the United States. To the unemployed the sound is muted. Second jobs are still being lost along with second incomes. Mortgage delinquencies continue to grow along with redundancies and private and corporate bankruptcies. With 95 percent of the families in the United States unable to afford to buy a medium-priced home, who will be available to purchase the homes that will be offered by those who can no longer continue to keep up their mortgage repayments? How low will the price of these homes have to be before American families can afford to purchase them? The housing bubble is about to burst. The results will be devastating.

ANATOMY OF A HOUSING CRASH

What will it be like? What will it do to you? How will it affect your life-style? When the price of your house comes plummeting down in value, will your life-style still be worth living? The questions are, of course, emotive . . . but so is the subject. So emotive is the subject that many people deliberately blind themselves to the history of housing activity as if it never existed, hoping the books have been burned and all the memories blurred. Many individuals will insist that house prices can only go up . . . never down . . . and have only gone up . . . never down since the dawn of creation. This is simply not true. Over the past few hundred years there have probably been more booms and busts in residential housing in the United States than in any other country. There are four specific periods when the prices of homes in the United States rose to absolutely fantastic heights. This was during the 1830s, 1880s, 1920s and 1970s. Each upsurge in house prices looked exactly the same as the other. So far, three out of four have collapsed with declines in prices reaching up to 50 percent according to John Wesley English in his book *The Coming Property Crash*. The only boom that hasn't yet collapsed is the most recent one. "This crash is yet to come," says English. The first two decades of the nineteenth century were a period of extravagant speculation and apparent prosperity in America. The long cycle of wars, both in Europe and the United States, ending only in 1815, had favored the erection of an unstable and overdeveloped credit structure which has been the seed corn of every major financial panic. During the first twenty years of the century, every type of economic activity had flourished, including industry, which grew into the proportions of a boom after 1808. The primary stimulus was domestic demand. At the time, America was a nation of people who were projecting an accidental and temporary bout of good fortune into the indefinite future.

The depression of 1819–1822 ushered in severe distress. In 1819, Matthew Carey estimated that 3 million people, approximately one-third of the population, were directly affected. From faraway Cincinnati came a report describing the "distress as beyond conception." Property values had drastically declined throughout the nation. Marshals and sheriffs were repossessing thousands of homes each day as bankers foreclosed on mortgages.

At the annual meeting of the Tennessee Agricultural Society, its president, Samuel Hopkins, addressed the members in October 1820:

> Last year we talked of the difficulties of paying for our lands; this year, the question is how to exist. The struggle is not now for property; from this time onwards we shall have to contend for clothing and a few other necessaries, without which we must become a miserable, and I fear, a barbarous people. . . .

Distress was equally acute in both the city and the country. Unemployment was widespread. Pauperism became a serious urban problem commanding concentrated attention for the very first time in American history. In Baltimore, twelve soup kitchens were established to help the poor in 1820. In Philadelphia, there was also daily distribution of soup at the rate of half a pint per person. In New York, soup kitchens were established through the generosity of local butchers and collections were raised in the city's churches. In 1819, the New York Society for the Prevention of Pauperism issued a statement proclaiming alarm at the increase in the number of paupers. There were 8,000 paupers in a city of 120,000 people. By 1820, the number of paupers had risen to between 12,000 and 13,000.

People living in Cincinnati were leaving for the backwoods to raise food while the newspapers were appealing for old clothes for the poor and for shoes to enable poor children to attend Sunday School.

The propertied classes suffered great hardships, having their wealth decimated during this period of depression. Property values declined precipitously. Added to the problem was the burden of debts against property which could only be liquidated by means of forced sheriffs' sales at auction. These forced sales depressed prices further and even more quickly. A committee of the Pennsylvania Senate reported that during 1819 there were 14,537 auctions for debt in the state. The value of real and personal property in New York State, as recorded at the comptroller's office, declined from $315 million in 1818 to $256 million in 1820. In Pennsylvania, land that had been boomed to $150 an acre in 1815 dropped to $35 an acre in 1819. In Baltimore, rentals plunged by approximately 50 percent.

The collapse in property values was a nationwide phenomenon. Similar conditions prevailed east and west, north and south. At Richmond, Virginia, property depreciated from 50 percent to 75 percent. Many of the homes of plantation owners were not salable at any price. They were valueless. Poverty was so widespread that it was nearly impossible to find anyone prepared to assume the cost of maintaining some of the more imposing residences. The reasons cited for the cause of the debacle had an old familiar ring to it . . . overextension of credit.

By 1835, Americans had forgotten the disaster of the 1820s and were ready to repeat the scenario all over again. The year 1835 was once characterized as the most prosperous the United States had ever known in its history. Harriet Martineau, a popular journalist of the time, said it seemed "as if the commercial credit of New York could withstand any shock short of an earthquake," since it had been able to stage such a rapid recovery from the losses of the great fire earlier that year. By 1837, not only New York but the entire nation was convulsed by a shock, no less devastating than any earthquake could ever have been. The nation was reeling from the shock waves that began with the crash in Chicago real estate that followed the speculative boom. While property investment in the United States was widespread during the 1830s, the proposed construction of the Illinois–Michigan Canal made Chicago an exceptionally dominant area of speculative activity. The construction of this canal would mean that the new Lake Michigan harbor would be joined with the Illinois River. The Illinois River flowed into the Mississippi at St. Louis. The canal would connect Chicago with the great inland waterway system, making it a strategically important center of commerce. Chicago would be serving the towns which rested on the banks of the Illinois River along with those of the state interior. In addition, the canal would open the city for business from St. Louis along with all of the other great cities that rest on the banks of the Mississippi. Chicago could then furnish these cities with an inexhaustible supply of pine lumber from the great forests of Michigan and Wisconsin. Great quantities of feed and grain would be available from the richly fertile land on the outskirts of Chicago. The immense prairies of the West would be available for the supply of huge herds of livestock. Chicago's influence would extend from the Atlantic seaboard to the slopes of the Rockies. Chicago was the boom town of the 1830s. Homesteaders came in droves. Land and property speculators were quick to exploit the conditions. Banks were lending on property as fast as they could push money across the counter.

Property prices ballooned. In 1830, the first parcels of land were sold. An 80-by-100-foot lot brought about $100 at auction. The same parcel of land that sold for $100 in 1830 sold for $3,000 in 1834. By 1835, it would have brought $15,000.

The bubble burst in 1837. The collapse of property, business and banking was only the beginning of a long and severe process of purgations. Between 1837 and 1843 American society passed through the deep hollow of a great economic cycle while society became heavy with doubt and distress. The nation had been drawing on the future and the future dishonored the check. As early as 1840 the estimated loss due to depression was calculated at a total of $6 billion. Some losses were incapable of measurement. Every class in the community was affected and economic interest deeply stirred. The propertied classes were once again among the hardest hit because they had absorbed the largest lines of credit. Distress selling meant that the land in Chicago that had been purchased at $11,000 an acre in the halcyon days of 1836 couldn't fetch $100 an acre four years later in 1840. Throughout the state of Illinois banks closed their doors and collapsed under the burden of defaulters whose property couldn't even pay the interest on the loans outstanding. The state itself defaulted on its obligations. Work on the canal was discontinued. Chicago property values fell further.

By 1841, what began in Chicago became a national calamity. Between 1841 and 1842 eight states went into default. Whole communities were involved in the general collapse. With the collapse of values and prices, the tide of bankruptcy rose, engulfing nearly everything and everyone. It was a nightmare that would cast a shadow over America for years to come. Not surprisingly, there was a concentrated effort to determine the cause of the Panic of 1837. It wasn't too difficult to trace the cause: overextension of credit when the pressure of an overinflated economy proved too great.

Next on the list of memorable property booms and busts in the history of the United States was California, circa 1880, about forty years after the Chicago fiasco, which to judge from contemporary accounts left scars that were no less deep. Theodore Van Dyke wrote the epitaph of the California real estate bubble in his book published in 1890, *Millionaires of a Day*:

> We were a lot of very ordinary toads whirled up by a cyclone until we thought we were eagles sailing with our own wings in the topmost of heaven.

It took irrigation and the spread of the railroad network to bring a land boom to California, for the heavy speculative money came from Easterners drawn by the warm climate of the West Coast. Originally many had come as winter tourists. But the growing prosperity of that fertile state drove real estate prices up, and in due course the Easterners made a casino of the market. "We never knew what the cussed land was worth until outsiders found it out, and now we are green enough to let them make all the money out of it." Van Dyke again.

Indeed. In Los Angeles and San Diego, a raging speculative epidemic drove the price of land up from perhaps $200 an acre in 1885 to nearly $10,000 by the summer of 1886. Borrowing was not quite as easy as it would be later, but it was common enough to be able to borrow 75 percent of cost price. The boom collapsed as all booms built on borrowed money always have collapsed throughout history. As is the case with all booms, the illusion was that prices were only rising to catch up with their real value. And since they were rising, the price paid was unimportant. The crash came in 1888 and continued through 1889. It was not the result of any setback to the general prosperity of California, though it certainly caused one. By the end of 1889, values had sunk by 75 percent, and thousands were ruined.

The plunge in property values during the depression of the 1820s, the boom and bust of Chicago real estate in the 1840s and the saga of the California land boom in the 1880s give clear evidence of the vulnerability of property as an investment. The greatest property fiasco of all time and the most momentous in living memory is without a doubt the Florida land boom of the mid-1920s and its awful dénouement.

Florida means a tropical climate with sandy beaches. Late in 1921, as the country was emerging from the recession of 1920–1921, land in Florida was cheap. The early comers, retired folk and farmers, were simply attracted by the quality of life. They were buying homes. But, as the prosperity of the state increased and the price of land rose, it was not long before speculators began coming in increasing numbers. And soon real estate combines were promoting the attractions of a home in Florida in the northern states. It was the Roaring Twenties and disposable income was rising rapidly. By 1925, the Florida land boom was in full swing, fueled by the widely promoted idea that Florida was the most desirable state in the union and by the popular notion that real estate prices could only go up. It was the old, old story of greed undeflected by thought.

The bankers financing the boom were no more cautious than the speculators indulging in it. In the single year of 1925, the loans on the books of the Florida banks practically doubled. The intending buyer only had to put down 10 percent of the purchase price and was frequently able to sell the contract on the land before it had expired. Immense paper fortunes were made by people who had no intention of living in the home, or building on the land they were buying. The city records of Miami show that one plot of land which was sold in 1914 at $1,500 changed hands in 1926 at $1,500,000.

The peak of the boom is usually put in the summer of 1925. It seems to have been about then that the momentum of price increases was at its highest. The railroad figures show passenger traffic still rising throughout the year, but there was a limit to the number of "greater fools" willing to pick up the baton—and a limit to the depth of their pockets. In any case, by early 1926, the slowdown was sufficiently apparent to elicit a number of statements from government spokesmen to the effect that this was a healthy breathing space. The general view was that the boom was good for several years more. Certainly that was the view from real estate agents and mortgage officers.

In the autumn of 1926, two hurricanes did some damage to property and a lot more to prices. Even after that *The Wall Street Journal* was to proclaim that the boom would go on, but it was already broken. Not only had prices crashed but the number of deals fell away to a trickle. The bubble had burst, and it left an appalling trail of defaults, including twenty-six of Florida's municipalities.

It was several decades before real estate prices in Florida returned to their peak levels of 1925–1926. Not until the 1960s, in fact. Those who had decided not to sell during the crash, preferring to wait for the next boom, were still waiting . . . thirty-five years later.

Of course it is true, "they don't make land anymore." But there is plenty of it. Its price rises and falls just like any other commodity. And the ups and downs have not just been confined to notorious booms and busts. In 1900, the average nationwide price of house-building plots was $780. In 1920 it was $1,507. And in 1940, it was back down again to $800. All this time the population was growing: it was up by nearly three-quarters over the period.

But something phenomenal did happen after the war. For between 1950 and 1980 the average plot price rose from $1,060 to over $30,000, an increase of around thirty times, whereas the debasement of the currency as measured by consumer prices was only 3.4 times. It was this phenomenal increase in the price of building land that lay behind the remarkable boom in house prices since World War II. Practically all of America's 57 million householders assume that the rise in prices will continue in the future much as it has in this recent past. It is a matter of vital concern too, since the wealth invested in housing amounts to more than all the wealth invested in all the stocks and bonds in the nation. And the assumption is almost certainly wrong. In fact it could be very badly wrong, as I propose to show.

THE POST-WAR HOUSE-PRICE BOOM

In 1981 the median price of new single-family houses was $69,800. A home is by far the most valuable possession most Americans have. Americans consider their homes much more than just a place to live. The home has become a store of value, a medium for saving, the financial bulwark for the average individual in America. Most people in America today are probably more concerned with house prices than any other item.

The best news most people can hear is that house prices will start moving up again and will continue to move up forever. It's always easy to convince people of the things that they want to believe in to begin with. Vested interests in the residential property industry prey on this tendency and real estate brokers, mortgage lenders, bankers and the media encour-

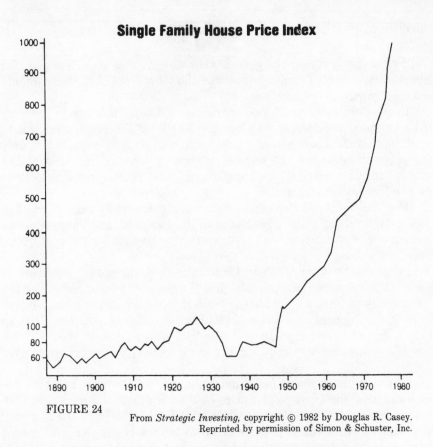

Single Family House Price Index

FIGURE 24

From *Strategic Investing,* copyright © 1982 by Douglas R. Casey.
Reprinted by permission of Simon & Schuster, Inc.

age it. Daydreaming has always been preferable to thinking among the masses. With stocks and bonds, diamonds, gold or stamps, only a modicum of harm is done. A home, which is a necessity of life, bought on borrowed money, requires considerably more careful consideration.

The end of World War II called the tune for the post-war housing bubble in America. Just after the war, house prices were understandably depressed. Adjusted for a low rate of inflation, prices were as low as they had been in 1919 or 1895. In the post-war reconstruction period, as servicemen returned from abroad, the baby-boom years of the upwave were just getting underway and the housing supply lagged behind demand. Prices began to rise . . . and rise . . . and rise.

There have been many factors that have combined to cause an exceptional rise in house prices since World War II—demographic, sociological, fiscal, monetary and psychological. These factors have all been reinforcing each other and have been at work throughout the period up to the end of the 1970s. With the coming of the decade of the 1980s, these factors started losing their potency and began to disintegrate. As the reasons for the revaluation of housing prices continue to decompose, the opposite process will come about and property prices will be devalued. As ye sow, so shall ye reap . . . as ye inflate so shall ye deflate!

Inflation, of course, has been the hallmark of the post-war era. There has usually been high inflation in times of war. So it was during World War II, and it was no surprise that, after a lull, inflation sped up again during the Korean War in the early fifties. Reassuringly, it calmed down again. During the rest of the 1950s and much of the 1960s, inflation was between 1 and 2 percent. That was more than zero, of course, and it was a very different matter from the deflation that had been the rule for much of the 1920s and early 1930s. Borrowing had been very expensive during those years of deflation.

In 1920, only about 40 percent of American householders had mortgages on their homes. (Now, only about 20 percent do not have them.) The experience of the twenties and thirties did little to encourage the spread of the mortgage habit. And, with one thing and another, the proportion was not much higher just after the war. But anyone looking back at the mid-1950s could see a succession of about twenty years during which general consumer prices had risen without a setback. Apartment rents, too, had been rising steadily. Anyone who had the cash, had already bought his own house, naturally. Every American wants to own his own house. However, the attraction of borrowing to buy your house was growing increasingly clear. The 4 percent mortgage was no longer available by the mid-1950s, but money could be had at 5 percent for 30 years. The financial figuring was very seductive compared with renting; so, although borrowing was dangerous, and to be avoided in general, the habit began to spread.

Naturally interest rates rose. House buyers were not the only ones in the market for borrowed dollars. Corporations could see the advantages too, not least that interest payments were tax deductible. That factor became a growing consideration for individuals concerned with increasingly high personal tax rates as their incomes swelled in the prosperous sixties.

By the start of the 1970s it was clear to most people that inflation was here to stay. No one had taken a wage cut in decades and they were not about to start. Rents could be expected to go up along with most other prices, including house prices. Furthermore, inflation had begun to accelerate in the late sixties. So, although mortgage rates had now climbed to the 7–8 percent area, they were still a steal when compared with paying rent out of net after-tax income.

Still, not everyone could afford to buy a house even with a mortgage. The down payment was a sizable sum. Kids just out of school did not have that kind of money. And there were lots of them. The famous post-war baby boom, which had begun around 1950 and peaked in 1957, was putting more than 4 million teenagers into their first jobs in the early 1970s. Something else was happening too, which sociologists called the breakup of the nuclear family. The kids did not want to stay at home with their parents. They wanted a place of their own, which meant a small or shared apartment, as close to the place of work as possible.

This new element in the supply/demand equation for apartments sent rents surging upward. During 1972 and 1973 it was possible to discern a veritable apartment boom, in which the public shared through the new Real Estate Investment Trusts (REITs) floated on Wall Street. There was a surge of speculative development of new apartments to meet the new demand. With the economy in full expansion and demand for office space buoyant, the boom spread to commercial real estate which had been a relatively calm market up to that date.

Then came the oil crisis and the economy was plunged into a slump. For many young people, it was their first experience of an economic dislocation which actually affected their lives. Jobs became harder to find, the automobile more expensive to run as inflation soared into double figures. In the urban real estate market it meant empty buildings, falling rents and many defaults.

But all was calm in the homes market. What the 1973–1975 slump did was to ram home the advantages of house ownership. There was no inflation in the cost of home ownership: the mortgage interest was fixed. The soaring rents of 1972–1973 had set even more of those who could afford it looking for a house to buy. The price of houses rose steadily through 1974 and 1975 even as apartment and commercial real estate values were slumping. Between 1972 and 1975 the average price of a new home rose from $12,000 to $43,900.

So, by the second half of the seventies, it was plain for all to see that you had to own your own home. There was no longer any room for doubt about that. Mortgages were still to be had at 9 percent, which was less than the typical house seemed to be appreciating in value every year. With income tax rates running up to 70 percent, the financial arguments were incontrovertible.

From 1975, there was an explosion in mortgage borrowing. It had started in the earlier days of easy money in 1971, but was checked in the squeeze of 1974. Prior to that mortgage borrowing had been under $20 billion and had seldom risen over $15 billion. In the second half of the 1970s, as Figure 25 shows, it soared over $100 billion, to $114 billion in 1978 and $124 billion in 1979. That is new mortgage loans on single family owner-occupied homes only. Net of repayments, the increase was a startling eight times from $10 billion in 1970 to $82 billion in 1978.

Initially, the impact of all this new borrowing on the homes market was quite orderly. America was just emerging from recession in 1976. In that year new house prices rose 9.5 percent. The next year they rose 12.5 percent on average, and that was well above the inflation rate of 7.5 percent for the year. By 1978 the house had become a sure thing. It had become the investment par excellence. Mortgage rates were still only 9.5 percent: easy money and a slowing inflation rate had kept them down. The increase in the average price of a new home jumped to 15 percent in 1978. House prices had doubled since 1970. And that national average concealed much greater rises in such parts of the country as California and Florida, New

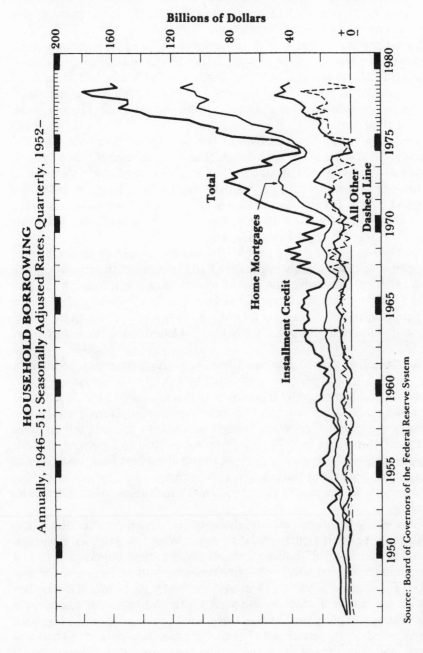

HOUSEHOLD BORROWING

Annually, 1946–51; Seasonally Adjusted Rates, Quarterly, 1952–

Billions of Dollars

200

160

120

80

40

+0

1950 1955 1960 1965 1970 1975 1980

Total

Home Mortgages

Installment Credit

All Other
Dashed Line

Source: Board of Governors of the Federal Reserve System

FIGURE 25

York and Chicago. Many could point to fourfold, even sixfold, rises in the prices of the homes they had been smart enough to buy. The bigger the home, and the more money they had borrowed to buy it, the greater was their personal equity in the investment.

Sometime during 1978–1979, the house became not a home, not even an investment, but a vehicle of speculation for thousands of Americans. Houses came to be bought, not necessarily even to live in, but to hold for the exhilaration of hearing that its price had risen in value. In some cases, these paper gains were more than the owners had earned in salaries in the whole of their lives.

That was certainly often true of the twenty-five-year-olds who had been born in the post-war baby boom. For now, of course, these young people had grown out of apartments, had children, and bought themselves a house—or sometimes two. It was the visitor to Chicago in 1836 who remarked that a friend "had realized, in two years, ten times as much money as he had before fixed upon as a competence for life"—from Charles Cleaver's *Early Chicago Reminiscences.*

To more and more young people who had not bought their own homes, it seemed in 1979 absolutely imperative to do so, even at the cost of considerable sacrifice. Otherwise, the cost of a house was going to run away and would never be affordable, ever. That year and into the early 1980s there was panic buying of homes, by people who in more ordinary times would have waited patiently for exactly what they wanted at the price they could afford.

As the 1970s turned into the 1980s, something happened to interest rates. Instead of mortgage rates climbing by a point or so every few years, they shot up, on average by 2 points in 1979 and nearly 3 whole points in 1980 and again in 1981 to reach 17 percent or more in places. Still the rise in new house prices carried on, though at a slower pace. It fell from an average of 15 percent in 1979 to 9.5 percent in 1980 to 4 percent in 1981. But once again these averages give not the smallest idea what was happening in certain pockets of the market. It is the mark of a speculative bubble that things strike the people as quite normal which seem to outsiders to be insane.

So it was with Tulipmania in eighteenth-century Holland, and so it now is with house prices in Southern California, in West Los Angeles, for example, where "entry-level" housing, homes for first-time buyers, starts at a very minimum of $400,000. That is five times the national average for new homes. The implied land values in very ordinary parts of suburban Los Angeles are maybe $2 million per acre, up to $5 million for fashionable areas. The opportunity cost of this entry-level housing—interest foregone on investment or the actual cost of borrowing the money—starts at around $50,000; and that is three times the national average disposable income, or after-tax earnings. The only place such prices can exist is on a carousel. For practical purposes, such prices can only be paid by people who have just sold another such object of speculation. That is the only way the carousel can go round. You too can buy a house in Beverly Hills . . . so long as you have just sold one. Or, maybe, so long as you are an Iranian or rich Mexican —but the world is running out of this commodity.

It is generally agreed that it was in the fall of 1981 that the spiral in residential real estate prices peaked out. The Federal Home Loan Bank believes that the 13 percent mortgage level is a threshold which stops a lot of new buyers. That level was passed back in 1980, and in 1981, even subsidized mortgage rates rose above 16 percent. That was the year in which the unthinkable happened and average house prices hesitated and actually started to fall. The fall continued through 1982, though it has been a relatively mild affair in terms of the national average.

In the rarefied world of the Manhattan coop and condominium market —inventions of the sixties and seventies which allowed apartments to pass into individual ownership—the slump in prices in the first half of 1982 was a rude shock. According to a well-known measure, the Douglas Elliman index, the average coop price dropped from $521,000 at the October 1981 peak to $390,000 in the second quarter of 1982. Total strangers to the market might think there is one nought too many in the figures. But there is not. The market is described as rarefied because the average buyer puts his net worth at $2.7 million, according to a recent survey.

If this was not a good old-fashioned bubble, it certainly got pretty wild at times. A "flipper" is a speculator who binds a contract with a down payment with the intention of reselling before closing date. A New York specialist tells this story of a flipper who got hurt late in 1981. The property, at a good East Side address, was contracted for at $1.2 million. The seller wanted cash and the buyer plunked down a $120,000 deposit. After four months of advertising, initially at $2 million, "the speculator was unable to flip, even for the original price. The contract expired, and the owner— $120,000 richer—put the property on the market again at $1.2 million. This time it sold for $875,000." The story was related in Barron's of November 2, 1981.

The Manhattan market picked up in the second half of 1982, but condo and coop prices ended the year down 10.5 percent across the board, 23 percent down at the fashionable end such as top Park Avenue addresses. No fun for a forced seller who had financed purchases at 17 percent. Recovery has been much slower in luxury condos in Florida, which was being described by real estate men as a "disaster area" in mid-1983. In Miami, at the end of 1982, there were 12,500 vacant units, compared with total sales in the $100,000-plus bracket of 3,000 during the year. Latin Americans are just not buying anymore. In San Diego, which was as badly hit as anywhere by the 1982 slump in house prices, the only visible recovery in demand early in 1983 was for entry-level housing priced at $70,000 and up, and financed by subsidized Federal Housing Administration (FHA)

mortgages with little or even no down payment. The average single de-
tached home in San Diego County sold for $107,000 in 1982.

END OF AN ERA

Early in 1983 house prices were recovering in many areas, and indeed
in terms of reported nationwide averages. So was house building. It is a
matter for speculation how far and for how long this recovery might proceed. But what is clear is that things have changed and the change is
seminal, not temporary.

In the 1980s a new word became fashionable and is now frequently
heard from the lips of mortgage officers, who are understandably preoccupied. It is less frequently uttered by real estate agents. The word is
"affordability." Don't blame me for it. I think it is as horrid as real estate
agents do.

What worries mortgage officers is the ability of first-time house buyers
to afford mortgage repayments when interest rates are sky-high and so are
house prices. In fact it isn't only first-time buyers that mortgage bankers
are worried about, but mortgagees in general. Early in 1983 the national
delinquency rate on mortgages—where payments were thirty days or more
overdue—was near 6 percent. In troubled San Diego County, foreclosures
on mortgages were up 120 percent in 1982, to 3,304. That is a lot of families
on the streets in just one year, in one county.

The problem has been building up for some years. In fact maybe it was
inherent all along in the particular circumstances of housing in the post-
war era. But it only seemed to show up around the mid-1970s. In the old
days, the rule of thumb was that housing costs should not exceed a fifth,
or at maximum a quarter, of the family income. In the days up to the
mid-1970s it probably did not, on average. But as house prices escalated in
the mid-1970s and as mortgage rates soared toward the end of that decade,
home ownership costs for mortgagees shattered that rule of thumb. The
table shows that typical mortgage costs broke through 35 percent of disposable income in 1977, through 50 percent in 1980 and through 60 percent
in 1981. The table ignores tax relief on interest payments, which varies
from household to household, but it also ignores real estate taxes and the
cost of utilities and maintenance. In any case it graphically illustrates the
change that took place at the end of the seventies.

National figures show that mortgage payments amount to about 30
percent of all householders' net income, inclusive of the 20 percent or so
that have no mortgages. The Federal Home Loan Bank of San Francisco
calculated in 1982 that housing accounted for 37 percent of consumer
spending on the basis of the new Consumer Price Index. Again, this is a
national average. Recent buyers on mortgage are worse off.

At first sight it would appear that the situation has improved dramatically since mid-1982. The FHA-subsidized mortgage rate has come down

Affordability of New Homes

Costs of Home Ownership (Conventional Mortgage) Compared to Median After-Tax Household Income

Year	Median New Home Price (Conv. Mtg.)	Median Household Income After Tax,* $	Ratio of Home Price to Median Income	Mortgage Rate, %	Mortgage Payment (25% down, 30 years), $	Mortgage Payment as a percentage of Median Income*
1964	$21,300	N/A	N/A	5¾	93.23	N/A
1965	22,700	N/A	N/A	5¾	99.36	N/A
1966	24,400	N/A	N/A	6¼	112.69	N/A
1967	26,600	6,207	4.29	6½	126.10	24.4
1968	28,500	6,646	4.28	6¾	138.64	25.0
1969	30,400	7,091	4.29	7¾	163.36	27.6
1970	30,800	7,477	4.12	8¼	173.55	27.9
1971	31,900	7,805	4.09	7¾	171.42	26.4
1972	31,600	8,245	3.83	7½	165.73	24.1
1973	35,200	9,006	3.91	8	193.72	25.8
1974	38,000	9,461	4.02	9	229.32	29.1
1975	43,900	10,236	4.29	9	265.95	31.2
1976	48,000	10,891	4.41	9	289.67	31.9
1977	53,400	11,574	4.61	9	339.22	35.2
1978	61,300	12,800	4.79	9½	385.97	36.2
1979	70,300	13,980	5.03	11¼	513.66	44.1
1980	76,900	14,930	5.15	14	685.15	55.1
1981	80,100	15,995	5.01	16¾	843.24	63.3

*Median after-tax income is calculated by multiplying median household income by the ratio of total disposable income to total personal income.

SOURCE: Federal Home Loan Bank Board; U.S. Bureau of the Census; Federal Home Loan Bank Board, Office of Economic Research; Board of Governors of the Federal Reserve System, *Federal Reserve Bulletin.*

FIGURE 26

through the 13 percent barrier, though conventional rates were still above 13 percent in mid-1983. They could come down further. Certainly people fixing up mortgages now are better off than those doing so in 1982. And those with variable rate mortgages are feeling the benefit of lower rates. But don't fool yourself.

Mortgage rates are a function of the whole complex structure of general interest rate and price expectations. Mortgage rates have fallen but price inflation has fallen faster. In fact house prices have fallen, period. Suppose inflation stays below 4 percent for a while, will a mortgage rate of 13 percent look low? Will it look lower than a rate of 16 percent looked when general prices had been rising at 12 percent and house prices even faster?

If you want to know what the general expectation is about future inflation you can take a line through long-term government bond yields. If they yield 10 percent then the general expectation is that inflation will be around 3 points less, that is, 7 percent. You can also be almost certain that that will prove to be wrong. It invariably has done. The general expectation is made up of past experience, with a slight adjustment for current monetary policy.

In the early 1950s, past experience included memories of the peacetime deflation of the 1920s and early 1930s and of the wartime inflation of 1939–1945 and 1951. That is why government bonds yielded only 2.5 percent. At around 4 percent in the first half of the 1960s, government bond yields were about right for the inflation rate of the previous decade, but of course very wrong for the one to come. So was the 6 percent yield of 1971–1972. So was the 8 percent average of the later 1970s. Throughout the entire period to 1980, price expectations and bond yields lagged behind the actual outcome of price inflation because it was increasing. And the lag was several years. Precisely the same thing has happened the other way round during this decade. The turning point was 1980. I believe it was a major watershed. But in any case, if inflation continues to diminish or even stays around where it is, price expectations, bond yields and—at last—mortgage rates will lag behind, for several years. They will stay very high in relation to inflation.

This is a key conclusion for homeowners and potential buyers. "Real" mortgage rates, that is, rates adjusted for inflation, are likely to stay very high for several years. It is a key conclusion because that has not been the case since the 1930s. And because the fundamental reason for the post-war house-price boom will have been turned on its head.

Not one person in a thousand believes this conclusion now. But consider. If quite a number did think like this, would house prices be where they are now? It is the very nature of the peak of a boom that the vast majority of the people concerned believe it is going to continue—as we have seen with bubble after bubble throughout recorded history.

The drop in mortgage rates to date has unquestionably helped the homes market. But there is a condition for further meaningful drops in long-term interest rates. You need lower expectations for inflation. But practically everyone links house prices with inflation rates over the long term. So lower inflation rates will imply lower growth in house prices for most people, which will make that mortgage rate still look expensive (as it really will be).

What will happen to house prices if they cease to look like a good investment? If houses were just homes to live in, there is no reason why anything should happen. But people see their own houses as an investment, including millions of houses which are not the homes of the owners and millions more which are secondary homes. (There are about 57 million owner-occupied homes in the United States. That is also roughly the number of two-generation families. But there are 87 million homes. Americans are very amply housed.) The answer is that if there seemed to be better investments around—like mortgages—there would be many more houses for sale and prices would collapse.

What is alarming is that the great American public has just made a massive vote of confidence that the old era is alive and well. During 1982 the trend toward adjustable rate mortgages—where the borrower benefits from falling interest rates but pays the cost when they rise—seemed to be gathering momentum. By September, over half of all new mortgages were adjustable. Since then, however, the trend has reversed. And by mid-1983 the old fixed-rate mortgage, for thirty years mostly, was back taking three-quarters of all new mortgage money. This made the savings and loan institutions very happy (though they all pretend they no longer do this business) since they have been making a turn of 3 to 4 points on the difference between these thirty-year fixed mortgages and their short-term borrowing. But there are two chances out of three that it will be a tragic and penal error for the borrowers—if interest rates fall, or if they stay roughly where they are. It would be only if interest rates rise significantly and stay up that the new fixed-rate borrowers would stand to benefit.

Of course there is a way out if the bet goes wrong. Repay the mortgage. Unfortunately, as the thrifts know very well, few people will be both willing and able to do this. For most it would mean selling their home. As interest rates come down, the temptation will be to argue that they will soon head back up again and people will just pay the price. In the end, if people redeem their mortgages, it will most likely be in distress and by constraint. Those who are both willing and able to redeem should be good and sure they stay that way.

AN INVISIBLE CRASH?

In January 1979, I told listeners to my daily radio broadcast that a recession would begin during the fourth quarter of 1979, but unlike previous recessions, this one would ultimately lead to a 1930s type of depression involving a decline in property values which would ultimately lead to a crash in residential property prices. Based on the global structure of the property market, I also felt the crash in residential property values would be taking place all over the world at the same time. My forecasts were treated with skepticism. My views on residential property were considered absurd.

In March 1980 I restated my view on property over another radio station. Again, I claimed that a collapse in residential property prices was imminent. After the broadcast, the switchboard at the station lit up like a Christmas tree. Irate callers insisted that a severe fall in house prices could not possibly occur. They accused me of making irresponsible forecasts without bearing. As a result of that fateful broadcast, nearly two years elapsed before I was invited to speak on that particular radio station again.

More vested interests dominate the residential property market than any other market. The information you are likely to receive and the views which are widely expressed will almost invariably favor those vested interests, not necessarily your interests. The residential real estate profession has a deeply vested interest in persuading us that house prices can only go up and up. Or if they dip, it will be no time before they start heading upward again. In fact, the real estate fraternity is far more committed to a rise in house prices . . . in perpetuity . . . than the financial brokerage community is committed to rising asset values. Stockbrokers can at least engender some sizable commissions through "short sales," where the customer sells first in the hope of buying back later at a lower price. As homeowners, most are ready to believe the progaganda that says house prices will rise forever. That is human nature.

The biggest vested interest of all is of course the government. With its various forms of subsidies to the housing industry, along with encouraging longer-term mortgages, it has been greatly responsible for the boom in house prices to start with. The government has clearly done everything in its power to get you to buy a house. With more than 60 percent of the people in the United States now owning their own homes, that's a very, very powerful political lobby. Any government ruling over a period when property prices collapse would certainly stand little chance at any subsequent election. House prices have become a more emotive political force than the level of unemployment . . . far more.

Aside from the cliché about not making land anymore, a favorite argument of the profession is that there will always be a growing demand from young people who are anxious to have their own homes. In recent years, this argument has had particular force as the famous post-war baby boom kids approached house-buying age. But as time went on the charts depicting this potential householder bulge have tended in a curious way to move the bulge farther and farther out, so that it still remains in the near future.

The facts suggest that demand for homes from the baby boom bulge has in reality passed its peak. The post-war birth rate peaked in 1957. When

THE BABY BOOM AND THE DEMAND
FOR HOUSING

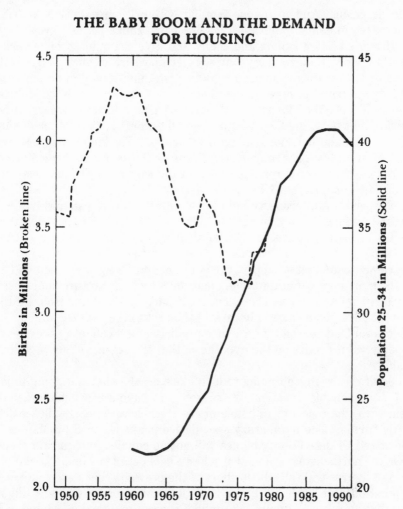

Source: Professor Dwight M. Jaffee, Princeton University

FIGURE 27

do people buy homes? The answer is when they are young. A study of the 1970 census revealed that 33 percent of homeowners owned their homes before the age of twenty-five; 22 percent between the age of twenty-five and twenty-nine; and 16 percent between twenty-nine and thirty-four. So the tradition that bunches the first-time home buyers between the ages of twenty-five and thirty-four, as the chart does, is inaccurate. In fact, the median or typical home-buying age is around the year twenty-four, say twenty-two to twenty-six. Add those numbers to the year 1957 and you get 1979–1983 as the peak of housing demand for the grown-up babies. Demand would only tail off very gradually. But the point is that it is unlikely to be increasing. And as anyone familiar with price mechanisms knows, it is increases in demand, not high levels, which cause prices to rise.

If you sit down calmly and coolly and give the subject some serious thought it won't take you very long to come up with the conclusion that this notion of houses (or diamonds, or gold or anything) rising in price forever and a day is nothing more than a delusion. It is a very attractive delusion because it suits the majority of Americans who are homeowners. It is a delusion that feeds on itself because we all encourage each other to share it. It is a "popular delusion," a "crowd delusion." The kind Charles Mackay wrote of in his book *Extraordinary Popular Delusions and the Madness of Crowds*, the favorite reading of one of the world's most famous exploiters of delusions, Bernard Baruch.

The residential property bubble has burst, and we can and will have a crash in values; it may be unthinkable, but it is a distinct possibility and a highly probable one at that. The political implications that I have outlined may appear as a flaw in the thesis. I can hear the voice now saying, "The government won't let it happen. It can't afford to. The government will bail out the mortgage defaulters. The government will make sure house prices keep on going up forever. There'll be a massacre in the White House if they don't." I have given extremely careful thought to the political implications and it is for that reason that my firm prediction of a collapse in residential property values relies on the hypothesis that the crash will not look like a crash.

So, if the crash isn't going to look like a crash, what is it going to look like? A reasonable question. We're going to have an invisible crash. To begin with, the recovery in house prices that began in early 1983 will go a little further. The more crazy speculative peaks reached by Manhattan condos and Orange County homes will not be equaled, but certain properties in the northeastern states will achieve new peaks in value. The national average figures will fall a little short of the previous peaks after adjusting for inflation. But lower mortgage rates will have encouraged new buyers. The inflation rate will fluctuate around 3 percent and the underlying trend in prices will appear upward in nominal terms. For a time, house prices will continue to fluctuate. All along the trend will continually be below the rate of inflation even though it will look like values are moving higher. Temporarily. Soon we'll see the end of the idea that a house is a good hedge against inflation. As the months go by, more and more people will perceive that borrowing costs are very high in relation to inflation and particularly to the sluggish performance in house prices. The investment market in coops and condos will edge steadily downward. A raging bull market in corporate banks and U.S. government securities will be drawing funds away from alternative investments. People will begin to question the viability of perceived inflation hedges. In the residential real estate market mortgage foreclosures will be on the increase although this will be given very little publicity. In the background, the level of unemployment will be reaching crisis level.

At the next cyclical downturn in the economy, due in late 1983 or early 1984, house prices will fall rather more than they did in 1982. There will be a number of people who will be suggesting the unthinkable, that investment in housing is a thing of the past, but most people will consider the drop in house prices means that bargains are once again available.

By late 1984, homes in the $1 million category will have fallen by as much as 25 percent. This trend will have gone unnoticed by most homeowners since it will not be reflected in the house price indices which concentrate on median prices. Cheaper homes could still be rising in price in late 1984 while the more expensive homes are falling sharply. It is unlikely that the average individual will have any idea of how the price of his own home is performing. At the early stages of a decline in property values, most people will blithely assume the decline in value among certain categories of housing in certain areas will not affect their particular home and therefore they will not be unduly alarmed.

As prices fall, many who had intended to sell unoccupied properties they were holding for investment purposes will withdraw from the market, preferring to rent them out in anticipation of a more buoyant market later on. There will be a bulge in the market for rented accommodation. The sudden appearance of many "For Rent" signs will exert downward pressure on an already vulnerable owner-occupier market. As the market for rented accommodation grows there will be competition and downward pressure on rents. That will mean the gap on the interest payable on a mortgage and the return which can be received in rent on the capital value of the property, will widen. It will become far cheaper to rent property than to spend money on a mortgage. This will further deter house purchases and depress the values of residential property, adding to the self-feeding downward spiral.

Throughout the long-term downward slide in residential property values, there will be many countermoves to the prevailing downtrend. Prices may fall for two or three months and then rise for a month or two. Prices may then fall for five or six months and then rise for three to four months. Prices are certainly not going to move down in a straight line . . . until we approach the end of the property crash. After a speculative bubble bursts there will be many traps and perceptible upswings in the property market that will catch the unwary.

Initially people will see the decline in property values as a fleeting opportunity to buy at a slightly lower price. Real estate agents will pounce on prospective buyers, selling "last chance" concepts . . . "get in quick before house prices start soaring again." Investors in commodity markets and stock markets often quote the adage, "A bull market climbs a wall of worry and a bear market flows down a river of hope." That means after a market has had a long fall and then begins to rise, even though the rise may last for a long time, many investors mistrust the rise, remembering all of the deceptive upswings that occurred while the market was falling.

After a time, the "wall of worry" abates, and investors begin to think prices will continue to go up forever. When the idea that rising prices will last indefinitely finally achieves universal recognition, that's when prices start to fall again and the psychology is reversed. Hope springs eternal at the early stages of a market decline. Each minor blip upward is considered to offer the promise of the next massive sustainable rise. Investors then reflect upon the deceptive downswings that occurred during the long-term upswing that preceded the fall. During the demise of the property market which I see in the years ahead, each dip in prices will be classified as a "healthy breathing spell" by most. Each rise in prices will be hailed as the beginning of the next property boom . . . as the residential property market flows inexorably down its "river of hope."

Because of the enormous level of participation in the house-buying boom of the past few decades, millions of Americans will be affected as they gradually become aware of the fact that property prices are steadily falling. Eventually they will think that house prices may not start rising again for quite some time. With the passage of time, an increasing number will begin to doubt the delusion that property prices "always go up" and will then become deeply troubled.

As confidence dwindles, lenders will be more restrictive in their lending policies. House builders will try to hold their stocks of unsold houses but many will be forced to sell at distressed prices to meet overdue bank loans. Professional property speculators will be unloading their holdings at an ever increasing rate. Restrictive policies of lending institutions and a deterioration in public sentiment will serve to curtail demand. The combination of the two factors will ensure that the fall in prices mounts in its severity. As the downward trend in home values becomes more pronounced it will become increasingly more difficult to reverse. Minor recoveries will become more brief and gains more modest. The decline in values will become sharper and last longer.

By 1986, it is likely that the sense of urgency to buy a home will have virtually vanished from the American scene. As the secondary depression bites deeper, other necessities of life will take priority over owning a home. Rented accommodation will be more plentiful by then. Investors who are in property will have no choice but to rent since buyers will be a rare breed. There will be a steady increase in the number of houses on the market in all sizes and shapes, but sales will be very, very poor.

By late 1986, losses on property will be making the headlines. It will be the heavy end of the market that's making all of the news. The owners of coops and condos will be reporting disastrous experiences. Building and construction companies will be going bankrupt at a frightening rate. Mortgage funds will have become virtually nonexistent, so severe will be the struggle for survival among mortgage lenders who are heavily burdened by defaulters. The savings and loan industry will have more casualties with runs on deposits of the weaker members. A rescue operation by the Fed will be almost a daily occurrence.

By 1987, there will be no real residential housing market to speak of in the United States for the owner/occupier. Some houses will be totally unsalable at any price. This has been the case during depressions in the housing industry throughout history. In America, from 1931 to 1934, many people were abandoning their homes, unable to keep up mortgage payments, crowding together in small ghettos and slums. Although 75 percent of the working population in America was employed at the time, the 25 percent that was unemployed, many of whom had defaulted on their mortgage payments, were sufficient to collapse the residential housing market. Those with jobs who may have sold their homes, or never had a home to start with, were certainly not prepared to risk their savings by purchasing a home that could fluctuate so violently in value. Those who had owned their homes were certainly not prepared to change homes if in so doing it meant an increase in the commitment to property. During the 1930s, the residential property market in America consisted only of sellers, no buyers. The 1980s are likely to offer similar prospects in the residential housing market.

The story of the U.S. house-price bubble could be written almost word for word for any free Western country. Everywhere the inflationary experience has been similar. Everywhere mortgage interest is deductible. Everywhere the same conclusions have been drawn to the effect that a home represents the ultimate infallible investment. Everywhere, since around 1980, the housing market has been turning sour. In some countries, such as Holland and maybe France, it is not clear whether there will be any recovery at all before the next downward spiral in house prices. In an increasingly international world, these issues cannot be isolated. The Dutch and especially the French have been buyers of real estate on the East and West Coasts of the United States. It is estimated that 22 percent of all investments in Manhattan coops come from abroad. When the apparently invulnerable image of homes as an investment is tarnished the global repercussions will be incalculable.

The housing market is a slow-moving market. The declines which I envisage will not be perceptible for the next two to three years as far as the majority of the population is concerned. By the late 1980s, it is my estimate that the average house price will have fallen by 30 to 40 percent. At the terminal stage of the decline in house prices, there will be an almighty flushout, with values falling as much as, or more than, the ground lost in the first ten years. I believe it is conceivable that house prices could plummet by up to 80 percent over the next ten to fifteen years. I expect half of that decline to take place over the next five to ten years. The rest will come in three to five years . . . the final panic sellout may only take twelve to eighteen months.

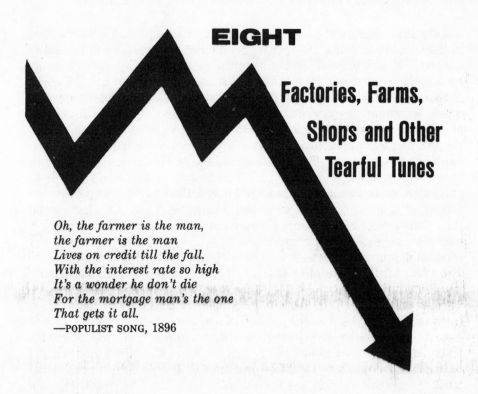

EIGHT

Factories, Farms, Shops and Other Tearful Tunes

Oh, the farmer is the man,
the farmer is the man
Lives on credit till the fall.
With the interest rate so high
It's a wonder he don't die
For the mortgage man's the one
That gets it all.
—POPULIST SONG, 1896

The great American dream is home ownership. An Englishman's home is his castle. These are the popular clichés. Karl Marx said religion was "the opium of the people." Today it is house prices. What price can be put on a dream? There is no limit. Those in the business of selling houses or encouraging people to take out a mortgage can always find justification for predicting that prices will rise forever. People in the home business very badly want to convince themselves that prices will always rise. They do just that. They convince themselves very badly.

While an excursion into the wide-screen, Vista Vision, Technicolor fantasy of owning a home will mean many people will be prepared to pay dream-world prices for a 3BR, 2Bth, in Orange County, rather more stringent criteria affect the value of commercial real estate. Ultimately, the price of a factory, office, shop, or farm even, is related to the profitability of the business occupying the property. This holds true for the greengrocer, winegrower, microchip manufacturer or porn merchant. The fantasy boom in house prices may be a phenomenon of the twentieth century. By contrast, booms and busts in commercial real estate, building sites and farms have been with us for centuries.

What causes a real estate bubble? What causes a crash? "Prices got too high," sing the chorus after the siren's song has been sung. The answer is correct, but it tells you nothing. In the final analysis the cause of a boom

156

and crash in real estate is no different from what it was for "Tulipmania" in Holland during the seventeenth century. Expectations of profit rise to the level of dreams and fantasies which cannot possibly be translated into reality. Prices then crash. In every case, without exception, the expectations which were admitted to be absurd after the crash were seen as completely reasonable before the crash.

The trick, of course, is to determine the level in the price cycle that represents absurdity. This can be extremely difficult when it comes to the determination of residential property values. You become involved with trying to quantify a dream. In the case of commercial property, although values there, too, have reached the level of absurdity in the past, essentially values are more readily quantifiable.

THE GROWTH ASSUMPTION

For nearly two decades after World War II, conditions in the U.S. real estate market could be described as stable. Memories of the 1920s and 1930s were still vivid. In fact, those two decades took in the bulk of the peacetime experience of most people's recollections. During the interwar period, real estate proved to be a risky investment. In the 1920s rents tended to move down, which didn't matter too much to the landlord who owned the property outright, but was hard on those who had financed on mortgage. In the 1930s, the problem was more that tenants could not afford the rent and were moving out, leaving city blocks half empty. Naturally landlords looked for a high return on their investments—much higher than on government bonds, for sure, which yielded only 2 percent or so at the start of the period. Eight percent was a fair rule of thumb for a top-grade property; maybe 12 percent for something in the second drawer. Since mortgage finance was to be had from life insurance companies and mortgage bankers at maybe 5 percent, a handy positive cash surplus was available to the investor.

By the mid-1960s, the real estate men had done pretty well, especially those who had used mortgage finance to the hilt, which meant 100 percent. For on top of the positive cash surplus they had enjoyed for some years, they also had useful capital gains to fall back on should they need to sell a building. Some, it is true, were beginning to get quite a taste for this business. The risks looked rather small in the prosperous 1960s, and when you could get 100 percent financing from Prudential, it was starting to look like a sure thing. Still, memories of the interwar period lingered. And besides, the big fortunes were being made on Wall Street, in the growth industries epitomized by IBM, Xerox, Polaroid, Syntex and in stock options.

So in the mid-1960s the real estate market was still stable, but the seeds of a speculative boom had been sown. As the decade progressed, it seemed more likely that rents could only rise. That meant real estate was a sure thing. So naturally more people were keen to get into the game. That meant that property prices moved up. In fact they tended to move up faster than rents. You could afford to accept a lower initial rental yield, because capital gains began to look practically assured. It was only a matter of time before capital growth would come to be taken for granted. If you could assume a 5 percent growth rate, you could settle for a lower return on a real estate investment. Some would say up to 5 percent lower. Suddenly, the impact on capital values becomes dramatic.

Imagine a city real estate development with an all-in cost of $1 million, which can be let for $100,000—a return of 10 percent on cost. If an investor were to assume a 5 percent growth rate in capital value, he might be willing to accept an initial rental return of 5 percent rather than 10 percent. So he might be prepared to pay $2 million for the building. Suddenly it is worth twice the cost price. And what if the growth assumption swells to 10 percent? Then you enter an unreal world in which investors might be prepared to buy properties on a rental yield of 4 percent, 3 percent or even 2.5 percent. It all depends on the degree to which people convince themselves about future growth. Now we are talking about a possible further doubling in price of the property. And if the growth assumption goes back again from 10 percent to 5 percent, real estate values can halve. All this on the basis of mere assumptions about future growth. The same thing can happen with stocks. This is how booms and busts are born.

Leave aside hypothetical assumptions, and look at current facts and figures. In recent years, we have seen growth projections based on an inflation rate of over 10 percent. At the turn of the decade, this is what the assumption was: we know this from the fact that government bond yields were up to 14 percent. Since then we have had "disinflation." The long-term inflation assumption has dropped to around 7 percent. Already this has caused a crisis in the commercial real estate market. But the current inflation rate is much lower than that: even projections for 1983 and 1984 are lower, not above 5 percent. Maybe inflation assumptions will have to come down further. If they come down to 5 percent, the effect on commercial real estate would be even more dramatic than the downward revision so far. Already it is possible to see how the real estate fantasy which has been built up over thirty-five post-war years would be completely shattered.

THE FARMERS' DILEMMA

Dr. Raymond Wheeler of the University of Kansas invested twenty years and a staff of over 200 to compile detailed charts covering 3,000 years of world weather, correlated with the exact dates of significant events in recorded history. With nearly 2 million data entries, supplemented by maps and charts, Wheeler concluded that man behaves differently, but predictably, according to climatic shifts. The earth's climate shifts from Warm-Wet phases to Warm-Dry phases, then from Cold-Wet to Cold-Dry phases, and back again in a continual circle. Significant economic events in history coincided with different climate phases. The worst depressions appear during the Cold-Dry weather. The Drought Clock indicates the world is entering a Cold-Dry phase. According to Wheeler, the drop in temperature will be accompanied by long, severe droughts, with a serious effect on world food production. Wheeler says that one-third of the last twenty-five years of this century will involve severely cold, dry periods.

The growing season began to shorten in late 1974 in the United States. An early September frost destroyed millions of dollars' worth of maturing corn in the Midwest. Once the cold phase has stabilized in the coming years, frost in June and August can be expected in the world's corn belt. Early and late frosts will become a serious menace in southern areas. Winters could become severe enough to cause serious problems for cattle and sheep raisers in the Northern Hemisphere. Blizzards will be much more common than for fifty years or more. Severe lengthy droughts and famines will strike worldwide.

According to Wheeler, the world should now be preparing for long shortages in water supplies and for shorter, not longer, growing seasons. Colder weather and longer droughts will bring a scarcity of food for the prosperous nations, famine and starvation for the less economically stable.

Along with the fall in temperature, there will be a serious decline in rainfall. This has happened consistently during the hundred-year cycle on the Drought Clock, twenty-six times since the days of Ancient Greece. Each of those long-term drops in temperature and rainfall can be seen in the sequoia tree-ring curves, the longest of which goes back to 350 B.C. In the fifth century, near the fall of the Roman Empire, world rainfall was so low that sequoias grew very slowly for decades. The Caspian Sea in Asia sank forty-five feet below its present level.

Wheeler contends that droughts and frost will influence the world economy, which he claims is linked to the weather cycle. The current climatic period is inevitably characterized by a succession of sudden and troublesome depressions. Prosperity as we have known it is due to decline for an extended period. "Times may have changed from the earlier terminations of 500-year cycles," says Wheeler, "but the laws of nature have not." According to the weather cycle, the next era of prosperity is not expected to develop until around 1995.

Wheeler's findings seem to conform to the long wave pattern of economic life, even though his findings are the result of considerable noneconomic data. There is little evidence in Wheeler's writing that he was aware of, or concerned with, the economic findings of Schumpeter, Kondratieff, Juglar and Kitchin.

The exact conditions Wheeler describes for the 1980s were experienced by American farmers in the 1930s in America's Midwestern states. The great Dust Bowl of Oklahoma gave farmers a double depression in the area. John Steinbeck described it in *The Grapes of Wrath* in 1939:

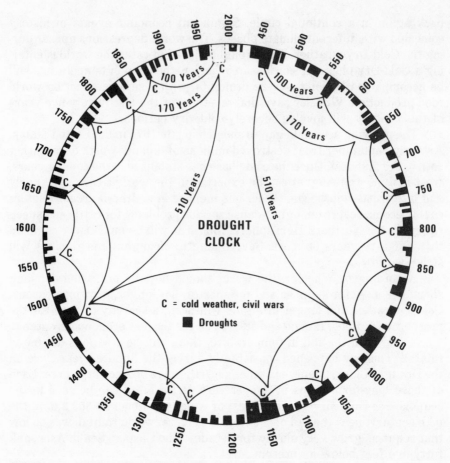

FIGURE 28   DR. RAYMOND WHEELER'S DROUGHT CLOCK

They were not farm men any more, but migrant men. And the thought, the
planning, the long staring silence that had gone out to the fields, went now to
the roads, to the distance, to the West. That man whose mind had been bound
with acres lived with narrow concrete miles. And his thought and his worry
were not any more with rainfall, with wind and dust, with the thirst of the
crops.

Whether economic depressions bring steep contractions in farm production, or disastrous falls in farm output from adverse weather conditions
lie at the root of cyclical depression is debatable. Obviously each affects the
other. Like all commodities, agricultural land prices have been subject to
widely swinging price trends, in sequence with our long-term patterns of
economic life.

When the Pope visits a new land, he kisses the earth. Man comes from
dust and must return to dust. Or clay. A prose as well as poetic tradition,

also dating back to biblical times, has man made from clay. Modern science even has room for a respectable theory that the humble clay of the earth's surface is the very origin of man; that in clay's crystalline structure are to be found the perfect conditions for the replication of the building matter of life. (See Lyall Watson's *Lifetide,* page 49 *et seq.*)

People need little encouragement to find in Mother Earth, in farmland, the most basic and most reassuring investment of all. In certain conditions, the conditions of the upwave, this has translated itself into a conviction that land, above all investments, can never lose its value and can only go up in price. But the hard facts of history show that land prices are just like any other prices. They rise and fall in great waves.

A lucky accident has given us some average farmland prices in Pennsylvania in the early nineteenth century. From $53 per acre in 1809, land prices had risen to $111 by 1813. They continued rising in the inflation following the War of 1812 in the United States and the Napoleonic Wars in Europe. From a separate record it seems land prices in Lancaster County, Pennsylvania, trebled between 1809 and 1818. Following the crisis of 1819 land prices plunged to well below the modest 1809 valuations—$38 per acre on average for Pennsylvania in 1820.

The crisis of 1819 put paid to speculation during the next fifteen years. But by the middle of the 1930s, the time of the Chicago urban land boom, it began building up. It reached such a peak in 1836 that the government issued a "specie circular" in July which restricted payment for farmland to hard metal cash. Farmland prices crashed once again in line with falls in commodity prices of 43 percent in New York City and 66 percent in Ohio between 1836 and 1843. The economic expansion that followed the depression of 1837–1843 was one of the greatest in American history. It was spurred by the discovery of gold in California in 1849 and the great railway boom of the 1850s. But it was the growth of American agricultural output and exports that paid for the imports which fueled the boom. Even in the 1870s, manufactures only accounted for 18 percent of American exports.

Farmland prices boomed across the nation. Yet, when the Great Depression of 1873–1895 had run its course, farmland prices were back where they had been at the start of the century in most states. The story was the same in Europe, in the countries with a history of stable currencies. In England, for example. In his book *Farm Business Management and Land Ownership* (1979), Peter Ashton constructs a table of agricultural land prices going back to 1770. It depicts the same rhythmic periodicity as the long wave pattern. In 1770, we begin with the low point in the price cycle at £22 per acre. After a high in 1810, land prices reverted to the same level forty-five years later in 1825. After two more peaks and a second trough later, in the depression year of 1933, farmland prices were almost back to the same level at £23 per acre. Then began the debasement of the pound that started in World War II and lasted into this decade.

Ashton found another periodicity in what he defines as the "land price: money value ratio," in which farmland prices are related to the general level of consumer prices. He notes a cycle which is apparently a hundred years long, with about fifty years from peak to trough and trough to peak. As it happens, the peaks coincide with the onset of the Cold-Dry period in Wheeler's Drought Clock. You can make what you like of that. A clear peak in this "inflation adjusted" measure of land prices came in 1972, at the start of the latest period of secondary prosperity.

The English historical experience confirms the American. We left U.S. farmland prices at their trough at the end of the nineteenth century. The first quarter of this century witnessed a remarkable buildup of mortgage debt on farms. Part of the buildup may be attributed to America's efforts to supply the Allies with grain, particularly after it entered World War I in 1917. One way or another, total farm mortgage debt across the nation in 1920 was three times its level of 1910. A terrible price was going to be exacted for this explosion of borrowing, in the 1930s.

The paradox of a depression is that if there is one class across the nation that should survive severe economic straits with comparatively little hardship it should be the farming community. Yet the evidence suggests it was precisely the farmers who were worst hit during the 1930s. The explanation, in a single word, was debt.

Between 1900 and 1914, when Figure 29 takes over the story of farmland and farm product prices, farm real estate had approximately doubled in price. The explosion of product prices in the last years of the war helped farm prices to a further 60 percent gain between 1916 and 1920. To encourage production the government had introduced a guaranteed price of $2.20 for wheat (per bushel), which compared with a prewar price fluctuating around 75 cents. The removal of the guarantee and the collapse of commodity prices generally in the panic of 1921 removed that special reason for high farmland prices. But though product prices held up well through the 1920s in relation to the general price level, this secondary prosperity was a profitless one for farmers in terms of land prices, particularly when compared with stock prices on Wall Street. By 1932, the bulk of the collapse for stocks was over, but the final slump in farmland was yet to come. In any case it was a buyers-only market. Where farms were changing hands it was mainly in foreclosures.

The economics of farming appear to be such that you cannot, in the long run, farm on borrowed money. Yet farmers are encouraged to borrow like no other class of the citizenry. Small wonder that the errors of the first quarter of this century were repeated again in the third—in spades. Farming in the past decade is a horror story of a bubble in land prices, soaring debt and ebbing profitability.

Between 1967 and 1981 U.S. farmland values more than quadrupled. But three-quarters of the rise came in the second half of this period, since 1973. That year there was a serious crop shortfall: the price of grain almost

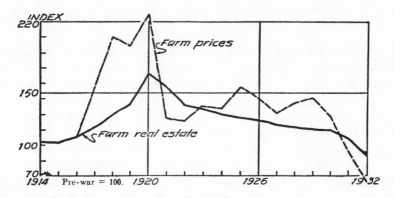

FIGURE 29   INDEX NUMBERS OF PRICES OF FARM PRODUCTS AND PRICES OF
FARM LAND IN THE UNITED STATES 1914–1932

From *The Prices Series* by G. F. Warren and F. A. Pearson.
Reprinted by permission of Chapman and Hall, Ltd.

doubled in two seasons and U.S. farmers made record profits of some $33
billion. The record has not subsequently been passed, not even in the boom
year of 1979, despite all the inflation since then. But farm borrowing has
more than tripled from $67 billion to $215 billion at the start of 1983, which
is way ahead of total gross farm income of $170 billion.

Without that frightening borrowing, land values would not of course
have soared as they have. But still, how could it happen, when farming
profitability has been declining all along? In 1976 and 1977, farm profits
barely topped $20 billion. Last year they slipped to an estimated $18 billion,
which is under $8,000 per farming family. They are expected to decline
again this year. With mortgage interest topping $22 billion, where is the
equity in U.S. farms?

Obviously other forces were at work, however delusive. In 1974, when
farmland prices rose almost a third, it was the aftermath of the first oil
crisis and U.S. farm exports that would provide America's answer to the
Arab oil tithe. The agriculture secretary at the time, Earl Butz, blazed
through the farm belt like a circuit-riding preacher urging farmers to plant
fencepost to fencepost with government credit and blessing. In the decade
after 1972, land under cultivation increased more than two-fifths, from 289
to 413 million acres. Russia provided an outlet until Carter's fateful grain
embargo in 1979, the year of a bumper U.S. crop. Economies of scale were
a further incentive to farmers to buy up neighboring lands.

But above all, farmland was real estate, and real estate rises in value,
as everyone knows. The "growth assumption" was as hard at work on the
farm as it was in homes and offices throughout the 1970s. Land, man's
beloved clay, was the ultimate "tangible," the archetype among "collectibles" in that strange era of the inflation hedge in the 1970s.

That story is all over, well and truly done with. The pain began in 1980,
when net farm incomes slumped $10 billion from $32 billion, and interest

payments leapt from under $12 billion to over $16 billion. That double whammy was nothing to what 1982 had in store, the year when U.S. farm exports declined (by 11 percent) for the first time in thirteen years, and wheat prices slipped a tenth and corn prices a fifth. Countries like Canada, Argentina, Australia and the EEC as a whole had not shared Carter's idealism over Afghanistan. Since 1979 they had been expanding wheat acreage by up to 7 percent per annum, and by 1982 the payoff was sizable in U.S. and world terms. Worse, a high dollar seemed to have made the United States actually uncompetitive on equal subsidy terms with her northern and southern neighbors. America was constantly being undercut in its traditional export markets.

In the fall of 1982, U.S. reserves had soared to 13.6 percent of domestic consumption for wheat and 46 percent for corn. Of a global wheat output surplus of 35 million tons in 1982, the United States accounted for 33 million. Washington's PIK (payment in kind) program for land retirement introduced in January 1983 was an imaginative response to the surplus—grain reserves in exchange for land retirement. On one estimate, it would pull 18 percent of wheat acreage out of production. But it will take time to make much impact on reserves and can only encourage America's competitors meanwhile.

In 1982, the pain that had begun in 1980 turned to agony. The price of farmland declined for the first time in most people's memory. A farmer in Nebraska in the spring of 1983 put the fall in the value of his land at $200 per acre to $750 in 1982, from the 1981 valuation of $950. This year he figured he would be lucky to get $650 for his 280 acres. With borrowings of $350,000, his agony is apparent. Another near Des Moines faced foreclosure with a debt of $1.5 million on his 1,400 acres. It was estimated that 5 percent of America's 2.4 million farmers were in imminent danger of bankruptcy; and another 10–15 percent were badly squeezed. It is doubtful whether Uncle Sam will give any more help: government outlays for 1983 are already up three-fifths this year to a record $19 billion. General distress among farmers compounded by a continued collapse in land prices seems inevitable. Overexpansion on credit is to blame, as it was in 1930.

FACTORIES FOR SALE, RENT AND DEMOLITION

Watching your house rise in value may make you feel good but it doesn't help you to pay your grocery bill. The real value of your home primarily rests in the shelter and pleasure you get from it. Institutional investors harbor dreams and illusions about the potential of future property and the rental values that may be assigned to factory premises when this world boom finally materializes. But the true value of a factory primarily rests in the ability of the business that occupies that factory to produce a profit. Factories involve a further problem which the house owner is not confronted with. That problem is marketability. Different businesses do not have the same use for the same factory. There is a limit to the appeal of a steel factory to a manufacturer of stuffed toys.

Further evidence that a depression is upon us is clear from the state of America's industrial centers. Major industrial areas throughout America are littered with "For Sale" and "To Let" signs as thousands of redundant factories continue to close. During 1982 bargain rents were being offered to encourage tenants. In mid-1983 America was making use of about 71 percent of its factory capacity. The rest was idle, and it is a good bet that it is likely to remain idle for quite some time to come. There is simply too much capacity in smokestack America and the reason these factories are never likely to be used again is that other nations can produce the output more efficiently and more cheaply than Americans can. Let's take the steel industry, for example. Over the past twenty years the industry has surrendered the enormous lead it once enjoyed in the scale of efficiency of its plants and is now in danger of falling even further behind. Today, 9 percent of all steel made in the United States is melted in inefficient, open-hearth furnaces, compared with virtually none in Japan and Europe where steel-making is done in basic oxygen and electric furnaces. The tardiness of America's conversion to continuous casting—a process that improves product yield, cuts energy use and boosts labor productivity—is even more pronounced. Only 26 percent of the steel turned out in the United States today is continuously cast versus 86 percent in Japan and 61 percent in Europe.

In the eight and a half years between 1974 and July 1982, 199 steel facilities were shut down in the United States. According to the report *Steel: Upheaval in a Basic Industry* by Donald F. Barnett and Louis M. Schorsch, by the year 2000 steel-making capacity among the integrated producers will fall by no less than 45 percent involving 53 percent fewer jobs. At the same time, it is indicated that there will be 133 percent more steel-making capacity in the minimals and productivity will increase by 55 percent. Translated into the effects on the market for plant, this will mean a massive bulge of space.

The spare capacity in smokestack property has no value. That's right. Zero. Zilch. Nothing. Nada. A proportion of the remaining 71 percent of capacity which is being used also has negligible value, since it cannot be employed at a profit over and above the cost of money. That proportion can only be guessed at. But one way or another, probably 50 percent of American industrial real estate has no value and is essentially worthless. This is extremely serious inasmuch as a great deal is done on the basis of balance sheets that contain overvalued assets. Take the leader of the steel industry, U.S. Steel. The company sees a hideous future in which it will have to close down about one-third of existing capacity. But the company has such massive debts that closing the plants will "wreak havoc with its balance sheet," as an analyst from Standard & Poor's credit rating division recently put it.

Corporate liquidity and indebtedness in the manufacturing industry are at their worst state since the early 1930s. In 1982, for the first time ever, debt interest payments exceeded 50 percent of corporate pretax profits. In the mid-1960s the figure was 15 percent. Debt was primarily of a short-term nature in the 1960s, short-term debt representing 70 percent of long-term debt. In the 1950s and 1960s, there was a tendency to borrow for longer periods and short-term debt dropped to 40 percent of long-term debt. In the meantime, corporate profits took a 14 percent share of national income. By 1982 the figure was 7 percent. This picture is typical of the plight of industry at the incipient stages of a depression. The financing of the manufacturing industry must be restored with a great wave of debt liquidation before the next period of sustainable growth can begin. Attempting to generate an economic recovery under current conditions is like pushing on a string.

The critical state of the manufacturing industry is a global phenomenon. Britain has been especially hard hit. Never in living memory have there been so many empty factories in Britain. At the beginning of 1982, one of Britain's leading industrial estate agents estimated that there were nearly 146 million square feet of vacant factory and warehouse space in England and Wales alone. That figure compares with 54 million square feet in 1979. The fact that vacant warehouse and factory space has almost trebled in three years gives some indication of the speed at which the depression has been eroding values in England and elsewhere. As in the United States, these vacant factory and warehouse premises are virtually worthless. Since 1973, the industrial property market has been the weakest of all the commercial property markets in England and western Europe.

It has been argued that as we approach the twenty-first century, America's future lies in high technology rather than manufacturing industry. This may be true but the move into new technologies will do little to mitigate the immediate difficulties and the financial holocaust likely to be attributable to the collapse in industrial land and property values. Despite an impressive array of post-war inventions—the fuel cell, the Hovercraft, the unraveling of the mysteries of DNA, the microelectronic revolution and the great strides that have been made in the efficient use of energy—the world of industry is slowly dying of technological anemia. The growth of investment, and thus productive potential, continues to decline, entailing a process of deindustrialization. Deindustrialization is a formal, academic word for the destruction of jobs, living standards and future prospects. It means rising imports, with a consequent crisis in trade; it means disintegration of industrial communities where for so long family life thrived on the salaries and employment of the factory; it means a dependence on foreign enterprises for the design, quality and operating characteristics of everyday products; it means the steady abandonment of those manufacturing skills that are the very cornerstone of a balanced economy. In the end it spells disaster for the vast service sector with its banking, insurance and other financial skills since these services exist only to assist and support the work of industry.

The prospects for the rest of the decade are daunting. America is faced with an illogical spiral of rising costs and a rising currency. If inflation in the United States continues to be curtailed at a faster rate than elsewhere, then the currency is likely to rise further and faster as American goods are priced out of the international marketplace through the rise in the currency, leading to a continued fall in the level of exports. Imports, in the meantime, will be flooding in to fill the gaps left by the collapse of industrial production. The consequences of the crisis in trade will be an unparalleled drift to national insolvency. The collapse of industry will, in turn, destroy millions of jobs. Entire regional populations, once prosperous on manufacturing, will be ravaged by the slow death of unemployment. On current trends of deindustrialization, there is likely to be a rise in unemployment levels approaching that of the 1930s by no later than 1985. Vacant factories will dot the landscape in increasing numbers.

As an investment, industrial building and land has left a great deal to be desired over the century. The combination of industrial buildings and land has involved a growth rate of under 1 percent per annum over the past hundred years. During the depression of the 1890s, the fall in the value of industrial real estate prices was greater than that of either shop properties or office properties. The same holds true for the depression of the 1930s. Compared to investment in other forms of property, industrial property has an extremely poor record. During periods of depression, the record of industrial land and property values looks horrifying. The current rage of deindustrialization and the continuing disuse of factory and warehouse space is something real estate investors have never been confronted with before, nor have those who value these premises on the balance sheets of many American companies. Factories and warehouses are likely to be the white elephants of the property market, ultimately becoming the most unattractive parcels of property anyone could conceivably own.

THE COMMERCIAL PROPERTY BUBBLE

If the corporate sector's ability to pay its rents were the only worry over the next few years, you could conclude that the commercial real estate market, as I shall call the rented market for shops and offices, was in for a tough time, no worse. But the trouble has been speculation. The kind that brought panic to Chicago in 1837, and that was the root of the depressions following 1873 and 1929.

According to a recent nationwide survey, the vacancy rate in offices was 10.8 percent in March 1983. Nearly a ninth of all the office space in the country was empty, tenantless. At the end of 1982, the figure was 10.3 percent and one year earlier 7.1 percent. A normal rate would be 3 percent or 4 percent. The empty space is the result of a "national boom in office building development of historic proportions" according to the surveyors. Just lately, the relationship between new rentings and new developments coming on stream has been deteriorating a little more slowly. So predictably, the voices of real estate agents can be heard crowing that the worst is over.

So it might prove to be if today's conditions were those of the upwave. The industry is aware that disinflation has changed the sums. As one put it: "Mistakes in the industry will not be paved over by inflation as they have in the past." But it goes much further than that. First, the mistake this time was the biggest in post-war history. A mighty speculative bandwagon sent 200 million square feet of office space into the air for completion by around the end of 1983. That was four years worth of projected annual demand.

Second, projections of office demand are based on past conditions. In 1972, no one dreamed that the projections that were being made for demand for supertankers could prove so completely wrong. Not only did subsequent demand *not* rise at 7 percent per annum as predicted: it actually fell away to less than nothing. The tanker glut of 1973 is still with us ten years later. Past demand for office space was based, first and foremost, on the belief that rents would rise and so would capital values. Many corporations, financial and otherwise, built or bought huge buildings for themselves in the belief that it was one of the best investments they could make. Often they bought more than they could use themselves and rented out the balance. Some, like Pan Am, ran into difficulties and had to sell out. There will be many more Pan Ams, but they may be just be a pinprick to the problems of the "downtown" real estate market.

For the first time since the war, office rents and building values suffered a severe decline in 1982. The decline in both has been put at over 20 percent when hidden incentives are taken into account. As it dawns on more and more fund managers and corporate treasurers that rents and values could go on falling—with fluctuations—for several years, the market in office space will be turned upside down. Ownership will be avoided instead of sought. Lease commitments will be minimized by renters instead of maximized. Many in the industry have difficulty in conceiving how this could happen. But it has happened regularly in the past.

The sharp drop in rents after the Civil War, in 1867, was a mere warning of things to come. And Figure 30 only tells half the story, for having declined from an index level of 187 in 1869 to 151 in 1880, city rents went on declining roughly to the end of the nineteenth century, plummeting after the Panic of 1893. By the late 1890s they were back close to the pre-Civil War levels. The same is true of the 1930s. By 1935, city rents were back down around the 1914 index level. The drop was much more severe in the smaller cities, which in those days included Houston, Los Angeles and San Francisco. An index for ten of these based on 100 for 1914 was already down to 103 by 1932, as against 126 for eight larger cities, from New York to Buffalo.

How fast could commercial real estate values fall? The "secondary banking crisis" in Britain in 1974 provided a dramatic illustration, in very recent memory. In the post-war period, real estate development has been

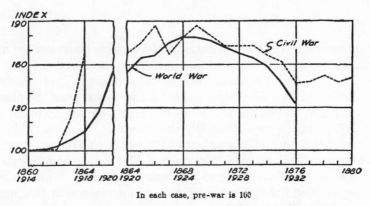

FIGURE 30   RENTS IN FIVE LARGE CITIES IN THE CIVIL WAR PERIOD AND IN
EIGHT LARGE CITIES IN THE WORLD WAR I PERIOD

From *The Prices Series* by G. F. Warren and F. A. Pearson.
Reprinted by permission of Chapman and Hall, Ltd.

the favorite game of British entrepreneurs. Circumstances were perhaps
particularly favorable. The capital market was better developed in Britain
than elsewhere in Europe. London's emergence as the world center of
international finance was a major factor. In the 1950s and 1960s, the personal fortunes accumulated in commercial real estate in Britain seemed to
make any other area of financial endeavor look pointless, and British developers were making their mark throughout the globe; in Canada, Australia,
France, Belgium and Holland—even in America.

By the early 1970s, the field had attracted a host of newcomers and a
frenzy of competitive bidding had sent commercial real estate values soaring far beyond their traditional relationships with rental incomes. Traditionally, the yield on top quality shops and offices had hovered, with great
consistency, around 6.5 percent. By late 1973, the average had been driven
down below 4 percent, which meant that capital values had jumped 60
percent above trend. In the typical case, the entire cost of the development,
and sometimes more than the cost, had been financed on short-term credit
from the mushrooming band of fringe banks that participated in the boom.
When the credit squeeze of 1974 pushed the price of government paper to
18 percent, something had to give. The bubble burst. In the space of six
months, average rental yields leapt to 8.5 percent. Where buyers could be
found at all, the price of commercial real estate had worse than halved in
half a year. With the likes of Jim Slater, Ronald Lyon and William Stern
toppled empires that had been valued at hundreds of millions of dollars.

The American experience in 1974, when a $21 billion debt balloon in
REITs went pop, was a tame affair by comparison. The speculation was
punctured in its infancy. Commercial real estate had been a relatively
sleepy market in the United States in the 1950s and 1960s. Unfortunately
this implied that the U.S. crash was yet to come.

It is generally agreed that 1977 marked the trough of the downtown

real estate market in the United States. In the ensuing boom it is estimated
that U.S. banks put $80 billion into short-term construction loans. The
"villains" in the speculative fever were the Canadian developers, backed by
some $15 billion of Canadian banking credit. Americans point the finger at
Cadillac Fairview, 36 percent owned by the Bronfman family of Seagers,
Nuwest Group and, biggest of all, Olympia and York. Canadian bidders, it
is said, forced the price of site values in Denver from $150 a square foot
to $700 between 1977 and 1982. The price of $1,900 a square foot paid by
Cadillac for its famous downtown Manhattan site may prove to be an
historic record. Cadillac walked away from the development at a reputed
loss of over $20 million in 1982.

It was early in 1982 that the boom broke and rents and capital values
started plunging. The interests vested in talking the market out of its
slump are measured by the $100 billion or so of short-term bank finance
which needed to be rolled into long-term mortgages from insurance companies and pension funds. But that debt is just a single thread in a web of
borrowing that enters every corner of American life and spans both the
Northern and Southern Hemispheres of the globe. It is now stretched so
tight that the parting of one strand could shatter the whole construction.

The love affair institutional investors have been having with property
can be short-lived. The introduction of deep discount bonds, zero coupon
bonds and other investment vehicles with a more certain rate of return than
growth projections leaves very little justification for further investment in
property. It is much more viable for the pension fund manager to lock in
a known rate of return for decades, than to be subjected to fluctuating
capital values. The more responsible trustees among institutional investors
have, in recent months, been increasing the fixed interest content of their
portfolios.

Financial institutions have, in recent years, been among the largest net
purchasers of property for investment. They have helped to support the
market, and push prices to levels which bear no relationship to the potential
profitability of the businesses on the sites they have been buying. Competition from alternative investments which promise equal, or higher returns
with lower risk, will bring a fall in institutional property purchases. Institutional investors will no longer prop an overvalued market. As long as
property is providing inadequate returns from a risk-evaluated standpoint,
premises will continue to be vacated and not taken up by purchasers. Even
after the secondary depression has run its course, I do not see how commercial property values can possibly return to the lofty levels of recent years.

The current state of the commercial property market and its likely
future is put quite succinctly in an article in the London *Times* of May 20,
1975:

> The great weakness of commercial property is that it depends on the level of
> domestic business activity; empty offices, as in Manhattan, mean cheap rents.

On the other hand the harvested value of a field of barley will always be based on its world market value; if the pound falls against the dollar, the value of a field of barley, or a field capable of growing barley, will rise. In effect commercial buildings gain their value from the domestic economy, residential property from the level of domestic wages, and farm land from the world price of farm products.

Look around you, and the prospects for commercial property values can readily be seen. As for farmland, one commodity market after the other is collapsing. In offices, the last defense in the economy, the service sector, is beginning to decline as the amount of office space available is swelling. Britain's manufacturing base is steadily shrinking, and the need for industrial premises is continually diminishing. Retail sales are in the early stages of a renewed decline as the secondary depression bites deeper into the consumer sector, and an increasing number of investors enter bankruptcies and sell up.

The current commercial property market is behaving precisely as expected in the early stages of a secondary depression. The latter stages of a secondary depression bring a collapse in values. This is likely to be evident early in 1983 and 1984.

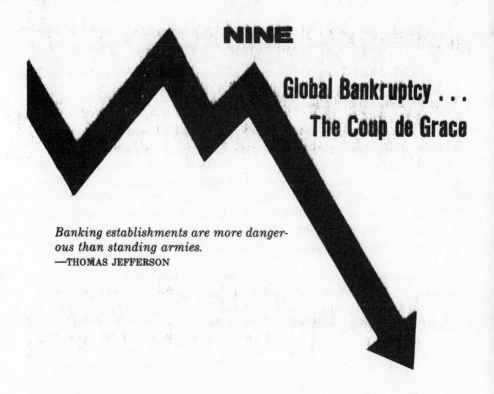

NINE

Global Bankruptcy . . .
The Coup de Grace

*Banking establishments are more danger-
ous than standing armies.*
—THOMAS JEFFERSON

The coup de grace is the final blow that ends all of the suffering. The type of suffering that much of the world has experienced over the last five years is likely to intensify. The developing countries are in the stranglehold of an insuperable debt burden. World trade, already contracting, is under threat from escalating protectionism. Domestic industry, agriculture and households are locked in a spiral of borrowing which is becoming even more menacing as inflation turns to disinflation and disinflation to deflation. The lenders, the banks, stare hopelessly at a black hole which swallows up more and more debt on the hopeless premise of staving off domino default. With the passage of time, the secondary depression of the 1980s will bring excruciatingly high unemployment, massive bankruptcies through industry, a collapse in capital markets, a sustained decline in property values and a great deal of hardship for many people. Throughout the process, international tensions will heighten. Countries will scramble to protect shrinking markets. Deficits for the developing countries will balloon while the temptation to default becomes increasingly more attractive. The coup de grace will be global bankruptcy as the nadir of the depression approaches.

Once again, using the 1930s as a model for what may lie ahead, we find that in repetition of what had happened several times before, as global demand for goods and services steadily contracted during the Great Depression, the world broke itself up into trade blocs. Each country attempted to gain a trade advantage over the other by depreciating its currency, instigating subsidies and erecting trade barriers. The idea was to increase exports one way or another so that individual nations could provide employment for their people. The game was called beggar-thy-neighbor. Every nation lost. None won. World trade was ultimately brought to a standstill. The collapse of financial institutions ricocheted from one country to the other. Bank moratoriums were declared and the United States experienced a "bank holiday" and a cashless society when all of the banks were closed. There is a Chinese philosophy that states life is a circle. We're still in the circle.

In 1944, the finance ministers of forty-four countries met at the mountain summer resort of Bretton Woods, New Hampshire. They did so to avoid currency and trade wars for the future, and to arrive at a system of greater international cooperation and stabilization of world trade. Out of the Bretton Woods agreement came the International Monetary Fund, to govern international monetary relations; the International Bank for Reconstruction and Development, to reconstruct a world that was in industrial shambles; and the General Agreement on Tariffs and Trade (GATT). The GATT rules against discriminatory tariffs were intended to prevent the misuse of devices to beggar your neighbor. GATT was incorporated into international law, rendering various methods which might restrict foreign trade "illegal." Among such barriers to trade were multiple exchange rates and discriminatory tariffs.

Before the Bretton Woods agreements could operate, massive currency depreciations against the U.S. dollar were required. With the exception of France, these were completed by 1949. By 1958 it appeared that Bretton Woods was a huge success. International trade was booming. Some countries were doing better than others, and ingenious administrators found little difficulty in devising new methods which, while outwardly respectable, would allow a competitive edge.

In the United States, there were "voluntary" restraints on the import of foreign textiles and on the export of U.S. portfolio capital and direct investments, the interest "equalization" tax, the reduction of duty-free import allowances for tourists, the order to government agencies to buy foreign products only if they were priced 60 percent below the U.S. substitutes, and the strict enforcement of sanitary rules and other rules on quality and labeling, which discriminated against foreign imports.

In Europe there have been "temporary" surcharges on imports, "import deposit schemes." Value-added taxes and turnover taxes are important revenue sources which subsidize exporters. Cheap export credits evade GATT rules. Among lesser-developed countries, complex tariff systems, producer cartels, buffer stocks twist the free market in world trade. America is at loggerheads with Europe. Japan is fair game for one and all.

In other words, the Bretton Woods agreement is now in shambles, and a fully fledged trade war is in the cards. Exactly the same type of trade barriers which fueled the last depression face us today. Then, it was done quite openly, since tariff warfare was not considered unsporting. Tariffs increased throughout the 1920s. The Smoot-Hawley Tariff Act was introduced in the United States in 1930, and prompted a further round of tariff competition. By 1931, tariff barriers in Europe averaged 51 percent. The widespread abandonment of gold standards opened the way for competitive devaluations. Speculative capital flows brought exchange rate chaos. Shrinking trade made debt service impossible for the developing countries and induced widespread defaults. Of the $60 billion in foreign government bonds issued in the United States between 1921 and 1929, 38 percent was in default by 1937. In the case of Latin America, the default rate was 72 percent.

Protectionist trends today are marginally more sophisticated. Standards are meticulously drafted to exclude foreign products on technicalities, be they turkeys or telecom systems. But such tactics are giving way to open warfare. It has already begun in agricultural trade, with America's open sale of subsidized flour to Egypt in early 1983. In steel, it is only a matter of time before the rift between the United States and the other steel producers develops into overt protectionism. Japan has begun a gradual tactical retreat in many products where countries have objected to the level of import penetration. This "tactical retreat" is soon likely to become a rout.

At the summit meeting of seven heads of state in Versailles, France, in 1982, and again at Williamsburg, Virginia, in 1983, pious intentions were expressed of taking concrete steps to restore some of the disciplinary elements of the Bretton Woods system. The first meeting ended in acrimony; the second in sweet nothings. The summits over the past few years have reflected deep, basic differences in national policies and priorities, and none of these basic differences have been resolved. The fundamental problem continues to be the inability of nations with widely differing social, political and economic characteristics to coordinate economic policies.

The global economic structure is interrelated now as never before through international trade. Yet there is no international will to promote interdependent free trade adequately. Throughout the 1970s and early 1980s, we have seen a direct return to beggar-thy-neighbor policies. Nations have ceased to seek free trade along the original intentions of the Bretton Woods agreement. As various economies have weakened, or been threatened by imports from other nations, political leaders have resorted to measures to protect their own self-interest by protective tariffs, embargoes and trade restrictions.

Early in 1977 the Japanese Prime Minister, Takeo Fukuda, warned that protectionism could take us back to the 1930s.

The world economic situation following the 1973 oil crisis was quite similar to the developments of that particular time. In the 1930s major countries, one after another, abandoned the open economic system of free trade, switching to the closed system of protectionism. I am not suggesting that we are once again on the road to World War. Yet, I feel deep anxiety about the social and political consequences with the world if we slide once again into protectionism or a breakup of the world economy into trade blocs.

An international trade war of horrifying dimensions looms. Everyone will suffer. The trade war will be the direct result of the underlying monetary crisis within the international system. A secondary depression of ostentatiously obvious dimensions will be needed before measures similar to Bretton Woods are once again instigated. A government usually reacts to crisis, rather than taking measures to prevent crisis. Accordingly, an international trade war, a collapse of the banking system and global bankruptcy, are virtually inevitable.

THE INTERNATIONAL DEBT MOUNTAIN

Following the global bankruptcy of the 1930s, a "new deal" was inaugurated. There were stricter controls over government spending; banking regulations were tightened and new regulatory bodies were set up to make certain that a calamity of such proportions would never happen again, and that so many seeds of debt would never be sown again.

For about a decade, the new regulations worked fairly well. Shortly after World War II and Bretton Woods, the seeds of the process that brought the international banking collapse of the 1930s were being sprinkled across the credit-thirsty field all over again, but on a much larger scale.

After World War II, governments wished to rebuild their economies. They borrowed to do so. Debt was piled upon debt. War recovery debt was followed by expansionary debt. Expansionary debt was expanded by anticontractionary debt. Debt spread throughout the developed world, and finally through to the Third World of lesser-developed countries. When consumers were creditworthy, they were urged to borrow well beyond their earning capacities. When saturation was reached in consumer borrowings, corporate borrowings were encouraged. When both consumers and corporations had reached the limit of their debt servicing capacities, further borrowing was encouraged to "remain afloat" until the next economic recovery. The monetary explosion of the past three decades involving the most tremendous expansion of credit in history transcended territorial borders.

Shortly before the oil crisis of 1973, there was a great boom in commodities. Prices very roughly doubled in that year alone, and Third World producers appeared eminently credit-worthy. Despite the tensions of the time, there followed a mad scramble among geobankers to lend to the developing countries for expansion of their productive capacities. Steel plants, hydroelectric power dams and all forms of capital projects were financed by American and European banks. The commodity boom faded. World growth slowed. Soon many of the new Third World projects turned out to be white elephants, and the borrowers were left with the burden of debts to service.

Prior to 1973, world trade had been increasing by nearly 9 percent per annum and trade in manufactures by 11 percent. After the fivefold increase in the oil price, both figures were cut in half. Following the oil crisis, an aggressive lobby among the lesser-developed countries (LDCs) was demanding a larger share of the profits of world trade. What they received was a global catastrophe . . . and credit. The oil price hike was expected to impel the industrialized world into chronic balance of trade dificits. It did not work that way. The petrodollars were deposited back in Western banks. The OPEC surpluses were filled by Western and Japanese goods. And the oil price burden lay on those countries least able to afford it, the poor LDCs.

By the end of 1979, the LDCs had external debts (medium term) to banks and international agencies of some $320 billion. This was more than a quarter of their total output, and over three times the level of their debt at the end of 1973. The second big oil price hike had hit them hard, raising their combined current payments deficits to $59 billion.

For some time it had been apparent that something very dangerous was happening—and not just apparent to me (for I had been following the matter closely for a while). A memorandum at the Office of the Comptroller of the Currency in Washington, dated May 17, 1977, offered this warning:

> Large outstanding international loans to developing countries and financially weak developed countries are a matter of great current concern. Such loans usually finance basic economic development in emerging nations and, more recently, cover national balance-of-payments deficits. In either case, the prospect that the country involved will be able to generate the sizable balance-of-payments necessary to pay loan interest and principal, in this author's opinion, is dim, even over the very long term.

In 1980, U.S. interest rates suddenly soared over 20 percent at one time, and the current payments surplus of the LDCs jumped to $86 billion. It was by then clear that the debt of the LDCs, so effortlessly acquired, was a monstrous albatross. But still the geobankers jetted around the world in a crazy race to outbid each other to thrust further borrowings on their impoverished clients. By now the LDCs were not borrowing from choice. In the next couple of years, their liquid reserves had been whittled away to nothing. They were borrowing for survival—and that's what the bankers were lending for . . . their own. By 1983, according to the IMF, overall LDC debt had doubled again to over $600 billion.

The "first wave" of the global debt store didn't even come initially from the LDCs. It came, in late 1981, form Poland and the Comecon bloc as a whole. In the light of what was to follow, all that is old hat now, and I won't drag up the details, except to recall that there is $80 billion out there, in Poland, Rumania, Bulgaria, Czechoslovakia, East Germany, Hungary, yes, and Russia, which will never be repaid, ever. Even by the summer of 1982 that was quite clear when a U.S. Treasury Department official let the usual mask of hypocrisy slip in a quote to *Business Week.* "Mexico is not Poland. They face an illiquidity problem but *they* [my italics] will be able to resume payment on their debt." Yet a year later, in June 1983, bankers picked up the farce of renewed negotiations on the rescheduling of Poland's debt.

Mexico, of course, was the next installment of the first wave. On August 20, 1982, at the Federal Reserve Bank of New York, Mexico's finance minister told more than a hundred bankers that his country could not repay its loans. Since Mexico's medium-term debt totaled as much as all the Comecon debt put together, there was little room for complacency this time; but a rescue package of $1.85 billion from a group of central banks operating through the Bank of International Settlements (BIS) in Basel was orchestrated within days, while geobankers and the IMF were putting together an $8.6 billion package to see Mexico out of the woods.

There were fears that the contagion must inevitably spread to Brazil (whose debts topped even Mexico's) or Argentina. But as the weeks went by, to the soothing accompaniment of falling U.S. interest rates, the fears subsided. And the world turned back to placing bets on when the United States and global economic recovery would start. It was against this background, on December 29, that the governor-elect of the Bank of England made a remark which may be destined to go down in history. "I think the crisis is over—if ever there was a crisis."

The very next day, Brazil unilaterally declared a moratorium (default) on its $90 billion or more of hard currency debts. On January 4, Rumania announced it was suspending repayments on $1 billion owing to banks. The next day Cuba declared it would pay back nothing before 1985 at the earliest. And Zambia suspended repayments of principal two days later.

Observers' attitudes to the "debt bomb" (Secretary of State George Schultz was one of the first users of the phrase) have varied between naïve, calculating, self-fooling and plain wistful. It is not always clear which. Referring to the possibility of a banking catastrophe on December 5, 1982, Walter Wriston, chairman of Citibank, put it "about as close to zero as anything that human beings can predict." Rather different words had been used earlier by the president of the Swiss National Bank and of the BIS, Fritz Leutwiler. In the alarming deterioration of financial markets he saw "the danger of a chain reaction" as banks called in loans in an "every man for himself mentality." Federal Reserve Chairman Paul Volcker sounded an even clearer note of warning on November 16, 1982, of a "threat without precedent in the post-war world," for "should we fail to understand the full extent of these difficulties or respond inappropriately, no country will escape the consequences."

Paul Volcker's position has been at the very interface between the vested interests of sovereign borrowers and their lenders. To those that had ears to hear, he was making a clear reference to a repeat of the financial conditions of the 1930s.

As 1983 wore on, it became clear that the ranks of the lending banks were splitting, with the big U.S. money centers on the one hand, and on the other the regional U.S. banks, allying with the European and Japanese internationals. The latter increasingly took the view that South America was a "money centers" problem—at least if the solution lay in constant new injections of cash. In May the BIS central bank members asserted that it would not be making further short-term loans to sovereign borrowers. Its president had earlier said it was not part of a central bank's job to put pressure on national banks to lend further funds to defaulters. The attitude of Congress and the great public in the United States and Europe hardened against the geobankers and their proposals for international agency solutions which smelt of a bailout.

By midyear, there was talk of a "second wave" in the global debt storm. Brazil was the chief worry. It was not meeting the economic targets it had undertaken as conditions for IMF borrowing. As late as March 1983, Brazil was insisting that it held reserves of over $3 billion which were adequate security for the bridging loans it had constantly been seeking. On examination, it emerged that these reserves consisted largely of credits with fellow Latin American governments, which were in no position to come forward with the cash. The same kind of problem has bedeviled Brazil's trade. More than a third of its exports used to be absorbed within Latin America. Now Brazil's neighbors cannot afford to buy its goods. Practically all the progress it had made in improving its trade balance toward a target of $60 billion surplus had been achieved by cutting back on imports, including imports of essential goods which someday it would have to start reordering. Brazil was going to need more money—maybe $2 billion or $3 billion—than the $4.4 billion the geobankers had already agreed to lend it.

An austerity program might bring it back within the IMF targets, but what political risks would that involve, with unemployment soaring and standards of living falling? Mexico and Argentina were meeting their IMF targets. In the case of Mexico, a huge $5.4 billion turnaround in current payments balance was achieved in the first third of 1983, but at the cost of a 67 percent slump in imports. Anyone could see such a situation was untenable. The economy would soon run out of the spare parts and equipment which are essential for its functioning. So if bankers lent money now, they would have to lend more next year and the year after, indefinitely.

The LDCs used to absorb about two-fifths of U.S. exports; South America alone, about 17 percent. This trade is drying up. That means jobs are being lost in the United States. It also means America can afford to buy that much less from the rest of the world or else it must go deeper and deeper into deficit on its trade account. The same is true for Europe and Japan. It is a rerun of what happened in the 1930s.

Argentina, Chile and Peru would all be asking for more money, like Brazil and Mexico. Venezuela had been reckoned a safe bet as recently as the fall of 1982. In the spring of 1983, it called for rescheduling of $16 billion of its $32 billion debt, and agreed to call in the IMF, something it had originally forsworn. All of South America is a black hole. Who will lend now? At any moment a coup, a change of government could bring in a faction that is in favor of deliberate unilateral default. As Figure 31 shows, the cost of servicing the interest and the annual capital amortization on their hard currency debt is becoming overwhelming for many developing countries. Yet Figure 31 only really presents half the picture, and half the problem. American Express has pointed out the lending banker is not just concerned with the servicing and refinancing of medium-term debts, which is what the debt table and others of the sort are confined to. There are also short-term debts incurred for less than one year, the most important being trade debts, incurred to finance imports, which do not usually exceed a term of six months.

Amex has produced figures which include such short-term debt refinancing with a suitable allowance for bona fide trade finance needs. On this more cautious view, the debt service pictures of some of the main LDC borrowers, particularly of Latin America, appear quite horrendous. The "real" debt service burden, Amex would say, for Brazil emerges at 80 percent, for Mexico at 110 percent and for Argentina at 150 percent. The figure is over 50 percent for Venezuela, Peru, Equador, Chile and the Philippines.

It is obvious that if your household income is $30,000 and you have to pay between $15,000 and $45,000 on mortgage payments and consumer and other debt service *before* you pay the groceries bill, you are in the kind of trouble that will get worse before it gets better. In fact it is likely to get worse so fast that it *never* will get better. That is the situation of these countries. Some of them have borrowed between 2.5 and 3.5 times their total income—with no security.

Bankers sometimes reply that sovereign risks are good risks. There may be temporary problems but overall they have done the right thing in shifting over a bit from lending to people and corporations to lending to countries. Said the vice-chairman of Chase Manhattan, William Ogden, last year, "We do have a problem—a serious problem. But it is a liquidity problem, not a solvency problem. . . . There is negligible risk of permanent default or debt denial in sovereign lending, because sovereign borrowers cannot cease to exist"—as corporations can, for instance.

Don't you believe it. What about that 72 percent of pre-1929 Latin American debt that was in default in 1937? Wasn't that "debt-denial"? What about the worthless debt certificates of China, Russia, Hungary, Rumania, Latvia, Dresden, Saxony, Bulgaria, Costa Rica, and U.S. Confederate borrowing? Several of them decorate my office walls, so I am not as optimistic as some bankers make out they are over the "certificates of

Estimated gross external debt and debt service of 21 major LDC borrowers

	Gross external debt at end-1982 $ billions	Debt service in 1983, % of exports[1]	
		Total	Excluding rollover of short-term debt
Latin America			
Argentina	38.0	154	88
Brazil	85.5	117	67
Chile	17.2	104	54
Colombia	10.3	95	38
Ecuador	6.6	102	58
Mexico	80.1	126	59
Peru	11.5	79	47
Venezuela	29.5	101	25
Subtotal	278.1	117	56
Asia			
Indonesia	25.4	28	14
Korea	36.0	49	17
Malaysia	10.4	15	7
Philippines	16.6	79	33
Taiwan	9.3	19	6
Thailand	11.0	50	19
Subtotal	108.8	36	14
Middle East and Africa			
Algeria	16.3	35	30
Egypt	19.2	46	16
Israel	26.7	126	26
Ivory Coast	9.2	76	34
Morocco	10.3	65	36
Nigeria	9.3	28	14
Turkey	22.8	65	20
Subtotal	113.8	58	16
Total of 21 LDCs	501.2	71	30

[1]Interest on gross debt plus all maturing debt, including amortization of medium- and long-term debt and all short-term debt as percent of exports of goods and services, including net private transfer payments.

FIGURE 31

From *World Financial Markets,* February 1983, p. 5.
Reprinted by permission of Morgan Guaranty Trust Company.

guaranteed confiscation," as monetary analyst Franz Pick has called these busted sovereign bonds.

There is, in fact, a very good reason why bankers should be concerned to make the point that their debt problem is one of liquidity, not of solvency. In many cases there are *legal* bars against lending to insolvent borrowers. In such cases, what the banks fear is that they may be vulnerable to lawsuits by shareholders or other interested parties.

The international banking system continues to hold most of these loans to Latin America, the Eastern bloc and elsewhere on its books as "assets," completely disguising the true state of illiquidity in the international banking system. If these debts were written off in the same manner as for a commercial company, the conditions would be terrifying. Lending is a matter of judgment, claim the polyglot bankers. As long as a country can avert default by borrowing more, and having its debt rescheduled, the dangers of not lending are as great as those of lending too much.

The emerging debt crisis is now actually more serious than that which led to the series of bank moratoriums and the bank holiday in the 1930s. The international financial problems of the 1920s and 1930s represented intergovernmental funding problems, and a rash of foreign debt failures, leading to losses mainly by individual bond holders. Historically, sovereign debt defaults did not necessarily undermine the international banking system. But such potential defaults are now threatening the solvency of all international lenders, rather than just governments and individual foreign bond holders.

The problems facing the international banking system are magnified by the level of indirect investment in potential defaulters. Whereas investors have not been prepared to purchase the debt instruments of Third World countries such as Argentina, Poland and Venezuela, they have placed deposits with commercial banks which have loaned out more than 100 percent of their capital resources to defunct borrowers.

In the United States, $200 billion has been placed in money funds. The assets of many of these money funds include certificates of deposit from bankers who have been exceptionally heavy lenders to the Eastern bloc, South and Central America. Accordingly, potential losses are not limited merely to bond holders, but extend to those whose savings have been invested in these banks. Recently, many of these money funds have been reducing the bank paper in their portfolios, while bond rating organizations have downgraded most of the major banks from AAA to AA or worse. There is a clear danger that depositors will begin to withdraw funds from those heavily exposed institutions once the scale of these debt problems becomes clearer to ordinary depositors, rather than just an open secret among informed members of the international banking community.

At this stage, international monetary policy can only take one of two directions, both of which lead to the same end. The system can continue to act in consort, rescheduling debts, rolling over credits, extending time limits for payment with printed fiat money. That would ultimately lead to global hyperinflation, and would merely postpone the inevitable. The price which would have to be paid would involve a far longer period of reconstruction than if the escalation of the debt pyramid was halted now. The deepening depression of the 1980s has meant that we have growing deflationary pressures built into the economic system in the form of steadily deteriorating liquidity and too much debt. Attempts have been made to offset these pressures by creating more inflationary credit. From 1974 to 1978, overborrowing on a vast scale was encouraged, and insolvent borrowers were supplied with a continual flow of credit. This climate has now disappeared, and the global economic environment is faced with depression which questions the sense of either extending or accepting further credit.

The second direction monetary policy could take would be to keep a tight prudent rein on lending. If defunct sovereign borrowers find their debts are written off as bad debts and they are no longer able to obtain credit, a major default will be precipitated either in Latin America or Eastern Europe. This would lead to a chain reaction of bank failures and a credit crisis, and a collapse in the international banking system which would make the 1930s look like an era of prosperity.

It is likely that bankers will attempt to pursue a policy of debt rescheduling and rollovers for as long as possible, thus blunting the deflationary pressures. There was evidence during the early part of 1982 that many central bankers were preparing for a liquidity crisis, shifting deposits between banks. There was little to suggest that major moves were being considered to avert an actual solvency crisis which would affect the viability of the international banking system.

The only remedy which has been suggested in stemming an actual solvency crisis has been the nationalization of the institutions concerned, and the large-scale injection of public funds. It is also likely that the international monetary system would have to consider extending loans by a special procedure to countries unable to service their debt in order to prevent the chain-reaction default from gaining momentum and running out of control. We have the mechanism available to the international banking system. The initiatives which have been suggested would require considerable coordination in the event of a major default, and probably could not be introduced in time to head off a multiple credit collapse. That would force a moratorium on international payments between banks, a temporary freeze on all bank deposits in major financial centers in order to avoid a "run on the banks" and possibly an interim nationalization of the banks.

THE PERILS OF THE DOMESTIC BANKING SYSTEM

We have referred to global debt as a mountain. When debt goes sour, the right comparison is with an iceberg. All outsiders ever see of an incipient bankruptcy, for instance, is the tiny visible fraction above the surface. The problems of the U.S. (and global) banking industry run very deep. You can never expect to see anything but the tip. And this is quite normal. The credit business depends on confidence. So do jobs. If a bank's energy department looks like running in to huge debts, the chairman will know nothing about it until the vice-president in charge of energy lending can hide the trouble no longer. And it goes further than that, of course. For the customer—a pipeline supplier, say—who depends on bank credit will do nothing to enlighten the lending vice-president as to the severity of his problems. And his customers, in turn, the buyers of his pipeline, are not going to let on that they can't pay for the pipeline just yet. And so it goes on.

When Penn Square went bust in 1982, there were precious few outsiders who knew that the problem was not just the difficulties of Penn Square, but rather a $2 billion loan portfolio it had sold around the marketplace, which was leaking bad debts like a sieve. It is certain that Continental Illinois didn't know what it was buying that was to give it serious indigestion for months, or Chase Manhattan, which bought a $212 million slice of the portfolio. In the same way Drysdale Government Securities kept so quiet about their troubles in the Treasury bond market that Chase and Manufacturers Hanover, backers of Drysdale, didn't know what hit them until they were looking at eight-figure losses.

So whatever horrors appear on the surface, they are only the tip of what lurks underneath. However, the fact that there is so much vested interest in keeping financial difficulties hidden has advantages. It means that what are actually corpses in hard times can be nursed until conditions improve and then brought back to life again. It means that conditions have to be quite exceptionally awful before the problems of individual accident cases infect others up and down a supply or credit chain and reach the epidemic proportions of domino collapse.

In fact such collapses, usually referred to as panics, were much commoner in the past, as we have seen. In the nineteenth century they seemed to occur every ten or twenty years. In this century, the year 1907 can be counted as a panic that devastated the banking sector but the only other collapse worthy of the name happened fifty-four years ago. People learned a few lessons from that one, because it was very bad. Or at least it seemed as if they had until the 1970s. Figure 32 suggests that maybe no lessons have been learned after all.

Figure 32 plots all the loans made by the domestic banks in relation to all the deposits which they have borrowed. There are two points to be made about this chart. The first is that when you have loaned out, say, only half or less of all the money you have borrowed and kept the rest in cash or safe liquid investments like Treasury bills, you have little to fear from the hard times when people run to you asking for their deposits back. When you have lent three-quarters, things can get most uncomfortably tight. The second is that the economic expansion we have enjoyed since the war has depended on the banks lending out as loans much more than they were taking in in deposits. For various reasons, it seems we have reached the end of that road.

During the 1960s and 1970s the banks went on a lending spree such as had never been seen in history. Already by the mid-1970s this resulted in the banks getting into such a tight position that they could henceforth only lend out as much as they took in. But the position of the borrowers was getting tight too. During the 1960s and 1970s there had been odd bankruptcies of note. There was Penn Central in 1969. That was a special case. The auto and aircraft industries were special cases too, so the fact that Lockheed (like Rolls-Royce in Britain) and Chrysler had to be bailed out by the government was not really such sensational news. Hard times

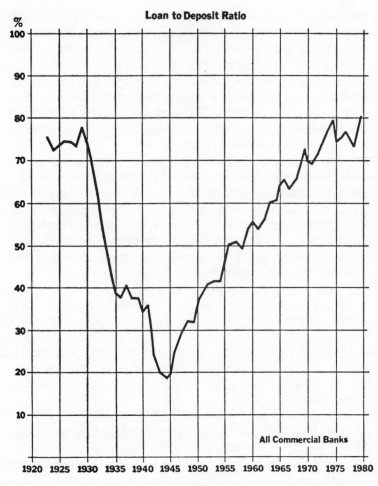

FIGURE 32

came with the 1974–1975 slump and bankruptcies across the nation rose to
a record of 11,629.

But in the 1980s two things happened that spelled "terminal" for the
great post-war debt accumulation. One was that interest rates soared to
heights that have not been seen this century. In fact long-term rates far
surpassed any peak on record. During the greatest period of sustained
inflation America has ever known it made sense to borrow. Borrowers could
get into difficulties, but the difficulties had to be very bad to prove fatal
simply because inflation was obliterating the pain of debt at such a pace.
The second thing was in a way more insidious, because it was the reversal
of a long-established trend: that was disinflation. The combination produced a completely new set of circumstances.

All this time, the financial position of corporations, households, municipalities and government had been undergoing an inexorable deterioration. In the corporate sector, the scale of the deterioration was dramatic. According to Data Resources, the leverage of nonfinancial companies—the ratio of debt to equity—rose from 0.5 in the mid-fifties to 1.3 in 1982. The debt, too, was getting shorter and shorter. On Salomon Brothers figures, in the early 1950s corporate short-term (under one year) debt was 33 percent of long-term debt; by the end of 1982 it was 100 percent. And the ratio of liquid assets to short-term debt has fallen over the period from over 2 to less than 0.5. In short, companies have very heavy debt in relation to net worth: they have to renew half their debt every year—and they have little cash to meet sudden calls.

Alarmingly, business failures accelerated suddenly in 1980 to surpass the peak of 1975—and then proceeded to more than double by 1982. Figure 33 shows that the phenomenon was not confined to the United States. Suddenly in 1982, it was no longer special cases that were in financial difficulty. The big bankruptcies were household names, like the Wickes stores group and Addressograph Multigraph. The walking dead included giants like International Harvester along with Massey Ferguson in Canada, and Dome Petroleum. In West Germany there was AEG, the giant electrical group employing 120,000, saved by government help. In France Poclain, in Britain Stone Platt.

All this, we must remember, is only the tip of the iceberg of corporations in distress. Companies were borrowing desperately for survival during the recession of 1982, when in normal times they would have had little need of funds. The disease is terminal, because the corporate debt burden is no longer being devalued by double-digit inflation: it is being further loaded by the weight of "real" interest costs. Debt service costs have

BUSINESS FAILURES IN THE UNITED STATES AND SELECTED FOREIGN COUNTRIES
Number of failures

	United States	United Kingdom	Germany	Canada
1973..................	9,571	2,575	3,996	2,718
1974..................	10,046	3,720	5,976	2,512
1975..................	11,629	5,398	6,948	2,863
1976..................	9,851	5,939	6,804	2,976
1977..................	7,988	5,831	6,924	4,131
1978..................	6,720	5,086	6,924	5,511
1979..................	7,757	4,537	5,484	5,648
1980..................	11,782	6,890	6,312	6,595
1981..................	17,217	8,596	8,496	8,055
1982..................	25,346	12,039	11,916	10,726

FIGURE 33

soared from 10 percent of gross internal revenues under President Dwight Eisenhower to 50 percent under Reagan, while corporate profitability has halved.

Inexorably, with a further downturn in the business cycle, corporate bankruptcies will explode with a quantum leap, involving massive writeoffs of bank assets. Inexorably more municipalities will go the way of the Washington Public Power Supply Service, though in this case the cost will be borne by bond holders, individual or other. Inexorably the plight of householders and farmers will deepen, with their debts transformed from boon to burden by disinflation. Of course, the vast majority will never declare bankruptcy: as always it will be a matter of scrimping, stalling off payments and trying to survive in the hope that, somehow or other, prospects will improve someday. During the downwave, that will call for patience. That is what the banks will need, too, since most of their loans to householders are as frozen as their loans to municipalities, businesses and sovereign states.

UNDERSTANDING THE BANKING MECHANISM

History tells us that sudden shocks leading to financial panic in the past have often come like bolts out of the blue. Who would have thought that the collapse of the Hatry Empire in 1929 could have led to one of the worst stock market crashes in history? Who could have dreamed that the collapse of a piggy bank like London & County in Britain in 1974 could have brought a large portion of the banking system of that country to its knees —requiring the support of the Bank of England?

A collapse in the international and domestic banking system could occur at any time, without warning. It is my firm belief that an international banking crisis similar to that in the 1930s is not a matter of "if" but simply a matter of "when." To understand how and why, a brief résumé of the way the system works may be helpful. Forgive the simple tone, but I find it useful once in a while.

At the root of the current problem is the "fractional reserve" banking system. What sounds like some sophisticated terminology is actually a relatively simple concept wherein, with just a little bit of money, a bank can create an awful lot of money. When you deposit money with a bank, that bank is not only able to lend out your deposit but it can also lend several multiples of that deposit. The number of multiples depends on what "fraction" of the loans a bank makes must be backed up by "reserves." If the reserve requirement is, say, 50 percent, then for every $1.00 you deposit, the bank can lend $2.00. If the reserve requirement is 10 percent, then for every $1.00 you deposit, the bank can lend another $9.00. And, if the reserve requirement is 5 percent, then a bank can lend $19.00 for every $1.00 you deposit and $19,000 for every $1,000 . . . $1,900,000 for every $100,000, which is the maxium amount you are insured for under the

Federal Deposit Insurance Corporation scheme. It all sounds a bit hairy, doesn't it? It would seem the system does lend itself in certain potential perils, but the problem is not with the system but the way the bankers operate the system.

The bulk of the money that keeps our economic and financial system in operation is the result of the credit that banks have created through the fractional reserve system. The system is sound and legitimate, providing the credit that is created is secured against some measure of real worth, such as property, or land, and is used in the promotion of productive activity such as farming and manufacturing, or in the construction of worthwhile capital projects. Ideally, the security offered to the lending banker should be of a nature that makes the debt self-liquidating. In other words, the project should be capable of producing a profit that can be used to repay the loan. Under such conditions, the fractional reserve system has an extremely useful and purposeful function. Bank lending can be secured against buildings or land or productive complexes already in existence—or as an act of faith, a banker's loan can be advanced against some tangible investment which has yet to be brought into existence. But what happens when this lending and borrowing cycle gets out of hand—when loan applicants become supplicants and the banks are sidetracked from their traditional role of financing agriculture and productive industry? What happens when banks become the pawns of government, induced to throw good money after bad by lending to defunct sovereign borrowers because the consequences of not lending are worse than the consequences of providing a loan that will never be paid? Then the fractional reserve banking system becomes a self-degenerating monster capable of the most heinous acts.

There are three major factors that are responsible for the maintenance of the banking system. Banks must be "solvent," "liquid" and inspire "confidence." When the banks are solvent and liquid they will automatically inspire confidence. At such times the banking system can be considered sound and stable. When the system becomes illiquid, solvency is threatened along with soundness and confidence. When the system becomes illiquid and insolvent, it becomes unsound and confidence deteriorates. When the system is illiquid, insolvent, unsound and there is no confidence ... the system collapses. The consequences are usually disastrous.

For a bank to be solvent, its assets must be equal or greater than its liabilities. As long as the assets are at least equal to the level of liabilities, the bank or banks can be considered to be in a solvent state. Of course, there is always the question of the quality of assets. If a bank lends to a developing country and that developing country is unable to pay back the money that has been loaned, this should no longer be considered an asset. In fact, if the borrower threatens the lender with the idea that he'll default and cause a banking crisis if more loans are not forthcoming, that asset actually becomes a liability. That's where we are today with the international banking system. Currently, solvency in the international banking system, like beauty, is in the eye of the beholder.

Now, let's look at the aspect of liquidity. Liquidity involves current assets as opposed to aggregate assets, principally cash on hand. A bank is fully liquid if cash on hand is equal to all of its liabilities. In other words, if every single depositor of a bank showed up at the same time, all demanding their cash immediately, if the bank was able to meet all of the withdrawals, the bank would be liquid. In the real world most banks would run out of money at the very early stages of the lineup, becoming illiquid quite quickly. Due to the very nature of the fractional reserve banking system, all banks are essentially illiquid.

By becoming a banker, through the use of other people's money, you can lend out much more than you have yourself. For example, if you had $1 million and then advertised for depositors, subsequently attracting $5 million, you could lend out $6 million plus whatever the reserve requirement would allow. On the other hand, if you had $1 million and took in deposits of $99 million, subsequently lending out $100 million, that would raise eyebrows, and much more. The Fed would certainly come down on you like a ton of bricks if they ever got to know about it. Such an activity would be stretching the boundaries of what is considered prudent for a banker. Even so, as long as you had enough cash in the till to pay off the odd depositor who came wandering in off the street, and as long as the assets of your loan portfolio maintained their value, you would still be able to remain in business. You would be considered liquid and solvent. There would be no entourage of indignant depositors clamoring for their money back and the $100 million you lent out (your assets) would be worth no less than the $99 million you managed to borrow in the form of deposits plus the $1 million of your own money (your liabilities). It may seem strange that your own money should be called a liability, but that's what it becomes when you use it to start a bank. It becomes a liability, to you.

Now, if by chance one of your loans goes sour and you lose, say $1 million (a mere 1 percent) of your loan portfolio, then you're in big trouble. You're an insolvent banker. You have liabilities of $100 million but your loan portfolio is only worth $99 million. And also, suppose one of your depositors found out about it and, as an act of altruism, circularized all of the other depositors, leading to a run on the bank, involving cash withdrawals that you don't have? Then you're really in big trouble. You're insolvent, illiquid and all of your depositors have lost confidence in you. The bank closes its doors and you then seek an alternative occupation, that is, providing you didn't put any of the bank's money in your pockets. If you did that, then you'd be invited to become a guest at one of the more secure federal institutions.

Now, let's go back to the real world of banking instead of the hypothetical world of piggy banking. The Federal Reserve is very anxious to keep its member banks solvent and liquid. It has rules about how much a banker with only $1 million can lend. The total liabilities of the top ten U.S. banks as of March 1983 were about $650 billion, of which $28 billion belonged to the owners of the banks which represented the equity, or net worth of the banks. This will give you some idea of the Fed's rule of thumb. In order to assuage fears over the stability of the banking system, in June 1983 the Federal Reserve Board acted in proposing that the nation's biggest banks be required to maintain their primary capital at 5 percent or more of total assets. These proposals came against a backdrop of increasing concern in Congress about the stability of both the United States and the international banking system.

A bank's "primary capital" represents money that either belongs to the shareholders or that must be converted into shareholders' money. That primary capital represents a cushion between potential losses on the one hand and money that belongs to depositors and other creditors on the other. The frightening aspect of the entire situation is that it has been well known for some time that some U.S. banks have actually lent more than their total capital to several Latin American countries that are having serious problems meeting their obligations. If, by some chance, all or most of those loans are never repaid, the entire capital of a number of large banks would be totally wiped out. Even though the federal government insures each depositor for $100,000, the far-reaching effects would be catastrophic. While the move to secure solvency and liquidity within the banking system is encouraging, there are two side effects that have daunting implications. The first is that, in order to maintain capital requirements, banks will be forced to restrict lending to Third World countries, which in turn will mean a further contraction in world trade, making a default in a lesser-developed country even more likely, ultimately leading to more pressure on the banks in the long run. Secondly, the move will direct funds toward the larger banks while exerting more pressure on the smaller banks as fears intensify. The net result will mean that small and medium-sized banks will become more vulnerable to a run from depositors, especially in the case where individual deposits exceed $100,000 or in those banks that are not members of the Federal Reserve system.

Primary capital of the top seventeen U.S. multinational banking companies averaged 5 percent of total assets at the end of 1982, up from 4.3 percent in 1979. The Fed's proposal that primary capital requirements are at least 5 percent of total assets of the average large bank holding company has pushed the banks into reaching that level. The banking companies that are included in the list in Figure 34 are those which are among the seventeen largest at the end of 1981. According to the chief bank stock analyst at Salomon Brothers, the year-end 1982 ratios of primary capital to assets of these seventeen banks were as follows:

RATIO OF PRIMARY CAPITAL
TO ASSETS OF 17 LEADING U.S. BANKS

Mellon National Corp.	6.1%	Chase Manhattan	4.8%
Marine Midland	5.7%	Security Pacific	4.8%
J. P. Morgan & Co.	5.6%	First Chicago	4.7%
Bank of Boston	5.5%	Irving Trust	4.6%
Continental Illinois	5.3%	Manufacturers Hanover	4.6%
Crocker National	5.3%	Bankers Trust New York	4.5%
Wells Fargo	5.2%	Bank of America	4.3%
First Interstate	5.1%	Citicorp	4.2%
Chemical New York	5.0%		

FIGURE 34

Currently, there is a prevailing consensus view that a sustained economic recovery is on the way and this recovery will enable a "rescue of the Third World." Therefore, as long as the bankers continue to manipulate and bend the rules, the end justifies the means since the wherewithal to return to normal is supposedly just around the corner. Since, in a fiat money environment, the element of confidence is of crucial importance, the present game of make-believe in which the international financial and political community is fully engaged, necessarily depends to an ever increasing extent on a continuous self-perpetuating process of deceit, such as carefully staged and orchestrated "economic recovery" propaganda. As each layer of deception is peeled away from the last, just as the promise of economic recovery in 1980 was peeled away from the deception of 1981, which was peeled away from the deception of 1982, which was peeled away from the deception of 1983, fresh dimensions of fabrications have to be invented and engineered by all involved.

By all accounts, the international banking system should now be under a state of siege. A careful scrutiny of the condition of the world banking system would reveal that the system is illiquid, and unsound. It has been in that condition for several years. But it continues. Why? Because the powers that be have miraculously been able to maintain confidence in the system. In spite of the number of banks that have failed in recent years, people are still prepared to leave copious amounts of their savings with the banking system. As long as depositors believe the banking system is sufficiently liquid to meet their needs, only a few will want their money at any given point in time. The banks, although illiquid, will therefore be perceived as solvent and continue to operate. However, if it is suddenly suspected that the system is insolvent and illiquid and people lose confidence in the system, a sudden rush of depositors could force bankers to liquidate investments at a loss, or suddenly be forced to write off bad debts. Under such circumstances, illiquidity could lead to immediate insolvency.

This is an intended oversimplification. As we move into the panic stage of the depression of the 1980s, the banking system is illiquid but solvent, at least on paper. Unfortunately, the situation is likely to deteriorate quite quickly as the depression and the increasing number of solvent borrowers mount. The bankers' current predicament can be best understood by considering those factors that are likely to mean the difference between insolvency and solvency among bankers. Let's take a closer look at the difference between a situation where assets exceed liabilities and the bank is solvent, against a situation where liabilities may suddenly exceed assets leaving a bank, or banks, insolvent.

There are four major assets that are held by bankers. These assets are the capital of the bank; cash on hand and with other banks; investments; and loans. The capital of a bank is the money that has been put up to establish the bank by its owners or shareholders. Cash is the money that is available over the counter from the till, along with deposits that have been made with other banks. The investments of a bank are usually Treasury bills, longer-term government paper and loans to municipalities. The loans of a bank are those which are outstanding from customers of the banks.

As can be envisaged, the assets of a bank can deteriorate quite quickly, leading to insolvency. A banker will always attempt to obtain the highest possible return on the capital of his bank for its shareholders. The profit of a bank is the difference between what a bank pays for the money it borrows from depositors and what it receives from borrowers. In most cases, the return on investments, including money on deposit with other banks, is barely sufficient to meet operating costs.

The greater the amount a bank can secure in deposits, the more a bank is able to lend. The more a bank can lend, the greater will be the return on the primary capital of the bank. In other words, if your primary capital is $1 million and you lend $2 million at 10 percent, your return is 20 percent of your primary capital, less what you have to pay to the depositors who gave you the extra million. If your primary capital is $1 million and you lend $2 million at 10 percent, your return is going to be 200 percent on your primary capital, less what you pay to depositors. A bank will, of course, lend at a higher rate than it pays depositors . . . in theory, but not always in practice.

A problem that arises from the aforementioned equation is that an increasing level of deposits in relation to primary capital often leaves less and less of a cushion to protect existing depositors of a bank against a major low loss. Let's say the deposits of Hypothetical Piggy Bank, Inc. are $10 million and the primary capital of the bank is $1 million. These deposits are a liability that must be paid back at some future date. Your deposits are ten times your original capital. Your liability-to-capital ratio is therefore 10 to 1. Now, if you get the job of managing the Hypothetical Piggy Bank, Inc. you may decide you're going to be a really prudent banker and avoid any situation that's going to force you to close your doors. You might then conclude that $2 million of that $10 million should be kept in cash in a highly liquid form, either in the till, or on deposit with some of the really big strong banks. You might also decide that you're going to be even more prudent with your investment policy and put $3 million in Treasury bills which are short-term obligations of the U.S. government. But, you're still going to have to show a profit and, as you know, the return from your investments and deposits may barely meet your operating costs. So your profit is going to come from lending the remaining $6 million of the bank's money to good customers of the bank. Of your original $1 million and your deposits of $10 million, you then lend $6 million, which is theoretically at risk. You would lose your capital and endanger your depositors' money, only if 17 percent of your loans went bad and arrived at money heaven. Placing $6 million of $11 million at risk would be considered excessively prudent banking. Your banking brothers might think you were anticipating the end of the world.

But, suppose you decide you don't really want to be a prudent banker? What you really want to be is whiz kid. You want to rise to the top of the banking profession like a meteor. Managing the Hypothetical Piggy Bank, Inc. may be a stopgap but you really can't wait to start rubbing elbows with the megamoney operators over at Chase. The first thing you're going to set out to do is to attract as many depositors as you can as fast as you can. Naturally, you will have to compete with other banks. You might try a line of nude chorus girls dancing outside the bank each Friday at pay time, but in the final analysis what you'll have to do is pay over the odds for your deposits and attract greedy investors. If you have to pay higher rates than other banks to your depositors, you're also going to have to charge higher rates to your borrowers if you're going to show good profits. Now, that's going to mean taking on some of the riskier loans that other banks have turned down. In addition, you'll probably want to lend out the maximum you can and keep the minimum on hand in cash, T-bills and at deposit with other banks. Of course, you might run the risk of a really big depositor coming in and asking for all his money back at once. You know he would be very unhappy if you told him that he might have to hang on a few months until your loans come in. You can protect yourself against that contingency by matching your loans. In other words, arrange the maturity of your deposits, with the maturity of your loans so that they match up. But, if you do, your bank will be about the only bank in the world that does that. As a potential high-flyer in the banking world, you know the only way to really make profits is deliberately to mismatch by borrowing short and lending long, or sometimes vice versa. A lot depends on the trend of interest rates. That also means adding more risk to the risky loans you'll be making, but risk is what banking is all about nowadays and with a bit of luck and aggressive management, you might find yourself in the enviable position where you have achieved management capabilities of the top ten U.S. banks whose assets (loans) are $650 for every $28 of net worth, a ratio of 23 to 1. Unlike the case of our prudent banker where it would have taken a bad debt level of 17 percent of the loan portfolio to render the Hypothetical Piggy Bank, Inc. insolvent, in the case of the top ten U.S. banks, if a fraction over 4 percent of those assets were turned into bad debts, the system would be insolvent.

However, if no one knew you were insolvent, it would not matter too much if you had stuck to matching your deposit and loan maturities. Then nobody could hit you with a withdrawal scare—as Continential Illinois came near to being hit last year—and you could nurse your bank back into solvency in due course. If worse happened, and you had given up all pretense at matching your maturities which had grown even more mismatched by the freezing of your assets in rollovers with no hope of ultimate redemption *but* your accountant did not insist that you reveal any of this, *then* take heart, for your position would be no worse than that of the top ten banks of the United States, and maybe those of West Germany, Austria, Japan and Swaziland for all I know.

When a bank maintains a high-risk profile and the ratio between investment-type assets (Treasury bills, etc.) to loans continues to fall, the bank becomes progressively more vulnerable. One of the major problems in recent years is that what was once considered an investment-type asset has turned into the most speculative holding in the portfolios of the international banking system. At one time, among the most secure assets a bank could have in the investment portfolio were loans to sovereign borrowers (countries), national government securities and loans to local authorities. These assets were supposedly highly liquid and convertible to cash at any time. The only problem was that loans of that nature acted as a drag on profits. Now we have a situation where many of those loans have turned out to be neither highly liquid nor convertible into immediate cash this side of eternity, but they still act as a drag on profits.

Loans to customers were always considered to be the riskier end of the banking business, but in terms of return, far better than funds held in cash deposit with other banks, or funds invested in long-term U.S. government obligations or Treasury bills. In the constant quest for profits and higher returns on capital employed, banks have consistently run down their investment in U.S. government obligations and cash equivalents over the years. This factor, coupled with the horrifying situation involved in sovereign lending, has increased the danger of many banks becoming insolvent as the number of defaulters required to wipe out a bank's capital has become progressively smaller. In the meantime, loans to customers in ailing industries, coupled with loans to defunct sovereign borrowers, leave banks in a situation where the funds that have been loaned out are not as rapidly convertible into cash as they should be, compounding the problems of potential insolvency with illiquidity.

Loans to customers can be divided into three categories: mortgage loans, business loans and consumer loans. Virtually every quarter, the number of new bankruptcies in America rises, along with the level of bad-debt writeoffs. Personal bankruptcies have also been reaching new all-time highs, encouraged by the most recent bankruptcy laws. Month by month consumer debt writeoffs continue to escalate.

Mortgage lending poses a severe threat because it involves the very dangerous practice of "borrowing short" to "lend long." We have already seen what this practice has done to the savings and loan associations. The escalation in mortgage lending began with the residential property boom.

When a bank forecloses on a mortgage it can often lose a significant part of the principal it loaned if the price of the property is unduly depressed. It is not mere coincidence that prices of residential property have been most depressed when mortgage defaulters and foreclosures were at a peak.

Mortgage lending involves commitments of twenty years or more. There is no long-term market for banking which can be matched against long-term mortgages. Like the savings and loan associations, bankers who have loaned funds on mortgages will have to fund these mortgages through short-term deposits. I have already described how a crash in residential property will come as the depression deepens. This needs no further elaboration. A withdrawal of depositors' funds from banking institutions, coupled with a collapse in property values and a surge of mortgage defaulters, in itself could trigger massive insolvency, without considering the other problem areas in banking.

The seemingly impervious asset of a bank would appear to be cash on deposit and cash held with other banks. Like the case for sovereign lending, maybe it was at one time, but it isn't anymore! If the entire banking system is in a precarious state, then cash with other banks is at risk also. If a major borrower of the Grabbitt & Runn Investment Bank, Inc. goes into default, this could cause the Grabbit & Runn Investment Bank to go into default if the borrower was large enough. If the Glad Hand Bank happens to be a depositor with Grabbit & Runn, then Glad Hand loses its deposit. If Glad Hand's deposit with Grabbit & Runn is big enough, then the loss of that deposit could make Glad Hand insolvent and trigger a moratorium. Now suppose the Happy Mousing Cat Food Company had all of its liquid cash with the Glad Hand Bank. When the Glad Hand Bank goes under, the Happy Mousing Cat Food Company, Inc. loses all its cash, but still owes money to the Consuming Credit Bank . . . and can't pay back. The Consuming Credit Bank may also have had funds on deposit with both Grabbit & Runn and Glad Hand. The default by the Happy Mousing Cat Food Company, Inc. could be the final straw that sends the Consuming Credit Bank down the tubes . . . which at the time may just happen to be holding a large deposit on behalf of the Amalgamated Trust Company for Bankrupts and Insolvents. Needless to say, the story could go on and on . . . and will. It can be strung out into extravagant complexity, and usually is. What I have described is known as the domino effect.

We now have a situation where the balance sheets of the entire international banking community are looking very, very fragile indeed. Furthermore, there are numerous items that are not readily apparent on the surface that must also be considered. As interest rates have moved higher in recent years, the value of fixed interest securities has aggravated what is a highly dangerous situation to start with. A few years ago, interest rates declined to their lowest level. There has been a reasonable fall in interest rates over the past two years but certainly not sufficient to restore the value of fixed-interest securities that may have been held for the past five or ten years. Yet these fixed-interest investments remain on the balance sheets of banks in the United States and elsewhere at cost. In a frightening number of instances, these current values are appreciably below cost levels and, in some cases where the borrower has defaulted, stand at nil. This is another example of where the solvency of bankers has been seriously impaired while current accounting practices permit the presentation of a somewhat misleading picture.

Finally, there is the international portfolio of the bankers. A large number of foreign loans are not actually listed as foreign loans, but appear disguised as investment-type assets in the bank's investment portfolio. Now, remember, investment-type assets are those which are supposed to be readily convertible into cash. However, many of these "investment-type assets" will never be repaid. The extent to which solvency and liquidity have been prejudiced by foreign defaulters who have not been declared in default is difficult to determine. It's something no banker really wants to talk about . . . or think about.

At the end of 1982, the U.S. banking system had $211 billion on loan to the LDCs. Of this Mexico owed $24.4 billion, Brazil $22.8 billion and Argentina $8.9 billion. In all, Latin America accounted for a little less than a third of total LDC lending. The Eastern bloc and the Philippines and South Korea accounted for a further 5 percent. As is implied by Figure 35, loans to developing countries which can at best be described as doubtful account for several times the equity, or net worth, of the money center banks.

As a general rule, the banks have not made serious provision in their published accounts against their sovereign loans. In March 1983, the amounts specified for "nonperforming" loans—loans that are in arrears on interest payments, roughly—were just $13.5 billion for the top ten U.S. banks. For the non-U.S. international banks, no figures are available. In a frank moment, most U.S. bankers would probably admit that their income

	Mexico	Brazil	Venezuela	Other	Total	Total as per cent of equity
Citicorp	3.27	4.36	1.09	1.09	9.81	203
BankAmerica	2.50	2.30	2.00	----	6.80	148
Chase Manhattan	1.69	2.36	1.01	1.01	6.07	220
Man. Hanover	1.72	2.01	1.10	1.97	6.81	245
Morgan Guaranty	1.08	1.69	0.54	0.76	4.07	150
Chemical	1.50	1.30	----	0.74	3.54	182
Cont. Illinois	0.70	0.49	0.46	0.38	2.03	119
First Interstate	0.68	0.47	----	----	1.15	64
Bankers Trust	0.87	0.87	0.47	----	2.23	143
Sec. Pacific	0.53	0.49	----	0.18	1.19	80

Source: The American Banker, March 1983

FIGURE 35   TOP TEN U.S. BANKS' LATIN DEBT EXPOSURE

statements bear no resemblance to the real state of their profitability on real asset values.

There are other specific areas of high danger among the U.S. banks' assets. The energy sector—the domestic oil supply industry—is one, where bank involvement has been put at around $30 billion. Tankers is another, at up to $15 billion. Less visible are letters of credit, which have been issued to guarantee the borrowings of companies and municipalities and the like, whose own credit rating precluded them from borrowing at the rates they wanted. In the early 1980s, at moments when the credit markets were very tight, they issued loans at preferential rates on the basis of bank guarantees stretching out up to ten years or more. One estimate for the amount of such letters of credit is $70 billion. It is an example of a semihidden area of vulnerability.

But as I have said, all that can ever be seen is the tip of the iceberg. The unprecedented buildup of debt in the post-war years to date has left businesses, households, municipalities, even government, in excruciatingly poor financial shape—stretched to the margin in many cases. Real estate, residential, agricultural and commercial, now represents an area of horrifying mismatchment for the whole credit industry. Internationally, sovereign debt is now a more hideous albatross to the lenders than to the borrowers. They at least can just call it a day and default. "Lend not to him who is mightier than thou, or if thou lendest, consider thy loan as lost" was the wise old Florentine adage.

Many see in the growth of the Eurodollar market into a $2 trillion colossus the area of greatest peril for world banking. It may be, because any break in confidence, any sudden withdrawal of funds, will ripple across the whole system of interlinked chains of deposits like toothache.

What is absolutely certain is that the entire U.S., and global, credit structure has reached a pitch of fever which can only be reduced by liquidation. It is a giant carbuncle which must be lanced or hemorrhage internally. It is almost equally certain that the main core of the world's major banks will emerge intact at the end of the day, if only because all the panic money withdrawn from the system at any time must end up with the banks perceived as the most solid.

THE APPROACHING BANK HOLIDAY

Yes, a nationwide bank holiday is in the cards. People will be living in a cashless society. Some will lose their entire savings. What will it be like? Will there be a warning? Can you protect yourself? Let's look back to the 1930s and see what happened then.

The 1920s had not been kind to America's farmers. Low prices for farm products had forced increasing numbers to seek recourse in debt. By the late 1920s up to 85 percent of all farms were mortgaged in some states. In 1929, world overproduction of wheat caused a precipitous fall in price and many, many U.S. farmers were bankrupted. The same applied to cotton. In regions that were particularly badly affected, the strain on the small regional banks was frequently intolerable, and yearly bank failures were numbered in the hundreds in the late 1920s.

Following the Wall Street Crash of 1929, the public was running scared and runs on banks were a regular occurrence. The number of bank failures jumped to 1,352 in 1930, then to 2,294 in 1931. But there was still no domino collapse, such as many feared. The situation was alarming, however, and there were calls for the government to step in and do something. In the fall of 1931, Hoover made an effort to get voluntary cooperation out of the banks. The National Credit Corporation was designed for the banks to pool their resources so that the big strong banks could help the weaker ones out of trouble. But it was a failure. So in early 1932, Congress created the Reconstruction Finance Corporation as a "banker's bank," with a capital of $2 billion, later raised to $3 billion, which was serious money in those days.

That seemed to help, and the rate of bank failures that year was cut to 1,456. But the tide that had been set in motion was unstoppable. The excesses had by no means been wrung from the bloated credit system. To many it must have seemed that things could hardly get worse than they looked in the winter of 1932–1933. The breadlines and soup kitchens, the apple sellers, the Hoovervilles (shanty towns in the city suburbs), the long disconsolate lines in front of closing bank doors . . . that scene of distress and desolation has been painted a hundred times in words and pictures.

Whether it was the result of currency and gold turmoil emanating from Europe at the time or merely the uncertainties surrounding the election of Franklin Delano Roosevelt in November 1932 is not clear. What seems fairly certain is that the 1930s banking crisis began rising to a crescendo during the winter of 1932.

As had been stated year after year since the depression began, most commentators were claiming the depression appeared to be bottoming out in the spring of 1932. Wholesale prices in the United States stopped falling. In July 1932 industrial production picked up. Gross investment hit bottom. An upturn was anticipated. Charles Kindleberger describes the background quite succinctly in *The World in Depression*:

> Gross domestic investment in the Unites States amounted to $16 billion in 1929. It fell to $1 billion in 1932 and net investment . . . to $66 billion. Inventories declined, durable goods wore out, depreciation reduced fixed capital. At some point, gross investment turns up again and the acceleration principle comes into its own. With purely financial theories of the business cycle, there is no need for the upturn. Liquidity squeezes, bank failures, price declines have no natural limits until the monetary system has been entirely wiped out and the system is converted to barter. With gross investment close to zero in 1932, the system was ready for an upturn. It was first necessary, however, to have an apocalyptic climax of bank failures.

The Reconstruction Finance Corporation was set up early in 1932 with $3.5 billion of government money. The scheme was intended to provide support for ailing banks and other large corporations that were having difficulties. In September 1932, the RFC published the figures for its first six months of operation. The sum that was intended to provide the substructure for America's entire financial system was seen to have virtually no effect. Over $1.5 billion of the $3.5 billion had already been lent by the RFC while banks and corporations were still falling like tenpins. When the details of those loans were published and the inadequacy of the measures fully recognized, the financial community was horrified. Runs on the banks intensified. Residents of the state of Nevada were the first to panic. Hordes lined up outside the banks to draw their money out. Many were disappointed. In October 1932 the state of Nevada closed all its banks, unable to meet the demands of depositors. Nevada was the first of several states to declare a bank holiday.

By January 1933 the panic had spread to Iowa. In early February, a feud between Henry Ford and Senator James Couzens over two rival groups of Detroit banks required the governor of Michigan to close the banks in order to prevent Ford from withdrawing a large deposit. By mid-February six more states were forced to suspend banking operations. A week later, the banks were closed in New Jersey. During the first three days of March sixteen states declared a bank moratorium. On the eve of Roosevelt's inauguration, Governor Lehman closed the banks of New York. From February 1, 1933, through March 4, the Federal Reserve Bank in New York lost $756 million in gold; it called in $709 million from other Federal Reserve banks which were also the objects of heavy runs from depositors.

It was a crisis of confidence which borders on the absurd. On the afternoon of Friday, March 3, 1933, Herbert Hoover made a desperate attempt to have Roosevelt join him in some form of proclamation reassuring the American people that the banks were fundamentally sound. Hoover believed that a part of the mood of panic was due to public distrust of Roosevelt's as yet undisclosed policies. Hoover also had a long abiding faith in the soothing qualities of exhortations from high places, not unlike some of America's recent senior executives. Roosevelt distrusted the effect of such incantations and refused all of Hoover's entreaties. Roosevelt did not want to commit himself to any program of action until he had the power to act. Although he had been elected president in November 1932, the government would not be his to command until March 4, 1933. In the meantime, news continued to pour into the Treasury of further bank runs and closings in various parts of the country. Reports revealed that during only one week another quarter-billion dollars had been drained out of the system and that the cash reserves in the nation's operating banks had dwindled to a mere $6 billion. At the time there were holders of savings account passbooks totaling $41 billion who wanted their money right then and there.

By Saturday, March 4, twenty-two states had declared either total or partial suspension of banking activities. It was clear to the men at the Treasury that the American banking system had by then reached a stage where it was completely unable to withstand the strain of even one more business day. As the control of the government changed hands on the Washington portico during that fateful day, the financial heartbeat of the greatest capitalist nation on earth had virtually come to a stop. Three major decisions were taken by Roosevelt. The first was to declare a national bank holiday and close all of the banks in the United States. The second was to call Congress into special session in order to decide how best to reconstruct the U.S. banking system. The third was to summon a group of the nation's leading bankers to Washington enlisting whatever help they could give. Ironically, the legal statute that Roosevelt invoked for the purpose of closing the banks was called the "Trading with the Enemy Act of 1917."

Initially, the bank holiday was intended to last for four days but it was later extended to eight days. A set of temporary procedures was adopted for deciding which banks would reopen after the holiday, which was intended to allow sufficient time for a close examination of the soundness of individual banks before their gradual opening.

Now what do you think it was like to wake up to a society that was cashless with every bank in the nation shut on Monday, March 6? What did it feel like when you suddenly came to realize that all the money you had was the cash and change in your pocket and that once that was spent there was noplace that you could go to get anymore? Would you be afraid to walk out on the street in dread fear of hysterical mobs rampaging through the city, storming banks with crowbars and dynamite, looting stores for food, money and weapons? Would you be tempted to bury the family jewels in the backyard and sit beside your door with a shotgun across your lap to repel invasion from the hungry mobs? Well, if that's the picture you envisage, you can be assured that the reality of the situation was not like that at all.

There may have been a few who panicked. There were probably some individuals who rushed in disbelief to their banks to find out if it was really true. Here and there you may have found a frightened housewife scraping together all the cash and change that could be found, converting it into a hoard of canned goods at the local grocery store. But these were the exceptions rather than the rule. Grim, even tragic, though the closing of the banks was, people often laughed and made jokes of their common dilemma . . . at least at the beginning.

As you can guess, the experiences endured by people in a moneyless society were immensely varied. Salesmen, stranded in cities away from home, would rummage through their sample cases selling whatever they had at high discounts in order to raise enough cash for a railroad ticket. Businessmen had to meet their payrolls with post-dated checks, promissory notes, company-backed scrip or even merchandise from their shelves. Hotels, restaurants, grocers, dairies, drugstores and gasoline stations went on an all-credit basis for their regular customers. Before long, the most critical shortage was not money per se but currency in usable denominations. If all you had was a twenty-dollar bill in your pocket and you wanted to buy a packet of cigarettes or ride on the subway, you were as good as broke unless you wanted to pay twenty dollars, less whatever change happened to be available for either of these privileges.

Shopkeepers often cruised the streets in search of newsboys or apple vendors who could sell them some change for paper money. The going rate for a dollar bill was eight cents in change. If you had coinage you could even buy bigger discounts on the larger notes.

Commuters who regularly rode short distances on the Long Island Railroad discovered they could raise a bit of cash and coinage by redeeming their commuter tickets. The cash reserves of the Long Island Railroad were subsequently drained. The promoters of a major boxing tournament at Madison Square Garden in New York announced that it would accept any reasonable and usable barter in exchange for tickets so they could fill up the house. It was said that included in the vast array was a pair of silk panties and a solid gold toothpick. Movie houses were empty. There were usually more ushers than people. One hotel in the Chicago Loop area decided it was going to launch a benevolent "stay now, pay later" scheme. After a few days they found the majority of their customers were former habitués of the nearby skid row.

But it certainly wasn't all fun and games. The humor of the situation wore thin fairly quickly. The depression had caused such severe hardships among so many people that very few wage earners could afford to miss a single payday without encountering severe distress. The depression brought a hand-to-mouth existence for a large number of people.

Applications for Home Relief soared. My mother was among the applicants. Thousands of Americans were suffering from hunger and cold. In Detroit the bank holiday entered its fourth week. Business activity dropped 60 percent during those four weeks. Workers with checks in their pockets that couldn't be cashed fainted on the job for lack of food.

In several states, barter was the only means of survival. People were often unwilling to accept any currency of any kind. They just wanted food and goods. Some states and municipalities began to print their own money. The city of Cleveland had its own dollar bills signed by the mayor and the city treasurer. A three-cent stamp had to be put on one of these bills each time it changed hands. When a bill had acquired thirty-six stamps the city promised to redeem it for "real money." There were many other innovative means for exchange. Telephone slugs, postage stamps, bus tokens, subway tokens, foreign coins and even cigarette coupons and baseball cards all played an important role in this "funny money" growth bank holiday when no other means of exchange was available.

On Monday, March 13, eight days after President Roosevelt instigated the bank holiday, banks began opening their doors once again. Treasury officials divided the nation's 5,000 Federal Reserve member banks and 14,000 nonmember banks into three categories of relative solvency. The Class A banks, which numbered 2,400, were considered to be sufficiently solvent so they could begin operations immediately. It was deemed that Class B banks would need some sort of financial support before they could reopen. The majority of banks were in the Class B category. Class C banks, which numbered about 900, were to remain closed under a "conservator" appointed by the Treasury. Most of the Class C banks never opened their doors again. It has been estimated that 14 percent of the aggregate amount of depositors' money was lost.

What causes the kind of panic that can bring an entire nation's banking system to a stop? "I remember the Bank Holiday," recalled Arthur Robertson, a prominent businessman, to Studs Terkel in *Hard Times*. "I was one of the lucky ones. I had a smart brother-in-law, an attorney. One day he said to me, 'I don't feel comfortable about the bank situation. I think we ought to have a lot of cash.' About eight weeks before the bank closings, we decided to take every dollar out of the banks. We must have taken out close to a million dollars." He was early as well as lucky. It is a question of confidence.

As Roosevelt's right-hand man, Raymond Moley, reminisced to the same author, "It's a crisis of confidence. People panic and grab their money. There's a story I like to tell. In my hometown, when I was a little boy, an Irishman came up from the quarry where he was working, went into a bank and said, 'If my money's here, I don't want it. If it's not here, I want it.' " And in the end, one bank collapse leads to a chain of domino failures. David Kennedy, later Treasury secretary under Nixon, recalled that in the wake of the closing of the Bank of the United States (of ill repute), 200 smaller banks closed—"because of the deposits in that bank from the others."

Nowadays people think it could not happen. We have the credit card for a start. No reason why Visa should not be honored. And you have the FDIC, the Federal Deposit Insurance Corporation, founded in 1933, which guarantees bank deposits up to $100,000. But it *does* happen. How did Penn Square go bankrupt in 1982? What about Seafirst Corporation, which failed this year despite a $1.5 billion credit lifeline from a group of major banks? And the Texas banks of Mr. C. H. Butcher? The $100,000 insurance is little comfort if your deposit is $1 million: runs start with the big money, the "lucky" guy with the brother-in-law. It is a question of confidence. We have seen that debts go bad. Who can be confident they are good, when the LDCs' plight is worsening every day?

Can anyone say with any degree of certainty that a crisis of confidence, sufficient to close all of the nation's banks, is not imminent? I believe it is not a matter of "if" . . . just a matter of "when."

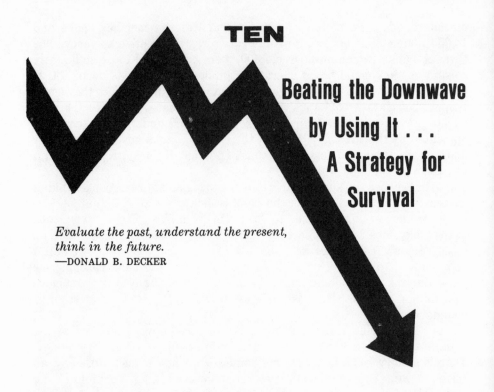

TEN

Beating the Downwave by Using It . . . A Strategy for Survival

Evaluate the past, understand the present, think in the future.
—DONALD B. DECKER

According to ancient mythology, the nymph Echo fell madly and hopelessly in love with the handsome youth Narcissus. She gave her love freely and willingly, but, in time, discovered her love was unrequited. Echo wept and pined at first, but her sorrow soon turned to a desire for vengeance. Accepting that her love for Narcissus was in vain, she demanded of the gods that Narcissus be punished for not loving her as she had hoped. Her wish was granted. Narcissus was made to fall in love with his own image reflected in a pool. He became mesmerized by it. Narcissus gradually wasted away, and perished, while gazing at his own reflection.

The gods of Greek mythology were a tricky sort. Although they sympathized with Echo's grief, they had little sympathy for her desire to inflict vengeance on poor Narcissus, whose only crime was a lack of desire for her. Echo's vindictive behavior certainly did not escape the action of the gods who condemned her to solitude, wandering through the hills, unseen but not unnoticed, fated to repeat continually "the last sounds which fell upon her ears."

There may be a corollary to Echo's fate in what has been happening in the world over the last few years. Large numbers of people seem to have been echoing the words of politicians, who spew forth optimism in an effort to placate the electorate. It seems that very little effort is being made to determine the validity of hopes for economic recovery and other excursions into wishful thinking.

Professional propagandists are fully aware that the public is always prone to believe what is palatable, and what it prefers to believe to start with. It is easy to be optimistic when almost everyone else is; it is also easier to echo optimistic sentiments than to seek out a scenario which may be pessimistically different from the official line. Politicians and others with a vested interest take full advantage of this tendency. As a result, very few people are prepared for the inexorable difficulties which occur with unfailing repetition. Since the early part of 1980, politicians have been promising improving conditions the world over. Others have echoed their sentiments. But the global economy has steadily deteriorated, and continues to do so. Many people have allowed themselves to be sheltered from reality by merely an echo.

Falling in love with your own image or opinions can be no less dangerous than the fate of Narcissus when it comes to planning your future. Successful planning involves the evaluation of circumstances as they exist rather than the way we would like them to be, or the way we have perceived them in the past. The only certainty we really have is the certainty of change. Narcissus and Echo could have avoided disaster had they been a little more open-minded, and a good many people are likely to do far better for themselves in the period ahead if they avoid the temptation to echo what they have heard.

I have often been reproached for making myself unpopular by telling people the things they don't like to hear. I could win a lot more friends and influence a greater number of people by telling them what they love to hear, even if it is a lie. But I will not.

I have spent most of my life enjoying the fruits of the upwave, the long prosperity which allowed me to borrow, speculate and steadily improve my standard of living. But all good things must end. As an investment adviser, it is my responsibility to determine when that end might come.

The upwave that began after the Great Depression of the 1930s ended in 1972. The recession that followed the end of the upwave from 1973 to 1975 was classic in every respect. The system experienced its biggest shock since the 1930s with the world economy contracting for much longer and falling far steeper than had ever been anticipated. The length and depth of the recession was greater than any seen throughout the post-war era. I recognized that recession as the type that always follows an exceptionally long period of prosperity, signaling the terminal stage of that prosperity as it has for over 200 years. But that was only the initial warning sign. The downwave had begun but people were going to get one last bite of the cherry of prosperity before the long sad years involving depression came along. The secondary prosperity was immediately around the corner as the 1973–1975 recession drew to its close. The secondary prosperity is the phase that usually provides the longest and strongest bull markets. Writing for subscribers to *Investors Bulletin* in late 1974, I told them to expect a share boom and economic recovery beginning in early 1975. Both the U.S. and the U.K. stock markets have duly fulfilled my forecasts and expectations.

But the secondary prosperity is over now. The period of a gradually declining plateau of economic activity will soon become another great depression as we now teeter on the brink of monetary collapse. We are faced with the prospect of the worst depression of this century, possibly the worst since the beginning of the Industrial Revolution. What that means in simple language is . . . breadlines, apple stands, bankruptcies, panic, rioting, anxiety, business foreclosures, the depletion of capital, bank failures, ruin, worry, joblessness, hunger, desperation . . . affecting at least 50 percent of Americans, possibly more. Yet, at the same time, there will be many opportunities.

The symbol for crisis in Chinese is composed of two separate symbols which represent two separate words. One of those symbols represents the word "risk," the other "opportunity." It is just conceivable that what is perceived by many as a period of crisis on the horizon could well turn out to be the most rewarding period ever for a large number of people. It is a fact that those who face problems and prepare for them courageously are most unlikely to experience them.

HOW TO STOP WORRYING AND LEARN TO LOVE THE DEPRESSION

The traditional view of the depression of the 1930s and depression in general is of hordes of people on the relief lines and "hunger marches." A closer study of the period of the 1930s shows that hardships were certainly not suffered by everyone. It is true that 25 percent of the workforce of America was unemployed. But 75 percent was employed and those with steady jobs enjoyed a rapid increase in their standard of living through the depression. While a raise in salary may have been difficult to come by, the price of goods and services fell steadily in those years, which meant you were getting a de facto increase in your salary each and every week without ever asking for it. It may seem hard to believe but the dollar in your pocket was actually increasing in value, buying more and more.

A study of the 1930s along with that of previous depressions is by no means a study in black. It is one of contrasts. We see America impoverished and unemployed. But we can also see America embracing a bustling society, the erection of skyscrapers and housing estates along with suburban luxury mansions and cocktail bars gleaming with chromium trim. The 1930s also saw the widespread introduction of automobiles, electric ovens, radios, rayon underwear and talking movies. It was a depression for many, but not for all.

High unemployment during the depression resulted in a redistribution of income from the unemployed to the employed. The man with a steady job fared well. The demise of the old staple industries brought businessmen face to face with economic reality, and gave a new sense of urgency and action to innovation. Businessmen who took advantage of the emerging industries of the 1930s built fortunes that lasted for decades. Labor productivity during the depression rose faster than at any time this century. Most of the growth in productivity was in the "new" industries, including chemicals, electrical engineering, vehicles, artificial fibers, precision instruments, paper and printing and utilities. Often new industries grew out of old industries, the tangible results of modernization.

Rayon production, for example, advanced sharply during the 1920s and continued to increase during the 1930s. But most important of all was the automobile industry. Beneath the surface of sluggishness and depression, all the way through until 1933, the automobile industry provided an important element of dynamism. By 1938, the automobile industry in the United States was the largest single consumer of steel output, absorbing 51 percent of all produced; of malleable iron, absorbing 53 percent of all produced; of alloy steel, absorbing 54 percent of all produced; of plate glass, absorbing 68 percent of all produced; of rubber, absorbing 80 percent of all produced; and of gasoline, as the car industry absorbed 90 percent of all produced. The auto industry, down to the eve of World War II, helped blunt the effects of depression to some degree and then sustain recovery. Directly and indirectly, the sectorial complex of the auto industry was a continuing vital "spring of technical progress" prior to the depression, through the depression and beyond.

During the depression years there was also a revolution in electricity production and consumption. So powerful was the trend in electricity production that the period of the Great Depression is reflected as merely a retardation in the rate of growth. The number of kilowatt hours corresponding in cost to one ton of coal used for household purposes increased by nearly 25 percent between 1929 and 1935 in the United States. The increase in the efficiency of electricity production was the basis for the emergence of a mass market in electricity consuming durable goods that proceeded rapidly in the United States throughout the depression years. Although electricity production itself is (like oil refining) a highly capital-intensive industry, the whole sectorial complex, including the building of power stations and lines, generators, radios, vacuum cleaners, refrigerators, irons and other electric-powered household gadgetry of high mass consumption, helped absorb the bulk of the American workforce during the depression.

Higher production and efforts to stimulate demand brought a marked fall in the prices of goods and services. Between 1929 and 1933, the cost of living fell by just over 25 percent in the United States. The average price of a popular family car fell by a similar amount during that period. In 1935, about one in every two families owned an automobile in the United States. It probably was either a holdover from better days or a secondhand car purchased for about $300. There was always someone in the family who was likely to be a good enough mechanic to grind the valves, change the oil, patch the tires and perform the majority of the tasks that were needed to keep the car in running order. It is said that the alleged mechanical genius of the American male undoubtedly owes much of its validity to the depression.

Britain, a country that suffered worse than most during the depression, overtook France as the largest producer of motor vehicles in Europe in 1930. While unemployment in Britain was 26 percent of the workforce, the number of electric stoves sold in the country rose from 75,000 in 1930 to 250,000 in 1935. The number of radio receivers in Britain increased from around 500,000 in 1930 to nearly 2 million by 1937.

After dispensing with the evening meal as quickly as possible, a ritual in millions of homes all over the world during the depression was to gather the family around the radio. Radio in the thirties occupied a place in family life comparable to that of television today. Programming was arranged to appeal to the housewife during the daylight hours. The housewife was offered a mixture of melodrama and helpful discussions on a wide range of feminine interests.

Helen Trent was a fictional heroine of one of the more endurable soap operas. The radio station was once showered with a bushel of get-well cards when the script required her to be in the hospital for a couple of installments.

In the late afternoon there was a wide variety of children's programs. These ranged from "Uncle Wiggly," who read stories for the tiny tots, to the hair-raising adventures of "The Lone Ranger" and "Superman." The prime evening hours were, naturally, reserved for top-rated newscasters like Floyd Gibbons, comics like Fannie Brice, along with items of a meatier texture. A poll by *Fortune* magazine in the late 1930s showed that people preferred getting their news by radio than by reading it in newspapers. Of course, this helped radio flourish since the growth in the number of radio sets meant advertisers had an expanding audience on radio, as opposed to newspaper advertising where the number of readers steadily contracted through the 1930s.

Despite the depression, the music on the variety shows like the "Chase and Sanborn Hour," the "Kraft Music Hall" and the "Maxwell House Showboat" demonstrated a chumminess in the air epitomized by the songs of Kate Smith. People gathered around their radios to be soothed by a sweeter and more sentimental kind of music than that of a decade earlier. For popular music in the grand style there was André Kostelanetz. Vocalists with the big bands developed a soft upper-class crooning style, perfectly elocuted. Rudy Vallee sang just that way. His voice delighted millions the world over.

Radio had a truly phenomenal growth during the 1930s, particularly in the United States after it was commercialized in 1920. During the depression, radio was considered to be on the threshold of a "Golden Age." It attracted top stars from the entertainment world and concert artists who were among the highest paid in the land. Such was the demand for "escapism" in any form.

THE BETTER PAID

During the depression professional workers increased rapidly as a percentage of the workforce and also in relative importance. This was the necessary offshoot of the rise in the new technologies in the chemical industry, rayons, electrical equipment, aircraft, as well as large-scale administration. Although the number of professional workers remained a small proportion of the working population of America, their absolute numbers increased dramatically as people rushed to acquire the new skills in order to better their chances for permanent employment. The biggest growth was in professionally trained employees in industrial firms and in local or federal government agencies provided there was a specific skill that could be employed. Technicians, draftsmen, supervisors, progress chasers, professional engineers and scientists were in great demand and commanded exceptionally high salaries, relatively speaking, while unemployment soared and wage rates declined across the nation. The brunt of the unemployment problem fell on the rank-and-file employees, where job losses mounted and salary cuts threatened those who remained in employment. For the skilled and the semiskilled real incomes steadily rose. In twenty-five leading manufacturing industries in the United States, the following is a record of monetary, and real, average hourly earnings during the period June 1929–March 1933.

It can be seen in Figure 36 that money wage rates continued to be maintained at almost the par of the peak secondary prosperity until the latter half of 1931, while real wage rates actually increased by over 10 percent during the depression years. For skilled workers and the professional classes, the growth in real wages was far higher.

During boom times and hard times there are always those who possess and accumulate wealth. It is true that those with million-dollar incomes numbered 207 in 1925, rising to 290 in 1927 and finally a record 513 in 1929 as the big bull market gushed blood money to all and sundry from every

AVERAGE HOURLY EARNINGS IN 25 MANUFACTURING INDUSTRIES
(100.0 = 1929)

	MONETARY	REAL
June 1929	100.0	100.7
December 1929	100.0	99.8
June 1930	100.0	102.7
December 1930	98.1	105.3
June 1931	96.1	111.0
December 1931	91.5	110.0
June 1932	83.9	108.2
December 1932	79.1	105.7
March 1933	77.1	108.3

FIGURE 36

office. But, by 1930, the number of individuals with million-dollar incomes had shrunk to 150 as the blood drained out of the bull. By 1931, the number was down to 77 and by 1932 there were a mere 20 Americans with an income of $1 million or more. The stock market that had produced so many millionaires during the 1921–1929 period had come full circle. By the end of the era the number of Americans with million-dollar incomes was at precisely the same level as 1921. Of course, those who made and lost were the nouveau riche. The massive concentration of capital among the older, well-established American families remained and was enhanced. Millions of dollars had been stashed away in that final push in Wall Street, for not everyone lost money in the crash.

During the early 1930s the rich were still indubitably rich. It has been estimated that 5 percent of the population with the highest incomes received about one-third of all the income. In fact, the proportion of personal incomes received in the form of interest, dividends and rental income from property, broadly speaking, of the well-to-do was about twice as great as in the years following World War II. On the whole, consumption was maintained by the wealthy, even if some of it had to come from reducing investment or temporarily spending capital. There was little sign of austerity for the rich.

The deep contrasts during the 1930s were divided by class and locality. In many areas of the United States it would be an understatement to describe conditions as horrifying. In other areas the effect of the depression was minimal. There was the glamorous side of the depression—the mansions on Long Island, the wild parties, the champagne and an endless stream of new debutantes entering the social scene throughout the depression years, filling the Stork Club and the Copacobana in New York.

London entered the 1930s with all the outward signs of opulent prosperity, and continued to do so in many areas. Throughout the 1930s, the London season remained in full glory, including the ritual of the debutantes' presentation at court in white dresses and ostrich feathers. A society or county family with a daughter of marriageable age in England was expected to provide the "coming-out" dance. Each dance cost several thousands of dollars, not including the cost of the dinner parties which the average deb was required to attend during the May to July season in London.

The fashionable world of the socialites of the 1930s with their clubs, parties and chic luxury mansions and apartments, continued to stamp a brittle smartness on Long Island and Park Avenue. Those catering to the rich prospered. Many were totally oblivious to the depression.

In many areas of the United States and in the prosperous luxury areas of Florida, California and New York, it seemed as if a large number of people refused to face the very existence of the depression. It has been said that the bank holiday of 1933 brought a certain kind of joyous, devil-may-care mood. People were determined to get by, somehow. The attitude of the times seemed to be based on the theory, "Things have gotten so bad, they just have to get better."

Barter became very popular, almost as popular as the various forms of entertainment. People would trade food and vegetables for movie tickets and tickets to variety shows. In 1932 a group called the Irish Players opened in Chicago and attracted a huge audience. People took potatoes to the box office and exchanged them for tickets. In general, musicians and entertainers fared well, either in terms of income, benefits in kind or both.

There was a new emphasis on popular democratic enjoyment among the lower and middle classes who had jobs. The general surroundings were more decorous than in the twenties, while a far more gentle spirit prevailed. There seemed to emerge a new camaraderie among people. The bright young things of the twenties had become the young couples of the thirties with families ensconced in their suburban houses. The wide-open-air parties, reached by gleaming sports cars in the twenties, were replaced by "road houses" and drive-in movies offering wholesome entertainment for all the family.

During the 1930s, the cult of the body suddenly became popular. Health centers were opened all over America. There was a craze for vitamins and anything that could provide a more youthful, healthier look. There was a craze for physical fitness without rhyme or reason. Physical fitness courses proliferated. Exercise machines were widely advertised. Some sociologists believe the craze for fitness and a more elegant style of dress came from the desire to present a better appearance and thus enhance one's employment prospects. Self-improvement in general became a byproduct of the war. There was a great vogue for self-improvement books. "Life is just a matter of good salesmanship" was the message Dale Carnegie sold to 100,000 readers of *How to Win Friends and Influence People*. Walter B. Pitkin helped to alleviate the fears associated with growing old in his book, *Life Begins at Forty*, another best seller. People sought self-improvement through the reading of history and biography, in which there was a marked revival of interest. Along with the chroniclers of the past were those authors who ventured to peer into the future. Lawyers, economists and engineers such as Stuart Chase, Davinia Coyle, John T. Flynn, Thurman Arnold, Lewis Mumford and others turned to writing as the would-be elucidators of the tangled web of modern society of the 1930s. *The Economy of Abundance*, by Chase in 1934, and *Folklore Capitalism*, by Arnold in 1937, took an irreverent view of the popular dogma of the time and enjoyed brisk sales and wide acclaim.

Hemlines lengthened after 1930. Hats became floppy and the ubiquitous cloche disappeared. Charmeuse and crepe de chine became the fabrics of fashion, and synthetics like rayon gained popularity for their practical features. The effect aimed at was for "sheerness" and "delicacy," particularly in women's stockings of "artificial silk." Long legs were definitely "in." From 1933 onward, there was a revival of the softer line. A great deal of muslin was used in women's clothing, and the "body line" of the previous era was reintroduced. There was a distinct period quality about women's clothes through the 1930s. This was helped a great deal by popular films like *Gone With the Wind*. Regency period and eighteenth-century fashions became exceptionally popular. Crinolined dolls made into telephone covers graced the bedrooms of the ladies of the richer suburbs. "Old Vienna" was also in vogue, and popularized in film and a popular operetta. Princess Marina was considered the best-dressed woman of 1934. Her wedding to the Duke of Kent was the fashion event of the year.

Social conduct involved a new morality. Entertaining was done at home. Married women were discouraged from working. There was greater emphasis on human relationships. For most people, divorce carried a heavy social and moral stigma, as King Edward's supporters found to their surprise in the abdication crisis.

Life went on during the depression for most people. We have been brainwashed into believing the depression of the 1930s represents an evil of the capitalist system under which we must all suffer. Suffering was widespread, but it was certainly not universal, in America or elsewhere. A large number of businesses failed, but many prospered. A large number of banking and financial institutions closed their doors, but most remained open.

While there were deep contrasts in social life during the depression, there were even deeper contrasts in industry. "These are really good times," said Henry Ford in March 1930, "but only a few know it."

In Studs Terkel's superb documentary, *Hard Times: An Oral History of the Depression*, William Benton tells of his career as a director with Benton & Bowles, an advertising agency. "As I solicited business, my chart was a kind of cross. The left-hand line started at the top corner and ended in the bottom of the right-hand corner. That was the stock market index. The other line was Benton & Bowles. It started at the bottom left-hand corner and ended at the top right-hand corner. As the stock market plummeted into oblivion, Benton & Bowles went up into stardom. When I sold the agency in 1935, it was the single biggest office in the world. And the most profitable office. We didn't know the depression was going on."

Benton arranged for the purchase of the "Amos and Andy Show" for Pepsodent toothpaste. The depression never hurt Pepsodent at all as a result of the skill employed in radio advertising. Pepsodent sales doubled and quadrupled. The company was ultimately sold to Lever Brothers at an astounding price, making a fortune for its owner. A similar success story involved Maxwell House coffee. "The Maxwell House Showboat" went on the air in 1933, which was just about the nadir of the depression. Sales of Maxwell House coffee were up by 85 percent in six months and kept right on zooming. Sales soon doubled and quadrupled. Maxwell House also did not know there was a depression on. Many other companies who manufactured a wide range of products did well, including Muzak Corporation, Coca-Cola and Encyclopaedia Brittanica, for far different reasons, each subscribing to a strategy involving progress through catastrophe.

Millions were made in various industries in a way which would not have been possible without the Great Depression. The same will hold true during the great depression of the 1980s, which is now on our doorstep. For those who are able to adjust, the coming depression can be a period of profit, opportunity, increased purchasing power, maintenance of real capital, better living standards, relaxation and a vastly improved quality of life. Believe it or not, each and every one can choose how to approach the current depression, and how to prepare for it.

I firmly believe that the chances of averting the natural course of the long-term economic pattern are no better than infinitesimal. There is absolutely no way the boom and bust, upwave and downwave pattern of economic behavior, which has been repeated for centuries, is suddenly going to change.

I run the risk of attack from critics who may think it illegal or immoral to show people how to profit from a calamity which is likely to cause hardship to millions. Is it immoral to buy your investments when they are cheap, and sell them when they are too high? Is it immoral to buy assets at a fraction of their future value? Is it immoral to postpone buying a house so that you can pick it up at half the price later on? Is it immoral to purchase an undervalued business or underpriced stocks when money is scarce, and you have the money? Is it immoral to save your money and live within your means? In short, is it immoral, illegal or unpatriotic to try to protect yourself, your family and your life savings, the results of a lifetime of toil and effort? These are the things I advocate.

If you believe that wishing will make things so or you believe in luck, or that some mystical power, some "regulation," some government edict, will spare you from the secondary depression, what I have to say will have little meaning for you. If you believe that over the past fifty years politicians have suddenly discovered something that eluded them in the preceding 300 years, preparing for what I believe is in store will appear to serve little purpose. If you are firmly convinced that, no matter what, government should take care of you, or will take care of you, nothing I have to say is likely to change your attitude.

But if you believe that the only help you are going to get is what you provide for yourself; that your personal destiny will be guided by you and no one else; that no one else is going to be more concerned with your personal savings and ambitions than you are, then the strategies I recommend for the next five to ten years could be of inestimable benefit. You may not see the benefits immediately. It could take a year, maybe longer. But the potential rewards are near enough for you to begin making your preparations now.

THE NATURE OF BUSINESS DURING THE DOWNWAVE

In order to plan your personal and financial strategies during the coming years, it is important to understand the drastic changes likely to take place. We are entering a long period of deflation. Deflation means falling prices. The effects of deflation on business are likely to be dramatic. We have lived through the period of inflation, and many assume that deflation, or falling prices, will be a boon to business. This is a misconception.

Coping with deflation is likely to be as difficult as living with constantly rising prices. As the prices of various goods and services level off and start to decline, more and more companies will discover that profits are squeezed, balance sheets are weakened and capital spending plans are thrown awry.

Price deflation is likely to occur far sooner than wage deflation. The benefits from lower labor costs will diminish as companies have difficulty maintaining prices and profit margins. Since prices will be falling faster than labor costs, the unit cost of production will rise as the volume of trade drops. The fall in general prices, and the decrease in volume, will mean that cost increases cannot be passed along to customers.

Deflation will mean that prices will be falling across an extremely broad front, from raw materials to services. The fall in raw material prices will mean that many companies will lose the paper stock profits which helped buoy balance sheets, and were of great assistance in obtaining credit. The fall in asset values will make it more difficult to borrow.

Some industries will be more vulnerable than others over the next two to three years. Industries where costs rise faster than prices, or fall more slowly than prices, will have the most difficulty. Primary industries like mining, steel, copper and metal fabricating will be worst hit. Wage levels have been the most stubborn in these industries, while markets are likely to be among the weakest. Prices for basic products have come down faster than the cost of items used in making these products.

Food retailers will have problems during the early stages of deflation, as rapid stock turnover quickly translates falling wholesale prices into lower shelf prices. The biggest problem for business is that the last link in the chain of costs to weaken during a deflationary spiral is wages.

Generally, when inflation is high, companies can expand profits by holding stocks and gradually increasing them. As inflation declines, so do stock profits. When inflation becomes deflation, these stock profits turn into stock losses. Many companies will find themselves with stock they bought at a higher price than they can now sell their goods. This in turn will add to the squeeze on profits.

Deflation will also aggravate the debt burdens of many companies. When inflation was roaring ahead just as we were about to complete the period of secondary prosperity, many companies were anticipating inflation in perpetuity. Many long-term investment projects were therefore undertaken at high interest rates on the assumption that a continually high rate of inflation would enable borrowing costs to be absorbed. The conventional wisdom suggested that if inflation were to reach, say, 20 percent, as many thought it would, it paid to borrow money at 14 percent, anticipating normal profit margins, on borrowed money, plus whatever the rate of inflation allowed between prices and costs. But with inflation likely soon to level off at 2 to 3 percent, followed by deflation, the cash flow generated by those borrowed funds would be insufficient to service the borrowing costs.

During most recessions, companies cut stocks, and reduce short-term borrowings. Since 1980, businesses have been slashing stocks but short-term borrowings have continued to rise. This is because high interest rates have made long-term borrowing prohibitive for all except government. Many companies have been unable to raise long-term debt, and have had to service the increase in the long-term borrowings by continually rolling over short-term debt. The result has been a steady increase in stock liquidation, and a steady increase in short-term borrowings.

The overall effect is self-feeding. Cuts in expenditure and planned layoffs will mean the depression must deepen. This in turn will mean that the pace of deflation will quicken, eroding corporate cash flows so that more firms in more industries will be forced to cut prices drastically, even though they will not be able to offset cuts by cost cuts. Decreasing demand will mean that companies will be unable to absorb price cuts through increased sales. Many companies will be forced to make further cuts in investment, and will slash payrolls as the economy keeps sliding. The deflationary spiral will ultimately resemble the inflationary spiral to which we have become accustomed, but upside down.

The strategy for businessmen during the downwave is opposite to that for the upwave. Borrowing must be steadily reduced, wherever possible. Borrowing today because rates will be higher tomorrow will be most imprudent. Borrowing must be cut to the bare bones. Cash is king during the downwave.

Many companies have been anxious to increase stocks during the upwave, allowing inflation to maximize both real profits and stock profits. Deflation will be the problem in the months ahead. The wise businessman will keep stocks at rock bottom, just sufficient to meet existing demand. Demand forecasts should be steadily revised, and downgraded periodically if necessary.

THE IMPLICATIONS FOR NEW BUSINESSES

Many businesses began life during the secondary prosperity, when it looked as if the world was returning to normal. In some areas, business opportunities looked marvelous during 1979 and 1980, despite inflation. Say our businessman decided to build a plant capable of producing a fixed amount of chromium-plated Coca-Cola bottles, which were in great demand in 1979 because many believed they would become art treasures, and would be a good hedge against inflation.

Any businessman who decides to form a corporate entity for the purpose of manufacturing goods is likely to use the traditional capital structure at the outset, involving a combination of equity capital and debt. Usually the plant and equipment will be used to secure the debt aspect, such plant and equipment being capable of producing a minimal and optimal amount of goods based on current demand projections for the product to be manufactured. If future demand projections are based on merely an extension of current trends into the future, big troubles could be in store for our embryonic manufacturer.

Say our prospective manufacturer of chromium-plated Coca-Cola bottles borrows $10 million on the basis of debenture capital secured against his factory and has to pay 12 percent interest on the bond to investors, the interest rate being fixed for the life of the bond. In other words he has taken out a twenty-five-year mortgage on his business and will pay 12 percent per annum until he repays the capital. If he is a prudent businessman he will start a sinking fund to be sure that the capital is available at the maturity of the bond. First, it must be recognized that the product that has been chosen is one that may have been popular during the inflationary phase of the cycle but, as a result of changes in consumer attitudes, is no longer going to be popular during the deflationary phase of the cycle. This is not only true of chromium-plated Coca-Cola bottles, but is also true of an extremely wide range of goods and services which are compatible with an inflationary environment but totally incompatible with a deflationary environment. But, suppose more by luck than judgment, our manufacturer of chromium-plated Coca-Cola bottles survives the next decade and there is renewed demand for his product. Then his problems are really going to start.

Ten years from now, it is likely that the cost of setting up a business for the manufacturer of chromium-plated Coca-Cola bottles is going to be a lot less than it is now. To start with, interest rates are likely to be a lot lower than they are now, in which case those who are starting businesses will be able to finance their needs at a lower cost as far as capital is concerned. This, in turn, will help profit margins and cash flow. Given the prospects of a steady decline in property values, rentals and raw material costs, it is likely that a competitor beginning the manufacture of chromium-plated Coca-Cola bottles in ten years will be able to erect his plant and equipment at much lower costs than the manufacturer who erects his plant now. The competitor who starts late in the cycle will also be able to purchase far more modern equipment capable of greater productivity and is also likely to be able to acquire a workforce at a lower cost since the long years of unemployment will have meant a higher premium is placed on having a job than is the case now. The net result is that the entrepreneur who waits until the final stages of the depression or the end of the deflationary cycle will be in a far better position than anyone who starts up in business at or near the inflationary peak. Those who invest in businesses later in the cycle will have the combined benefits of lower overheads and higher productivity, enabling the entrepreneur to sell his goods at a lower cost while operating at a higher profit margin since the costs of production will be lower.

During the latter stages of inflation, price sensitivity barely exists. People stampede into the shops, car showrooms and a wide range of suppliers and retailers, paying whatever prices are asked just to acquire what they want. During the early stages of deflation, such as we have now, price sensitivity for goods and services steadily intensifies. In a price-sensitive environment and when demand is falling, the first major move that is carried out by manufacturers is to cut prices in order to compete with other manufacturers who are also cutting prices. Price competition for the average manufacturer is the kiss of death for any business. In the first instance, those who respond to price competition and start cutting their prices are likely to be competing with others whose manufacturing costs are lower, or with businesses that are about to go bankrupt.

On a global basis, deflation means trade wars as individual countries fight to protect their markets by any means possible. Domestically, deflation means price wars. If a manufacturer has overhead that is lower than that of his competitors he can often cut his prices and still produce a profit if he is in a relatively liquid state. If a manufacturer is forced to cut prices below his production costs in order to move inventories that are eating up credit charges, more often than not he will go bankrupt. During the deflationary spiral of the downwave many firms will be driven out of business, but a nucleus of well-managed firms that are innovative and imaginative, and that plan for the type of environment that lies ahead, will remain highly profitable, left to form the base for the next sustainable recovery, just like the lemmings who remain on shore, devouring the available vegetation while others continue the ritual of mass suicide. Some people make things happen; others watch things happen and a prodigious multitude allow things to happen to them. During the upwave, many businessmen simply ride with the trend, profiting in the slipstream of what the early innovators left behind.

During the remainder of this decade such a strategy will no longer be viable. The rewards of the future will belong to the innovators, the creators, the imaginative, the forward planners . . . those who are capable of thinking independently of the crowd. The great philosopher Kierkegaard claimed progress is made through shocks to the system. During the second great depression of this century, many will be shocked into total inertia, others will be shocked into action.

THE WINNERS OF THE DOWNWAVE

The method most widely adopted to combat price competition and falling prices during the previous downwave was to form monopolies and cartels. Firms combined into increasingly larger companies, fixing prices among themselves once the number of competitors had been reduced. This was particularly widespread during the 1870s and 1880s in the United States, in the era of the magnate, the railroad baron and monopolist. Only the downwave made these activities possible. They never occurred during the upwave, since they were unnecessary with rising prices. Most activity of this type was aimed at limiting the steady erosion in prices by reducing competition.

In the great depressions of the past, industrialists joined with some competitors, and sought to destroy others. Many were destroyed. Markets were divided among cartel members, both geographically and on a percentage basis. John D. Rockefeller set out to create a monopoly in oil. Those who did not join him had to fight, and usually lost. The downwave, with its pressure on prices, provided exactly the right climate for business to seek relief through monopolistic combination, and this can be expected to happen again during the years to come.

In the end, most cartels are doomed to failure. No matter how large the combine, no matter how great the force on the marketplace, economic forces are greater. The one entrepreneur who demonstrated the weakness of cartels and managed to master the nature of the downward spiral better than any other was Andrew Carnegie. Playing the downward price spiral was far from the sole reason for Carnegie's fantastic success, but it was a significant factor, a perfect long-range strategy in which he demonstrated far more diligence and foresight than his contemporaries.

Carnegie's plan was basically very simple. It required tremendous nerve and self-discipline to succeed. The downwave involves long periods of contraction and short periods of recovery. During the brief prosperity that followed the U.S. Civil War, Carnegie began selling his assets and steadily accumulating cash, building his liquidity as quickly as he could. During the next depression, Carnegie held the cash generated during the early part of the depression. As the depressionary trough neared, he began to expand as quickly as he could. Carnegie's core of operations was in steel, and he purchased as much plant and equipment as he could afford to expand his manufacturing capacity. This was roughly opposite to most other entrepreneurs, who were suffering the contraction in demand in what they considered the worst depression in history. The steel industry has habitually suffered worse than most in a depression.

Most businessmen are trend followers. They expand capacity and production while demand is increasing. They cut back when demand decreases. At the trough of the depression in the latter part of the nineteenth century, steel stocks were being slashed. Plant and equipment were being sold for a song. No matter how desperately the steel cartel tried to maintain prices, many broke away and ran in different directions for survival. It must have taken great discipline and enormous courage and self-confidence for Carnegie to have spent huge sums, adding to his steel production capacity while his steel works were idle. Yet he accumulated while his contemporaries were distributing.

There were many offsetting factors in Carnegie's grand design. The materials and goods he needed for production came at bargain prices during the depression. Because he had planned ahead he was highly liquid, with strong assets, and represented a good credit risk. He found it easy to borrow at low interest rates, while many of his contemporaries were poor credit risks and could not borrow at any price.

It was customary for America's steel magnates to meet at least once a year. Then they would set the price of steel to ward off competition, and to ensure that they themselves made an adequate profit. Carnegie boldly announced that he could deliver finished steel to any user at a price far below that which any member of the cartel could afford. As a consequence, he demanded the largest stake in the distribution. Carnegie had singlehandedly broken the steel cartel. Before long, he dominated the entire steel industry.

Andrew Carnegie emigrated to America from Scotland intent on building a fortune. By the age of thirty-four he had amassed several million dollars, owned an iron company, locomotive works, railroads, a bridge-building company and, of course, Carnegie Steel. These were the rewards for acting contrary to those who were failing. These were the rewards for anticipating events, and adopting the appropriate strategy at a time of desperation.

EXPECTATIONS DURING THE DOWNWAVE

Not everyone can be an Andrew Carnegie. But even the wage earner or small proprietor can improve his lot by being able to anticipate changes coming.

As part of the survival kit for businessmen, I have prepared a list of expectations during the downwave, in contrast to the upwave of the previous decade. Top priority is to build liquidity and reduce debt to the bare minimum. Many people feel that if they abide by these old-fashioned rules, they will be missing out on something. This may have been true during the upwave, but it is no longer so. Profitable borrowing comes only in an inflationary environment. The world of the borrower has been turned upside down. Over the past few years those who have raised liquidity, and kept commitments low, have generally done far better than those struggling with accumulated debt costing more and more as the days pass.

Some of the greatest fortunes in history were built during panics, collapses and depressions, when businessmen were able to expand, when cash could be used to purchase assets at five and ten cents on the dollar. Wherever possible, the shrewd businessman should be building his liquidity in anticipation of a similar phenomenon. Study the following expectations for the downwave. The idea is to put yourself in a position to take advantage of the many changes in the business environment that the next few years will offer. You want to beat the downwave by using it.

NORMAL ACTIVITY DURING THE UPWAVE	NORMAL ACTIVITY DURING THE DOWNWAVE
1. Commodity prices soar until it appears that an explosive curve has developed.	Commodity prices enter a long cyclical downtrend.
2. Debts are easy to pay and the rate of debt repayment is low.	Lenders have difficulty in obtaining repayments. Slow payers and defaulters increase.
3. New bankruptcies fall.	New bankruptcies rise.
4. Holders of debt issue do badly, but can get capital repayments.	Holders of debt issue profit handsomely, so long as borrowers are stable.
5. Earnings in life insurance companies rise.	Earnings in life insurance companies fall sharply.
6. The buying power of charities decreases, but new funds come in.	Charities suffer, because new funds fall off, and income declines by more than the likely increase in purchasing power.
7. Buying on credit is very popular and is strongly encouraged.	The creation of debt is abhorrent.
8. Government revenue is brisk, and taxes are easy to pay.	Government has difficulty in collecting taxes.
9. Government expenditure on public services increases as does expenditure by local municipalities.	There is a sharp drop in the standard of public services. Taxpayers form protest groups. Little is accomplished.
10. The derelict element of the community disappears. Soup kitchens are virtually unheard of.	Soup kitchens proliferate. Many self-respecting citizens have to be fed at public expense.
11. This is the era of the nouveau riche.	This is the era of the nouveau poor.
12. There is a sharp increase in trade union membership. Trade unions wield extraordinary powers.	Labor union membership falls. Labor unions steadily lose ground.
13. Salaries lag behind the rise in prices but there is plenty of work.	Salaries stagnate while prices fall. Jobs disappear.
14. Salaries for rank-and-file employees rise faster than the incomes of professional classes.	Salaries for skilled employees in high-tech industries rise rapidly.
15. Workers find easier promotion.	Promotions are slow. Demotions and layoffs are common.

16. Farmers prosper steadily.

Farmers are among the worst hit, and face a long and severe depression.

17. The standard of living in industrial areas improves sharply.

The standard of living in industrial areas declines sharply.

18. Construction in urban centers escalates.

Construction in urban centers is overdone and then checked.

19. Fire insurance losses fall.

Fire insurance losses escalate.

20. Goods are hoarded.

Cash is hoarded.

21. Services like laundries, TV repairs, dry cleaning, auto repairs and home improvements prosper.

There is a sharp decrease in the demand for labor intensive services, and do-it-yourself movements appear.

22. Doctors' fees lag behind price increases, but business increases, and outstanding bills are easy to collect.

Doctors' fees continue to lag. Business decreases, outstanding bills are difficult to collect.

23. Suicides decrease.

Suicides increase.

24. Interest rates rise.

Interest rates fall.

25. There is a decrease in crime against property, but an increase in violent crime.

There is a decrease in violent crime, but more crimes against property, and fraud and deception.

26. The size of life insurance and commercial insurance cover increases.

There is a sharp decline in the amount of insurance cover applied for.

27. Property prices steadily advance.

Property prices steadily fall.

28. Rents steadily increase, but are easy to collect. There is a shortage of commercial property.

Rents fall more slowly than most prices, and are difficult to collect. There is an overabundance of commercial property.

29. During the latter stages of the upwave fortunes are made in equities and collectibles.

During the early stages of deflation, fortunes will be lost in collectibles and equities.

30. Taxes steadily increase.

Taxes will be regularly cut.

31. The rate of savings steadily decreases.

The rate of savings will steadily increase.

32. The number of mergers and acquisitions steadily expands.

There is a standstill in merger and acquisition activity.

Gary Shilling and Kiril Sokoloff produced a Table of Winners and Losers during a period of falling inflation in their most useful book, *Is*

Inflation Ending? Are You Ready? (Copyright © 1983). That table is reproduced with the kind permission of the publishers, McGraw-Hill:

WINNERS	LOSERS
Savers	Individuals and businesses heavily in debt Municipalities
Businesses with little or no debt	Art auctioneers Real estate and commodity brokers
Quality stocks and bonds	Commodities and commodity producers Housing speculators
Producers of proprietary products, where competition will not erode pricing power	Farmland investors Investors in hotels, office buildings and shopping centers Producers of farm equipment
Low-cost producers	Collectibles, objets d'art, antiques and their dealers
Venture capitalists	Previous buyers of tangible asset-rich companies
Research and development	Investment letters which stress trading and speculation Publications geared toward instant gratification
Efficiency and quality control experts	Luxury, foreign-made automobiles Non U.S. government money market funds
Entrepreneurs	Publications oriented toward real-estate speculation French wines and other foreign-produced "collectibles"
Companies that derive profits from increased volume rather than high prices	Foreign investments with an emphasis on natural resources Companies that earlier bought their stock and ran down liquidity
New products and those with the talents to develop them	International commodity cartels Countries with high external debts denominated in U.S. dollars
Pensioners and others on fixed income	Noncompetitive businesses that were shielded from competition by inflation
Marketing and production people	Undercapitalized businesses Advertising activity

U.S.-made automobiles	Bureaucracy, corporate staffs, overhead and staff functions
Conservative investment practices	Regulation-oriented lawyers and publications
The U.S. dollar	Unionized labor in previously regulated industries Washington consultants and lobbyists
Strict family budgeting	Creative finance people Conglomerates
Specialized education, continuing education for professional people, and trade schools	Merger and acquisition specialists and activities Arbitrageurs Those who were overindexed to inflation
Consumers with low debts, high savings and productive jobs	The federal government Newly deregulated industries such as airlines and trucking (initially)
Renters	Many tax shelters
Money market funds backed by U.S. government securities	Firms that merely mark up costs OPEC
Importers	The United Kingdom, Mexico and other non-OPEC oil exporters Executive recruiters
U.S. tourists abroad	Those who rely on government bailouts Companies with long-term, fixed-rate supply contracts Leveraged buy-outs and those who specialize in them
Consumers of imported goods	Joint venture partners of OPEC countries Employees of local governments
Users of internationally traded commodities	Businesses that depend heavily on municipal spending

HINTS FOR BUSINESSMEN

Many businessmen extend credit in order to keep their customers. Others will allow customers to delay payment of invoices for the same reason. This practice could be disastrous for the small businessman who is normally undercapitalized and who could suffer considerably from delayed payment. It would certainly be wise to subscribe to one of the major credit-rating organizations such as Dun & Bradstreet. It would also be wise to consider credit insurance provided your current bad debt ratio would justify the premium, bearing in mind your sales to bad debt ratio is likely to deteriorate in the years ahead. Generally, as a businessman, you must only allow credit to customers who have a superior credit rating even if it means losing business. You're going to lose a lot more than your profit margin if your customer suddenly finds he is unable to pay you. Profit margins can also be eaten up by financing the outstanding invoices that are due you. Larger companies are often the worst perpetrators when it comes to delaying payments during periods of financial pressure. You must be tough and be certain your invoices are promptly paid.

Keep your borrowings to a minimum. Avoid the use of factoring organizations or other forms of alternative credit. Wherever possible, finance your activities through cash flow. Your level of cash flow will tell you about the viability of your efforts. Listen to it. For example, suppose you are a retailer of the latest home computer and decide you want to advertise the product. Do not engage in an advertising campaign that's going to extend your indebtedness. Start your campaign with a small ad. If the return from your ad gives you a profit, then reinvest the profit in a larger ad, retaining a small portion of the profit for your business. Continue this practice until such time as your ads begin to show a loss. That will mean you've saturated your market. If the small ads at the beginning of your campaign fail to produce a profit, the market is telling you that demand for your product is simply not there. If the demand for your product isn't there, all the advertising in the world is not going to create that demand.

If you are in a business where transport is essential, give careful thought to developing your own independent road transport, providing this can be financed through cash flow. You may find that by developing your own fleet of transport vehicles, you're in a position to deliver goods while your competitors cannot, because of a variety of dislocations that can be expected for the period ahead. The ability to effect prompt deliveries could mean the difference between growth and failure in your business.

If possible, concentrate your business activities in areas that are the least likely to be affected by a contraction in demand. If you are in a consumer-oriented business, study local unemployment trends. You'll find they vary enormously from city to city and from state to state. Areas with the highest levels of unemployment are likely to suffer inordinately as the depression continues to bite deeper. The underlying cause for current weakness will be the cause for extended weakness. Remember the South Bronx!

If you happen to own your own business premises, investigate the prospects of a "sale and leaseback." The last thing you want is to have the capital of your business frozen in what is likely to turn out to be a depreciating and illiquid asset. If a "sale and leaseback" cannot be arranged in your locality, consider the sale of your business premises in favor of rented accommodation. The cost of renting is likely to be far less than the return you could get on the free capital as long as interest rates remain at current levels. For quite some time it's likely to be cheaper to rent property than it is to rent money. Your basic objective in the period ahead should be to maximize liquidity and minimize fixed asset investment.

Leasing equipment is likely to be a better bet than buying equipment, particularly for a new business. The improvement in cash flow is likely to supersede the benefits of any depreciations allowance. The ruthless preservation of cash flow will put you in a position where you can purchase goods at vast discounts by paying cash. This will allow you to maintain your profit margins while undercutting your competitors, most of whom will be deeply in debt. You must always be on the lookout for opportunities where you can buy at low cost or reduce your business overheads.

Inventories must be kept at levels sufficient only to meet existing demand. Stock profits will be a thing of the past. Essentially, your business strategy should be geared to volume expansion, turning over your inventory as quickly as possible, even if it means at reduced profit margins.

Reduce the number of your suppliers to the bare minimum. You want to give your existing suppliers every incentive to give you discounts by providing them with a reasonable volume of your business. The bigger the size of your orders to suppliers the greater will be your chances for negotiating lower prices on the goods you need for your business.

There will be a vast labor pool from which you can draw executive talent. Most personnel techniques are completely outmoded. Be on the lookout for imaginative, innovative individuals who will be willing to accept salaries at far lower levels than those to which they have been previously accustomed. Employing people that "make things happen" will be the key to your future success in business. Do not allow preconceptions to affect your judgment. Many talented women will be looking for work in the months ahead. Talk to them. In fact, make a concentrated effort to talk to as many people as possible who may be able to help you with your business. Only the fittest will survive.

Fraud, deception, embezzlement and crimes against property will soar in the years ahead, although crimes of violence will decrease. You must therefore place a very high priority on making certain your business is adequately insured for these contingencies. There's a little story that offers further implications as far as the importance of insurance is concerned but this should not be treated as a recommendation of any kind.

It was during a bright sunny day in mid-July that Sol, on vacation in Atlantic City, meets his long-lost pal, Abe, strolling along the boardwalk.

"Abe! I haven't seen you in years. What are you doing down here? On vacation?"

"Sol! Is it you? I live down here now. I'm retired. Remember the factory? Well, the furniture caught fire and the factory burned to the ground. The insurance company paid me five million dollars. I decided I'd

had enough of the furniture business so I decided to come down here and
retire. What about you Sol? How are you doing?"

"Oh, I'm still in the plastics business. I'm down here on vacation."

The two friends part but the following year both meet in the same
place at the same time again. This time Abe spots Sol first.

"Sol! It's you again. So, you've decided to have another vacation in
Atlantic City?"

"No, Abe. I decided to retire just like you. Remember the plastics
factory? Well, last year we had a flood. The insurance company paid me six
million dollars so I decided to retire too."

Abe became pensive; hesitated; and then whispered gently into Sol's
ear, "Tell me, Sol, how do you start a flood?"

ADVICE FOR PROPERTY DEVELOPERS

For those in the property business there are a number of very special
considerations. During the early 1970s when commercial property seemed
to be heading for trouble, I mapped out a list of strategies intended for
commercial property developers. All of the individuals with whom I am
personally acquainted profited by these strategies at the time. I am now
revising the strategies to include residential property.

▾ If you are currently engaged in the construction of any type of property
development, this should cease. Unsold projects and expansions everywhere should be discontinued regardless of the stage of development,
whether or not foundations have been laid. These projects should be
offered for sale and turned into cash as quickly as possible.
▾ If you are an investor in property you must cut down on your property
holdings and try to make your business more efficient. The prudent
businessman will attempt to cut back on any loss-making items that he
distributes. The prudent property developer will want to cut back on any
properties that are currently producing a negative cash flow, regardless
of what may be perceived as the value of the reversionary interest.
Reversionary interest is likely to turn out to be nothing more than an
illusion.
▾ Creative financing should play an important role in your property dealings. Bear in mind you'll be ahead of the crowd if you're distributing
your low-income-producing properties now. Most will continue to believe
in the sanctity of property investing. If you act quickly, you can make
your low-income-producing properties seem more attractive by offering
them to buyers on what is perceived as reasonable terms. If necessary,
issue a first mortgage and a top up mortgage. If you're dealing with a
private buyer and he defaults, you'll still have the initial deposit along
with whatever payments he made in the meantime to cushion your risk
and you'll also wind up with the property back again. When financing a

buyer it would be best to act on the assumption that he's going to default and arrange your strategy accordingly.

▼ As a general rule, you'll want to raise as much of your outstanding debt as possible through the sale of the less desirable properties that you have and shorten the maturities on the remaining debts. As would be the case for any business, you must strive to improve liquidity so that you'll be in a position to pick up bargains as property prices decline and liquidity gets tighter. Many dealers have been issuing long-term nonrecourse obligations secured against their low income or nonincome-producing properties in order to improve liquidity. Essentially, these are de facto sales.

▼ Owners of commercial properties should carry out an assessment of the nature of their tenancies. Where a tenant is in good financial standing and earning a good profit from the premises he occupies it would be reasonable to raise the rent to the optimal level the traffic will bear. Essentially, renting property is far cheaper than owning property at this time. Any astute businessman is aware of this. There should be little resistance to rent increases in these cases.

▼ As far as residential property is concerned it would be wise to dispose of as much residential property as you can, particularly in the low-priced areas. In times of trouble, mass hysteria will always seek scapegoats. One of the first has always been what is described as the "blood-sucking landlord." As the depression deepens and as troubles surface, property will again become the favorite political football of our leaders. There will be public indignation over the amount of money that has gone into property, depriving industry of investment. The do-gooders will then begin to tamper with tax legislation in an effort to redirect funds away from residential property into industry. Expect a host of controls, one of which will be rent controls. Residential property will be used as a scapegoat to draw attention away from other areas of bureaucratic ineptitude. Rental values and capital values will plunge accordingly.

▼ If you wish to retain some of your property interests concentrate on the top end of the market. Take advantage by providing furnished offices to companies that are doing well. Try to upgrade the rental value of your premises with a minimum of expenditure. A good interior designer can be of inestimable value in this respect. Talent and imagination will continue to command a high premium as will the creation of affluent illusions.

▼ What holds true for commercial premises also holds true for residential premises as far as upgrading rentals is concerned. The luxury end of the furnished rental market will be the most resilient, particularly if taste and imagination are employed. The medium- to lower-priced end of the rented market will be disastrous.

▼ If you want to dispose of your larger property holdings the best way is to concentrate on dealing with those real estate agents that are active in the institutional investment market. Most institutional investors are likely to cling to the illusion of property as a good investment long after most individuals have recognized the futility of it all. The structure of the institutional investment market and the sums involved have regularly encouraged overpayment and poor assessment of risk in a variety of investments.

Institutional investment managers rarely have a talent for reading balance sheets as well as they are able to read pro forma cash flows. They are unlikely to be able to assess operational problems or future potential at terminal junctures any better than they can read balance sheets. They will form a vast market to whom you will be able to dispose of your larger properties.

Many institutional managers have suffered considerably in the fixed-income market and have performed very poorly in the equity market. There is currently considerable demand for property since this is the one area in which most have done well. Most institutional investment managers are not genuine investors. They work for a salary. They think like private investors who are keen to purchase shares after a long rise but, unlike private investors, these managers are investing other people's money, not their own. The incompetence that normally weeds out loss-making amateur investors does not operate among institutional investors.

Institutional investors are human. Like all of us, their first priority is to protect themselves. Attempting to achieve superior performance has little to do with the institutional investment manager's keeping his job, which is the first priority. They protect themselves by doing subconsciously (and/or consciously) what they think everybody else is doing. No institutional investment manager is going to get fired for losing 50 percent of the value of the portfolio by investing in property if all of the other managers did the same. On the other hand, the investment manager could well lose his job if he loses a sizable chunk of his fund by investing in bonds while his peers were investing in property. The institutional investment manager has everything to lose (his job) and very little to gain by attempting to achieve superior performance by leaving the herd.

The herd is likely to remain mesmerized by property until the very end of the collapse, when the decline in property values becomes ostentatiously obvious and most believe that property investment is the most foolhardy and dangerous thing anyone could do. In the meantime, institutional investment managers will continue to follow the trend of mass opinion and provide a relatively constant market for the larger properties. "Property is safe," they will say. "Property isn't volatile like other markets. Property is a basic necessity. They're not making land anymore."

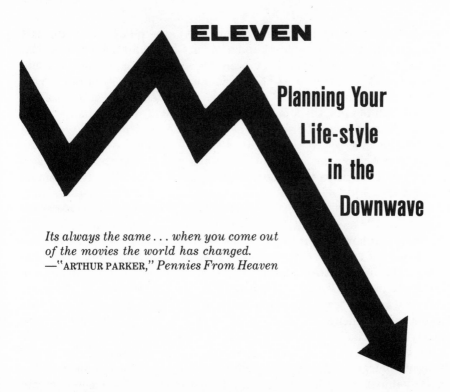

ELEVEN

Planning Your Life-style in the Downwave

Its always the same . . . when you come out of the movies the world has changed.
—"ARTHUR PARKER," *Pennies From Heaven*

"I want to live in a world where the songs come true," says Arthur Parker, antihero of the MGM hit musical, *Pennies from Heaven* starring Steve Martin and Bernadette Peters. The time is 1934. The place is the suburbs of Chicago. America is eyebrows-deep in the worst depression of its history. People pack the movie houses, flock to the dance halls and rivet themselves before their radio sets, trying to get a glimpse of the other side of the rainbow. The pink-chiffon-candy-floss world that dreams are made of, as portrayed by the popular songs with optimistic lyrics that promise love, romance and happiness, is certainly preferable to the humdrum day-to-day existence that has become a seemingly permanent life-style for many.

But this is 1983. The place is Detroit. The movie is over. It's had its run in the big cities and the suburbs. *Pennies from Heaven* is now just another episode in cinema history. The onset of hot weather marks the fourth anniversary of Detroit's economic slump. A kind of economic solstice could be observed with the opening of a second Capuchin Brothers' soup kitchen. Detroit is in a depression. It has lived with the depression for so long now that the 1.2 million inhabitants wonder whether the economic recovery that politicians have been talking about will ever come to visit Detroit. Many other people in many other cities are thinking along the same lines. When the State of Michigan began taking applications for 25,000 minimum-wage summer jobs for young people, Detroiters put in enough applications to

227

take all of the jobs with none left for anyone in the rest of the state. But most people have a television set and a radio. Cinema attendance has been creeping up and the discos don't seem to be suffering unduly. The big automakers have applied a bit of muscle and made Detroit the last downtown where a Grand Prix auto race is held and offshore speedboat racing has begun. In the fall, the Montreux Jazz Festival attracted musicians and jazz fans from all over the world. The movie is over. Ironically, the world hasn't changed.

I began writing this book in the summer of 1979. At that time, I was forecasting a recession that would ultimately lead to a 1930s-type depression or worse. I am no longer forecasting a depression. The depression is here. It's in Detroit, Chicago, New York, Los Angeles and many other areas of America. It's only a matter of how deep the depression bites, how far it spreads and how long it lasts. My estimation is that it will bite deeper, spread further and last longer than anybody believes possible. When the depression is over, in two to three years time, then the further implications of the downwave will be the inexorable force that shapes people's lives.

There are two ways to become poorer and two ways to get richer. You become poorer when your income goes down or when your income goes up but buys less. You become richer when your income goes up or when your income goes down but buys more. Many people have seen their incomes rise strongly during the inflationary years but they have been impoverished just the same. In the years ahead, the majority of the workforce will remain employed. Even during the worst years of the depression to come, I am certain that the majority of people who hold on to their jobs and businesses will be better off than they were during the most recent period of excruciatingly high inflation.

As the depression deepens there may be an improvement in some incomes but the benefits in the period ahead will come from the dramatic fall in the cost of living which I envisage. The price of food and manufactured goods is likely to fall most. This will bring a real improvement in the standard of comfort for the bulk of the community, especially the middle classes. There will be a complete change in emphasis on labor relations. No longer will the worker be able to assume it is his inalienable right to a continued series of wage increases if he is merely physically present on the job. The premium will shift from the worker to the job. Most people will be happy just to have a job whether or not there are prospects for advancement or wage increases. Salary increases in most industries and in government service will be difficult to come by.

Family units are likely to be smaller. Those who are working will benefit from a correspondingly higher disposable income and greater affluence than was experienced during the 1970s when the prices of goods and services rose beyond the reach of many households. Keen price competition in the consumer durable industries will mean that more people will have more radios, televisions sets, home computers and the like than ever before even while the depression deepens.

Outside the consumer areas, the output of many of the old staple industries such as steel manufacturing, machine tool makers and heavy industry in general, will decline to their lowest levels ever as we see a relentless shift of many basic industries to developing countries and a massive dislocation of traditional employment patterns. Yet, during the next four years, "new" industries will be forging ahead at an unprecedented rate. A new economic order will emerge in the wake of the global depression driven by an "information revolution" that has its roots in the rapidly expanding microelectronics industry and associated technologies. With this new economic order will come untold opportunities for those who can recognize the trend and adjust to the changing life-styles, attitudes and the inevitable technological innovations that are overtaking the world economy.

TIME FOR A BIT OF INTROSPECTION

Those of you who have digested what I have said up until now must decide for yourselves whether or not the evidence I have presented is sufficient to justify the changes in the world's political, financial, sociological and technological framework along the lines I have suggested. If you feel that the scenario I have given for the future is probably the correct one you must carefully evaluate your personal prospects, your existing job or business and the manner in which you have planned your future. What I have outlined could mean you would be better off changing your job, learning a new trade or perhaps moving to another state where the economic climate may be better suited to you particular skills over the shorter term. Many of the developments that I believe will take place over the near term could well be unpalatable to you. But remember, if you stick your head in the sand, your tail becomes the target. Those who are likely to benefit over the longer term will be those who accept that a drastic revision of their life-style may be necessary and that current expectations may not be compatible with what the future actually holds in store.

Many people may feel they do not have sufficient knowledge to decide for themselves if the course of the next decade will take the shape I have predicted. At the same time, vested interests will bombard members of the public with a plethora of disinformation which refutes my forecasts. The sum total of all the knowledge accumulated in the recorded history of mankind—going back 5,000 years—is now doubling every ten years. Yet, extraordinarily, few people seem to understand the mechanics of disinformation and how disinformation has contributed to the reluctance of Western democracies to face certain unfashionable facts.

Change is certain. It requires courage to adapt to change. Courage is doing what you may be afraid to do. There can be no courage unless you are afraid. Obviously, it is very difficult for any politician, in a partisan, take-it-easy, consumer society, to explain that it is only the strong and courageous who will inherit the future. So important are the decisions for you right now that I implore you to take the time and effort that you need to plan your future and to decide what that future is likely to hold. Your decision must not be deflected by the propaganda of those who will benefit from your ignorance. Ignorance usually carries the worst of all possible penalties.

Compare the conclusions I have drawn and the reasons for those conclusions with those of the opposing view. Read the reference sources listed in the bibliography. The material and knowledge that you need to help you plan your future and to make decisions is available. You must not allow yourself to be blinded by the opinion of the masses and the vested interests who govern the decision making process of the masses. Think for yourself, objectively, without preconception or prejudice. Look at the facts and evidence. Only a fool argues with fact.

History repeats itself when men and women who have come to be apathetic and easygoing conveniently forget the past. Plan your future with conviction and determination. No one is likely to care as much about your future as you do. After all, you're going to spend the rest of your life there. Those who prepare for the future, firmly, decisively and courageously, are the least likely to encounter the problems that may be perceived as associated with the terminal juncture of a period in society that is no longer viable.

THE SOCIAL, CULTURAL AND POLITICAL ENVIRONMENT

As we move through the downwave, into the depression, then into the more tranquil period of slow growth, fashions will change to reflect the shift in public psychology. Craftsmanship will return to the fore. Manufacturers will once again take pride in the quality of their garments rather than merely the fashionable element. Fashion will not change as frequently as has been the recent experience. Clothes will be bought and made "to last." In general, dress will become more conservative and be of an appreciably higher standard. Skirts will be longer and necklines higher for at least the next four to five years. Designers will fashion clothes for a slim, youthful, feminine form. A return to the fashion of previous depression years can already be seen. It is one hundred years since the bustle reached its fullest flowering. Never before or since the depression years of the 1880s has so much material been gathered for the sole purpose of focusing on the posterior. Now, here we are, a second depression after the bottom fell out the bustle business, and it is suddenly fashionable to wear a dress with a fine exit line. Bare backs plunge to a posterior cleavage and ruffles and bows outline the rear of most of the glamorous fashions for 1983. "Nineteen eighty-three is set fair to the Year of the Derriere—just like 1883 before it . . . and 1785 . . . and 1584," says Suzy Menkes, a well-known London fashion editor.

In the 1930s, an extremely laborious and exhaustive study of the history of fashion was undertaken by Agnes Brooks Young. Her book was published in 1937 by Harper Brothers under the title *Recurring Cycles in Fashion*. Her study of fashion through the ages led to the conclusion that there was one common denominator that ran through several hundred years of design which was the contour of the skirt. She found there have been only three fundamental types of skirt contour, viz:

FULL BACK: Skirts that are close fitting in the front but loose and gathered at the back.

TUBULAR: These are the skirts that closely follow the contours of the body in the front, back and sides.

BELL: Bell shaped skirts obviously look like a bell, narrow at the waist and becoming fuller through to the hem which is the widest part.

The periods of these fashions were defined by Mrs. Young as follows:

1740   1815   1875

1790   1860   1910

1. BELL	1725–1759	5. FULL BACK	1869–1899
2. FULL BACK	1760–1795	6. TUBULAR	1900–1935
3. TUBULAR	1796–1829	7. BELL	1934–?
4. BELL	1830–1868		

FIGURE 37   SKIRT SILHOUETTES THROUGHOUT HISTORY

Mrs. Young's study of fashion was totally independent of macro-economic activity. There is no reference to long-term economic activity in any part of her work. The data that are introduced would seem to add further supporting evidence to the long wave economic cycle insomuch as it appears that changes in the nonliving universe are associated with human enotion and behavior and expressed in the style of dress. Mrs. Young did make the casual observation that in the 1840s, 1870s and 1930s —all of which were years of severe economic depression—style in dress seemed to leave the natural lines of the body and became heavier, more elaborate, more constrictive, and had lower hemlines. The choice of colors was invariably somber, almost funereal.

The one underlying element of dress in all of these periods of economic

hardship was the loss in the amount of physical freedom and bodily exposure. The choice of heavy materials, extra yards of cloth, expensive and
elaborate haberdashery, would appear to be the reverse of what designers
are likely to anticipate during periods of hard times. On the other hand, it's
possible that designers were not actually anticipating hard times and stum-
bled upon the correct fashion, cycle after cycle, purely by accident. The
style of dress is consistent with the psychological atmosphere associated
with periods of sobriety, suggesting a heavier, constricted emotional and
physical state of the population during these times. When there is an
abundance of optimism, opulence and apathy, one would expect the opposite extreme in dress.

If we bring Mrs. Young's observations up-to-date, we find that the last
major reversal in fashion was the collapse of the microminiskirt hemlines
in 1968. Since that time, we've been in a transitional period from the standpoint of both fashion and economics. Alvin Toffler refers to the period as
one of "ecospace."

It would thus appear that both people in general and those in the
fashion industry could benefit strongly from a thorough knowledge of
long-term macroeconomic activity as outlined in these pages. Clothing designers and merchants should realize that styles in fashion are neither
random, nor capricious, nor directionless . . . but rather regular, an orderly
expression of the psychological state of people at given points in history.
The wise fashion designer will recognize that it would be totally imprudent
to force upon an unwilling market styles that many people may be neuro-
logically incapable of accepting at the time.

The record of skirt widths during the depression years demonstrates
this, and although 1931 was a depressionary year, fashion was relatively
constant. In mid-1932, people began to question the incessant claims of
economic recovery and skirt widths began to change. As the depression
reached its nadir, the changes were more pronounced. There was a very
short-term change in fashion trends in early 1934 in response to the abort-
ive economic recovery that got underway but failed. In 1935, there was firm
evidence of economic improvement. The change in fashion was dramatic
and sustained.

Women's fashion will range from the severely tailored look for business wear and day wear, to the ultra-feminine look for the evening. Expect
a revival of taffeta petticoats and crinolines. The idea will be to emphasize
the female form although covering it. The trend will reflect a return to the
traditional role of women who will no longer have the desire to compete on
male terms on the one hand, and the businesswomen who will want to
portray the image of efficiency on the other.

Producers of natural fibers are likely to be engaged in bitter price wars
as the depression deepens. This will affect the choice of materials used by
designers. Cotton is likely to be one of the worst victims of the fall in
commodity prices. Cotton will feature prominently in many designers' fash-

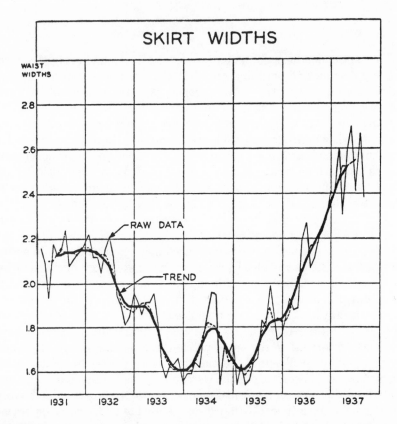

FIGURE 38

ions. Natural fibers, like linen, wool and silk will also be treasured once again. Synthetics will hardly be used in fashionable garments.

Men's fashions will be stable for quite some time. Ties and lapels will no longer contract and expand with trouser bottoms. Extremes will be out. There will be little of the narrow lapels of the late 1970s nor are we likely to see the very wide lapels of the 1960s for quite some time. A middle-of-the-road look will be in vogue. The well-dressed man will want to look conspicuously inconspicuous. Men's clothing will be less colorful and more somber, veering toward the elegant, involving fine hand-tailoring and only superior cloths. Many of the fashions of the 1930s are currently experiencing a revival. We have seen the return of the wing-collared dress shirt and the one-inch bow tie. Jeans, of course, will lose their popularity completely, even for leisure wear. People will be expected to conduct themselves with more decorum and be more decorous, emphasizing a rejuvenated morality and a dismissal of decadence. It will be unheard of for a gentleman to dine at a more fashionable restaurant without a jacket and tie. Even the less fashionable restaurants are likely to join the trend. In general, there will be a return to sobriety and conservatism.

The frantic, mindless popular music of the 1970s and early 1980s will completely disappear from the scene. Initially, we can expect a revival of nostalgia. This has already begun. Recordings of the 1940s and 1950s are currently being reissued and are experiencing a renewed popularity. The change in people's attitudes will also be reflected in the popular dances and rhythms. Music will be slower and more romantic. Couples will once again be seen holding and caressing each other on the dance floor. The narcissistic gyrations and spastic writhing that were part of the frenetic discotheque mania of the 1970s will no longer be seen. People will begin listening to the words of the songs, associating the lyrics with a more subdued, idealistic romanticism that they find compatible with their new life-styles and the tranquility of noninflationary times.

The changes in fashion and music, accompanied by a desire to escape the prevailing realities will also be reflected in the literature of the next few years. There will be a boom in self-help books ranging from diet books and books on physical fitness to do-it-yourself books on auto mechanics, carpentry, generally any area which might help people save money. There will also be a boom in "get-rich-quick books." Any book that promises to tell people how to make a fortune in the stock market, real estate or any other area of endeavor will do well—until the market crashes. After the crash, books of this nature will become extinct. Also among the best selling nonfiction books will be those of an historical nature, particularly economic history. Those who have the intellect to digest nonfiction literature will desperately try to find guidelines to help them understand what is happening to them. The period of the 1930s has been referred to as a "golden age" of literary sociology. There was a strange alchemy which blended the Marxist revolutionary class struggle and Walt Whitman's sense of American oneness. We can see this happening now. These tendencies are likely to be expressed in both the nonfiction and the fiction that gains popularity over the next few years.

Although publishers and fashion designers who are able to keep pace with the changes in the public mood are likely to prosper in the hard times ahead, works of art, particularly contemporary art, are among the more dispensible human needs when times are hard and money is short. The depression that I see coming is likely to literally obliterate any meaningful source of income for all but a handful of American artists while erecting a barrier across the path of many young people who may be seeking a career in art. The impact of the depression on the visual arts is likely to be closely akin to what it will be like for literature.

Artists can be expected to experience a sudden upsurge in social consciousness and many will proclaim themselves revolutionaries or communists or anarchists. We can expect to see considerable experimentation with new art fads and styles in which social and aesthetic impulses are blended. Artists will rediscover the American scene as a source of artistic inspiration. At the same time, most of these canvases will be unsalable and the artists can be expected pour their bitter resentment onto their canvases and sculpture; there will be bitter caricatures of capitalist bosses and tycoons, stolid muscular workers being ground to death by robots, and the pinched, hopeless faces of the jobless trapped in gloomy ghettoes all combined in an endless array of indecipherable montages of harsh color and angularities that reveal the inchoate anger and frustration of their creators.

Puritanism is likely to return. Sex shops will be closed. Censorship will be tightened. New laws will lead to a return to more prudent moral standards. Church attendance will rise, and alternative religions will lose their followers. There will be fewer working wives, but more working youngsters. All of this will strengthen the family unit. A deterioration in human relationships is characteristic of the upwave. Morality is low. Divorce is high. Cohabitation is the norm. During the upwave it has been said that married people live like single people, and single people live like married people. This trend is reversed during the downwave. During the upwave, the emphasis is on materialism, and people become progressively more insular in their human relationships. Empathy is a forgotten word. During the downwave, brotherly love is rediscovered. People become aware of far greater fulfilment in the family than in a second car; that a good friend is a far greater asset than a minicomputer; that a woman's love and undivided loyalty are a far more meaningful symbol of a man's success than a Rolls-Royce.

During the downwave, there is a distinct tendency toward right-wing politics and strong political leadership. The government elected during the middle of the 1980s is likely to have a strong leader, and remain in power for quite some time. Generally, the middle 1980s to the middle 1990s will be a period of relative stability, unlike anything in the past two decades. While the affluence of the "swinging sixties" will not be repeated for quite some time, the recurring crises of the "sobering seventies" and "agonizing eighties" will also not be repeatable. In general, the decade that lies ahead will be one of sobriety, peace and tranquility.

The depression will leave its mark for quite some time, and will take considerable steam out of the industrial society, slowing it down, making it less intimidating to people even after the downwave is over. People will move closer to the resources, to land, water and woods. There will be all sorts of new opportunities for small-scale economic activities. The big corporations will find themselves in bitter trade wars, with contracting markets, and will find it progressively more difficult to sell everything they produce. As the vast scale of society contracts, the need for a "big brother" government providing all will also contract. It will be more of a face-to-face world.

The period immediately ahead will be one of rampaging unemployment and considerable economic disruption. Most people will feel threatened by the changes, but those who are willing to adapt efficiently and quickly will actually enhance their position.

Those who hold on to a declining way of life, to a job in a declining industry, to a business with little future, merely because they are unwilling to accept change, will find the next few years extremely difficult.

Those who are probably best prepared for the years ahead are those who have never been wealthy, but have engaged in physical labor, have skills, and are prepared to get by on reduced material goals. The repairman, the car mechanic, the artisan, the craftsman, the handyman, will all be able to channel their skills into areas that will be resilient to the changes in society.

The individual likely to suffer more than most, unable to adjust to a short frugal period, is today's vociferous wheeler-dealer in property, the stock exchange and other business enterprises that are a product of a bygone era. This type of individual, who is probably carrying an enormous debt burden, will be wiped out by any prolonged setback, and will find his life-style rested on quicksand. Suddenly he will be faced with poverty. He has probably never worked with his hands for $5 an hour, and knows very little beyond exploiting the angles.

Over the next three to four years, there is likely to be less of everything in material terms. Less clothing, fewer cars, fewer possessions. But there will be more spare time, more time to enjoy friends and family, more individual opportunities, more physical work, more community, more contact with nature, generally a more challenging life-style. People will have more time to enjoy what there is to enjoy. People are likely to become more alive to opportunities and ideas. People will be able to afford to take themselves less seriously. The frowns will become smiles, and people may once again be able to laugh at themselves. Those who adapt will find more pleasure from simple things, with a new set of standards geared to the quality of life.

Warren Johnson, in his book *Muddling Toward Frugality* (1978), offers suggestions on the best way of preparing for the changes over the next few years, changes which will bring smaller cars, bankruptcies, high unemployment, and all the symptoms of a society that has been living beyond its means.

DON'T	DO
1. Don't get involved with status symbols.	Savor the simple pleasures of life.
2. Don't be too acquisitive, and wrap yourself up in your private successes.	Learn to appreciate them. Build your life around family, friends and work.
3. Don't become so involved in debt that your freedom is restricted.	Always be willing to adapt to change and be aware of change.
4. Don't become too specialized. The need for your skill could disappear.	Save your money to allow you the flexibility change may warrant.

5. Avoid positions in industry that depend on nonrenewable energy.	Find work that will expand should existing resources become scarce.
6. Don't become addicted to affluence.	Learn as many skills as you possibly can.
7. Don't live in areas that depend on transport for basic necessities.	Try to live in an area where there are renewable resources—good water, wood and so on.
8. Don't buy land in remote, inaccessible places.	The best place to live is in or near a small town.
9. Don't be greedy, and get caught holding a speculative bubble when it bursts.	Repay the mortgage on your home before undertaking any investment or assuming any other debt.
10. Don't keep yourself too much to yourself, and risk isolation and hostility.	Develop loyalties with neighbors in your community.

While several of the do's and don'ts which Johnson recommends are totally in keeping with what the future will hold, there are certain suggestions that are based on assumptions that I do not believe will materialize. Firstly, I do not believe energy will present any problem whatever in the years ahead. Great strides have been made toward energy conservation while I envisage a drastic fall in the price of oil. Alternative energy sources will continue to be developed at increasingly competitive prices offering more competition for fossil fuels. We are entering a period of abundant, cheap energy as the result of the technological advances of recent years. I do not feel that nonrenewable energy prospects should be a remote consideration in future planning. Nor do I believe the conventional wisdom that has projected recent energy scarcity into the future indefinitely. Contrary to the assumptions of Johnson, I am firm in my conviction that transportation will be readily available and cheaper. I do not feel there is any necessity to avoid land purchases in remote and distant places because of transportation difficulties. I would certainly advocate all of the "do's" on Warren Johnson's list but would be highly suspicious of the assumptions on which items 5, 6 and 7 of the "don'ts" are based.

A PEEK AT THE OILY PAST AND A GLIMPSE AT THE SLIPPERY FUTURE

The optimists of the oil industry insist that what we are seeing now is just a bout of temporary indigestion for the oil price. It is claimed that for the remainder of the century the price of oil will rise by about 10 percent. According to the argument, crude prices must ultimately go up because the world is using up its oil. The growing scarcity of oil plus an inflation rate of at least 6 percent means that a 10 percent rise per annum in the price of oil is a reasonable expectation. That particular argument is pure unmitigated verbal garbage. To begin with, it is becoming clear that demand for oil will certainly not be able to keep up with the pace of potential supply over the next two decades. In real terms, all prices are therefore destined to decline, lagging behind the pace of inflation and accelerating in the case of deflation. Those who claimed "inelastic demand" for oil, citing oil as a special commodity were talking pure fiction. Oil is just like any other commodity. If oil follows the fate of many commodities, which had been the subject of a speculative bubble, an 80 percent decline in the price is not an unreasonable expectation. History shows that the crash that follows a speculative boom serves to retrace an average of 80 percent from an historic peak.

The oil glut is likely to be no less a permanent fixture of the current decade than was the oil shortage of the previous decade. Energy efficiency has been heightened through innovation and technology far more quickly than most "experts" ever thought possible. Several fossil fuel alternatives such as photovoltaics are already cheap enough to compete with oil in certain circumstances. Thousands of research analysts are now tinkering with new techniques and technologies. In the meantime, increasing numbers of fields are coming on stream while many producers must keep production in full swing in order to gain revenues to make transfer payments against dwindling tax revenues in economies that continue to weaken.

The illusions of the past are now disintegrating rapidly and with them the probable disintegration of OPEC as a meaningful cartel. To be technical, OPEC never existed as a true cartel (by definition, a group that controls prices by controlling production). The organization thrived as long as there was a seller's market, but until recently it has never had to prove that its members could also operate in a buyer's market with unity and abide by agreements to limit production. The collapse of the talks in Geneva demonstrated that such discipline may be beyond them. As cameras flashed and video recorders whirred, OPEC's most powerful leader, Sheikh Ahmed Zaki Yamani, curtly announced: "The meeting has ended. There has been complete failure." This simple pronouncement could hardly have been loaded with more significance. The mighty organization that once seemed to bend the world to its will was sinking deeper into its worst crisis. OPEC was badly split, if not permanently shattered.

With OPEC about to dissolve as a unified influence it is likely that oil producing nations will enter a "free for all" of overproduction and price cutting. For some nations it will be a last-ditch effort to save tottering governments and sagging economies. At the same time, demand will certainly not increase. Demand is far more likely to slip from current levels as the economies of importing nations continue to stagnate and decline in the year ahead. While we were alone when we first forecast the likely demise of the oil sector, now there is an increasing number of analysts who see deflation, depression and a huge oil glut combining to bring oil prices down with a terrible thud to perhaps as low as $8 a barrel, representing an 80 percent decline from the peak. While such a forecast may seem outlandish to many, it must be looked at in perspective. (After all, the price of silver experienced a similar thud in 1980.) To begin with, spot oil prices have already fallen from a peak of $40 a barrel to the recent price of $29 a barrel. That's a 28 percent decline in nominal terms. The consensus is that oil will fall to a low of $25 to $26 a barrel. Those who believe the price of oil is capable of falling to $25 a barrel do not consider such a concession of any great magnitude. William Brown, the director of energy studies at New York's Hudson Institute, argues that OPEC has never been able to control either production or prices. Instead of managing the market, he says OPEC merely follows the price dictated by supply and demand. In 1979, for example, prices exploded not by OPEC decree but because the Iranian revolution dramatically reduced supplies. Brown, who two and a half years ago accurately predicted the current oil glut and OPEC's troubles, now forecasts "the complete demise of what is erroneously called OPEC cartel" and a plunge in prices to as low as $20 a barrel. That would leave the price of oil with a 50 percent decline from its peak. (What's another 30 percent here or there?) Of course, many are still unable to conceive of such a decline in the price of oil but the doors of perception have usually been closed to the consensus. Even the current price level of oil would have been thought totally absurd a few years ago—"Oil prices can go only one way: up." Remember? (*Ed. Note*: The prospects that were held for oil prices a few years ago are currently reserved for property prices!)

We are fully aware that the suggestion that oil prices could fall by up to 80 percent in price strains the credulity of most. This would mean an $8 oil price involving a further decline of 70 percent from current levels. We can hear the outcry from here. "That just couldn't happen. It's unthinkable. It's unprecedented." While it may be unthinkable it is certainly not unprecedented and it certainly could happen.

Before harboring preconceptions, it would be wise to determine whether these preconceptions have any foundation. Those who insist a drop of 80 percent in the oil price "could never happen" and who believe it is unprecedented and "has never happened" are simply unaware of the history of oil. There are two documents that provide some excellent reference material. One is *The History of the Standard Oil Company*. You can also obtain a special 1927 congressional study from the Library of Congress entitled, *Prices, Profits and Competition in the Petroleum Industry*.

Prior to 1900, crude oil (such as kerosene) was used primarily for illumination. Other important uses included oil for heating and in asphalt and lubricants. The most significant market force was John D. Rockefeller. Standard Oil Company, at that time, attempted to function as a form of OPEC, setting prices and controlling supply all by itself. Rockefeller developed a union of refiners, limiting their output of oil to an allotment he assigned, even getting them to accept freight rates that he personally arranged. For a time, Standard Oil not only controlled domestic pricing and output, but it also controlled foreign exports of oil at a time when the United States was the world's leading oil export country.

In spite of the tremendous influence exerted by Rockefeller and his Standard Oil Company, the combine was still unable to always maintain margins and price stability. The ebb and flow of inflation, the elastic nature of demand and the continuing emergence of new producers—much the same forces that are at work today—triggered price swings of tremendous magnitude. For example, between 1867 and 1869, well-head crude oil prices climbed from $1.68 a barrel to $6.72 a barrel. That was a price hike of 300 percent. However, by 1874, the price had fallen back to eighty-four cents a barrel, a decline of a whopping *87 percent*.

From 1874 through 1876 it was boom time again. There was a massive increase in the price of oil which galloped from eighty-four cents a barrel in 1874 to $3.78 a barrel in 1876, a gain of 350 percent in just two years. Then came the downturn. During the next three years the price of oil plunged downward once more, back to eighty-four cents, a decline of *78 percent*.

Then for quite a long stretch, Standard Oil was able to run the show according to its dictates. In other words, market forces allowed the price of oil to succumb to the wishes of John D. Rockefeller. From 1879 through 1894 prices remained relatively stable in the eighty cents to $1 range. Therefore, for a period of fifteen years, margins were more or less constant. During 1894 prices began to edge higher and by 1895 hit an exponential uptrend. The oil price doubled between 1894 and late 1895. Between 1895 and 1897 the price of oil plummeted again, losing 50 percent of its value back down to $1 a barrel. Happy days were here again for the oil barons between 1897 and 1900. Over those years the price of oil rose by 125 percent.

At the turn of the century, enter the automobile and exit the restrictions on both the supply and demand side of the equation. New discoveries in Texas, Oklahoma, Wyoming and California expanded supplies that previ-

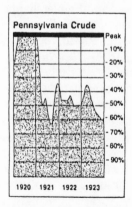

FIGURE 39

ously came from Pennsylvania. A new source of demand for oil in the form of the automobile, along with post-World War I inflation, kept the price fairly steadily upward until 1920 when the price of Pennsylvania crude reached $6.10 a barrel, a gain of 510 percent from the 1897 low. In 1921 the world was in the grip of a deep post-peak-inflation recession. Commodity prices collapsed. The total collapse in commodity markets was also shared by oil. Crude oil prices actually set the pace on the downside, suffering a decline of 70 percent in just twelve months.

Whether or not history will repeat itself in the same manner is of course debatable. The implications and indications are that it will. A similar 70 percent fall from the current benchmark price of $34 would take the price down to $10 a barrel. That may be unthinkable but hardly unprecedented or improbable. Those who cannot learn from the lessons of history are condemned to repeat it. Given the current attitudes toward the prospective prices of oil along with the lack of any integrated strategy to protect the financial community from the ravages a savage drop in the oil price will ultimately produce, it would appear evident that very few have learned anything at all from history.

Over the past decade, Western banks have received tens of billions of surplus petrodollars from OPEC and recycled them as loans to developing countries. If OPEC now decides to reclaim those petrodollars the banks will obviously no longer be able to continue carrying those loans. The international banking system now finds itself perched on a tenuously constructed financial pyramid that will crash if the oil price tumbles, which adds to the potential vulnerability resulting from loans to companies in all facets of the energy business. Many oil and oil service companies are now heavily in debt and any appreciable drop in the price of crude, whether slow or fast, will bankrupt them.

In the meantime, we are in a teeter-totter position. If the price of oil falls, the nations that produce oil could be forced to a default situation. If the price of oil doesn't fall, big borrowers that have to import oil will remain in hot water, providing additional default problems. Since the oil monster was turned loose in the early 1970s, the international monetary system has never been the same . . . the toothpaste just can't be crammed back into the tube without destroying the tube.

The OPEC cartel appears to have completely lost control and will no longer be able to exert any influence on the oil price structure, much to the dismay of the hard-line members of the cartel and to that of the British government, which has based its plans on the assumption that the world oil price structure would remain undisturbed. Its contingency plan, in the event of any oil price weakness, is to allow the currency to depreciate so as to compensate for the lower oil price through windfall sterling gains from exports of oil denominated in dollars. In the meantime, one must pay even closer attention to the prospects of deflation. As individuals borrow, the shrewd investor should repay. If the stock market soars, investors

must treat these as selling opportunities. If you don't sell when you can
. . . you may sell when you are forced to.

Further falls in oil prices will reflect weakness in industrial demand on
a global basis which will also be reflected by falls in output and industrial
demand for commodities. Recently, commodities have been experiencing
bear market rallies which are due to terminate within weeks. As these
markets slump, the true state of the global economy will be revealed. This
in turn will be translated into falls in equity markets around the world.
There is only one market that will truly benefit from falling oil prices. That
is the high quality end of the bond market along with the U.S. government
securities market. A debt crisis will soon surface once again. Only those
borrowers such as the U.S. government, with an outstanding reputation for
repaying external debt, are likely to show any capital gain potential in the
months ahead.

CAREER OPPORTUNITIES DURING THE DOWNWAVE

As the world dips deeper into depression and then emerges from it,
there will be a distinct shift in career and job opportunities and also in
employment patterns. Industries where jobs are at risk over both the short
term and longer term fall into two categories: the labor intensive and
industries that are producers of nonessential items. Some industries are
vulnerable on both counts.

The shape of work and the time spent at work will change dramatically. The traditional blindly accepted demarcation lines between full employment and part-time employment, unemployment and leisure will become increasingly blurred and meaningless. At a time when unemployment
is rampaging ahead and is likely to continue to do so, it is absolutely vital
that people are not distracted by the false agendas proposed by politicians,
bureaucrats, academics and trade union leaders whose mouthings are continually promoted in the media. It is a fact that no industrialized country
in either the East or West can blithely return to the full employment, nine
to five, one-or-two-jobs-for-life simplicities that were possible during the
upwave that ended in the early 1970s.

During the 1960s and early 1970s, it was widely thought that the
service industries were capable of soaking up those displaced from manufacturing industries, together with the new influx of recruits to the labor
force. Now it can be seen that service industries are no less vulnerable to
technological and social changes than manufacturing industries. Predicted
increases of as much as 35 percent for office productivity through the use
of technological innovations are expected to dampen the prospects for
white-collar employment for the next decade, without considering the
effects of a depression. Numerous service industries have already collapsed
and contracted in the same manner as industries in the primary and secondary sectors. In the United States, employment in private households of

serving staff and employment in the amusement industries has fallen sharply throughout the period from 1948 through 1978.

Lora S. Collins, who conducted a study for CB Business Conditions Analysis, has concluded that the shift to service industries in the United States "has not meant rapid growth in the traditional service occupations that spring to mind . . . beauticians, repairmen, laundry workers, for example." It is quite clear that "service" in those kinds of occupations has suffered a marked deterioration over the years. "The sharpest employment shifts," says Collins, "have been toward government . . . mainly in health and education . . . plus private medical work and business functions like data processing." Areas that have recently served to absorb those that were displaced by the decline in manufacturing industries and certain service industries are no longer able to employ those whose skills are no longer required at the same rate.

A leading industrialist, Mr. van den Hoven, chairman of Unilever NV, says that he does not think employment in terms of job activity will be a problem in the Western world by the year 2010. In a paper that was delivered at Columbia University, van den Hoven suggested that because of a static population, more flexible retirement, a shorter working week, longer holidays and relatively fewer job entrants coming onto the labor market, feelings of insecurity in this respect will fade away. Social pressures against technological developments will greatly disappear. Herman Kahn and Daniel Bell share a similar view. Be that as it may, that's thirty years in the future. What do people do in the meantime who must toil for their loaf of bread . . . twiddle their thumbs while praying for manna from heaven?

Most of the academic trivia and minutiae that pretend to offer us a view of the future fails in most respects to prepare people for that future. We must eat and find food and clothing, today and tomorrow, next week and next month and next year.

I believe I have covered as much meaningful material on futurology as is currently available. What I find is a distinct lack of pragmatism and causation, particularly with regard to the manner in which the average individual should use the work of futurologists for the purpose of planning his future in the years that lie immediately ahead. Indulging in futuristic fantasies is as much fun as any other game that you can play with your clothes on, but when your life depends on the application of the forecasts, a more meaningful approach than is currently available is surely needed. Let me see if I can fill in a few gaps.

The automobile industry, and those industries upon which it relies, will remain in decline for the simple reason that an automobile is a wholly inefficient item and its existing technology is totally incompatible with the needs of the populace. An inefficient automobile has become more of a status symbol than anything else. In the years ahead, status symbols will lose their importance with all but a small nucleus. The automobile is an inefficient consumer of energy. While I believe that energy costs will fall sharply, they will still not fall to the level of the 1940s and 1950s in real terms. Car sales are likely to continue to decline, especially in the medium-priced models. The continued contraction in the auto industry, along with planned production techniques that will reduce the use of labor and increase productivity, means that no job under the management level is safe in the motor industry. It must also be remembered that sharp contraction in the motor industry will hit other industries such as steel, rubber, heavy engineering and heavy electronics.

The construction industry will also be an exceptionally vulnerable one in the period ahead for many reasons. On the one hand there will be a contraction in building. There can be an expected slowdown in building roads, shopping complexes and manufacturing plants. The industry will also suffer from the lag between the fall in the price of building materials and the easier trend in property values across a broad front. A construction company that undertakes the erection of a plant or office building now may find that by the time the work is completed its client has gone bankrupt. Devious methods will be used to break contracts by those ordering construction projects, since similar accommodation is likely to have become available at a lower price between the inception of construction and the finished building.

Service industries like marketing, finance and banking will suffer indirectly, influenced by the general contraction in the "smokestack" industries. During the long period of prosperity many businesses in these areas have been riding the crest of a wave, benefiting from an environment where demand continued to expand to the point where even the most incompetent have survived. The period ahead will offer little opportunity for the incompetents. Only those who are geniunely talented, inventive and imaginative will reap the benefits that society has to offer. Financially, depressions are supposed to have a cleansing effect. There is also a cleansing effect sociologically.

During a depression retail sales suffer. While the affluent will retain large portions of their wealth and at least 75 percent of the population will remain employed, those who are unemployed will exert a drag on retail sales both in physical and psychological terms. The retail industry is geared to the mass market. The contraction in mass market demand will affect large department stores to a greater extent than specialized boutiques.

Industries associated with the affluent society concept will be seriously at risk. With the exception of equipment intended to improve the mind and body (exercise equipment, home computers, etc.), manufacturers of recreational equipment, electronic games, peripheral electrical appliances (car vacuums, steam valets, trouser presses, compact disc players, low and medium quality hi-fidelity equipment, etc.), jewelry, furniture, carpets and retailers of "big ticket items," offer very poor employment prospects. In general, over the next few years, people will tend to make do with what they have. Planned obsolescence will become self-defeating. As was the case when disposable income was high, people will no longer be anxious to run out and buy the latest sonic degradation modifier or the newest fad in TV games. Materialism will take a backseat to practicality. Status symbols will generally be frowned upon. A man's worth will be judged by his intellectual and physical abilities rather than his possessions.

Jobs in service industries linked to the affluent society will also be suspect. These include banking, advertising, public relations, accounting, the legal profession, insurance services and investment services geared to the small and medium-sized investor. During a depression a large number of bankers and stockbrokers go broke. To some people this in itself is often sufficient justification for a depression. Many people feel exactly the same about lawyers and accountants. There will always be lawyers but there will not be as many of them ten years from now because the demand will not be as great. There will not be as many doctors, accountants or stockbrokers for the same reason. As far as locations are concerned, jobs in urban areas are likely to be more vulnerable than jobs that are some distance from major city centers. There is likely to be a large decentralization of work as companies move out of high rent, high priced urban centers and cut costs by moving to cheaper suburban areas. This will also be accompanied by a decentralization of the population involving an increasing number of self-sufficient homogenous communities all over the nation.

The textile industry will be hit badly by the shift away from man-made fibers to natural fibers while its labor intensity will also be a factor that will impede the performance of the industry. Essentially, there will be jobs in all of the industries I have just mentioned, but there will be a far smaller number. There will be fewer textile workers, car workers and steelworkers. The enormous advances in robotics, coupled with the high cost of labor will see to that. There will not be as many filing clerks, clerical workers, sales assistants, stock assistants, forecourt attendants (ushers in movie houses are now virtually unheard of), waiters, waitresses, margin clerks, ad infinitum, ad perpetuatum. Now I know what you're thinking. What in hell is left? The answer is, plenty!

Most job opportunities in the years to come will be related to science and engineering as will be the major career opportunities. The next generation of robots will be able to see, touch, hear, smell and even talk to you and—during the latter stages of the next upwave—they will probably be able to fornicate. But robots will never become human. Robots are mechanical devices. They will be subject to technical failure periodically and will require skilled technicians to look after them. Until such time as they are designed to look after themselves, they will need the extra loving care which can only be supplied by the highly trained, skilled technician. It has been forecast that by the year 1990 there will be 1.5 million jobs available for those who are skilled in one or more of the various areas of robotics. Career opportunities for robot engineers are indeed bright during the years of depression that are now ravaging the untrained and unskilled.

The drive to become completely independent of fossil fuel is likely to continue for the foreseeable future. This will mean a growing number of new job opportunities as energy sources alternative to fossil fuels steadily become available. In the nuclear power stations, right now, demand for skilled and semi-skilled workers greatly exceeds the manpower available to fill these jobs. Great strides have been made in the manufacture of solar systems for home use. An increasing number of jobs will be available in this area in the processing, distribution and installation of solar systems for both industrial and domestic use. The manufacture of synthetic fuels will continue at an accelerating pace. Many of the major oil companies are now engaged in these projects. While the smaller oil companies who depend solely on fossil fuel development are likely to disappear this will not be the case for the multinational energy producers who are currently exploiting all known energy sources outside of fossil fuels. There are also smaller specialist companies solely engaged in bio-mass facilities operations while others have been concentrating on low cost methods of coal, tar sands and shale extraction. Jobs in these areas will be plentiful for geologists, mining engineers and all the way through the infrastructure of these industries.

Manufacturing industries are not going to disappear into oblivion nor will cheap Third World labor be able to accomplish what computerized technology will accomplish. Swedish engineers and scientists are currently designing a series of model steelworks for the early 1990s. There are two basic concepts. One is that continued automation will allow small batches of specialized steel to be made to order, without a massive economic penalty. The other is that automation will remove most of the manual input of the steelworker's job. This process is already well advanced in many modern steel mills where the operator's job is becoming increasingly one of monitoring dials.

In the case of assembly line automation, there are numerous examples of what can be expected. Fiat, the car manufacturer, has used the high degree of automation currently employed in its plants as a major advertising feature. According to Fiat:

> The introduction of automation processes results in an overall professional growth in two directions: on the one hand, by eliminating or reducing the more simple and repetitive work positions, the average level of skill is raised; on the other hand, the need for greater knowledge of integrative systems for the planning and control of production and maintenance of the plant leads to the introduction of a new professionality or an enrichment of existing professionality.

The implications are that tomorrow's production workers will, in general, be more highly trained, adaptable and intelligent than has generally been the case for many years. As manual factory employment shrinks due to the demand for goods and services and the nature of the work involved, the people who retain factory floor jobs will become increasingly elite employees. Of course, higher standards of education and ability will be required, but for those who recognize and adapt to the changes in the nature and availability of the various types of employment, the future could indeed be a rosy one, even during the depression years.

The world population is expected to double in the next thirty-five years. The need for low-cost housing will intensify as the downwave deepens. Low-cost housing was actually a feature of the 1930s depression. Those builders and construction companies who concentrated their efforts on providing low-cost housing were the survivors of the disaster that struck most of the construction industry. Engineers are currently investigating the viability of mass-produced modular housing. New low-cost housing unity will be more energy efficient and employ radically new constructions, techniques and materials. It is intended that modular housing will be fabricated with heating, electric waste disposals and automated recycling with communications systems already installed. Many jobs will be open to those who acquire skills in the new methods of design and construction both on a skilled and semi-skilled level. Those currently employed in the construction industry should either seek employment in companies that are willing to enroll you in a training program or else seek private tuition.

In 1948 the first practical application of the transistor became available. At the time it was difficult to see what the ensuing possibilities of transistor technology might be. Initially, the transistor seemed to be little more than a replacement for the vacuum tube but took up less space. How little we know! How limited are our perceptions! How finite our imagination! The transistor led to the development of the silicon chip which led to microcircuitry upon which massive industries have been built. We can now place in our pockets a calculator that will perform functions that would have needed a whole desk top of equipment to perform twenty years ago. What will be the "transistor" of the next few decades? No less dramatic than the transistor is the laser. The laser is likely to replace machine and foundry tools in every tool- and die-making shop in the world. The machine tool makers of the future will be laser technicians. Hospitals of the future will require laser technicians due to the increasing use of laser surgery. Every sound engineer will also have to be a laser technician or employ one. The music of the future will be digital rather than analog. Lasers are being used in the chemical industry, in the printing industry and in the communications industry. A recent advance in laser technology is the microwelder, in which the laser is contained in a head fitted with a telescope through which the operator can view the surfaces to be welded. Through the laser, holography has become an important industrial technique. It has been estimated that by the end of the decade, 2.5 million laser technicians will be required. These laser technicians will be among the highest paid employees, along with robot technicians.

The industry that is likely to make the most dramatic impact on society in the future will be that of genetic engineering. I don't mean the far distant future, but within the course of the decade. The field of genetic engineering involves biotechnology, cloning, gene therapy, nitrogen fixation and planned breeding. Among the many biotechnological processes now in operation are the production of industrial alcohol (Gasohol), protein for animal feed, a variety of medicines and the extraction of minerals from ores (Microbial Mining). Prospects for the future are even more exciting. Imperial Chemical Industries is developing a biological polymer that may replace many types of plastics that are currently derived from oil. In addition, scientists are discovering many new ways of rendering pollutants harmless through developments in biotechnology. The potential applications of genetic engineering are legion, spanning many areas of agriculture, medicine and industry; the 1980s will show us how far these techniques can really take us. The years ahead will witness some truly amazing feats, like the genetic alteration of corn and wheat to suck the nitrogen out of the air and eliminate the need for ammonia fertilizers. The genetic engineers believe they will be able to produce fuel from wastes, plastics from sugar, sweeteners from cheese, extract metals from ores and clean up oil spills . . . that is, if we actually continue to use oil. Those who wish to enter this field are likely to require a minimum education qualification of a B.S. in chemistry, biology or medicine for initial industrial production work. Demand for Ph.D. biologists and chemists from genetic engineering firms and those in allied fields will explode. As the field widens, a great deal of the production operations will be accomplished by process technicians with lesser qualifications involving perhaps a year or two at a technical college after receiving a high school diploma. If you can get in on the ground floor in this field, run . . . don't walk. There will certainly be no depression for you.

Although the "total integrated information system" still lies in the future, a good deal of progress has been made toward it. Such an office will include word processors, intelligent computer printers with an internal programming capacity; automatic dictation and telephone message switching systems; private automatic branch exchanges; electronic filing systems that are stored in computer memory and accessed on a visual display unit; photosetting equipment incorporating laser scanners or cathode ray tubes; video communication facilities incorporating closed-circuit television; facsimile transmission (electronic mail) and access to external computerized data bases such as view data bases. The message is that no skill is likely to be in greater demand over the next decade than that of the computer programmer. Harvard University now insists that all undergraduates be able to write a simple, two-step computer program before graduating, regardless of their chosen career. Even as the depression deepens, the demand for competent computer programmers outstrips the supply. So, why not put that electronic toilet of yours to some good use and hook it up to a home computer? The aging pop idol, Jack Jones, has become a home computer enthusiast, an ideal strategy for an alternative career.

Broadly speaking, there are three different scenarios for the future of energy. One involves the shift from wasting and politically unstable energy sources such as oil to the still plentiful ones such as coal. This will largely be brought about by the changes in the price mechanism. The second scenario is more exotic. This consists of the grand idea of orbiting solar power stations, of water taking over from oil and of biomass fuels. One American writer has estimated that a hybrid polar tree known as Clone 388 (or more fondly as the "Btu bush") grown on marginal land, is capable of providing enough cellulose fuel to fire all of America's power stations for the rest of eternity. The third scenario rests on the assumption that energy demand in the West need not inevitably grow. Now that the need for conservation has been recognized, after the excessively prodigal use of energy during the 1950s and 1960s, it is argued that economic growth should not be assumed to require commensurate growth in energy consumption. In all three scenarios, the centralized energy systems survive, particularly the big electricity grids. Alternative energies only play a marginal role. In this particular instance we have an industry that is likely to remain stable and therefore jobs related to any area of electricity production are likely to be safer than most.

In the years ahead, certain established trades will continue to flourish while new trades appear alongside. There will be change, but not everything will change. Work will continue to be available for operating engineers, men who are experienced at running cranes and bulldozers, motor mechanics, heating, cooling and refrigeration mechanics, skilled craftsmen and appliance men. Need for these types will be based on the large number of businesses which will not be able to invest in the new technologies just yet while people in general will be slow to move away from those appliances which they have become accustomed to or replace them. Repairmen and servicemen who can attend to these appliances are likely to be in even greater demand as the recession deepens. In order for retailers to compete, they will have to improve dramatically the service they provide. The "discount house" of the past, where you walk in, buy the appliance and then hope and pray it works, will be a dying breed.

In the years to come, there will be no genuine shortage of jobs. The major shortage will be in adaptable, creative, imaginative people needed to fill these jobs. The help wanted columns are unlikely to be barren, even during the depths of the depression.

BUSINESS OPPORTUNITIES DURING THE DOWNWAVE

The downwave will last from ten to fifteen years. First, we will have a 1930s type depression, followed by short periods of expansion, but longer periods of recession. When the downwave is complete, there will be a change as significant as when the world shifted from an agricultural society to an industrialized society. By the year 2000, post-industrialized society is likely to be in full swing. Individuals who have adapted to the down-wave, preserving their capital and energies, will reap the greatest benefits. The initial problem will be to make certain that the changes in the coming years do not set you back too far to share in the rewards of the next upwave, which will certainly come.

The man with a steady job in an established company attuned to the needs of the future will fare much better than the entrepreneur over the next few years. Business opportunities for the remainder of the 1980s and early 1990s are going to be limited. The small businessman will do far better than the big businessman. The entrepreneur who can sell his personal specialist skills will do far better than the man who has nothing to offer but a dash of accountancy skills and the ability to buy and sell things.

By this I don't mean individuals with more ambition than sense who seek to get rich quick on borrowed money. The bankruptcy figures, over 25,000 last year up from 11,000 in 1975, show that today's climate is already most unhelpful to the average entrepreneur. He is still living in the age of inflation, which is over. I mean the computer programmer, the designer, the electronics engineer and so on. Business opportunities during the depression and its aftermath are limited, but there are some.

The seamstress will reappear. Men will want their socks darned, instead of chucking them out, and women will patch up their nylons. People will turn back to the now overgrown garden patch and sow their own vegetables. True, agricultural and horticultural produce will be dirt cheap in the traditional areas of production. But distribution costs will keep them exorbitant in the suburbs. Suppliers of garden seeds will prosper, as will manufacturers of garden tools. Home preserves will come back in fashion and Grandma will make apple pie again instead of buying it at McDonald's.

Time magazine recently published a table of expanding and contracting job markets up to 1990. Admittedly it leaned rather heavily on a projection of past trends. But it showed a big increase in the demand for secretaries, nurses and their assistants, sales cashiers and other jobs in which women have been traditionally predominant. With numbers of women withdrawing from the workforce in favor of jobs of one sort or another at home, it is likely that female unemployment will drop further below male unemployment. It is also possible that home-based cottage industries will thrive, along with a great increase in husband and wife teams in the computer and telecommunications peripheral and software fields.

As budgets tighten and more people are thrown out of work, the demand for cash will increase. Watch for the reappearance of pawnbrokers. A pawnbroker will lend money at what is usually an exceptionally high rate of interest. He will take your goods and hold them until you repay the loan, or cease to pay the interest on the loan. If you do not repay the loan, he sells your goods. This type of lending is exceptionally secure since most will only lend a small portion of the resale value of the goods they hold. When there is no one to turn to for immediate borrowing, the pawnbroker can help. It is likely to be very profitable in the years ahead.

Remember Charles Atlas and the ninety-eight-pound weakling? This summer, as the sand-kicking season comes up, the tiny coupons will come pouring in asking for the thirty-two-page booklet "showing how dynamic tension can make a new man." Ectomorphic adolescents, hungering for the great triangular chest Charles Atlas sports in the advertisements, find their salvation in body-building.

Charles Atlas, born Angelo Siciliano in Brooklyn, New York, the Horatio Alger of the human body, died about a decade ago, but the business continues under the direction of Charles P. Roman. Every month, he sends out thousands of Charles Atlas lessons. The package costs $25, the same price as when Angelo Siciliano and Charles Roman began in 1929. As a fledgling advertising man, Roman was given the Charles Atlas account, and decided that the best endorsement for the body-building plan called "dynamic tension," was Charles Atlas in swimming trunks. The two men incorporated their efforts in 1929, a year when most men had nothing more than their bodies to bank on. The Charles Atlas technique was an immediate success. It is easy to imagine how profitable it must have been. The price of the course has been able to withstand inflation over fifty years. During a depression, people become more concerned with their appearance and wish to look more attractive, possibly to enhance job prospects. Businesses designed to exploit this could prove profitable.

During the 1930s they said radio would kill the movies. During the 1940s they said television would kill the movies. During the 1970s they said video would kill the movies. The movies are still alive. Have you ever thought of opening a drive-in movie? At the moment they're doing a thriving business. During the depths of the depression in 1933, Richard Hollingshead Jr. took a movie projector into the streets and flashed a movie on the side of a building, then sat in his car and watched it. Before the people with the big butterfly nets could come to take him away, he patented a ramp system allowing occupants of a car to see a screen over the car in front of them and on June 6, 1933, the world's first drive-in movie was opened on Admiral Wilson Boulevard in Camden, New Jersey. Hollingshead duly proved he was a genius rather than a mental defective.

Some self-styled experts have called drive-in movies "the buggy whip of the 80s." Such a view conflicts with the experience of drive-in movie operators across America, one of whom is Frances Smith, who attracted hundreds of motorists to her Ledgewood Drive-In in Morris County, New Jersey when she was showing *Psycho II*. One viewer noted that he brought his wife and two children to the double feature for $7 (adults $3.50; children under twelve free). He had no babysitter to pay. The family packed its own snacks and drank beer while watching the movie. He said that when the weather is good he brings a lawn chair and sits outside the car.

Between 1948 and 1958, the number of drive-in theaters in the United States rose from 820 to 4,000. Industry officials touted the drive-in movie as the only way to combat the onslaught of television. They were right. Since television and video, movie theaters have been closing down and are being converted to other uses at a rapid rate; yet there remain 3,178 drive-in theaters in America. Most of them are in the outer fringes of suburbia or in rural areas where land is cheap and getting cheaper.

Many drive-in theaters hold flea markets and other events during daylight hours in order to keep revenues up. Drive-in theaters also sport miniature golf courses and special nights when bingo games and live music precede the movie or when families can bring outdoor grills for cookouts. Following the trend of indoor movies, drive-ins have been erecting two, three and even four screens. One drive-in in Florida has eight screens. The Westerbury (New York) Drive-In has three screens and shows first-run films and the owner says business has improved in each of the past five years in spite of a period that has been disastrous for the indoor movie theaters and for other elements of the entertainment industry. Any business that can provide family entertainment at a low cost will be a sure winner during the next five to ten years.

As an increasing number of firms are squeezed for cash during the depression, there is a normal tendency to delay payments. In some cases payments are not made at all. Debt collectors do a brisk trade, along with companies who specialize in credit investigations and credit ratings.

As the depression deepens, more companies will be declaring voluntary and involuntary liquidation. There will be a booming trade in buying and reselling bankrupt stock. Receivers and auctioneers will also find businesses thriving.

An increasing number of unemployed will have a considerable amount of time on their hands. Do-it-yourself businesses and businesses leasing tools and equipment for the do-it-yourselfer will benefit.

Fast-food chains usually thrive in a depression. The demand for cheap food increases as people seek to fill their stomachs cheaply. During the 1930s, the Horn & Hardart chain was born. These "automats" employed minimal labor, and dispensed hot food from coin-operated units. Throughout the 1930s, 1940s and 1950s the Horn & Hardart chain was among the most profitable catering businesses in America.

Businesses that help people save money are good propositions. High quality, slightly used secondhand clothing shops should prosper. Appliance repairs, tailoring alterations, car repair and maintenance and general repair work should do well. So will businesses involving salvage work, recycling old cars and other equipment and reclaimed building materials. It would also be worthwhile pursuing handyman skills such as carpentry, plumbing, welding and electrical repair work.

Currently there is considerable growth in centers for small manufacturing units serving regional needs. As the downwave goes on, people will try to avoid buying expensive items which are produced elsewhere. This will create opportunities for local producers and manufacturers. The town tradesman could find his business is recession-proof. The shopkeeper, the baker, the butcher, café operator, secondhand shop proprietor, tool sharpener and the general repairman may well find their small-town businesses prospering. Until recently, small towns were drying up, but now they are expanding again. No one is getting rich, but there are opportunities for people moving into smaller towns. The small entrepreneurs are living a good life, and they are independent.

For the skilled craftsman, the idea should be to make things that are superior to machine-made ones. Leatherwork, pottery, musical instruments, quilts, knitwear and exclusive made-to-measure clothing should all find a ready market, providing the price is right. Make it better, make it cheaper, and you will not have to worry too much about the depression.

A CONSUMER STRATEGY FOR THE DOWNWAVE

At the early stages of the downwave, you can expect extremely wide price variations in routine items. At the time of this writing, the price of a gallon of gas varies from station to station. Between the end of the secondary prosperity and the beginning of the depression, this type of price variation is normal. Shoppers should constantly be making price comparisons on food, clothing and the necessities of life. On high-priced goods, never pay the asking price; haggle. Do not be shy. Everybody does it. I do it all the time.

"January sales" . . . "winter sales" . . . "summer sales" . . . "autumn sales" . . . "fire sales" . . . "end of season sales" . . . "beginning of season sales" . . . "closing sales" . . . "opening sales" . . . and all manner of sales will come with greater frequency as retailers attempt to unload stock. Postpone your purchases wherever possible to take advantage of the retail price wars as depression bites into consumer industries.

As we move deeper into depression, price variations will disappear, and prices will decline in unison. Shoppers should only purchase sufficient for immediate needs. Buy daily, particularly with fresh produce like meat, fish, fruit and vegetables. Prices could fall day by day.

Secondhand "big ticket" items are going to be available at enormous discounts in the months ahead. Stereos, videos and other electrical items, prams, bicycles, gold jewelry and such will be the most difficult to sell. The longer the purchases are postponed, the cheaper they will be.

YOUR HOME DURING THE DOWNWAVE

Any form of property, commercial or residential, will be severely affected by the downwave for many years to come. Unfortunately, many homeowners who bought over the past year or so will also be exposed to great difficulties. People who took out a recent mortgage of 85–100 percent will be looking at very large losses if they sell, and fairly hefty paper losses if they do not. Often the deposit for a home represents the entire family savings. Already, many families have lost their entire savings, and do not realize it. I believe house prices will continue to fall, with fluctuations, for the next ten to fifteen years. Many people view their homes as a nest egg, a source of money in the future, to be used for a second mortgage or security for bank borrowing.

When the day of reckoning comes, these people will be disappointed. They may find that their mortgage exceeds the value of their house, leaving their savings wiped out. Others are hoping to "trade up" to more expensive homes, assuming an increase in the value of their existing homes will let them make a larger deposit on a more expensive home. They too will be disappointed.

The math is quite simple. Say you put down a deposit of $15,000, and bought an average-priced home of $80,000. You would have $15,000 of equity and owe $65,000 on a first mortgage. Suppose the house falls in value by 20 percent, a conservative estimate given the likely conditions over the next year or two. A 20 percent fall would mean your home was only worth $60,000. You still owe most of $65,000 on the mortgage. That means your $15,000 savings have been wiped out. If you sell, you will have to dip into your pocket to repay the balance of the mortgage.

For those who recently took out a 100 percent mortgage, the math gets worse. Say you borrowed $50,000 on a $50,000 condo. If values fall 20 percent, it would be worth $40,000. Before thinking of moving you would need $10,000. If the price of homes falls faster than your mortgage repayments, it could be a long time before you build up sufficient equity to repay the mortgage from the proceeds of the sale. Your little castle could become your dungeon.

So far I have only dealt with the possibility of a 20 percent fall in house prices, assuming that most people will manage to meet their mortgage payments. Say you had been trading up, putting down larger deposits on more expensive homes, with larger mortgages. Suppose you made a profit of $30,000 on your previous home, and put it all down on another home costing $150,000, with a mortgage of $120,000. With interest rates at 12 percent, that will involve a pretty hefty monthly outgoing. Higher-priced properties fell much faster in the recent slump than lower-priced ones. It is quite conceivable cheaper properties could fall by 20 percent, and prices at the upper end of the market could fall by 40 percent.

If you suddenly find difficulty in meeting your mortgage repayments, and find that you must sell and move to a cheaper home, you have problems. Your $150,000 house will be worth $90,000. Your $30,000 deposit will have evaporated and you will still owe up to $120,000 on the mortgage. Somehow, you will have to find $30,000 to make up the difference between the sale price and the amount owed to the bank. Technically you could be insolvent, with liabilities greater than your assets. If you cannot keep up your mortgage, the bank can foreclose, and you face Skid Row. That could be what home ownership means during the downwave. Bear in mind, this example involves a relatively small fall in house prices. My forecast is of a fall of as much as 80 percent over the next ten to fifteen years.

The homeowner must be fully aware that such a decline in house values will represent a *real* loss of spendable money. This may not be as clear to most homeowners as it appears. Many bought their homes ten to fifteen years ago, perhaps even longer, at relatively modest prices, and rest happy that they are risking no more than their original investment, if that. Not so.

If the average man had put aside $50,000 in a bank fifteen years ago, that $50,000 would have grown to over $100,000, assuming a modest 5 percent average compound return of 5 percent after tax. If, as a result of a bank failure or other catastrophe, you lost $30,000 of your accumulated capital, you would be very upset. The homeowner must accept that his loss from the coming collapse in house prices will be the same type of loss. Money you thought was yours will no longer be yours; the same kind of spendable money that could be used to pay medical expenses, send a child through school or buy a new car.

There is a thing called opportunity cost in leaving your money in a depreciating asset. If you took $100,000 and put it into a safe fixed-interest investment such as Treasury bonds yielding 10 percent, in three years time you would have $133,000 (ignoring tax), a rise of $33,000 as opposed to a $30,000 loss which would hit you if your house fell in value by 30 percent.

Without a doubt, given the current high return on safe investments, to sell your house, if practicable, is the most positive course of action any homeowner can take. If you have a home worth $100,000, with an equity of $70,000 and an outstanding mortgage of $30,000, you can take your tax-free capital gain and achieve an additional gross income of $7,000 or more before that $70,000 disappears in the property melee. You will have no further mortgage payments to make, no property taxes, property insurance payments or repairs. Depending on your area you should be able to rent accomodations as good as those you sell, given the increase in income which the investment revenue and savings on home ownership will allow. Yes, you will pay more taxes. But you will freeze your $70,000 or maybe do much better than that. If you can only get outside the almost universal preconception that house prices (and rents) can only go up, you will see that the math speaks for itself.

My recommended strategy for the downwave is that, if you are thinking of buying a house, do not if you can possibly avoid it. Wait! If you own a home with substantial equity, sell if possible, and rent.

The best deals in rented accommodation are in *short leases*, the unexpired portions of longer leases. Real estate agents have been finding it difficult to sell these tail-end leases. Rents are well below market rents. Currently, most people are unwilling to pay a high premium for a short lease. Most people harbor the illusion of continued inflation and rising property values. It is therefore generally believed there will be an astronomical increase in rent when the short lease expires. This is incorrect, but explains why short leases can be had at bargain prices. A two-to-six-year-lease on residential property offers excellent value. It is now a buyer's market for short leases, and this should continue for quite some time, though newly created leases should be viewed with suspicion.

If you do not, or cannot, become a renter, and are unable or unwilling to part with your existing home, there are other options. These are not so satisfactory, but they will offer some additional protection, and are better than taking no action at all.

It would be wise to investigate refinancing your home, and investing the proceeds. The object will be to achieve an after-tax return on the additional borrowed funds in excess of the interest payments after tax. In some cases this may be possible, and could increase your income.

Perhaps the chief danger in home ownership is that you may lose your job. Look into the possibility of taking out an insurance policy against this risk. U.S. Home Corporation has offered such a mortgage protection plan to buyers of its houses. Mortgage Guaranty Insurance Corporation has offered such a plan in the Pittsburgh area. Search around. You should find others prepared to provide some such service. It might be a selling point too, if your mortgage is assumable by the buyer.

There are numerous possibilities in what has been called "creative financing." They are all to do with making it financially easier for the owner or acquirer of a property to pay for it.

At the height of the house-price boom, it became common practice for the buyer of a home both to assume the seller's mortgage and to issue a note in lieu of cash for the rump of the purchase. It was not uncommon for the buyer to put down only 90 percent of the full purchase price in cash and the seller to settle for a note for the rest. This was a very foolish practice indeed for the seller. My advice to sellers today is to have no truck with anything but cash payment, and to use a price discount if necessary to clinch the deal. For the rest, an appeals court ruling went against the practice of assumption of the seller's mortgage by the buyer in the case of "due on sale" mortgages. This has frankly made it less attractive for long-standing mortgage holders to sell their houses. A 7 percent mortgage which has fifteen years to run is currently a rather valuable commodity to throw away.

If you have a recent mortgage at a high rate—equal to or higher than current rates—redeem it if you can. Much better, in today's circumstances, is an "adjustable" or "variable rate" mortgage which, as the name suggests, is varied more or less in line with current shorter-term interest rates. Better still is a relatively new arrival, the profit-sharing loan or "shared appreciation mortgage," in which the lending institution reduces the interest rate in return for a share of the profit on sale. You got it! If the "profit on sale" ends up as a loss, the institution takes part of it off you—the biggest part you can get, I would recommend.

If you have absolutely no alternative and *must* buy a house, do it with the biggest mortgage possible—preferably a profit-sharing loan, otherwise an adjustable one. This may appear as a direct contradiction of my previous recommendations to avoid mortgaged property ownership like the plague. Bear in mind this is only directed to those who are forced to buy a home or be homeless. I hope you are not in that position. If you are, here is why I recommend the maximum possible mortgage.

a) Mortgage money—especially the great bulk of mortgages which are advanced by the FHA (Federal Housing Administration) or VA (Veterans Administration)—is, to taxpayers, the cheapest money you can borrow. In fact you can probably invest in tax-exempt municipal bonds at a profit. Just make sure they are of better quality than Whoops, as the failing Washington power authority, WPPSS, is understandably known.

b) The home will be a horribly illiquid "investment" as prices slump. Personal liquidity will be of paramount importance in the difficult days ahead. The money borrowed from the mortgage institution will give you the flexibility that is crucial at such times. In the downwave, cash is king.

c) If the worst of all things happens, and you are unable to make your mortgage payments, the greater the negative margin between the value of your house and the outstanding mortgage, the further back you will be in the queue when the lender considers calling in the loan. Say you take out a 95 percent mortgage on a $100,000 home. You will own the lender $95,000. If you are forced into foreclosure on the mortgage, the lender will have to write off $5,000 on a 10 percent fall in the property ($10,000 less your $5,000). Given the same decline in property values, another borrower in trouble with a 90 percent mortgage instead of a 95 percent one would leave the lender nothing to write off. It would be far more tempting for the lender to foreclose where it did not have to take the write-off, than where a bad debt will arise.

YOUR VACATION HOME

While buying a home is unlikely to be a good investment in the years ahead, vacation homes are likely to be an even worse investment. Vacation homes in less industrialized nations are likely to fall steeply in value, with many countries being forced to impose exchange controls. The weaker countries will get weaker. Unfortunately, many of the sun-drenched villas are in areas with exceptionally weak economies, like Italy, Malta, Spain and France. These areas are also becoming more politically unstable.

A recent study by Forecasting International, using a technique which predicted upheavals in Iran, Poland and Afghanistan several years before they occurred, shows turbulent times ahead for Italy and Spain. The Forecasting International model devises a set of "vital signs" for each nation. These include general welfare figures, the number of fertile females and their offspring, the trade balance and energy dependence, the number of guest workers, the treatment of dissidents, arms sales and the rate of increase of military salaries (if military pay doubles in two years, someone is attempting to buy loyalty). Also considered are the income gap between the top and bottom tenths, racial and ethnic tensions and the number of educated males between eighteen and twenty-eight living in cities and unemployed (a prime source of political dissidents). These are all related to potential world events in nonrenewable energy resources, capital formation, inflation, deflation, population and food.

In the years ahead, some of the most dramatic changes in outlook will affect nations now in the mid-range of economic and political stability. Italy is expected to fall to twentieth place, putting it on par with a country like Nigeria. Italy's decline in stability corresponds with the end of the brief cooperation between the Italian Communist Party and the ruling coalition that followed the dramatic Moro kidnapping in 1978. Continuing terrorist activities could ultimately lead to the collapse of Italy's constitutional government. Italy is also vulnerable to many political, social and economic weaknesses which will be exacerbated by global trends over the next few years. The worst Italian problems will be related to food, population, energy and raw materials.

Spain is another country likely to suffer a dramatic decline in political and economic stability. In 1980, Spain ranked fifteenth in terms of stability. It is forecast that Spain will fall to twenty-fifth place, making it one of the world's most unstable countries. Spain is troubled by economic stagnation and burdened with one of the heaviest external debt problems in recent history. The deteriorating world trends over the next few years will have a greater destabilizing effect on Spain than on other nations. Over the short term, Spain faces serious problems that include a lack of energy resources, dependence on foreign capital and technology and internal strife caused by the separatist activities of the Basque and Catalan parties.

Israel is expected to fall from fourteenth place in terms of political and economic stability, to twenty-third, placing it among the five least stable countries. The decline can be attributed to increasing violence between Arabs and Jews in the occupied territories, the increasing influence of the West on Israel's Arab neighbors and the continued lack of ideological unity among the Israelis. Inflation in Israel is an incredible 130 percent. The birthrate for Israel's Arabs is more than six times greater than that of Israel's Jews, and will aggravate internal tensions. The admission of Spain and Portugal to the EEC will mean an Israeli loss of citrus and flour exports, adding to the weakness of the economy.

People who purchased vacation homes in Wales have been the subject of bitter resentment launched by an angry nationalistic populace. Unemployment in Wales is chronic. Homelessness is nationwide. Those who purchased low-priced vacation housing in Wales have now found their homes have been burglarized, burned, vandalized and often turned into worthless rubble by those who feel foreign ownership of homes they can't afford to buy is rubbing salt into the wounds of their poverty.

In April of 1983, the Greek Supreme Court ruled that foreigners cannot acquire real estate in the "frontier areas." As a result of the ruling, those who originally sold the land to Americans, Britons, West Germans and others, can now reclaim the property in return for the purchase price they paid. If the buyer just happened to put in a tennis court, swimming pool, Jacuzzi and other refinements in the meantime . . . tough luck. The original seller gets it back lock, stock and barrel.

The law barring foreigners from acquiring property in Greek border areas actually dates back to 1927. In recent years, because Greece was keen to promote tourism, foreigners were encouraged to buy island estates by setting up corporations based in Greece. These corporations enjoyed all the rights of Greek nationals. During the military dictatorship between 1967 and 1975, the National Tourist Organization even advertised and encouraged these transactions as a matter of national interest.

One very wealthy millionaire, induced to buy a sumptuous spot on the lovely island of Corfu, was Jacob Rothschild, a member of the famous banking clan. In 1969 he purchased fifteen acres of land for just under $70,000. He then spent a considerable sum converting an old farmhouse into a modern luxury home with every conceivable refinement. Today, that estate is worth over $750,000, but the original seller now gets the whole thing back for $70,000. The Greek Supreme Court has already ruled in favor of the original seller, who was a Greek national. The ruling, to which there is no recourse in Greek law, will affect foreign-owned property on Rhodes, Crete and the other Ionian islands, along with the islands of the eastern Aegean.

While the value of vacation homes in various areas of America is likely to fall dramatically, many individuals will be forced to liquidate homes originally purchased for investment purposes, finding they subsequently turned out to be bad investments. Generally, Americans are about to embark upon a period of retrenchment where only the basic necessities of life are going to be harbored. A vacation home is not one of those basic necessities. The world depression is likely to affect Europeans and others to an even greater extent than Americans. The vacation homes that fall into the low- and medium-price category owned by Europeans in Florida, California and elsewhere, are likely to be offered for sale in droves.

While the problems facing vacation homeowners in America will be abundant, those Americans who may have purchased homes outside the United States could suffer far greater problems. They could find the home has been confiscated, destroyed or subject to the whim of a government edict as was the case for vacation homeowners in Greece. Furthermore, the value of the home is likely to be severely affected by currency considerations since vacation homes that are the most popular have been in areas of severe instability and currency weakness. In addition, not only will the threat of currency devaluation affect the value of the home but exchange control regulations may prevent you from taking the proceeds of the sale out of the country. And finally, in areas of growing instability and civil unrest, aside from finding difficulty in getting your investment out, should

you decide to visit your vacation home, you might even find difficulties in
getting yourself out.

IF YOU'VE GOT IT . . . DON'T FLAUNT IT

Crime is going to be an even bigger problem than it is now during the
next two to three years. When people become desperate they do desperate
things. If a man is hungry and unemployed he may have no alternative but
to turn to theft. You don't want to be the target. Therefore, you must
maintain a low profile and protect what you have.

In Europe, particularly Italy, kidnapping is very big business. There
are bands of organized kidnappers who execute their kidnapping and ransom with the skill of commando units. They are able to keep track of
foreign millionaires who enter the country, where they live and what their
habits are. Recently, the ex-wife of one of the Rothschilds was kidnapped
in Italy and has never been seen alive again. In a London restaurant the
owners were held captive by a group of thugs until an agreed-upon ransom
was paid. The daughter of an Italian millionaire was kidnapped and he
subsequently paid millions for her return. She was never returned alive.
The father belatedly recognized that the reason his daughter had been
kidnapped was because he had purchased a Rolls-Royce. Professional
thieves will often canvas the upper-class neighborhoods, jotting down the
license plates of the most expensive cars in the area before each three-day
weekend. They then return to the area, burglarizing those houses where
the expensive automobiles are no longer parked.

I happen to live in a building that has attracted an exceptionally
wealthy Arab clientele. In their home country, if someone is caught stealing, the penalty is to have his hands chopped off. Theft in the Middle East
is at a very low level. Not being accustomed to the crime level in our
Western society, these people will leave large sums of cash and valuable
jewels casually tossed on the tops of bedroom tables, chests of drawers or
whatever may be convenient. This tendency has become so well known that
criminals come to this building from all over Europe. My home has been
burglarized five times in the past six years. The complex in which I live
averages eight burglaries a week.

While many criminals will steal for survival, the element of vandalism
is another threat to your existence. If you happen to be among those who
have managed to be prudent and cautious, protecting your wealth and
valuables, should this be known to large numbers of people, it is likely that
you could become the victim of envy as an increasing number of people fall
on hard times. As I walk through the car park underneath my building I
see Rolls-Royces with key scratches along the side and other expensive
cars vandalized with spray paint or doused with brake fluid.

Now is the time for you to maintain a low profile. Attempting to gain
the respect of your friends and neighbors through conspicuous and ostenta-

tious living is likely to be counterproductive. We are now living in an age of growing envy and desperation.

In addition, you must consider the aspect of fraud. You may be a target at this moment. Criminals are known to solicit insurance companies and entice employees to supply information on burglar alarm systems and the value of jewelry and other items kept in the house, along with detailed entry systems for those who are heavily insured. Commercial enterprises are continually compiling data on your life-style, your preferences, the amount of assets you control and other aspects of your existence that could be damaging to you if allowed to fall into the wrong hands.

Here are a few safeguards you may wish to consider. Do not give your name and address to firms or companies unless absolutely required to do so. If you purchase goods in a shop there is absolutely no reason for you to give your name and address, information that can become part of a mailing list that's sold, resold and sold again to parties of whom you have no knowledge. Where practical, effect your purchases in cash or money orders, minimizing the records that are kept of any transactions that you make. It would be wise to conduct your banking affairs with several banks so that your overall transactions are diluted. Restrict the use of credit cards to routine expenditures only. Do not give your social security number for identification purposes unless required to do so by law. Make use of a safe deposit box for cash and valuables. Try to avoid providing financial details wherever possible. In general, keep your affairs discreet.

In no circumstances should you deal with any investment or business firm that will not reveal its address or salient financial information. You will want to have access to the principals of any firm or firms that you are having financial dealings with. It would be wise to have an unlisted telephone number in order to avoid telephone calls from high pressure salesmen and other persons with whom you do not wish to have contact. You must be in a position to select whom you wish to invade your privacy. It would also be wise to rent a post office box for the purpose of receiving merchandise or information that you order by mail. When answering advertisements, this type of correspondence should be carried out under a name other than your own or a company name. It would be a good idea to have a registered company name for similar purposes. For anonymity, a Delaware corporation is the best.

I cannot overstress the importance of maintaining a low profile. You should not have your name on the front of your house or on your mailbox. Don't put your initials or any unusual signs on your car. Don't use a conspicuous low number license plate. Don't brag about what you have. Take a vacation from being conspicuous for the next couple of years. In other words, don't make yourself a target for the criminally inclined.

TWELVE

Investment During the Downwave

Much has been written about panics and manias, much more than with the most out-stretched intellect we are able to follow or conceive; but one thing is certain, that at particular times a great deal of stupid people have a great deal of stupid money ... At intervals, from causes which are not to the present purpose, the money of these people—the blind capital, as we call it, of the country—is particularly large and craving; it seeks for someone to devour it, and there is a "plethora"; it finds someone, and there is "speculation"; it is devoured, and there is "panic."
—WALTER BAGEHOT,
"Essay on Edward Gibbon"

Make no mistake about it, investment during the downwave, after the secondary prosperity has faded, means investment in a world turned upside-down. It means that all the rules that have been a faithful guide during the upwave are turned on their heads. Survival will call for a diametrically opposite approach. It's a bit like going out into the real world after years of school and finding that everything has to be relearned.

I often begin a lecture by referring to a comic strip by Charles Schulz and his band of precious youngsters. One particular episode begins with Charlie Brown and his little friend Pig Pen sitting on a curb while Lucy and Linus can be seen in the background gazing up at the star-lit sky. "Now Linus, see all those twinkling lights up there," says Lucy. "They're really big candles hanging from very long strings. There's a little man who sits in that big white crescent, and as soon as he sees this big yellow ball coming up in the other side of the sky, he gets on a rocket and puts out all those candles. Then he goes back to the big white crescent. When he sees the big yellow ball begin to go down, he gets back on his rocket and lights all the candles." At that stage, Charlie Brown turns to Pig Pen and says, "Poor Linus. It's going to take him years to unlearn all the things Lucy is teaching him." It will take most investors years to unlearn all the things they think they know, given the vast changes that have taken place in the investment arena.

The final stages of a secondary prosperity have always produced a speculative orgy. In the 1970s, this took the form of an unprecedented public stampede into tangibles and all manner of collectibles, from condos to coins. Prices at the peak (and even now) bore no resemblance to any known values—$2,000 for a case of young claret wine, for example. During the course of the downwave, there is likely to be a total collapse in the value of these collectibles. At the start of the 1980s, supercyclical corrections began to be felt in many of them. Diamonds and other gems, coins and stamps had lost as much as 50 percent of their previous values by the end of 1982. The downtrends in their values are likely to continue for the next ten or fifteen years. In 1983, there were signs of the beginnings of a recovery in some markets—in jewelry first, then in old master paintings. Many people still harbor the belief that they will return to their peak prices. So they may, but it could take forty to fifty years. In the meantime, the fall in values may have amounted to 90 percent, at least when adjusted for inflation.

When we reach the panic phase of the downwave, which cannot be far off, there will be a collapse in equity markets across the board. On the other hand, there is likely to be a complete rejuvenation of fixed interest markets. During the early stages of the panic, individuals who take advantage of the high yields in high-quality fixed-interest investments will be able to enjoy the capital gains falling interest rates provide, along with high income. As the downwave progresses, the yield gap between equity investment and fixed-interest investment will disappear. Ultimately, equities will yield more than fixed-interest investments to compensate for what is likely to be perceived as higher risk. First and foremost, investors must make every effort possible to protect their capital during the downwave. This means avoiding speculative endeavors like poison, and discarding any investment where there is a risk to nominal capital. If you are merely able to emerge from the panic phase of the downwave with your capital base intact, you will have done far better than a great many investors. You must exercise extreme caution.

FRAUDS, SWINDLES AND DECEPTIONS IN THE DOWNWAVE

As businesses become overextended during the upwave, there is an increasing tendency toward financial mismanagement. Commercial and financial crises are intimately linked with transactions that overstep the confines of law and morality, shadowy though these confines may be. The propensity to swindle and be swindled runs parallel to the propensity to speculate during a boom. Crash and panic, with their motto *sauve qui peut*, prompt still more people to cheat to save themselves.

Greed not only creates suckers to be swindled by professionals, but also pushes some of the amateurs over the line into fraud, embezzlement, defalcation and such. The forms of financial felony are legion. In addition to outright stealing, misrepresentation and simple lying, there are many other practices close to the line of morality and legality: diversion of funds from the stated use to an alternative use; paying dividends out of capital; dealing in shares on insider knowledge; taking orders but not executing them; borrowing against shares owned by another; selling securities without full disclosure of prior knowledge; using company funds to benefit insiders; mixing clients' funds with personal funds; using discretionary powers for matters of self-interest; altering a company's books; falsifying confirmations and contract notes; dealing to the disadvantage of individual clients. The list of tricks the trickster can get up to to feather his nest at your expense is virtually endless.

It would be comforting to believe that illicit financial practices have declined over the past 250 years or so. Yet, recent evidence suggests that the terminal phase of each economic cycle brings a vast array of swindles and the collapse of an uncomfortable number of financial institutions. The last cycle brought the saga of Investors Overseas Services. The securities sold by IOS were not sold in the United States because the Securities and Exchange Commission stopped it. Many U.K. financial institutions refused to handle IOS securities long before the scandal broke. Yet, many greedy investors saw IOS as a safe haven for European money seeking to escape withholding taxes and wanting action in the world's stock markets. The plungers at IOS also proved to be losers. When Bernie Cornfeld went to prison for his role in the operation, Robert Vesco took over. It is rumored that Vesco looted $200 million.

In addition to IOS, there was the usual sprinkling of bank frauds and banking failures. There was a scandal at the Chiasso branch of Credit Suisse. The bank suffered large losses from speculation through a Liechtenstein subsidiary which was believed to be illegally exporting Italian capital.

During the last recession, the Franklin National Bank in New York failed, and so did the Herstatt Bank of Cologne. Both failures were deemed to be aided and abetted by unauthorized foreign exchange speculation by employees of the banks. As the shock waves of these financial difficulties traveled around the world, many other banks were brought to the brink of failure. The First National City Bank in Brussels, the Banque de Bruxelles, also in Brussels, and Lloyds Bank in Trentino were brought to their knees.

Finally, the secondary banking crisis in Britain in 1974 revealed a degree of sharp practice and financial deceit in the City of London of which the general public had no inkling. "The unacceptable face of capitalism," Britain's Prime Minister Edward Heath branded it at the time. The closing of establishment ranks behind the Bank of England was as much concerned with hiding this "face" as containing the spread of financial panic.

What worms will the can reveal as we approach the panic stage of the downwave? The can is already open. A financial panic does not happen all at once. It begins with a series of crises which build in size and frequency until the glowing embers burst into flames. When historians look back, they may date the beginnings of the recent round of troubles to the Hunt brothers. Their heavy losses in silver in early 1980 nearly brought on a major crisis among the world's leading brokerage houses, a crisis narrowly averted by the Federal Reserve Board.

Since the Hunt brothers affair, we have seen the collapse of Drysdale & Co., the government securities dealing firm, in early 1982, and the fall of Penn Square in a $2 billion flurry of doubtful energy loans which shook the credit rating of Continental Illinois and even Chase Manhattan. In the summer of 1982, the default of Banco Ambrosiano in Luxembourg cast a shadow over the financial reputation of the mighty Vatican. This year's attempted lifeline from the major banks to Seafirst Corporation of Seattle ended in failure and the FDIC was left holding the bag of depositors' claims, prior to a bailout by Bank of America. Suspicions have been deepened further over the extent of the hidden iceberg of bad energy loans with the troubles of a bevy of Texas banks. So history is seen to be repeating itself as the sums of the defaults stretch from hundreds into thousands of millions of dollars and the number of defaults swells in the approach to the panic phase of the downturn.

A depression brings bank failures and bankruptcies because the decline in business activity means that people will have to use money they have been holding as cash. When these funds are exhausted, people have to sell assets to survive. As the initial withdrawals increase, money becomes still tighter. Borrowers find it increasingly difficult to make repayments, and to refinance their debts. The result is a decline in the value of the assets which financial institutions are holding as a security against loans, and in the liquidity of these financial institutions. The problems are compounded by inevitable loan defaulters. More and bigger companies go into liquidation. The financial institutions face soaring provisions for bad debts. During mid-1982, 226 companies a week were going bankrupt in Britain. There were over 450 reported bankruptcies each week in the United States.

HOW SAFE ARE YOUR SAVINGS?

There are two major threats to the international banking system as we enter the most serious and disruptive portion of the downwave. The first is the possibility of a major default among the lesser-developed country borrowers, who are heavily indebted to the commercial banking system. The second is the threat of a major withdrawal without notice of Arab money from both American and British banks. I am not alone in believing that the global banking system is in a very delicate condition, racing toward the most serious test it has had to face since the 1930s.

Banks can get into trouble from both sides of the balance sheet:

1. There could be a horrendous cumulative default by several of the lesser-
   developed countries, hitting banks already troubled by failing companies. That
   threatens the bank's assets.
2. Savings accounts maintained by the banks, plus Certificates of Deposit, could be
   withdrawn or not renewed. That would affect liabilities. A rapid withdrawal of
   funds represents the classic "run on the banks." The result could be catastrophic.
   Worldwide, it has been estimated that about 5 percent of bank assets represents
   cash on hand. The other 95 percent is lent or invested.
3. Banks operate under the assumption that conditions are always relatively normal, and nothing could happen to seriously enough endanger their assets or
   liabilities to cause a run, or bring about abnormal losses. Banks operate on a
   foundation of public confidence. As we have seen in the past, public confidence
   can suddenly turn to panic. The long list of failed financial institutions proves it.
   History shows many lost bank deposits.

The foundations of banking practices involve borrowing short and
lending long. Quite simply, in its extreme, this means taking money from
depositors that may be withdrawn without notice the following day while
lending it out on a twenty-year mortgage. Banks also honor checks drawn
on other banks and allow their customers and depositors to draw money on
these checks before they have cleared through the issuer. A sudden and
abrupt failure of a major bank or any emotive factor that leads to a crisis
in confidence could produce chaos in the weak and less prudent banks and
have a devastating effect on all of the banks.

When one bank goes down, if it's large enough, it will take others with
it in a domino effect. The banking panic of the 1930s began with the collapse
of the Creditanstalt in Austria. The banking panic in Britain during the
early 1970s began with the failure of London & County. Both of these
banking institutions were really minnows in the world of international
banking yet there were international repercussions of awesome dimensions. This time around, the names are going to get bigger and so is the
size of the defaults. The debts of Creditanstalt and London & County were
minuscule when compared with the size of recent defaults such as Drysdale, Penn Square, Banco Ambrosiano, Seafirst and the rest. But, no one
really knows at what point just a small failure or relatively modest dislocation will be the straw that finally breaks the back of public confidence.

The real uncertainty comes when depositors become aware of bank
problems, and begin to worry. In a real panic, the public does not distinguish between good and bad, or between sound and unsound banks. They
run to all of the banks to get their money out. All banks become suspect.
The classic public reaction is to withdraw money while the bank is still
solvent. This in itself leads to insolvency. The only thing that prevents
people from running regularly to get their money out is their belief that
the banks are not likely to fail. Once that changes, the banks will fail.

At the moment, the majority of financial institutions around the world,
whether they be finance companies, banks, building societies or other
forms of lending institutions, are essentially illiquid. Any institutions

predominantly in mortgages or consumer borrowing or heavily into other long-term lending could fail, regardless of how sound they now appear. It is time to take a very close look at where your liquid funds are tucked away, and to think very carefully about their safety.

HOW TO PROTECT YOURSELF FROM A BANKING CRISIS

What would a banking crisis mean to you as an individual? I am defining a banking crisis as a situation that would lead to a large number of bank moratoriums and possibly the closure of all banks for a short period. Under such circumstances, at best, there is no possible way that you could avoid considerable inconvenience. You may have bills that are due that have to be paid in cash. You simply might not have enough cash to live on. You could be stranded away from home with no access to funds. The ramifications are staggering.

A collapse in the banking system that leads to a banking crisis along the lines described could also mean a failure of the currency, should the monetary authorities decide to expand the money supply as a means of easing the situation. The Federal Reserve may not actually have to instigate such a policy. The currency would fail if sufficient numbers merely believed they would instigate such a policy and anticipated same. The failure of currency, as happened in Germany during the 1920s, would mean the near total loss of purchasing power of your money. Within weeks you could find that the price of a loaf of bread had soared from $1 to $10, to $10,000, to $1 zillion. These numbers are not as outlandish as they seem. Any German who lived in Berlin during 1923 will be totally familiar with the phenomenon, as will historians.

At the bottom line, in the event of a banking crisis, should you have all of your savings tucked away in a bank or thrift institution that goes bankrupt and never reopens—and that is not insured by the Federal Deposit Insurance Corporation—you will lose every penny of your savings.

That raises a very serious practical problem. What should you do? I cannot forecast just when the banks are going to hit some severe trouble, or how badly the coming banking crisis will affect the average depositor. All I do know is that risks are astronomically high. If, on any given day, depositors representing a mere 5 percent of sums on deposit at the banks demanded their funds (Arab money alone could do it), even the strongest would fail. Obviously, conditions would have to deteriorate quite considerably before this kind of panic developed. But depressions breed this type of panic. We are now in a worldwide depression.

It should be obvious that you must exercise the utmost caution as to where and with whom you put your savings, especially if you are dealing with financial institutions outside the United States. To begin with, foreign banks are not subject to the same banking regulations as U.S. banks. Should a branch of a French bank in Luxembourg experience difficulties, it is unlikely that the parent bank in France will support the branch office in a foreign country. And, furthermore, it is still not clear whether the branch bank of a U.S. bank located outside the United States will receive the support of the parent under international banking law. Depositors in the branch of a major U.S. bank located in Saigon learned to their cost that the supposed cover by the FDIC did not provide the guarantee they could have normally counted on had the bank been on U.S. soil. As a general rule, avoid putting funds on deposit outside the United States. If this is not a practical proposition, be absolutely certain that funds you may have outside the United States are being held by a branch of one of the U.S. "big ten," such as Citicorp, Chase, Bank of America, etc. The bigger the bank, the greater will be your safety. In the case of the large U.S. banks, moral suasion is likely to take precedent over international law. Fortunately, the U.S. banking system remains the strongest in the world and banking laws are designed to protect U.S. citizens to a greater degree than in any other country.

In America, banks that belong to the Federal Reserve System are likely to offer far greater security than those that do not. Under the Federal Reserve System, each account is insured for up to $100,000 by government guarantee of the FDIC. I would not recommend a deposit of more than $100,000 with any bank outside the U.S. top ten. Banks have been leaving the Federal Reserve System because that allows them to hold lower reserves against liabilities than if they were members. U.S. banks are more highly geared than any others in major Western countries. Be certain only to deposit funds with a member of the Federal Reserve System. The same considerations apply to the savings and loans.

The liquidity policies of finance companies and banks differ widely. Deal only with those which invest mainly in short-term government securities for their liquid funds. Always spread deposits between different institutions. If one of them experiences difficulties, only part of your assets will be hit. It would be very unwise to leave your funds with only one institution, regardless of how sound it may appear.

Most important of all . . . in fact it's absolutely vital . . . do not . . . do not . . . do not . . . under any circumstances . . . deal with any financial institution offering a deposit rate appreciably higher than the major banks, no matter who. Each day *The Wall Street Journal* reports money market rates. Use these rates as your guidelines.

Any financial institution offering a higher-than-market return gives rise to serious suspicions. If they are going to pay you more than the average rate, it means that they find it difficult to attract funds at the market rate. There are likely to be good reasons for that. If they are to make a profit on the high rate, they must also receive a much higher-than-market return themselves on their investments. They can only do that if they entertain above-average risk investments. The last thing you want is to have your funds supposedly safely tucked away, and then find they are being used for above-average risk investment. In practically every case of financial failure, failure occurred because of high risk investment.

It is possible, but not probable, that we may have a banking crisis of such severity that it will make no difference which banks or thrift institutions have your money. If the bank with your money is small and among the first to go broke, it will be rescued. If the thrift is small, you will find it merging with another thrift or bank, and you should be able to get your money without difficulty.

Should the entire system be threatened and shut down for a while, practically everyone with a deposit account will find themselves in difficulty. If there is a widespread banking moratorium like that of the 1930s, it will not make much difference which bank you were patronizing. The banks most likely to reopen first after a crisis are the flagship banks, the top ten or so "money center" banks in the United States. The nation will have to restore a monetary system of some kind in a crisis, and can only do it through the banking system. The banks that will receive the strongest support will be those with the highest safety for the greatest number, even though these may be the very banks exposed to the biggest defaulters.

There will be an escalating number of failures of financial institutions over the next two to three years. I have no way of knowing which companies are going under, and which will be the first of the banks to suffer catastrophe. I have no idea to what extent the government might be able to protect the interests of depositors, or whether the larger banks will be able to save the smaller banks, and thus protect the reputation of the banking system. What I am absolutely sure of is that there will be failures, and that some financial institutions will file Chapter 11. It is certainly not a matter of *if*, it is a matter of *when*. There is certainly a possibility that you may now be dealing with a company that could end up in bankruptcy. In many cases, it will mean a 100 percent loss of your savings. That chance is not worth the risk, when all that may be gained is an extra one or two percent per annum in interest.

SEVENTY YEARS OF INVESTMENT

Safety first must be the objective during the downwave. The rewards of such a policy may be far greater than you think. Money saved now and properly invested should yield many times its purchasing power in the years to come. We are entering the current phase of the downwave with exceptionally high yields which, if compounded, can produce staggering returns. Bernard Baruch was once asked if he knew of the seven wonders of the world. He replied: "I'm not too sure about the seven wonders of the world, but I can tell you about the eighth wonder . . . that's compounded interest."

There's a little calculation called "The Rule of 72." If you divide the number 72 by the yield on an investment, that is about how long it will take to double your money at a compound rate. At a yield of 12 percent, you double your money every six years. At 14 percent, you double it in just over five years. At 16 percent, you double it every four-and-a-half years. As we continue along the downwave, these rewards are available with fixed interest investments carrying the lowest possible risk.

Just as trends in fashion, religion, invention, literature, public morality and various other phenomena are related to economic activity, as one would expect, so too are investments. To maximize your investment returns and protect your capital, your investment strategy must be compatible with the economic environment in which you're operating. Most investors have developed their investment strategies on the basis of post-World War II experience. This is likely to turn out to be a disastrous and costly mistake. The post-World War II experience was the experience of the upwave. We are now in the downwave.

The Chinese philosophers believe that life is a circle. This philosophy certainly holds true for investment. During the early stages of the upwave, when interest rates are falling and investors are still licking their wounds from the ravages of a downwave, the most popular medium of investment is fixed-interest securities. At the early stages of the upwave real rates of return are high and it is perceived that safety in high-quality, low-risk investment is a better bet than common stocks where capital values fluctuate. As the upwave progresses, a new element comes into the equation— the element of inflation. The upward escalation in inflation during the upwave means that value in fixed-interest investments is eroded while real rates of return begin to fall. Money then moves out of fixed-interest investment into common stock investment which is more suitable for an inflationary environment. As the upwave reaches a peak, even common stock can't keep pace with inflation. Money moves out of common stock into "things." Collectibles become the only items capable of keeping up with the rampaging inflation: gold, silver, antiques, property and the like. When inflation peaks and a disinflationary environment sets in, collectible things collapse. Interest rates are usually sky-high at the inflationary peak. Investors find that yields are so high that they are getting a better return from simply leaving their money on deposit than they would be investing it in any of the alternatives. After the peak of the upwave, we get the downwave. Interest rates begin to fall and investors then move their funds out of cash or cash equivalents into fixed-interest investment for the duration of the downwave. At the end of the downwave, the upwave emerges and the circle begins anew. The best way to demonstrate this phenomenon is through the experience of long-term history.

1910–1920: Taking real returns, the decade from 1910 to 1920 was the worst of this century. Adjusted for inflation, real losses on fixed interest bonds, common stock or equities were quite heavy. Fixed interest issues fared worst, and equities best, but both groups suffered losses in real terms. For a brief period, there was a commodity price explosion and investors able to spot the terminal stage of the upwave and the way inflation hedges behave then, made fortunes. The profits were short-lived. The decade of 1910–1920 was similar to 1960–1970 in terms of investment performance.

1920–1930: The decade from 1920 to 1930 presented those once-in-a-lifetime years. Both major groups of stock exchange securities did well, with high real rates of return. Although the 1920–1930 decade was the first of the downwave, and included the Crash of '29, the decade ended with a satisfactory performance, except for those riding the commodity boom who failed to take their profits when the boom was over. There was a crash in commodity markets from 1920 to 1922, annihilating commodity speculators. Inflation hedges stopped working.

The 1920–1930 decade included the 1922–1929 period of secondary prosperity. The crash in commodity prices and in Florida land values sent a large flow of funds back into stock exchange investment.

During the decade, fixed-interest investments fared best. During those years, bonds began to emerge as an excellent hedge against deflation, although, during the previous decade, fixed-interest investment showed the worst negative real rate of return.

The decade 1920–1930 cannot quite be compared with 1970–80 in terms of the securities markets: the inflationary experience was so very different. Deep down, however, very comparable financial tides were at work. The equivalent of the stock market boom of the Roaring Twenties was the "tangibles" boom of the 1970s, particularly the boom in home prices. By comparison, the performance of the bond markets in both decades was thoroughly pedestrian. And perhaps this is why the beginning of the 1930s coincided with the highest real bond yields for the next fifty years, i.e., until the beginning of the 1980s.

1930–1940: For investors who were able to hold high-grade bonds through the depression years, the 1930s provided some of the best real rates of return of the twentieth century. Common stocks produced the lowest real returns for many decades on either side.

In the severe deflation of the early 1930s, funds initially flowed into secure cash equivalents such as Treasury bills, as the safety of the banks came into question. But as the fall in interest rates became clear for all to see, investors wished to lock in the high yields available on longer-term fixed-interest issues. Funds flowed out of cash into top-grade bonds offering high real returns as well as security. The trick was to spot the deflationary environment. Most investors missed it until much later in the decade. The double outcome was that while stocks crashed, top-grade bonds held up and then launched one of the longest and strongest advances in the history of the securities markets. It eventually saw Treasury bond yields down from 5 percent to under 2 percent, giving tremendous gains in capital as well as high real interest yields.

The decade 1930–1940 could well offer revealing guidelines to what lies in store during the decade 1980–1990—in that respect, and one another. That was the staggering gap that opened up between the highest and the lowest grade of bonds, between Treasury bonds and BBB corporate issues, which nearly reached double figures at one point.

1940–1950: By the 1940s it was accepted that, after nearly twenty years of deflation, deflation was likely to be a permanent way of life. War brought the beginning of the long inflationary upwave. At the time, this inflationary trend was considered the overriding deflation. The temporary respite in the upwave had begun, but very few people were aware of it. Fixed-interest investments continued to gain popularity during the 1940s. But over the decade, a long-term decline began in fixed-interest investments as inflation began to look ingrained. During the latter part of the decade, common stocks began to demonstrate their ability to cope with the gradually rising inflationary trend.

1950–1960: During the latter part of the 1950s, the "cult of the equity" was born. Inflation was recognized as a serious problem, and it was thought that the best way to beat it was with common stock. Inflation was growing moderately after World War II, and the cycle for fixed-interest investments had turned decidedly down. For the next two decades, fixed-interest investment was totally inadequate as a hedge against inflation. During the 1950s, only common stock produced a positive real return. For the decade, long-term bonds produced negative real returns.

1960–1970: Investment attitudes during the 1960s, the third decade of the upwave, were a restatement of the previous decade. Common stocks were once again the best performers. Bonds were still in the doldrums. In real terms, common stocks did not perform that well, and bonds produced a negative return. During the latter half of the decade, common stocks lost their luster completely. The Dow Jones Industrial Averages touched 1,000 interday in 1966 and spent the remainder of the decade below that level. To the surprise of many, inflation continued to move higher but investment in common stocks failed to benefit from the upsurge in inflation which marked the culmination of the Vietnam war: the supposed "growth stocks," the "nifty fifty" favorites of the megabuck institutional operators, in particular, fell from grace. During the second half of the decade of the sixties sinister forces were at work that would mean a decided shift in investment strategies if a positive real rate of return was to be achieved.

1970–1980: The great inflation of the 1970s in due course completely undermined the morale of investors in bonds. During this decade Treasury bond yields soared from around 6 percent to 14 percent, cutting the price of some long-dated issues by nearly half. In 1980, many observers were reconciled to the prospect of double-digit inflation, on and off, forever and ever. Bonds were dogs. They were even called "certificates of guaranteed

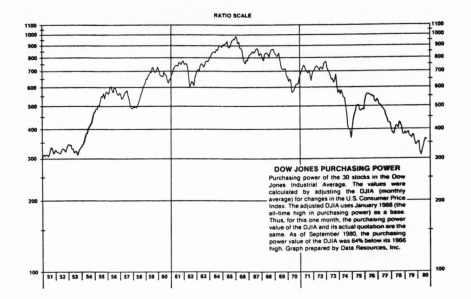

RATIO SCALE

DOW JONES PURCHASING POWER
Purchasing power of the 30 stocks in the Dow
Jones Industrial Average. The values were
calculated by adjusting the DJIA (monthly
average) for changes in the U.S. Consumer Price
Index. The adjusted DJIA uses January 1966 (the
all-time high in purchasing power) as a base.
Thus, for this one month, the purchasing power
value of the DJIA and its actual quotation are the
same. As of September 1980, the purchasing
power value of the DJIA was 64% below its 1966
high. Graph prepared by Data Resources, Inc.

FIGURE 40

From *Inflation-Proofing Your Investments* by Harry Browne and Terry Coxon,
copyright © 1981 by Harry Browne and Terry Coxon.
Reprinted by permission of William Morrow & Company.

confiscation" (by Franz Pick). Money funds were invented, and grew into
a $200 billion industry, to allow individuals to benefit from high interest
rates without the terrible loss of capital endured by long-bond holders in
times of rising yields—all compounded by high inflation.

Yet equities performed little better. Stocks had been sluggish throughout the latter half of the 1960s. In the early 1970s they failed to make any
headway on their mid-1960s peaks. When they crashed in 1974, it was at
last clear to one and all that the notion that common stocks provided
effective protection against inflation was just another myth. Adjusted for
inflation, the Dow Jones index at the end of 1980 was down to one-third of
its value at the 1966 peak. So it was that people turned to tangibles and the
decade ended in a speculative mania for precious metals and the like. The
peak of this mania was neatly symbolized in the peak of the gold price in
January 1980 at over $800—precisely double the level at the time of this
writing in summer 1983.

A closer study of investment in the seventy years from 1910 to 1980
is revealing. Before the peak inflation of 1920, the negative real return on
fixed-interest investment was at its highest for years. During the 1930s,
what had previously been the highest negative return became the highest
positive return in the fixed-interest market. During the 1940s, fixed-interest
holdings continued to produce a positive return. But in the 1950s, 1960s and
1970s, the negative return in fixed interest was far greater than during the
1960s, suggesting that the long-term trend was changing again.

In years of above-average inflation, no class of stock exchange security
proved an adequate inflation hedge. The only investments capable of pro-

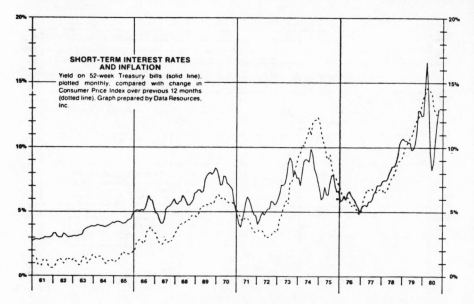

FIGURE 41

ducing a positive return against above-average inflation were commodities and collectibles, but only for a short period during the final stages of the upwave. During periods of average inflation, the best returns were in the equity market. When deflation ruled, the best returns came from fixed-interest investments.

The long-term record shows that fixed-interest securities, decade by decade, seem to be a better hedge against deflation than equity investment is against inflation. Since 1910, there were thirty-five years when the inflation rate was below average for the decade. For those thirty-five years, in only six years did the fixed-interest investments fail to produce a real return. Where there was a negative return, the performance was only marginally poor. Thus, on average, the return on fixed-interest investment was positive.

The net positive real return for each decade proved particularly important during the 1920s and 1930s, the first two decades of the last downwave. In twelve of the thirty-five years when inflation was below the average of the decade, common stocks failed to produce a positive real return. The performance of common stocks during the deflationary 1930s was disastrous.

This does not mean that fixed-interest securities are a better long-term investment than common stocks. On the contrary, although there were years in which common stocks generated a negative real return worse than that on fixed-interest investment, overall returns for equities were greater than for fixed-interest securities for most of the past seventy years.

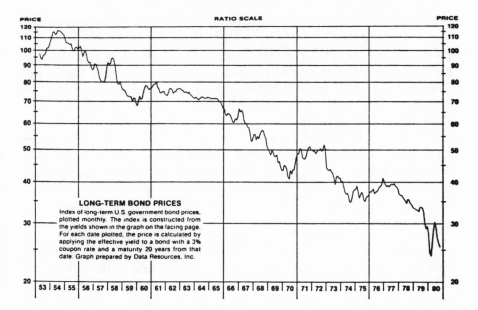

PRICE | RATIO SCALE | PRICE

LONG-TERM BOND PRICES
Index of long-term U.S. government bond prices,
plotted monthly. The index is constructed from
the yields shown in the graph on the facing page.
For each date plotted, the price is calculated by
applying the effective yield to a bond with a 3%
coupon rate and a maturity 20 years from that
date. Graph prepared by Data Resources, Inc.

FIGURE 42

From *Inflation-Proofing Your Investments* by Harry Browne and Terry Coxon,
copyright © 1981 by Harry Browne and Terry Coxon.
Reprinted by permission of William Morrow & Company.

The early 1980s: By early 1982 some people—a minority for sure—
began seriously wondering whether the long downtrend in bonds might be
over. Disinflation was here, a new era was in the making. Those 20 percent
prime rates of 1980 and 1982 were just a nasty memory. A further plunge
in interest rates in the summer won more converts to the new-bull-era-for-
bonds theory. But meanwhile something else was happening that was far
more seductive. The Dow Jones Industrials index, which for fifteen years
had consistently shrunk back from a barrier around the level of 1,000,
bounded clean over that barrier with stock turnover at record volumes. The
new era, it now seemed, was for stocks, not bonds. *Newsweek* ran a banner
headline proclaiming the new gospel.

Well, this is the moment of truth. It is up to you, the reader, to make
your choice. If you have followed me so far you know my views on the
matter. I see a huge scarlet sign with the word RISK written on it, and
beyond that a slope leading to a precipice. The slope is covered with the
furry bodies of lemmings rushing in the direction you can guess at. But the
decision is yours to make. I should merely like to make a suggestion of
what you should be deciding about. I suggest you should decide now where
the DJI will be in two or three years time, *not* where it will go in the
meantime.

There is a perfectly good psychological explanation for this rebirth of
the equity dream. It is nostalgia. After fifteen years of traumatic frustration, fund managers and investors are filled with heady nostalgia for the
good old days of the "growth stock," for the go-go days of easy money that

are the proper reward for fifteen years in the wilderness. But financial markets "have no memory and no conscience," as Dostoevski said of the roulette wheel. The only rewards they offer are treachery, at least to those who are unable to rid themselves of the dream of easy money. There is profound wisdom behind the Rothschild dictum for acquiring great wealth: *get rich slowly.* It normally takes quite smart people decades to acquire this understanding: most people never do. It may seem odd, but the downwave offers the chance to get rich slowly *quicker* than during the upwave.

INVESTMENT RECOMMENDATIONS DURING THE DOWNWAVE

When the long economic tide turns and the financial world is turned upside down, as it has been so many times in the past, every aspect of investment has to be reexamined in a new light. Think of the upwave as a period when money loses its value and the downwave as a period when money increases in value. When viewing the investment environment in this way, it is obvious that investments linked to nonmoney items will increase in value with the rapidity of the increase in inflation, while money-linked items will decrease in value. During the downwave, when we have disinflation ultimately leading to deflation, nonmoney items will lose value as the value of money increases. Accordingly, money-linked investment will become more attractive as deflation gains momentum.

The value of money is best determined by its cost in real terms. During the downwave the cost of money gets higher. During the upwave, money becomes cheaper, because governments print it as fast as they can. The true cost of money is the difference between the rate of inflation and interest rates. If inflation is at 15 percent and the prevailing price of bor-rowing money is 14 percent, then the cost of money is cheap. Only 1 percent. On the other hand, if prices are falling at the rate of 6 percent per annum and we have interest rates at 2 percent, the cost of borrowing money is 8 percent. Although nominal interest rates may appear high, the cost of money is very cheap. During a period of high inflation, the borrower profits by borrowing dear money and paying back in cheap devalued money. Quite clearly the lender suffers. During a period of deflation, the lender provides cheap money and later receives dear money when he gets paid back. The lender profits and the borrower suffers. During the down-wave, nominal interest rates are going to rise along with the rise in defla-tion. The process has already begun in earnest. The peak in interest rates occurred in 1980–1981 in the United States. In some other countries, like Britain and Japan, the peak in nominal rates came as early as 1974; there the trend of inflation and interest rates has been down for eight years. In other words, the long post-war trend of money value has been reversed. This phenomenon will have a truly drastic effect on your investment policy for the remainder of the downwave. The attitude toward many classes of investment will have to change, particularly life insurance.

Life Insurance: In one respect, the name of Connecticut is mud. As the home of the life insurance industry, it has come in recent years to be seen as the perpetrator of one of the biggest con-tricks in the history of savings. For in the post-war inflation era, a "whole life" or endowment "savings" policy has been one of the fastest known paths to the erosion of a lifetime of savings.

There are two main reasons for this unhappy phenomenon. The first is that life insurance is expensive to put on the books. Not only does a force of salesmen have to be retained and motivated, but huge back offices must be run to process paperwork. Everyone knows that costs in the service industries have been most vulnerable to the post-war inflation as salaries have risen faster than the cost of living. The life insurance industry is a service industry. It offers to take over the business of saving and death insurance from the individual, and such a service costs money.

The second reason is that the industry is mighty prudent. Some would argue too prudent. But in making their assumptions about how much money they will pay out in thirty years or more, a life insurer tends not to wish to take too many chances. If a widow were to hear from the insurer, "Listen, we were a little optimistic back in 1950. We don't actually have all that money we promised to pay back then, so you'll have to settle for just two-thirds," the widow will pass her grumbles on not just to the neighbors but to her legal advisers as well. Knowing what we know about the past thirty years, we feel this is a pretty improbable plea from a life insurance company today. But thirty years ago, nobody knew what we know today.

Thirty years ago, remember, the government was able to borrow money at 2 percent for two or three decades—from people like life insurers. Even when rates rose to 3, 4 and 5 percent not all the wisdom in Wall Street could foresee that by 1981, the government would have to pay 14 percent for its money. Whenever rates have gone up, the betting usually is that they will go down again—especially among prudent citizens. And life insurers feel they have to be among the most prudent citizens around.

So, the life insurance industry has been rather slow in raising the rates it feels it can "assume" for the future, hence the sums it offers to pay out on death or redemption. That has given it very big reserves of "profit," which in the case of stock companies belongs theoretically to the stockholders, but in the case of mutuals belongs to the policyholders.

Meanwhile, assumed rates of interest benefit may have been rising slowly, but they have been rising. Also, the hidden reserves accumulated by the companies have given them confidence. They have been encouraged to offer increasingly generous terms to compete for new business, and this process probably has some way to go. Now, what is going to happen if long-term interest rates go on falling—into single figures, and then through "hat sizes" right into single dice numbers? You've got it! *At some point,* the assumptions being made by the life insurers will be *too generous.*

Today, no one believes this will ever happen. In the late 1920s, life insurance didn't look like a very hot proposition either. Yet from the 1920s through the 1940s, life insurance was in fact one of the best savings propositions available. It could be that life insurance will be a key factor in the fight against savings erosion in the rest of this century.

At one time, the bulk of an average person's estate could be found in their insurance policies. Whole life and endowment policies have long been sold as savings plans. Before the inflation explosion, most of them adequately served their purpose. Over the past fifteen years, inflation has wrecked life insurance savings. Whereas $10,000 was a considerable sum twenty years ago, that $10,000 now looks a pittance in terms of purchasing power.

Right now, about the only thing that can be said in favor of endowment or savings-type policies is that they force some people to save who otherwise never would. But even now, any family head who does not hold a sufficient hoard of cash committed to safe, government guaranteed holdings, should be the holder of a term life policy, sufficient to guarantee the family's security on his or her death. That can be done for a comparatively tiny premium. Right now, this is probably the only insurance that makes total financial sense—death insurance.

The other kind of contractual saving that makes total financial sense today is a pension plan. If you save under a corporate pension plan, there is nothing further for you to do. It may not be a good plan, but you are most probably stuck with it. But if you are free to fix up your own pension plan —because you control your own company (or could do so) or are self-employed, you should know this. "In the name of retirement, the tax law allows you to divert money from your taxable income, put it in a pension plan, make investments with it, and shield the investment's earnings from all taxes. The tax deferral continues until you withdraw the money from the plan—which may be many years from now." Read the section on "Creating your own Pension Plan" in Harry Browne and Terry Coxon's excellent book *Inflation-Proofing Your Investments*, from which this quote is taken.

The most powerful and tax-efficient pension plan is your own corporate plan; the next best is a Keogh plan; and the last resort is an IRA or Individual Retirement Plan. In all three cases, the actual pension payments —the premiums—are tax-deductible up to certain limits. In all cases your investments should be confined to top-quality paper—through mutual funds if need be—split, say, two-thirds / one-third between bonds and short-term investments. If you could have a pension plan and don't, act now. It makes sense.

Life insurance premiums are not tax-deductible. However, there is one kind of "savings" policy to which the objections cited above to whole-life or endowment schemes, namely high company costs and low assumed interest rates, do not apply. It is the deferred annuity. This is a single premium policy that incurs no explicit sales charge, and guarantees an annuity or lump sum after a fixed number of years.

The amount of the future sum is not guaranteed: it consists of the initial principal compounded by floating interest payments. However, the interest is compounded without deduction of tax, and tax is only payable on payments at termination of the annuity period, or on earlier withdrawals. In this respect, it is as tax efficient as a pension plan and amounts to a savings account with full tax deferral. There is also a minimum guaranteed interest rate, usually a rather lowly 4 percent or so, but sometimes higher. The current interest rate will be below top market rates, but the next after-tax rate will be higher for many taxpayers. If you have $10,000 that you are just about to invest in gold, take my advice and stick it in a deferred annuity instead. If the "real," inflation-adjusted interest rate were to average about 3.5 percent, that would be $20,000 in *today's* money after twenty years. But I can guess you are not impressed!

So what of endowment insurance? My guess is that its day will come, and it will offer unique value. As the inflation rate keeps on getting lower, and those interest rates drop through hat sizes and dice numbers, the life assurance companies are going to start figuring they will go back up, not further down. We shall have come full circle—back to the way it seemed in the 1930s. The rates they assume will in fact gradually become more and more *imprudent,* but it will not matter much because of all the fat that was built up in their reserves during the post-war inflation. Those reserves will then go to benefit a new generation of policyholders. The "foolish children" of the last generation will become the "wise children" of the next one. Only there will be very, very few of them. These wise children will then enjoy net returns of maybe 7 or 8 percent for thirty years ahead, during which gross long-term interest rates may go rarely above 5 percent. They will be much in demand as marriage partners!

Gold: For at least 4,000 years, gold, silver and other metals were the world's money. The metals themselves were the principal form of exchange. All along, paper I.O.U.s had been the natural way of financing trade. But when governments came to print paper I.O.U.s, or banknotes, it was felt for a long time that such notes should be "backed" by gold. They should only issue notes in proportion to physical gold that they actually possessed. In fact, it did not have to be gold. Iran used the crown jewels at one time to back the note issue, and people seemed quite comfortable with the idea that the Persian crown jewels were as good as gold.

The "gold standard" came under pressure from time to time. After World War I, gold got mighty scarce around the world as most of it was owed to America for war debts. In Genoa, in 1922, it was decided that any foreign exchange issued by countries with some form of gold standard was itself as good as gold. This new "gold exchange standard" greatly increased the the pool of "effective" gold in the world. But this was only a palliative. There still was not enough gold to finance world trade. In 1926, Winston Churchill had the bright idea of confining the promise of "convertibility" to international exchanges. He introduced a "gold bullion standard" under which money was only convertible in very large amounts, for bullion.

So the currency was no longer effectively convertible for the citizens of Britain, or other small claimants. The United States pulled a similar trick in 1933, at the time of the famous bank holiday proclaimed by Roosevelt just after his inauguration. Americans were forbidden to hold gold. America too was on a "gold bullion standard." This was formalized by the Gold Reserve Act in January 1934. Gold was then revalued from $20.67 to $35, where it was to remain for thirty-seven years.

Once more, gold had been salvaged from a system in which it was playing an increasingly uneasy role. Its near 70 percent revaluation gave it a new lease on life. But the explosion of dollar credit during the post-war expansion placed increasing strains on gold. By then few countries were still on any gold standard. The world had moved to a dollar standard, but since the dollar still had its gold backing, gold was still—at the start of the 1970s—the linchpin of the system. Finally the strains became too great. Having first refused convertibility, the United States in 1973 abandoned all the dollar's links with gold.

Money no longer rested ultimately on any physical entity. It reverted to a simple symbol of confidence that had been the day-to-day status of all promissory notes throughout history. But for gold the change was more fundamental. Earlier silver, and now gold, was reduced to the state of a simple commodity, no different from platinum, copper or molybdenum. Gold no longer has any monetary value whatever, for the first time in at least four millenia.

It is hard for some people to come to terms with this change. In the old days, it made sense to hold gold at times because its monetary value was fixed in certain currencies. In the German hyperinflation of 1923, for example, gold, with its value fixed in dollars and pounds, gave good protection against the erosion of the mark. Some still feel the metal would have special value at a time of financial crisis. Nothing could be further from the truth. Since no one will know what value should be put on it, it will be spurned. It will be unloaded in vast quantities against that which has a known value—dollar bills—or unquestioned use, such as a hamburger.

It is conceivable that the monetary function of gold could some day be restored. But in the meantime it is just a counter for buying and selling among cranks and dreamers. Its price can just as well be $1,000 or $100.

Money Funds: The notion of pooling the resources of smaller investors, to allow them to take advantage of near-wholesale rates normally only available to the bigger fish, became real over a decade ago. The prototype of the mutual money funds, the Reserve Fund, was launched in spring 1972. It was the forerunner of a business that was to swell to $200 billion.

It was after the inflation—and stock collapse—of the first oil crisis that money funds really took off. The message that the public progressively came to understand during the latter 1970s and early 1980s was that here, at last, was a holding (it is not an *investment* in the traditional sense of that word) that was both safe and capable of affording a high measure of protection against inflation. For did not interest rates tend to rise when inflation accelerated? Yes they did, and even sometimes when inflation was declining. Money fund holders have known boom times of real interest rates, after inflation, at record levels during the 1980s.

For reasons I have already spelled out, there is good reason to believe these high real interest rates will be around for some appreciable time. Enjoy them. The money fund, or its equivalent, will be a central plank in the investment strategy for the downwave. The deregulation of the banking sector in the past year or so has provided a proliferation of choice of money outlets at near-market rates for investors great and small. All you need do is follow the two ancient criteria of liquidity and security.

The ultimate secure liquid investment is the Treasury bill—dealt with in Chapter Thirteen. Among money funds, the short-cut is to go only for those that invest exclusively in government paper, like the Capital Preservation Fund. Always be prepared to sacrifice a point of yield for security during the downwave. Among bank services, choose between money market deposits and super-NOW accounts according to your pocket and liquidity needs. And just make sure urgent liquidity needs can be met by more than one bank.

It must be recognized that money funds are not a one-way street. You can lose money in a money fund. Given the size of money funds, and the competition, there could also be a crisis in one or two. Money funds buy commercial paper. It is more than likely in the years ahead that several issuers of commercial paper will default. This will mean a loss in the money fund. Furthermore, even those money funds that deal only in government securities will be involved in repurchase agreements. The repurchase agreement is only as strong as the parties to that agreement, which in turn defeats the object of a money fund that deals only with government securities. Finally, if interest rates fall, the return from your money fund investment will also fall. There is no chance of "locking-in" high yields with a money fund.

THE BIG X

Prudence and caution are the investment dicta of the downwave. Cash or cash equivalents will serve you well. The average saver is going to benefit more than most simply by having his money in a bank account and making regular payments into one or more of the various life insurance plans that are offered. As far as everything else is concerned, take a big broad brush, dip it in red paint, and then mark them with a big X. Equity investment is a no-no during the downwave. Of course, there will always be those shares that move ahead while the majority tumble, but trying to find those most elusive areas that most only see after the event could be a costly exercise. You'll be playing the game with the odds against you, which is not a good idea. In a high-risk environment you must maintain a low-risk profile. The investment environment is going to present enormous risks for quite some time to come.

Property, jewelry, antiques, gem stones, stamps, coins, works of art, rare books, old newspapers and generally all collectibles are "things." These are the nonmoney items which produce no income but cost money to hold and store. During a period of rampant inflation they represent a store of value and, being perceived as such, they rise in value. During the down-wave, money is the best store of value that anyone could possible have. Cash is king during the downwave. Nonmoney items must therefore be avoided and cancelled from your list of possible investment vehicles for consideration.

The tyroinvestor, who often bombards himself with investment litera-ture, will be quick to come up with strategies that go beyond what may be perceived as an oversimplistic stance on my part. Pick up any literature on the option market and you'll find that it should be enormously profitable to purchase put options during the downwave, raking in the profits as prices plummet. In the back of the same book you'll also find a section that explains how enormously profitable it will be for you to sell put options during the downwave. So profitable is the option game for both buyer and seller, as described by the various popular literature, that it seems the problem of unemployment could quite easily be solved by the unemployed buying and selling options to each other at their appointed park benches. The fact of the matter is that during falling and rising markets, most people who attempt CBOE options lose money. Once again, this is a game where the odds are against both buyer and seller. Do not try to exploit the down-wave by buying put options. It is most unlikely that you'll be able to handle that type of risk.

What about selling short? This also seems like an obvious play. Were not fortunes made by the black-hearted short sellers during the 1930s? Joe Granville, the recently dethroned king of the bears, recommended short selling to his followers and annihilated all of them just before the U.S. stock market embarked on a ten-month bull run. For reasons that are too numer-ous to monitor in detail, very few investors profited by their short selling campaigns during the market crash of the 1930s. What they made on the initial downswing they lost on the subsequent upswing. What most inves-tors failed to recognize is that, during a cyclical bear market, shares spend more time rising than they do falling. This crucial timing factor has spelled the demise of many short sellers. Very few individuals can handle the risk involved in short selling. Don't try it!

Actually, "hedge funds" are supposed to help iron out some of the risk associated with short selling. There are several "hedge funds" which will soon be coming to the fore, trying to tempt you into parting with your speculative funds. As it so happens, professionals have shown no greater ability in assessing risk and dealing with contracting markets than have amateurs. If you think that someone else is likely to be able to handle a risk that you can't handle, forget it! No one is really going to care as much about your money as you do. It's going to be your responsibility to protect it.

In the final analysis, there are two points about financial markets that take most people, even hardened professionals, years to understand. Some never understand even though they may be partly aware of them. It's the difference between having twenty-five years experience and one year experience repeated twenty-five times. Often we can grasp principles on a skin-deep surface level. But, for the knowledge to be of any real practical value, the principles have to be felt in your gut and deep in your bones. The most important notion of all when it comes to dealing with financial markets is the element of risk and reward. Reward is always fully acknowledged but risk never, never, really reaches that gut level for most investors. The prospects of loss, yes. But not risk. The siren call of the marketplace is and always has been, "Never mind the risk, feel the reward." Conceptually, when all is said and done, the risk represents the gulf between the buyer and the seller. During the upwave the perceived gap between buyer and seller tends to be acceptably narrow. During the downwave it widens appreciably. At some time during the downwave the gap will widen to what could be described as infinity in many markets, for there will be all sellers and no buyers at all. Risk perception is probably the most valuable but least exploited area of investment. All you have to know is that you are entering a period of high risk which is like nothing you've ever seen in your lifetime. When you're standing on the railroad tracks and a locomotive is rushing toward you at 200 miles an hour, step off the tracks. You can always get back on the tracks if you want to after the train passes by.

The second aspect of investment consideration probably does not elude the stockbrokers and mutual fund salesmen but, with their assistance, conveniently eludes the average investor: cost of acquisition. In most cases, the agent who sells you a life insurance policy will receive a commission for the sale. The cost of his commission will be readily absorbed over the term of the policy without undue harm to the holder, providing he doesn't take out an endowment policy for forty years and decides he wants to cash it in during the first year after he's paid one monthly premium. Investments in stock market and commodity market securities are not intended for the same duration as life insurance policies, and the subject of commission costs is one that consistently gnaws away at quite skilled speculators until they must abandon or lose all. It has been estimated by a leading commodity broking house that the average amount paid out annually in commissions on private speculative accounts was just over 40 percent of the original capital sum committed. While stock market commissions are likely to be lower, they are certainly oppressive for the inveterate trader. No man alive can expect to consistently win against those odds, especially the average nonprofessional. Hence, the famous question of the novice on Wall Street, being shown all the yachts of the famous bankers and brokers in the New York harbor, "But where are the customers' yachts?"

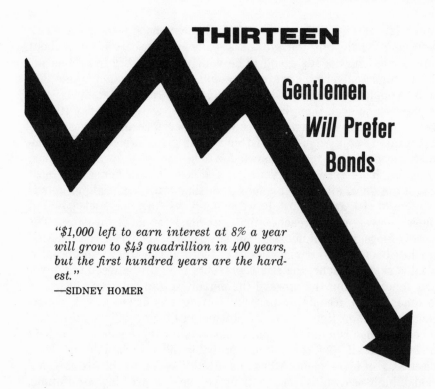

THIRTEEN

Gentlemen *Will* Prefer Bonds

"$1,000 left to earn interest at 8% a year will grow to $43 quadrillion in 400 years, but the first hundred years are the hardest."
—SIDNEY HOMER

In the late 1920s many Americans discovered the stock market for the first time in their lives. Before then, it was generally accepted that the stock market was some form of secret society only for the rich. But, in the late 1920s, anybody could play and everybody was playing. Americans also discovered they could buy on margin. With $10 down, they could buy $100 worth of stock. If the stock went up and was worth, say $200, they could sell the stock, put $200 down on margin and buy $2,000 worth of stock. If the $2,000 worth of stock doubled, they could then put down $3,800 on margin and buy $38,000 worth of stock. Many Americans actually parlayed their $10 into sums of this nature, and continued to do so until they reached the lofty level of financial suicide. All good things must come to an end. The stock market boom of the 1920s came to an end with an absolutely devastating financial holocaust.

After Americans discovered the stock market, margin and financial leverage, the final discovery was the margin call. That was a very sorry discovery. When a stock market continues to make new highs, the financially unwashed usually act on the assumption that it will go up forever and continue to plow more and more money in. People were borrowing on their homes, jewelry, paintings, antiques . . . everything conceivable to play the stock market . . . a considerable amount on margin. If you've borrowed to your maximum and are leveraged to the maximum when you get a margin

284

call, unless you put up some more money you're automatically sold out. The speed at which profits were compounded during the rising market was nothing like the speed at which the losses were compounded during the post-1929 market. The stock market has a tendency to fall faster than it rises. If you had $10,000 worth of stock, of which $1,000 was paid for, should the values of your stock fall by $1,000, your margin is wiped out. You get a margin call asking for sufficient dollars to restore your 10 percent equity stake. If you don't have the money, the stock market automatically sells sufficient of your stock to meet the margin call. If the stock falls further, you then get another margin call. Once again, if you don't have the cash to put up, you're automatically sold out. During the crash of 1929 the process merely fed upon itself until most people were totally wiped out. During the early 1930s, a majority of Americans were flat on their derrieres due to the stock market disaster. It took many, many years before enough confidence was restored in the stock market to tempt investors back again. Large numbers of those who managed to salvage some of their money after the crash concentrated their efforts on the safety of high-quality bonds and government securities during the late 1930s and early 1940s, preferring to avoid the hazards of the stock market. As it turned out, those who were merely seeking safety and security actually made great fortunes in their pursuits, purely as a result of their prudence and caution at that particular time.

Somewhere around the middle of the 1950s, the age of affluence began to peek its nose above the horizon. An increasing number began nibbling at the stock market again. During the early part of the decade of the 1960s most businessmen and those who were steadily employed began hearing the sweet symphonic music of coins jangling in their pockets as the personal disposable income of the nation began to rise strongly. By the second half of the 1960s, in spite of the rise in the rate of inflation—or maybe as a result of it—most Americans had managed to put aside some money that had been accumulated above and beyond day-to-day living expenses. The decade of the 1960s became known as the "swinging sixties."

To most Americans alive in the second half of the 1960s, the stock market crash of 1929 was a vague echo with little meaning. Most Americans were remarkably unsophisticated about investment at the time and the traditional store of savings was the friendly local bank. The newly affluent merely placed their surplus funds into savings bank accounts that were paying 4.5 to 5 percent at the time. "War" bonds were also resurrected during the second half of the 1960s, along with U.S. savings certificates among the unwashed. The rest of the monetary unsophisticates—a goodly percentage of the total of newly affluent—suddenly "discovered" the stock market. A whole new generation was seduced by the promise of making a killing in the stock market for the first time ever. Initially, indirect investment through mutual funds caught the eye of the public. Later, it was direct investment on margin. In the early 1960s a nightclub dancer named Nicolas

Darvas wrote a book called *How I Made $2,000,000 in the Stock Market*. The book told how the dancer worked out a method called the "box system" and used it to play the stock market from his various dressing rooms during nightclub engagements around the world. He made the operation look as easy as pie. The book became a best-seller. Although then-Attorney General Louis Lefkowitz accused Darvas of misleading members of the public, at the time no one knew what the outcome would be. The public was hooked by the easy get-rich-quick method suggested by Darvas. Many novice investors spent their days under the influence of Darvas's "box," mesmerized by their new discovery of the stock market.

As was the case in the 1920s, for most Americans the discovery of the stock market in the mid-1960s was a sad experience. In 1966 the Dow Jones Industrial Averages hit a peak and began one of the longest and most treacherous periods in market history. From 1966 through 1974, a falling market was an almost annual event. It wasn't a market that went down for nine whole years, it was a "roller coaster" affair involving sporadic stock market breaks interspersed with a few sharp upswings. By and large, it was the most frustrating and unprofitable period of stock market activity since the 1930s. The biggest dive of all took place in tandem with the 1973–1976 recession. By late 1974, when the American stock market was experiencing the last throes of distress selling, prior to the emergence of the secondary prosperity, millions of plumbers, barbers, waiters, bricklayers, dishwashers and migratory fruit pickers had lost all of their savings. Many vanished from the stock market completely, disillusioned for the rest of their lives. Ironically, the timid souls who had simply put their money on deposit with a savings bank because they didn't know of any other place to put it, did a far better job of preserving their capital than those who ventured forth in pursuit of easy riches. According to the performance records of the securities industry during the period from 1966 to 1974, even at a meager return of only 5 percent a year on their money, the people who had savings accounts wound up in far better shape than the more adventurous ones. The savers also did better than a large number of Wall Street "experts" and institutional portfolio managers.

The story certainly doesn't end there. In 1975, the period of secondary prosperity began. As I've mentioned, during the period of secondary prosperity, people have a chance to relive the experience of three decades, compressed into one decade. The investment experience of 1966 through 1974 was similar to the investment experience of the period 1918 through 1922. In 1974, the Dow Jones Industrial Averages touched 631. By early 1983, those averages had doubled, while individual shares in hi-tech companies had tripled and quadrupled in yet another public-sponsored speculative orgy. While those numbers may look impressive, rather than assuming the risk of the stock market, either through ignorance or desire, an exceptionally large number of American investors have chosen to invest the spoils of secondary prosperity in money market funds, as an alternative to the savings account. As it so happens, despite the stock market boom, most Americans who invested their money in money market funds are ultimately going to show better rates of return than the stock market players, as the market plummets downward in a crash that will make the 1929 affair look like a garden tea party. Rates of return have been falling for the money market funds as interest rates have fallen. As rates fall, the income receivable from money market funds will be lower. Before interest rates get too low, a number of investors will want to lock in the high yields for as long as possible. Thus, as interest rates fall, and it is perceived that investment in the stock market is one of the riskiest and most foolhardy areas where anyone could invest his money—as it was perceived in the early 1930s—a new investment mode will be rediscovered and achieve growing popularity. We have come full circle. The bond market has recently been playing a return engagement after ravaging investors for nearly three decades.

THE EIGHTH WONDER OF THE WORLD

Essentially, when you invest in money funds or the bond market, you have two intentions. The first is safety and the preservation of your capital. The second is income. On the surface, neither approach may seem particularly exciting. The reason it does not seem exciting is that most people are so desperately attracted to the idea that the stock market is a way to get rich quick, they fail to appreciate the far greater benefits that can accrue by a program designed to help you get rich slowly, but almost surely. In this maddening desire to get rich quick, most people fail to appreciate the dynamic power of compound interest. This is understandable when all you're going to get is 5–6 percent from a savings account and you're unlikely to reinvest the income. But, when you can lock in yields of 10–15 percent for ten years or more on a compound basis, the entire affair takes on a totally different perspective.

It has been said—with far more truth than humor—that if the Indians who sold Manhattan Island for $24 had placed the $24 in a bank that paid the prevailing rate of interest of 6 percent at that time, and if the interest had been added to the principal annually and both were reinvested at the subsequent prevailing rates of interest over the years since the sale, by 1950 the original $24 would have grown to more than the value of all the real estate in Manhattan today.

Now let's look at another equation. A close friend of mine recently purchased a poplar plantation in central France. When he purchased that plantation he calculated that the financial return on a suitably located poplar plantation in the area averaged 8.45 percent per annum in real terms over the past 2,000 years . . . adjusted for inflation. As such, being a conservative investor, he figured a real rate of return of 8.45 percent per annum was a pretty good deal, so he bought the plantation. He then carried out a few more calculations. He is in the process of building a family and it is his intention to keep the plantation in the family, passing it down through the generations. If his subsequent dynasty continues to replant at an 8.45 percent average rate of return every year—in other words, "plough back" the assumed yearly return for decades—it is his contention that his generation and all future generations in his family will be financially secure.

After twenty years, the value of the enlarged plantation will be five times the original stake, in constant money. After fifty years, the value will be fifty-six times the original stake. And—make sure you're sitting down before you attempt to digest the next few numbers—after 100 years the original stake would be multiplied 3,813 times, and after 200 years the growth in value would be over 10 million times the initial outlay *in real terms*. Don't forget, "real terms" means *after* any projected rate of inflation has been accounted for. There you have the lessons of—not 200 years of history—but 2,000.

Of course, there are certain problems involved in the equation. One would be to find sufficient suitable space for the program of expansion that would be needed if the process was to be continued for 200 years. This is one unquantifiable element of the program that anyone who wishes to try it should consider. Moreover, the kind of dynamic mentality required for such a single-minded program is not to be encountered every day. Certainly not in Wall Street today. But the exercise illustrates the process by which great fortunes have been amassed . . . perhaps *all* great fortunes.

Financial markets have never offered such *real* rates of return over long periods. Three or four percent has been more like the norm. But the long waves of expansion and contraction in prices and in economic life have produced variations from the norm that, when recognized, were capable of building fortunes with very little risk for those of independent thought and farsightedness. In certain types of securities, at certain times, the returns have been even double the 8.45 percent a poplar plantation could have produced over the past 2,000 years. On some occasions, compound returns that could have been secured for as long as thirty or forty years were even better than that. At other times, real rates of return have been negative for very long periods.

All the evidence suggests that the early 1980s offer a once-in-a-lifetime opportunity to profit from one of the long periods of far above average returns in an investment area that currently also offers one of the lowest risks—high-grade bonds and U.S. government securities.

Investors who bought U.S. government bonds in 1982 could have received a rate of return of 15 percent per annum without considering the capital gain that accrued between 1982 and 1983. During the summer of 1983, investors in long-term U.S. bonds could still have obtained returns of 11.75 percent. Of course, there was a big boom in bond prices between 1982 and 1983. But there's still plenty to go for at current rates of return. If interest rates happen to move up again, there'll be even more to go for. But don't forget the words of Jesse Livermore, who was probably the greatest market operator the world has ever known: "A man may know what to do and lose money if he doesn't do it quickly enough."

The following table shows you what to expect if you save a constant sum of money each month and reinvest the income through a bond fund or by direct investment in high-grade bonds or U.S. government securities with maturities ranging from 10 to 30 years.

ANNUAL YIELD OF 6%

	10 Years	20 Years	30 Years
$ 10	$ 1,638	$ 4,620	$ 10,045
25	4,097	11,551	25,113
100	16,387	46,204	100,451
200	32,774	92,408	200,902
500	81,939	231,020	502,257
1,000	163,879	462,040	1,004,515

ANNUAL YIELD OF 10%

	10 Years	20 Years	30 Years
$ 10	$ 2,048	$ 7,593	$ 22,604
25	5,120	18,982	56,510
100	20,484	75,936	226,048
200	40,968	151,872	452,096
500	102,422	379,684	1,130,244
1,000	204,844	759,368	2,260,487

ANNUAL YIELD OF 15%

	10 Years	20 Years	30 Years
$ 10	$ 2,752	$ 14,972	$ 69,232
25	6,880	37,430	173,080
100	27,521	149,723	692,321
200	55,042	299,446	1,384,642
500	137,605	748,619	3,461,605
1,000	275,217	1,497,239	6,923,210

BUY U.S. BONDS NOW. . . . "YOU CAN'T LOSE"

That was the message of David L. Lindsay of Babson & Co., Boston, in a feature article in the January 1982 issue of *Pensions & Investment Age*. Most people are aware that if interest rates start to fall the capital value of the bonds will increase and profits will be made. According to Lindsay, what most people have yet to discover is that even if interest rates move higher over the next few years and the interest rate picture worsens, it will still not be possible to lose money on U.S. domestic bonds, regardless of what happens.

"Even supposing that interest rates move higher than the fiercest bears are right at the moment predicting," says Lindsay, "under virtually any plausible pattern of interest rate behavior, nominal returns on U.S. bonds would stay positive just on the strength of income payments alone." The reason behind Lindsay's optimism is that interest rates on U.S. bonds can now be seen to have reached levels where the income components of the total return on bonds have become larger than ever before in relation to the price change components. In order to demonstrate the principle in simpler terms, let's go back a few years in history. Back in the middle of the 1970s, the prevailing rate of interest was in the area of 7 percent. The expectation was that should interest rates rise to 8 percent, that would cause a fall in the U.S. Treasury thirty-year-bond of 11 percent. Given a current coupon bond trading at par, the 11 percent drop in the capital value would offset the 7 percent coupon, in which case the bond gives you a negative return of 4 percent or more, depending upon your income tax bracket. What can be seen is that the change in prices as a result of the rise in interest rates was 50 percent more than the coupon. But things have changed considerably. Now, interest rates are in the area of 15 percent rather than 7 percent and the price change relative to the coupon in the event of a 1 percent rise in interest rates is no longer 50 percent more than the coupon. Should prevailing interest rates rise from 15 percent to 16 percent, that would mean your current coupon bond would only fall in price by 6 percent. Since you're getting a 15 percent coupon, you're still not losing. That 1 percent change in interest rates leaves you with a positive rate of return of 9 percent. The fascinating aspect is that even if interest rates stage an advance as spectacular as that which took place during the 1970s, you'd still come out ahead of the game. (Bear in mind we're dealing with long-term rates as opposed to the wild gyrations in short-term rates.) A comparable increase to that which took place in the mid-1970s would be an upward gain of 210 basis points. Should the prevailing level of interest rates advance from 15 percent to 17.1 percent, your bond would fall in value by 12.2. Considering the 15 percent coupon, you wind up with a positive return of 2.8 percent.

The typical bond portfolio in the United States currently has an average maturity of 15 percent and a yield of close to 15 percent. Given the support that this level of income provides for total return, according to Lindsay, "it is almost impossible to envisage an economic climate over the next five years that could result in a loss in these bond portfolios from current levels." Developing a worst case scenario, let's say the U.S. economy, along with the financial system, experiences even greater difficulties during the 1980s than it did in the 1970s. Once again, on the basis of a worst case scenario, let's assume the most negative predictions are right and that interest rates rise to 25 percent on the long end. (Should interest rates actually rise to 25 percent and remain there for any appreciable time, the shock to the business community would be such that the ultimate wave of bankruptcies would ensure that rates began falling even more rapidly than they rose . . . but that's actually beside the point.) Furthermore, let's make another assumption that is quite reasonable: that the 1000-basis-point rise in interest rates takes place at regular intervals over a five-year period, advancing at the rate of 0.5 percent every six months. Now for the magic of compound interest. On the basis of a bond portfolio with an average maturity of fifteen years with coupons updated throughout the next five years, even under the horrible conditions of a steady rise in long-term interest rates to 25 percent, the portfolio would still yield an average return of 10.4 percent and an aggregate increase over the period of 64 percent. Let's say you started with $10,000 at an average yield of 15 percent, the loss in market value of the portfolio would be much more than offset by the interest and interest on interest as reinvestment takes place at continually higher rates, leaving you with $16,424.35.

Year	Interest rate level	Portfolio value before interest	Interest income	Portfolio value
0	15.00	$10,000,000	–	$10,000,000
½	16.00	9,442,080	$ 750,000	10,192,030
1	17.00	9,648,826	815,366	10,464,192
1½	18.00	9,930,608	889,456	10,820,064
2	19.00	10,291,557	973,806	11,265,363
2½	20.00	10,737,603	1,070,209	11,807,812
3	21.00	11,276,613	1,180,781	12,457,394
3½	22.00	11,918,605	1,308,026	13,226,631
4	23.00	12,676,037	1,454,929	14,130,966
4½	24.00	13,564,187	1,625,061	15,189,248
5	25.00	14,601,639	1,822,710	16,424,349

Compound annual rate of return   10.4%

Lindsay produced the above table to demonstrate the effect of the compound annual return on a bond portfolio of $10 million. Now, of course, there's always the unexpected. If suggested interest rates could rise to 10 percent in the mid-1970s, this would be considered horrendous but conceivable. If you had suggested that interest rates might rise to 22 percent, as they have done, this would be considered catastrophic and a most unlikely possibility. At the moment, a rise in interest rates to say, 35 percent, would seem an unlikely possibility and bordering on potential catastrophe. Many believe bond markets would be totally wiped out and credit markets would cease to exist. But in all actuality, the world would still continue and we would survive an interest rate of even 35 percent. What would happen to the bond portfolio on the basis of a compound interest rate with interest reinvested at the progressively higher levels? If we construct tables similar to that which has been illustrated, it will be found that if long bond rates move from 15 percent to 35 percent over the next five years, you still come out with a positive return in spite of the decline in capital value. In fact, you would end up with a portfolio worth 50 percent more than you paid for it today involving an 8.5 percent compound rate of return.

Should we take the matter to still further extremes? Let's say interest rates explode at the rate of 10 percent per year over the next five years, leaving us with prevailing interest rates of 55 percent per annum at the end. The dramatic increase in interest rates and the total return received by investors would be so tremendous that, arithmetically at least, the compound return with interest rates at 55 percent would be even greater than if interest rates were 35 percent. A point is reached where the income will increase faster than capital value declines as a result of the rise in interest rates. At 35 percent your compound rate of return is 8.5 percent. At 55 percent the compound rate of return is 8.8 percent. Things have sure changed since the days when a 1 percent rise in interest rates meant a wipeout of your coupon and a chunk of capital to boot. As usual, very few have recognized the nature of the change.

In the examples that have been presented it has been assumed that interest rates would rise steadily from current levels of around 15 percent in equal amounts half-yearly over the five year period. Actually, it would be to the advantage of the bond holder for interest rates to rise sharply and hold the higher levels throughout the five-year period. This would ensure the possible reinvestment returns and the greatest amount of interest on interest in the years to follow. The worst equation would result if interest rates remained relatively stable over the next four years and then advanced sharply in the fifth year. But, even if that did happen, on a worst case basis, bond holders still come out with a positive rate of return.

I have tried to present a bottomline case for the prospective bond purchaser, using the most pessimistic numbers that are remotely within the realms of possibility. It should be fairly clear that even if interest rates soar to the unprecedented rate of 55 percent, you still won't lose money on bond holdings that are acquired within the parameters mentioned. Now I'm going to turn the equation around and show you what will happen to your bond investments if interest rates fall. Once again, I am using the 15 percent yield as a maginot line. In 1982 yields were over 15 percent. During 1983 the average so far is 11.25 percent. The following table demonstrates what would happen if interest rates actually retraced half of the rise that has taken place since the mid-1970s, falling back to 11.5 percent. As we have seen, in only one year, interest rates made that retracement. I don't know whether or not this situation will stabilize and we can maintain such an average over the next four years, but this would not be an unreasonable expectation. It should also be noted that, in a period of falling interest rates, the lower the peak from which we start, the greater the capital gain for each 0.5 percent fall in rates. Once again I am assuming a bond portfolio that maintains an average maturity of fifteen years and that coupons are regularly updated to prevailing yield levels throughout the five-year period. The following table shows that you'll end up with a gain of 136 percent over the next five years through the combination of capital gain and compound interest.

Year	Interest rate level	Portfolio value before interest	Interest income	Portfolio value
0	15.00	$10,000,000	–	$10,000,000
½	14.65	10,208,154	$ 750,000	10,958,154
1	14.30	11,190,162	802,685	11,992,847
1½	13.95	12,251,160	857,489	13,108,649
2	13.60	I3,395,941	914,328	14,310,269
2½	13.25	14,629,448	973,098	15,602,546
3	12.90	15,956,775	1,033,669	16,990,444
3½	12.55	17,383,161	1,095,884	18,479,045
4	12.20	18,913,981	1,159,560	20,073,541
4½	11.85	20,554,740	1,224,486	21,779,226
5	11.50	22,311,069	1,290,419	23,601,488

Compound rate of return   18.7%

There you have it. If rates rise to a level of 25 percent over the next five years, should you start with a bond portfolio producing a yield of 15 percent, although the rise in interest rates will mean that you suffer a loss in capital value, you still come out with an increase in the aggregate return of 64 percent. On the other hand, if you start with a bond portfolio yielding 15 percent and rates yield an average 11.5 percent over five years, you end up with a gain of 136 percent. In the case of rising interest rates, compound interest offsets the loss in capital value. In the case of falling interest rates, you receive the benefit of compound interest and an increase in capital values.

Obviously, the single most important aspect of bond investment is interest rates. I have shown you what will happen if interest rates fall. I have also demonstrated what is likely to happen if interest rates rise. But what are interest rates likely to do during the downwave? Obviously, the answer to that question will play an important role in your investment planning. If interest rates are likely to rise, then it could be that you would be better off with a money fund or a bank account than you would be with a bond portfolio. On the other hand, if you have a money fund or a bond portfolio and interest rates fall, ultimately you will find yourself with a very low return while having missed the opportunity of the huge capital gains that would have been made in the bond market. While it is interesting to look at both sides of the bond return equation, it really is important to take a position on interest rates.

As it so happens, the interest cycle is one of the most consistent and dependable financial phenomena known to investors. The fact that the interest rate cycle has been so reliable and infallible, involving parameters that can be seen to date back several *thousand* years, is probably why so few professionals talk about it, keeping the information to themselves. Just as sure as night follows day and winter follows fall, interest rates will decline to periodic lows and rise to cyclical peaks. Sometimes the rate of ascent or descent will be slow and gradual. Yet, there are other occasions when moves in interest rates can be explosive. Interest rates rose quite sharply during 1969–1970. There was another rapid rise in rates during 1973–1975. One of the most explosive moves in interest rates took place during 1981 and 1982.

Up until 1982 the frequency of tight money conditions had led to a situation where succeeding peaks in interest rates were successively higher than the previous ones and the complete cycle of interest rates from peak to trough was becoming progressively shorter. The shortening of the interest rates cycle was primarily the effect of an unfolding economic story in the United States and other countries—the tremendous growth of industry in the second half of the century, the great proliferation of government expenditures, higher standards of living for millions of families—all of which have fueled continuing inflation year after year and an incessant demand for money and credit. Industry kept on expanding through the early 1970s as the population increased; consumers demanded more and more credit and further credit was required for capital expenditures. Consumers have never been interest-rate sensitive and have always been willing to pay usurious rates of interest if immediate gratification was offered by way of a new home, TV set, video recorder and other items that allowed them to live in a manner to which they would like to be accustomed.

During the post-war era, we've seen a series of business contractions that were relatively short in duration. Industry overexpanded, workers lost their jobs, they defaulted on their mortgage repayments and were unable to keep up with their installment commitments. Mortgages were foreclosed, cars repossessed, television sets, furniture and other goods were carted off in trucks. When this happens, the demand for money falls. Interest rates fall too. The stock market goes down. But, eventually, the process of debt liquidation spends its force. The whole process starts all over again and interest rates begin sneaking up once more until another peak is reached.

Up until the early 1970s, the periods when interest rates fell were much shorter than the periods when interest rates rose, because the periods of economic expansion were longer than the periods of contraction. As we now know, this is the normal pattern of the upwave. When the upwave reaches a terminal stage, the periods of contraction occur with a greater frequency and the interest rate cycle from peak to trough becomes shorter and shorter until the entire relationship is reversed. This is what we've already witnessed. The recession between 1973 and 1975 was steeper than all of the recessions since the upwave began. The most recent period of economic contraction, that politicians claim we are moving out of, was even deeper than that one. Between November 1981 and December 1982 we saw the sharpest fall in interest rates since the 1930s. The yield on a thirty-year U.S. government bond fell to just under 10.5 percent. During the upwave, there were six bull markets in bonds. The average decline in yields during these six bull markets was 20 percent. The decline in yields between November 1981 and December 1982 was actually 31 percent. The fourteen-point upward drive in bond prices between November 1981 and December 1982 was 50 percent greater than the average of the six complete bull markets in bonds during the three decades of the post-war era, and as I will demonstrate, the current long-term cyclical bull market in bonds is likely to be only at its very early stages. The interest cycle has now been fully reversed. During the next decade we can expect to see long periods when interest rates will fall and correspondingly short periods when interest rates will rise. The long-term history of interest rates tells the rest of the story.

THE LONG-TERM TREND IN INTEREST RATES

The history of interest rates in America is highly instructive. Over the past forty-eight years, interest rates in America have been at their lowest in history, and also at their highest. The lowest rate of interest ever recorded in the United States was in about the middle of 1946. During 1946, stockbrokers were charging their clients an interest rate of 0.75 percent per annum on the debit balances in their accounts. At the time, if you wanted to purchase a home in America, the interest rate on the mortgage would have been somewhere in the area of 3.75 percent. Long-term U.S. government bonds were selling on a yield basis of 2.25 percent. You could buy those bonds on margin with a stake of only 7 percent of the capital value and be charged an interest rate on the margin account of a mere 0.75 percent. Obviously, if interest rates fell a fraction, you would stand to make a quick fortune. That was the extreme low point of interest rates in American history. Since the time of the extreme lows in interest rates we have also experienced the extreme highs, in early 1982.

A few years ago an absolutely fascinating book was published called *The History of Interest Rates*, by Sidney Homer. In his book, there is a record of minimum interest rates in Babylonia, Greece and Rome, beginning in 3000 B.C. and continuing until A.D. 350. While the recordkeeping may be somewhat suspect, a picture is produced of long-term interest rate activity involving a period of extremely important statistical significance. Obviously, a record of sequential repetition that spans nearly 4000 years is going to be more meaningful than interest rate behavior over the past ten, twenty or thirty years.

What can be seen from this very long picture is that interest rates, like trends in property prices, involve long-term cyclical sequences. Within these long-term sequences parameters of interest rates can be seen. Be-

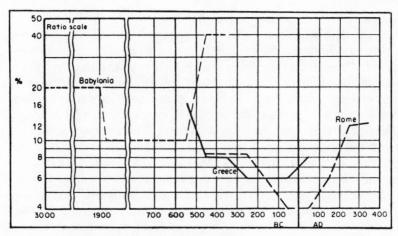

FIGURE 43   INTEREST RATES 3000 B.C.–A.D. 350

From *A History of Interest Rates* by Sidney Homer, copyright © 1977.
Reprinted by permission of Rutgers State University.

tween 3000 B.C. and A.D. 350 the normative peak in the long-term interest
rate cycle was approximately 15 percent. The normative low for the sequences was approximately 4 percent. There are a few very brief periods
when interest rates moved up into the 20–30 percent area, but never remained there for very long. There we have a picture of the trends in interest
rates over 3350 years in Babylon, Egypt, Greece and Rome. When interest
rates fell to 4 percent it would have been reasonable to assume that interest rates had fallen about as far as they were going to fall. When interest
rates rose to 15 percent, it would be no less reasonable to assume that rates
had risen about as far as they were likely to rise.

The trend in interest rates in America for the 170 years from 1800
through 1970 involves parameters of approximately 8 percent at peaks and
3 percent at troughs on average. The dots in Figure 44 indicate monthly
high or low yields at cyclical turning points in this century. In this period
we can begin to see some cyclical continuity. From 1862 through 1898
interest rates declined steadily. The falling trend of interest rates lasted
thirty-six years as did the bull market in bonds. From 1898 through 1920,
interest rates rose. The rising trend in interest rates lasted twenty-two
years as did the bear market in bonds. From 1920 through 1946 interest
rates fell. There was a bull market in bonds lasting for twenty-six years.
From 1946 through 1982 interest rates rose. The bear market in bonds
lasted thirty-five years. We have now begun a new long-term secular downtrend in interest rates and a secular uptrend in bond markets. What these
historical sequences demonstrate is that the long-term uptrend that is now
underway is unlikely to be a short-term affair since the trend in interest
rates is nowhere near as volatile as trends in other capital markets.

The period from the 1940s through the early 1980s was an unusual one.
The yield on U.S. government securities spanned a range involving the

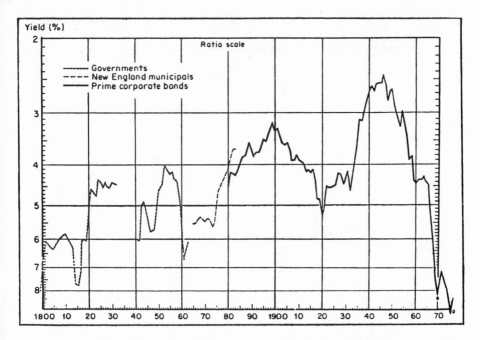

FIGURE 44   THE TREND IN INTEREST RATES IN THE U.S. 1800–1970

Reprinted from Salomon Brothers Inc's Interest Rate Chartbook.

lowest interest rates in U.S. history to the highest. The normal parameters for interest rates in America involve 12 percent at the peaks and 2.5 percent at the lows, excepting for temporary trend deviations.

During the period that spanned the lows of interest rates in the 1940s and the highs in the early 1980s, the yield on U.S. government bonds moved from a 1946 low of 2.125 percent to a high level of 14.25 percent. The extreme yield in U.S. government bond prices, exceeding the normal parameters by a significant margin, was responsible for the tremendous downward drive in yields and upward push in bond prices that followed. The low in U.S. bond prices was made in the summer of 1981. Between the summer of 1981 and October 1982, bond prices advanced by 38 percent.

Municipal bonds in the United States did not make their lows until February 1982 to produce a 15 percent yield. Between February and July of 1982, municipal bond prices rose by 43 percent to yield just under 9 percent.

The long-term Kondratieff wave cycle involves a fifty-four-year average. This fifty-four-year average, involving an upwave and a downwave, has been superimposed on the Moody's industrial bond yield for the corresponding period. The actual interest rate experience and the terminal junctures suggested by the periodicity of the long Kondratieff wave is extremely significant statistically and could only be violated over several thousand repetitions of history. Since there is a strong relationship between interest rates and inflation, the long-term behavior of interest rates is coincident to the long-term pattern of price behavior.

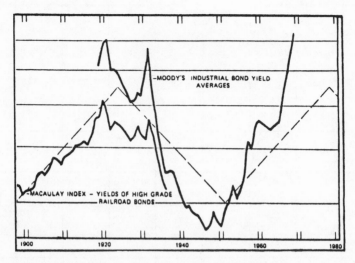

FIGURE 45   KONDRATIEFF APPLIED TO THE MOODY'S INDUSTRIAL BOND YIELD
AVERAGES

Americans have now endured a period of steadily rising interest rates
for no less than thirty-six years. People have been brainwashed to anticipate higher interest rates. We've practically come to the point where every
individual in the United States is acutely aware of what banks may be
willing to pay for one month-, two month- or three-month deposits virtually
on a day-to-day basis. People have never been so aware of interest rates
as they have been over the past few years. The perception is that interest
rates will continue to rise in perpetuity and the recent fall in interest rates
is merely a temporary aberration. Most people believe that, as the current
economic recovery gains momentum and governments are forced to continue to bail out sick companies, demand for money will increase, pushing
interest rates up into the stratosphere again. This is the conventional wisdom among amateur investors and professionals alike. One thing we know
about conventional wisdom is that it usually reflects the lowest common
denominator of intellectual achievement.
    The value of these long-term historical trends in interest rates is cer-
tainly not intended to provide a magic formula. I'm a pragmatist. I don't
believe in magic formulas. The value of this study is in the knowledge that
trend persistency in interest rates does exist and it is advisable to take the
trouble to utilize the knowledge that can be gained by a study of the
characteristics of interest rates that seem to override short-term factors.
Several characteristics are apparent in the long-term behavior pattern of
interest rates that can be useful in planning your investment strategy in
the years ahead. It can be seen quite clearly that once a long-term interest
rate trend has been established, the level of interest rates has moved in that
direction for quite an extended period, involving decades. The second im-

portant characteristic is that there is a reasonable normative level for high interest rates and for low interest rates. This can be seen over several thousand years of history. The successful investor buys his investments when they are low and sells them when they are high. The problem for most investors is quantifying what is low and what is high. The use of the long-term interest rate pattern which spans nearly 5,000 years goes a long way toward telling us what is low and what is high as far as interest rates are concerned.

I am certainly not suggesting that investors become slaves to these long-term secular trends. When it comes to the shorter-term timing of interest rates, these long-term secular trends are not particularly helpful; in that case, if you are involved in speculating on interest rate trends through the financial futures market or through fast-moving bond warrants, and even "zero" coupon bonds, you could sometimes run a big risk of sitting through some pretty hairy moves by ignoring short-term trend deviations.

Awareness of the long-term secular trends is vital but you should do no more than put these long-term trends in the back of your mind as one of the tools of judgment. You should not discard the shorter considerations suggested by economics nor should you ignore the current facts of life. At the same time, never forget that we are coming out of what is the greatest change that has taken place in thirty-five years and what is also likely to be the greatest change in interest rates that has ever occurred in 5000 years of recorded history . . . which also means some fantastic opportunities.

In the summer of 1982, we saw a tremendous rise in the value of interest rate-related securities. That sharp rise was only the first in what is likely to be at least two more sudden and sharp drops in interest rates that correspond with at least two more explosive rises in fixed-interest markets. These may not occur immediately, or even within the next six to nine months. But the good thing about bond investment is that, while you're waiting for these explosive rises to occur, you're not losing money. You're still getting a reasonable return on your investment and you also know that if the cycle doesn't give you the capital growth that you're looking for, at least the passage of time will. There are guaranteed maturity levels in the bonds that you buy that are certainly not available to holders of any other form of investment such as commodities or equities.

The value that bond markets currently offer in contrast to the historical trends should astound you. Current coupon long-term municipal bonds with a maturity of approximately twenty-five years have produced an average yield of 3.75 percent over the past eighty years. When deciding what is "low" and what is "high," compare the current yield of municipal bonds with the average.

High-quality corporate bonds with AAA and AA ratings have produced an average yield of approximately 5 percent over the past eighty years. Forty years ago, American Telephone and Telegraph issued a bond with a coupon of 2.875 percent. That bond was sold at par to eager retail and institutional buyers. In the late 1940s, New York State bond issues carried a coupon of 1 percent. At the time, for every $1,000 you could only get $10 a year, but these bonds attracted a premium as soon as they were issued. Now, pick up your newspaper and look at the current yields for AAA, AA and municipal bonds. There should be little doubt that you still have the bargains of a lifetime staring you in the face in spite of the explosive move in bond markets during 1982.

A CORNUCOPIA OF OPPORTUNITY

Gaining a true understanding of what the bond market has to offer and how all of the securities work is vitally important, particularly since the best move for one investor may not necessarily be the appropriate move for another whose goals and objectives may be vastly different. Finding the correct path to profit is further complicated by some of the paradoxes that are inherent in the U.S. fixed income market. For example, you can purchase bonds on margin. This means it is only necessary to put up a percentage of the purchase price of the bonds to actually buy the bonds. In the case of U.S. government bonds, the margin is 25 percent. Investors lodge 25 percent of the purchase price of the bonds with their brokers and borrow the balance of 75 percent. Investors have an increased cost by dealing in this way since there is an interest charge for the borrowed money, which, of course, further amplifies the element of risk.

Fixed-income securities in the United States are incredibly diverse with literally thousands of issues of different maturities, quality ratings, coupons and structures to choose from. Yet, with few exceptions, all of these securities react in the same way to the same major determinant of bond prices: prevailing interest rates. The only difference is the amount of change an issue is likely to experience given a particular change in prevailing interest rates.

Fixed-income securities, generally, are thought to be safe, stodgy and conservative. This idea is totally erroneous. By incorporating margin and by seeking highly geared bond issues, such as bond warrants or long dated zero coupon bonds, the action can be much faster than either the financial futures market or the traded option market. The general idea that fixed-interest issues are dull and slow-moving is a perception born of ignorance since bond markets have been out of favor for such a long time. At the moment equity markets are saturated with ignorant investors who believe that equity investment is the only area where capital gains can be achieved with reasonable speed. Investors believe that equity markets are the markets that really "offer the action"—I would certainly agree. In the months ahead, equity markets are likely to offer plenty of action—downside action.

Fixed-income securities pay interest in one of two ways. The security can be issued to the investor at a discount from par value, in which case the investor achieves a rate of return purely on the difference between the price at the date of issue and par when the obligation falls due. In other words, it's like borrowing $90 from Joe and promising to repay him $100 at the end of six months. Joe would have had a return of over 10 percent on his money for that six months.

The result of this type of transaction is a noninterest-bearing certificate that generally has a short maturity of five days to one year. Securities of this nature include Treasury bills, the discounted notes of several U.S. government agencies and commercial paper. In the United States there are more forms of noninterest-bearing certificates than in any other market and for longer durations, with many maturities stretching for over a year. In the case of some of the zero coupon issues, which are essentially noninterest-bearing securities, maturities stretch to twenty-five years.

Most bonds and other fixed-income securities quoted in the United States are in denominations of $1,000. (There are some with denominations of $10,000 and even more.) The price of fixed-income securities is quoted as a percentage of par value, which, of course, is $1,000. For example, a price of 80 for a $1,000 bond or note represents 80 percent of $1,000, or $800. Similarly, a price of 110.5 represents 110.5 percent of $1,000. The price would therefore be $1,105 per bond. There are also bonds in denominations of $500 and $100. These are known as "baby bonds" or "small pieces." These should be avoided because they are unmarketable. The U.S. bond market is geared to trading in "round lots." A round lot is 1,000 bonds. Bonds can also be purchased in "odd lots" which are amounts that are less than the round lot unit of trading. It should be noted that it is often extremely difficult to find buyers for small amounts of bonds in less than the normal unit of trading in the U.S. bond market. As such, there is usually a substantial premium that has to be paid by the buyers when purchasing an odd lot of bonds. The seller will also usually suffer a substantial discount when trying to distribute an odd lot of bonds. Of course, if these issues are held to maturity there will be no problem on the sell side.

The premium or discount that an investor may have to pay for purchasing or selling a parcel of bonds in an odd lot will often be contingent upon the marketability of the individual issue. There are occasions when the cost of dealing in an odd lot is relatively small. There are also occasions when the cost of dealing in an odd lot makes the entire transaction prohibitive. If you wish to deal in the U.S. bond market in an odd lot of bonds, *always* check the round lot price first so that you can determine the cost to you of dealing in an odd lot. If the cost is more than a point, I wouldn't recommend dealing. On average, expect to pay a commission of $5 a bond, which works out at about 0.5 percent on small purchases. The larger the purchase, the greater the savings on commissions.

HOW BOND PRICES MOVE

What almost all fixed-income securities have in common is that they are paid back at par, at 100 percent, on maturity. Their price in the market will be a pure reflection of this, plus their coupon, if they have one. The coupon divided by the price gives the "running" or current yield. The current yield may be a lowly 6 percent or a lofty 13 percent or zero . . . depending on the coupon. It will only dictate the price of the bond by coincidence. What dictates the price of the bond (or note or bill) is the return to maturity. If maturity is a month away, the bond will stand very close to 100, unless default is expected. If maturity is thirty years away, it may stand at 50 if the coupon is low enough (say 5 percent) or 130 if the coupon is high enough (say 15 percent). The capital gain in the first instance compensates for the low current yield, and the capital loss in the second is the price of the high current yield. Other things being equal, the overall return, the "yield to maturity" will tend to be the same in both instances. Bond prices move in accordance with the level of maturity yield that is acceptable to investors at any given moment.

As we examine how the maturity, the coupon rate and the level of interest rates can influence the degree of price fluctuations of fixed-income securities, we will observe what happens when security prices are falling (a 100 basis point, or a 1 percent rise in interest rates) and when prices are rising (a 200 basis point, or a 2 percent decline in interest rates). We have intentionally used different figures for the magnitude of price falls and price rises in order to demonstrate what may happen under a variety of conditions. Similarly, the coupon rate, maturities and interest rate levels in the examples that follow have been arbitrarily chosen for the purpose of illustrating the general principles. The most important aspect of following the fixed-income market in the United States is to gain some intuitive awareness of how certain aspects of fixed-income securities can influence the magnitude of price fluctuations when there is a shift in the interest rate cycle.

THE ASPECT OF MATURITY

The following table demonstrates what happens to fixed-income securities of various maturities when interest rates move up or down. It can be observed that for a given change in interest rates the longer the time remaining for maturity for a security, the greater the price fluctuation that is likely to occur. In other words, the longest-dated fixed-income securities are going to rise faster than the remainder of the market during a period when interest rates are falling or are anticipated to fall. When interest rates rise the longer-dated fixed-income securities will fall faster than the rest.

In the following table we can see that when interest rates rise from 7 to 8 percent an issue with a 7 percent coupon with one year remaining to maturity will decline by 1 percent in value whereas if the same security with a 7 percent coupon had twenty years remaining to maturity it would decline by 10 percent in value. In other words, a 1 percent hike in interest rates will result in a 1 percent decline in the short end of the market against a 10 percent decline in the long end. The long end is therefore inherently more speculative than the short end offering a gearing factor of nearly ten to one on the same interest rate fluctuation.

A similar degree of price fluctuation is involved when interest rates are declining. If there is a fall in interest rates from 7 percent to 5 percent an investor holding a security with a 7 percent coupon that has six months left to maturity will experience a rise in capital value of 88 percent. An investor holding a security with a similar coupon but with ten years to maturity will show an increase in capital value of 15.5 percent on the same fall in interest rates. It should be noted that past a certain point all bonds with a very long maturity will fluctuate virtually equally in price for a given change in interest rates. For example, a fixed-income security with a twenty-five-year maturity will usually fluctuate at precisely the same degree as a fixed-income security with a maturity of thirty or forty years or longer. Generally, if interest rates are expected to rise, investors should only be holding fixed-income securities with short maturities. If interest rates are expected to fall, then investors should be holding fixed-income securities with long maturities, if the objective is capital gains. The following table is an example of the price changes that will occur in the varying maturities assuming a rise in interest rates of 1 percent:

MATURITY	7% PIR. Price	8% PIR Price	Change
6 months	100	$99\frac{1}{2}$	- 0.50
1 year	100	99	- 1.00
2 years	100	$98\frac{1}{8}$	- 1.88
5 years	100	96	- 4.00
10 years	100	$93\frac{1}{4}$	- 6.75
20 years	100	90	-10.00

The following table illustrates the effect of price changes in the event of a fall in interest rates by 2 percent:

MATURITY	7% PIR Price	5% PIR Price	Change
6 months	100	$100\frac{7}{8}$	+ 0.88
1 year	100	101	+ 1.00
2 years	100	$103\frac{3}{4}$	+ 3.75
5 years	100	$108\frac{3}{4}$	+ 8.75
10 years	100	$115\frac{1}{2}$	+15.50
20 years	100	$125\frac{1}{8}$	+25.13

THE COUPON RATE CONSIDERATION

In the case of maturity we have seen that the longer the maturity the greater will be the fluctuation in the price. A similar rule applies to coupons. In the case of the coupon, the lower the coupon the greater will be the fluctuation in the price. Therefore, the issues with the greatest capital potential during a period of falling interest rates will be those with a low coupon and a long maturity.

As can be seen in the tables that follow, when a twenty-year maturity issue with a 4 percent coupon experiences a situation where the general level on interest rates rises from 7 percent to 8 percent, the price of the issue will fall by 11.3 percent. A bond with the same maturity and an 8 percent coupon will fall in price by 9.5 percent for an equivalent rise in market interest rates. A lower coupon security also moves faster percentage-wise during a period of falling interest rates. If a 4 percent twenty-year bond moves from a 7 percent yield to maturity to a 5 percent yield to maturity it gains 28.7 percent in price but an 8 percent twenty-year bond gains only 24.4 percent for the same shift in interest yields.

Thus we have another general principle which can be established with regard to fixed-income investing. If interest rates are expected to rise, it is better to own securities with a high coupon. If interest rates are expected to fall, it is better to own a security with a low coupon. For optimal capital gain during a period of falling interest rates the best possible fixed-income securities to own would be low-coupon securities with maturities over twenty years. An important factor to consider when dealing in corporate fixed-income issues is the fact that, in a period of falling interest rates, when fixed-income securities are likely to rise in price, lower-coupon securities not only move faster in price but also are much less likely to be called by the issuer, since they will already have been paying a low rate of interest vis-a-vis their par value.

The following table shows the effect of a 1 percent rise in the level of interest rates on a bond with a twenty-year maturity with coupon rates varying from 4 percent to 8 percent:

COUPON	7% PIR Price	8% PIR Price	Change
4	68	$60\frac{3}{8}$	-11.3
5	$78\frac{5}{8}$	$70\frac{3}{8}$	-10.5
6	$89\frac{3}{8}$	$80\frac{1}{4}$	-10.0
7	100	$90\frac{1}{8}$	- 9.8
8	$110\frac{5}{8}$	100	- 9.5

The following table shows the effect of a 2 percent fall in interest rates on a bond with a twenty-year maturity with coupon rates varying from 4 percent to 8 percent:

COUPON	7% PIR Price	5% PIR Price	Change
4	68	$87\frac{1}{2}$	+28.7
5	$78\frac{5}{8}$	100	+27.1
6	$89\frac{3}{8}$	$112\frac{1}{2}$	+25.8
7	100	$125\frac{1}{8}$	+25.1
8	$110\frac{5}{8}$	$137\frac{3}{8}$	+24.4

Several observations can be made from the tables submitted so far. The first is that in terms of mitigating risk and amplifying reward, the maturity of the fixed-interest issue is the overriding factor. The longer the maturity the higher the risk and the greater the reward. The shorter the maturity the lower the risk and the lower the potential reward. The reward potential can be amplified by using a lower coupon while the rise can be modified by using a higher coupon. The coupon does not have as marked an effect as the maturity factor however, in terms of capital gain potential or capital loss potential, given a specific fall in the level of interest rates.

THE QUALITY FACTOR

Triple A or C minus? That is the question. Many bond analysts use a "quality spread." A quality spread shows the difference between the yield on the higher quality bonds and the yield on the lower quality bonds. The lower the quality, the higher the yield. The higher the quality, the lower the yield. But the difference in the yields between low quality bonds and high quality bonds is a product of investment sentiment. When investors are optimistic about the future, the difference between yield on low-quality bonds and high-quality bonds can be very small, as little as 0.5 percent. When investors are pessimitic about the future, then the difference between the yield on low- and high-quality bonds can be massive, as much as 4 or 5 percent, depending on the prevailing level of interest rates. Prevailing interest rates have little to do with the quality spread. If investors begin to worry about whether or not the issuer of the bond is going to be able to pay interest on the loan, or possibly default on capital payment, interest rate considerations disappear. During 1981, when Triple A corporate bond yields were 10.5 percent, the bond of Chrysler actually yielded as much as 24 percent because investors believed that Chrysler was going bankrupt. The same holds true for International Harvester where there was a spread between the yield on International Harvester bonds and that of Triple A bonds. If interest rates fall, although high-quality bonds will rise with every fall in interest rates, in the case of a low-quality bond, you could find that your holding is going down while most other bonds are going up in price. During the 1930s, even Triple A bonds fell under suspicion. There were many good quality corporate bond issues that yielded as much as 10 percent while Treasury bond yields were falling through 4 percent. During the upwave, the quality factor seems to be of secondary importance. Investor optimism increases with the exponential trend of inflation. A point is reached where investors believe even the poorest companies will be bailed out by the endless prosperity. During the upwave investors in lower-grade issues tend to come out very well, especially if they get their timing right and confine their purchases to periods of temporary correction when the lower-grade issues are at their cheapest and the quality spread is at its widest. In mid-1983, the investment community was discounting a robust economic recovery capable of improving the fates of even the most disastrously managed companies with massive debt burdens. As a result, the yield between low-grade issues and high-grade issues fell to one of its narrowest levels in years. Buying low-grade issues at a time like that is about the most hazardous thing any bond investor could do. During the downwave the most rewarding long-term policy will be to deliberately sacrifice yield in favor of quality.

You might now say to yourself, "Well, perhaps I should confine all of my bond investments to Treasury issues. After all, they're the highest quality of all." Not necessarily. Particularly when it comes to the current high-coupon Treasury issues. Government policy can change, and so too can the potential rewards on government bonds. The power of government places it beyond the commercial law, which the corporate sector must abide by. Suppose long-term interest rates decline to low single figures, which would be compatible with the deflationary environment I envisage in the years ahead. High-coupon Treasury bonds issued at 14 percent and 15 percent are going to look like very expensive money indeed . . . money that the government is paying out of taxpayer revenue. In addition, those who bought Treasury bonds with high coupons at par are going to look "excessively fortunate" since a fall in interest rates to 5 percent or lower would mean these long-term Treasury bonds issued at 14 or 15 percent are likely to have risen in value by as much as 200 percent. Such a tremendous profit at the expense of the taxpayer could easily arouse envy and resentment among large sections of the population who will have directly, or indirectly, lost fortunes in the equity market. The high-coupon bond holder who, through prudence and caution, builds a fortune, could find himself in the same position as the short seller, often referred to as "He of the Black Heart" during bear markets. In November 1984 there will be another presidential election. According to my timetable, we could be at the nadir of the depression at that time. If we are at the nadir of a depression, obviously President Reagan will get the blame for it, just as President Hoover was held responsible for the depression of the 1930s. There could conceivably be a shift to an extreme leftist Democratic government . . . like that of the Roosevelt administration of the 1930s. Those who profited by the depression, such as government bond holders, would present an ideal political scapegoat. There are many methods government can use to penal-

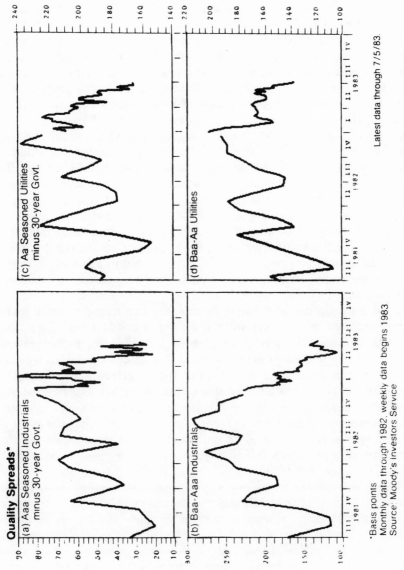

Quality Spreads*

(a) Aaa Seasoned Industrials minus 30-year Govt.

(b) Baa-Aaa Industrials

(c) Aa Seasoned Utilities minus 30-year Govt.

(d) Baa-Aa Utilities

*Basis points
Monthly data through 1982, weekly data begins 1983
Source: Moody's Investors Service

Latest data through 7/5/83

From *Interest Rate Weekly*, July 7, 1983.
Reprinted by permission of Prudential-Bache.

FIGURE 46

ize what the public perceives as an "excessive fortune" from which political capital could be made. Fortunes that are made in the government bond market could be neutralized through taxes or by some kind of mischievous but "lethal" early redemption proposition. I would point out this is a low probability, but a possibility just the same. A possibility that is more likely with Treasury issues than with corporate bonds.

There is a very strong case for avoiding a portfolio that is wholly government issues and includes a reasonable proportion of corporate bonds during the downwave. The job of evaluating the relative security and safety of corporate issues is taken care of by well-known rating services, such as Moody's and Standard & Poor's. The top rating of Moody's is Aaa. The top rating for Standard & Poor's is AAA. The next grade for Moody's is Aa and for Standard & Poor's AA. The scale of ratings for Moody's ranges from three grades of C through three grades of A. Single C is the lowest. Triple A is the highest. The same holds true for Standard & Poor's, except that S & P also has a D grade rating for bonds that are actually in default. During the downwave it would be unwise to settle for anything other than the Single A through Triple A category. Conservative investors may wish to confine all of their activities to Triple A. However, by doing so, some outstanding opportunities could be missed in some of the more exciting types of fixed-interest issues other than deep discount or current coupon bonds.

If we consider the way bonds behave, we find that for every given change in interest rates, prices will move further and faster on the longer maturities. These are the most volatile, more risky and more highly geared. This price volatility is compounded on the low-coupon, long-dated issues of corresponding maturation. The portion of the overall return to maturity that consists of capital gain (or loss) is a *compound* return, whereas the current interest yield is not. Interest on bonds can, of course, be reinvested so as to compound upward—in the same bond, if desired. But the yield at which reinvestment can be made is unlikely to be the same as the yield to redemption. In a period of falling interest rates, the yield on reinvested income will be progressively lower.

During the upwave, bond yields rose. During the downwave they can be expected to fall. If they fall far, the difference in ultimate compound returns from high-coupon bonds on the one hand, and low-coupon bonds on the other, will be highly significant. By far the highest overall returns will in fact accrue to holders of long-dated bonds with no coupon at all, since the entire return will be compounding at today's high yields.

THE "ZERO" COUPON FACTOR

The very best possible way to exploit the potential in the U.S. bond market in the period ahead is through zero coupon holdings, the only investment available where you can receive the benefit of pure compound interest and a capital gain potential which exceeds the compound interest factor. If the whole thing goes awry, the worst thing that can happen to you is that you double or triple or quadruple your money between now and the date of maturity on your bonds and then pay tax on a chunk of that . . . that's the worst thing. The best thing that can happen to you is that you double your money in a year or two, pay capital gains tax on the capital element and income tax on the far lower income element. I do not feel there is another investment available for long-term holders that can possibly compete with the potential of zero coupon bonds.

The following tabulation will demonstrate the profit potential on zero coupon bonds relative to a specific fall in interest rates. This immensely helpful table should astound you. The table gives the price of zero coupon bonds given various redemption yields.

Here's how to use the table. Let's say you have a zero coupon bond with nine years to run. (Put your finger on 9.) Now let's say you want to know what your capital gains potential is going to be if interest rates fall to 2 percent. The current yield on a good quality zero coupon bond is 10.5 percent. At 10.5 percent you will find the price of a nine-year bond is 40.71. If interest rates fall, causing a drop in the yield on zero coupon bonds by 2 percent to 8.5 percent, the price that would give you an 8.5 percent yield is 47.99. A 2 percent drop in interest rates would thus give you a capital gain of nearly 20 percent.

Now suppose there's a really tremendous fall in rates, similar to that which we saw in the summer of 1982. If interest rates drop from 10.5 percent to, say 5.5 percent, the price of your zero coupon bond would jump to 61.76, a gain of more than 50 percent.

Now let's take a look at what happens with some of the longer maturities such as the American Medical "0" with twenty-eight years to run. As you can see from the table, the price of a zero coupon bond with twenty-eight years to run at a 10.5 percent yield will be 6.11. If interest rates fall by 2 percent and the yield on the bond shows a corresponding fall, the price jumps to 10.19 for a gain of nearly 60 percent in a 2 percent drop in rates. If by chance there is a dramatic fall in rates, to say 5 percent, the price jumps to 25.51, and you've made more than four times your money. If that happened to take place over a two-year time frame, you'd pay income tax on two years interest at 10.5 percent. The remaining 280 percent gain would attract capital gains tax—and bear in mind you're dealing with the senior security of a company—not the equity. You'll receive this benefit whether or not the profits increase or decrease, regardless of the state of the economy and regardless of the outlook for the corporate sector. Finally, anyone who prefers to invest in equity markets while there are these kinds of values in debt markets simply has no idea of what investment is really about.

Investors who participate in either the IRA or Keogh retirement plans can incorporate zero coupon bonds without incurring any tax liability. For

Interest rates

Yrs to run	12 %	11.5 %	11 %	10.5 %	10 %	9.5 %	9 %	8.5 %	8 %	7.5 %	7 %	6.5 %	6 %	5.5 %	5 %
29	3.74	4.26	4.85	5.53	6.3	7.19	8.22	9.39	10.73	12.28	14.06	16.1	18.46	21.17	24.29
28	4.19	4.75	5.38	6.11	6.93	7.88	8.95	10.19	11.59	13.2	15.04	17.15	19.56	22.33	25.51
27	4.69	5.29	5.97	6.75	7.63	8.63	9.76	11.05	12.52	14.19	16.09	18.26	20.74	23.56	26.78
26	5.25	5.9	6.63	7.46	8.39	9.45	10.64	11.99	13.52	15.25	17.22	19.45	21.98	24.86	28.12
25	5.88	6.58	7.36	8.24	9.23	10.34	11.6	13.01	14.6	16.4	18.42	20.71	23.3	26.22	29.53
24	6.59	7.34	8.17	9.11	10.15	11.33	12.64	14.12	15.77	17.63	19.71	22.06	24.7	27.67	31.01
23	7.38	8.18	9.07	10.0b	11.17	12.4	13.78	15.31	17.03	18.95	21.09	23.49	26.18	29.19	32.56
22	8.26	9.12	10.07	11.12	12.28	13.58	15.02	16.62	18.39	20.37	22.57	25.02	27.75	30.79	34.19
21	9.26	10.17	11.17	12.29	13.51	14.87	16.37	18.03	19.87	21.9	24.15	26.65	29.42	32.49	35.89
20	10.37	11.34	12.4	13.58	14.86	16.28	17.84	19.56	21.45	23.54	25.84	28.38	31.18	34.27	37.69
19	11.61	12.64	13.77	15	16.35	17.83	19.45	21.22	23.17	25.31	27.65	30.22	33.05	36.16	39.57
18	13	14.09	15.28	16.58	17.99	19.52	21.2	23.03	25.02	27.2	29.59	32.19	35.03	38.15	41.55
17	14.56	15.72	16.96	18.32	19.78	21.38	23.11	24.99	27.03	29.25	31.66	34.28	37.14	40.24	43.63
16	16.31	17.52	18.83	20.24	21.76	23.41	25.19	27.11	29.19	31.44	33.87	36.51	39.36	42.46	45.81
15	18.27	19.54	20.9	22.36	23.94	25.63	27.45	29.41	31.52	33.8	36.24	38.88	41.73	44.79	48.1
14	20.46	21.78	23.2	24.71	26.33	28.07	29.92	31.91	34.05	36.33	38.78	41.41	44.23	47.26	50.51
13	22.92	24.29	25.75	27.31	28.97	30.73	32.62	34.63	36.77	39.06	41.5	44.1	46.88	49.86	53.03
12	25.67	27.08	28.58	30.18	31.86	33.65	35.55	37.57	39.71	41.99	44.4	46.97	49.7	52.6	55.68
11	28.75	30.2	31.73	33.34	35.05	36.85	38.75	40.76	42.89	45.13	47.51	50.02	52.68	55.49	58.47
10	32.2	33.67	35.22	36.84	38.55	40.35	42.24	44.23	46.32	48.52	50.83	53.27	55.84	58.54	61.39
9	36.06	37.54	39.09	40.71	42.41	44.18	46.04	47.99	50.02	52.16	54.39	56.74	59.19	61.76	64.46
8	40.39	41.86	43.39	44.99	46.65	48.38	50.19	52.07	54.03	56.07	58.2	60.42	62.74	65.16	67.68
7	45.23	46.67	48.17	49.71	51.32	52.98	54.7	56.49	58.35	60.28	62.27	64.35	66.51	68.74	71.07
6	50.66	52.04	53.46	54.93	56.45	58.01	59.63	61.29	63.02	64.8	66.63	68.53	70.5	72.52	74.62
5	56.74	58.03	59.35	60.7	62.09	63.52	64.99	66.5	68.06	69.66	71.3	72.99	74.73	76.51	78.35
4	63.55	64.7	65.87	67.07	68.3	69.56	70.84	72.16	73.5	74.88	76.29	77.73	79.21	80.72	82.27
3	71.18	72.14	73.12	74.12	75.13	76.17	77.22	78.29	79.38	80.5	81.63	82.78	83.96	85.16	86.38
2	79.72	80.44	81.16	81.9	82.64	83.4	84.17	84.95	85.73	86.53	87.34	88.17	89	89.85	90.7
1	89.29	89.69	90.09	90.5	90.91	91.32	91.74	92.17	92.59	93.02	93.46	93.9	94.34	94.79	95.24

Table prepared by Charles H. Coultas

the first time ever, investors can achieve the full benefits of compound interest through investing in the bond market. The results that can be obtained with relatively low risk if the investor confines his activities to the quality issues are truly amazing. For example, Swedish Export Credit Zero Coupon, quoted on the Eurodollar market and guaranteed by the Swedish government, is currently selling at 31. The bond matures in 1994. An individual who doesn't pay any tax will show over three times his initial investment if the bonds are held to maturity. The Dow Jones Index is only 200 points higher than it was twelve years ago. It is more unlikely that many investors have made three times their money in the equity market over the past twelve years.

Not all zero coupon bonds are of long-term maturities. ITT Zero Coupon, quoted in the domestic market, matures in 1990. It currently sells at 41. Over the next seven years investors can more than double their money if they have a tax-free status. Security Pacific Zero Coupon, priced at 68, will give you a return of just under 50 percent over the next three years. Pepsico Zero Coupon, priced at 90, will give you a return of just over 10 percent in the next eleven months.

CATS, TIGRS, AND OTHER "STREAKERS"

Unfortunately, the choice of zero coupon bonds is limited. There are only a few bonds that have a Triple A rating. The only form of government zero coupon bond is the "Freddie Mac," a government agency paper. During the period ahead it will be the quality bonds that perform the best. The higher the quality the greater will be the safety and the potential demand, and therefore the better will be the performance.

The highest quality paper of all in the United States is Treasury paper. To solve the problem of compounding returns on quality paper, Salomon Brothers and Prudential–Bache have come up with "CATS," "Certificates of Accrual on Treasury Securities." Those investors who purchase CATS receive what is described as "Money Multiplier Receipts" for which a secondary market now exists on the New York Stock Exchange. According to the offering memorandum, purchasers of Money Multiplier Receipts will receive two to ten times their original investment if these receipts are held to maturity. The Money Multiplier Receipts are actual evidence of ownership of serially maturing interest payments on United States Treasury notes and bonds which are the direct obligation of the United States of America. There are no periodic interest payments on these receipts, which are held by the Morgan Guaranty Trust Company of New York on behalf of the owners. Hence the name "Streakers"—the interest coupons have been stripped off!

Each receipt represents the right to receive a single payment at maturity. The face amount of the receipt is the amount the investor will receive at maturity. The receipts are sold at an "original issue discount" from the amount payable at maturity. The price of the receipts will fluctuate in accordance with prevailing interest rates and market conditions between the date of issue and maturity, in the same manner as a zero coupon bond.

Prior to issue, the anticipated yield to maturity was approximately 11.5 percent for the various different classes of issue. The table shows the price the receipts would sell at in order to provide 11.5 percent compound between the date of purchase and the date of maturity.

Price to the Public per Receipt	Amount Payable at Maturity per Receipt	Approximate Maturity
$500.00	$1,000	November 1988
$333.33	$1,000	May 1992
$250.00	$1,000	May 1995
$200.00	$1,000	May 1997
$166.67	$1,000	November 1998
$142.86	$1,000	May 2000
$125.00	$1,000	November 2001
$111.11	$1,000	November 2002
$100.00	$1,000	November 2003

As can be seen, an investment of $100 grows tenfold over the next twenty years on the basis of 11.5 percent compound. The minimum investment is $1,000. Over twenty years $1,000 worth of Money Multiplier Receipts will grow to $10,000 in the safest form of security that the U.S. bond market has to offer.

Another form of zero coupon U.S. Treasury security is a product of Merrill Lynch White Weld Capital Markets Group. Similar to CATS are these TIGRs, "Treasury Investment Growth Receipts," based on the same zero coupon principle as CATS but offering a marginally higher return. Payment on the TIGRs consists of the interest payments due on the bonds to which the individual series TIGR relates. Like zero coupon bonds, no payments are made until the maturity date. The purchase price of each TIGR is the present value of the payment or payments to be received thereon. The present value is calculated by discounting such payment or payments at the yield at which the particular series TIGR is offered, compounded semiannually for the period from the date of purchase to maturity. Like CATS, trading in the secondary market will affect the price that is paid and the return that is received.

Both TIGRs and CATS are excellent investments for investors who are able to take advantage of the zero coupon principle (self-administered pension funds, etc.) and perhaps for those who are unable to deal in round lots in the U.S. Treasury market, and prefer to avoid interest payments.

As the depression reaches its nadir, the only safe issues to hold will be short-term Treasury issues since, under such conditions, purchasers of any long-term debt instructions may have to sit through a period of substantial loss. Accordingly, short-term CATS and TIGRs could be an ideal complement to the portfolio during periods when only the safest securities will be able to protect the investor.

BOND WARRANTS

A famous philosopher once said, "Ninety percent of everything is garbage." In the field of investment 99 percent of everything is garbage because we have "gearing." Sophisticated investors have long been familiar with the use of gearing as a method of enhancing the profitability of their stock market operations. The basic principles are not new and the fundamentals are not terribly difficult to understand. Archimedes, the great third-century philosopher, is credited with the discovery of gearing or leverage. In this sense, leverage is the use of a lever—a bar or rod—supported on a fulcrum. Archimedes discovered that a small force applied at a considerable distance from the fulcrum would create a much larger force closer to the fulcrum on the other side. The same idea lies behind the use of gearing in the financial sense, the idea being to use a small amount of capital to do the work of a large amount of capital.

Many individuals are attracted to the equity market because of the various forms of financial gearing offered that promise a quick profit. These same individuals are often loath to become involved in bond markets because they feel that profits are too slow to come by and the element of financial gearing and fast profits is lacking. That may have been the case at one time, but it's certainly not the case any longer. We have a whole new ball game in the bond market.

Streakers provide the ultimate in a deep discount and therefore offer the greatest capital gain potential in the bond market. Since the discount is 100 percent of the return, it would be impossible to increase the gearing when using the deep discount method of bond selection for building a geared bond portfolio. However, there is another vehicle that can be used to increase the gearing that much more and accelerate the profit potential during a period of falling interest rates. That vehicle is the bond warrant, a recent addition to the arsenal of tools now available to the investor that will enable him to maximize his return in the bond market during a perid of falling interest rates.

In itself a warrant is like a long-term traded option. An option gives the holder the right to purchase an item at a given price over a given period. If the underlying security or commodity rises in price, the price of the option will rise. If the underlying security falls in price, the price of the option will fall. In the case of an option, whereas the duration of a contract varies from weeks to months, a warrant will often have several years to run.

There are two types of bond warrants: those that give the holder the right to purchase a zero coupon bond and those that give the holder the right to purchase a bond with coupon during the exercise period. The warrants bestow the right to buy at a price that provides a specific yield at the date of issue when combined with the price of the warrant. If yields fall, then the warrant price must rise if the yield resulting from the combined cost of the warrant and the exercise price is to remain compatible with prevailing yields.

For example, the exercise price of most bond warrants attached to a coupon bearing bond is par. One bond warrant allows the holder to purchase $1,000 of bonds. At the issue of 26 the total cost of exercising the Manufacturers Hanover Trust 14.125 percent 15.5.89 bond warrant worked out at $1,026 per bond. ($1,000 = cost of bond at par + $26 per bond warrant.) Each bid warrant allows the purchaser to buy one bond at par, the combination of which produces a yield of 13.45 percent to maturity on the investment. The exercise price will remain at par. If prevailing yields for an issue such as Manufacturers Hanover Trust with a 1989 maturity fell to say 12 percent, the price of the warrant had to rise to 91, since a coupon bond with a yield of 14.125 percent would sell at 109.10 to produce a yield of 12 percent. If by chance the prevailing yields for this type of issue indicate 10 percent, then the price of the warrant would have to rise to 190. A bond with a 14.125 percent coupon would sell at 119 to yield 10 percent.

The most highly geared of all bond warrants are those that are attached to zero coupon bonds, since zero coupon bonds are the most highly geared of all bonds. However, since we would be dealing with a discounted issue, the exercise price would be relative to the guaranteed yield to maturity at issue which would rise with the passage of time. The shorter the period of the zero coupon bond the higher would be the price needed to produce the initial guaranteed yield to maturity.

In August 1981, Citicorp issued 200,000 bond warrants. At an exercise price of $422.60 per $1,000, the warrant price of 24 would have produced accrued amortization to maturity of 13.5 percent, combining the exercise price of the zero coupon with the price of the warrant. If interest rates on zero coupon issues fell, the price of the bond warrant would have to rise to compensate for the fall. As it so happens, a fall in the yield to maturity of the zero coupon bond of 1 percent should produce a theoretical rise to 50 in Citicorp Warrants. If the yield on the zero coupon bonds fell by 2 percent, this should have produced a rise to 77 in Citicorp Warrants, and a fall in yields of 3 percent in the zero coupon bonds would have produced a rise to 106 in Citicorp Warrants. These figures are calculated by combining the cost of the warrant and the exercise price of the warrant to produce a yield that is compatible with prevailing yields.

Close followers of the bond markets will know why this example was chosen: because it exemplifies the risk in highly-geared issues. During the summer months of 1981 there was a panic in banking paper. Investment in the debt issues of banks was considered one of the riskiest ventures imaginable. As a result, while several bond warrant issues exploded in price, Citicorp Warrants expired valueless on August 18th because the yield on the Citicorp zero coupon rose while the yields on other bonds with warrants fell.

THE CONCEPT OF RISK: THE CONCEPT OF INVESTMENT

During the year 1932, interest rates on prime commercial paper declined from a peak of 3.9 percent to just 1.5 percent. The yield on prime railroad bonds also declined from a high point of 4.8 percent to 4.3 percent: in due course they would reach 2.3 percent. But during 1932, the yields on some fair-quality corporate bonds soared to over 10 percent. Such was the degree of polarization between good and bad risks at a time of financial panic. The market's assessment was by no means infallible, of course. There were many defaults. But most of the medium-quality bonds that touched 10 percent yields in 1932 were yielding 3 or 4 percent fifteen years later.

That was no comfort to many. In troubled times many sell out of fear, or indeed because they need the cash. There are troubled times ahead. It is as well to take action now to ensure that one's need for cash will not oblige him or her to sell bonds at what may be an unfortunate moment. It is even more crucial to minimize the chances of being driven to sell out of fear. This is why I urge you to confine your bond purchases to the very highest quality paper—preferably Treasury bonds or their equivalent (CATS and TIGRs) or other government backed paper—and build a high liquidity ratio into your portfolio with up to a third in Treasury bills or something equivalent.

The point is not merely that such holdings are inherently safer. It is that the "polarization" that tends to happen in troubled times actually confers a significant further premium on the very highest grade holdings. If Treasury bonds yield half a point less than AAA corporates now, they may yield 2 or 3 points less during moments of panic—with obvious implications for the relative price performance.

There is a further point to be made about risk and the concept of investments. It has been fashionable in recent years for market theoreticians to equate risk with volatility—such has been the preoccupation of this generation of investors with short-term price performance. For many actuaries in life insurance companies, this equation is simply not true. They have a contractual obligation to meet a claim in, say, twenty years. So long as it *is* rapid, what the price does inbetween times is wholly irrelevant.

I manage funds—my own and other people's. Since the start of this decade, something has happened that I have not known before in thirty years in the investment field. I have bought securities that, other things being equal, I envisage holding to maturity—always of top quality, but sometimes with strange names . . . like CATS, TIGRS and Streakers.

FOURTEEN

An Alternative
Scenario

*"The prophets prophesy falsely, and the
priests bear rule by their means; and my
people love to have it so."*
—JER. 5:31

Anyone who has a vague acquaintance with the Bible will certainly remember the story of God calling upon Jonah to proclaim the destruction of Nineveh because of the wanton wickedness in the city. Initially, Jonah could not believe that God would willfully destroy an entire population and was somewhat reluctant to carry out the assignment. But, after being passed through the bowels of a whale, Jonah was persuaded that evil must be punished. Jonah then made the necessary arrangements with the local TV station and announced on the six o'clock news, "Yet forty days, and Nineveh shall be overthrown." At that point, the Ninevehians decided the jig was up and the cookie was crumbling. All good things must come to an end. The coke, the hash, the pot, the wife-swapping, the love-ins, were all great fun but they certainly weren't worth dying for. The Ninevehians decided to repent, proclaimed a fast and covered themselves with sackcloth, "from the greatest of them even to the least of them." The wrath of God was thus assuaged and He decided to spare the city after all. But where did that leave Jonah? Jonah had staked his professional reputation on predicting the destruction of the city in forty days and, as it turned out, there was going to be no destruction, leaving Jonah in the role of a false prophet. "I've been had," squealed Jonah.

Of course there is a happy ending to the story. God persuaded Jonah that he should be pleased with having made a wrong forecast. After all, if Jonah's forecast had turned out to be correct, all the Ninevehians would have met their demise. The false prophet soon recognized that rather than offend God he was better off giving thanks to God for having spared Nineveh, "that great city, wherein are more than six score thousand persons that cannot discern between their right hand and their left hand; and also much cattle." Although the Old Testament doesn't tell it that way, what finally brought Jonah to a reluctant acceptance of God's change of heart was the acceptance that, but for his wrong forecast, the iniquity of Nineveh's population would never have been turned into repentance and his wrong forecast was directly responsible for a return to righteousness.

In that little story we have the principles of forecast-feedback, conditional predicting and vested interest forecasting all rolled into one. If God had told Jonah to inform the people of Nineveh that if they didn't mend their ways they would be annihilated, that would be a threat rather than a prediction. Instead, Jonah believed God had intended to destroy the city no matter what, and predicted the city would be destroyed in forty days. Obviously, God knew all about the power of forecast-feedback. It was in His best interests to get Jonah to make a false forecast given the value of the prediction-feedback. Had Jonah merely forecast the possibility of punishment, the people of Nineveh might not have repented with the same fervor as they had when they thought they faced inevitable death. Forecasting, rather than conditional predicting, obviously generates a far stronger feedback for those vested interests who use economic forecasting in this way.

For some time I've been at odds with the traditional forecasters who continue to predict economic recovery around the corner in the same way that Herbert Hoover did in 1929. "In no nation are the fruits of accomplishment more secure. I have no fears for the future of our country." That was Herbert Hoover's brand of economic forecast-feedback when the U.S. economy was just about ready to burst apart at the seams.

I've often been asked to explain why I think I'm right and most other people are wrong. To begin with, large numbers of negative economic forecasts which are at variance with the establishment forecasts never find their way into the media or are tucked away in the back pages in small print where nobody can find them. I'm really not alone in my negative views at all. More important, I have no vested interest. I make my living by being an accurate forecaster. I'm not running for political office nor am I the managing director of a multinational bank who must maintain confidence at all times. My vested interest is to be right in my forecasts and to help people improve their investment performance as a result of those forecasts. Forecast-feedback or self-fulfilling prophecies play no part in what I do.

Essentially, there are three different approaches to the subject of economic forecasting:

1. *Projecting*: Projecting involves studying the trend of a line that's already been drawn and subsequently extending that line, assuming the line that is drawn will take the shape of the line that has already been drawn, which in this case is our future. A projection is a more or less routine extrapolation which says that the future will be nothing more than a repetition of the recent past. The only thing that may differ is the placement of the decimal points on the predicted growth in the economic aggregates, assuming we are projecting a period of recent growth. This is the most simplistic method of predicting the future. It is also the most popular during periods of prosperity. Projecting is distinctly unpopular when the recent past is not suitable for projecting due to circumstances which are unpalatable. For example, if we have recently been experiencing economic strength, it is popular to *project* that strength into the future since we all like economic strength. If the recent past was a serious recession, then it becomes popular to forecast an end to the recession rather than project the recession into the future. There should be no assertion that any projection is valid or even meaningful. A projection cannot be used for the purpose of anticipating terminal junctures in existing economic conditions. A projection relies on the assumption that all things will remain relatively equal and continue in the same direction they had been taking in the recent past. A projection is therefore only of value in anticipating the future during periods when all things remain equal and continue in the same direction. This is rarely, if ever, the case when it comes to the aggregate behavior of the inhabitants of this planet.

2. *Forecasting*: A forecast is a somewhat more meaningful tool than a projection when it comes to anticipating the future. A forecast tries to describe as many economic variables as possible and assesses the possible consequences of changes in the variables. A forecast can be used to tell you when a recession is going to end. It can also be used to tell you when a prosperity might end and a recession could begin. Forecasting is more popular during periods of recession that everybody wants to see end than during periods of prosperity that most people want to see continue. The task of the forecaster is similar to that of the more astute members of the race tipping brigade. They will study all of the horses in a race and then determine the odds that each one has for winning.

3. *Predicting*: Ostensibly, predictions are useless. A prediction tries to call the race. A prediction suggests there are absolutes in the universe that can be determined with precision and these absolutes can be applied to economic forecasting. There is no hitching post in the universe. There are no absolutes. There can be no predictions of any meaningful use. We have possibilities and probabilities, risks and uncertainties, variables and alternatives. That's what life on earth is about. The most useful studies in

probability forecasting fall under the category of "game theory." A most appropriate title.

Essentially, this report is a forecast, subject to possibilities, probabilities and variables. The basic methodology that should be used when attempting to establish a likely prognostication for future events should involve a series of sustained, skeptical, systematic, emperor-has-no-clothes examinations of the important issues, their alternative resolutions and the long-term consequences. The imagination should be stretched as far as possible. Fashionable answers and preconceptions must be avoided completely. The forecaster must begin with a blank pad and come to a conclusion, only after the data have been assembled, not before. The forecaster must be prepared to tell people things they do not want to hear and be free to do so with regard to personal recriminations. There is a constant tendency on the part of forecasters to reinforce existing prejudices for the sake of popularity. I believe I have successfully avoided falling into those traps.

If anyone is going to determine the direction of the flow of a river it would be futile to study the water of the river under a microscope the way econometricians isolate irrelevant economic developments in their econometric models. If you want to find out the direction of the flow of a river you have to stand back from the river. Far back. Maybe 300 years back. Or 5,000 years. In a real sense there would appear to have been considerable retrogression in the ability to plan and anticipate the future. The modern intellectual involved in future forecasting tends to be educated mainly in relatively technical matters involving computer technology, differential calculus, the theory of sets and other arcane matters that blunt the sense of history. The modern economist feels that the suggestion that economic developments may be preordained is anathema to his intellect. The single answer cannot be satisfactory. Every answer must be carried out to the fifteenth decimal place. The only allowable deviation from the established norm is the decimal place. Simply stated, the quality of the people who have been attempting to predict the future may not be as good, or as moral, as were those confronted with the task one or two centuries ago. Since then we have abdicated creative thinking to the finite world of the computer that is not yet capable of creative thought. A computer is simply a moron with total selective recall. Garbage input = garbage output.

PLAYING THE DEVIL'S ADVOCATE

Modern economics, the harbinger of which is computer technology, will refute the findings of my long-term cyclical approach to macroeconomics on several grounds. Overriding most criticisms will be the intellectual distaste for projecting what will be seen as a somewhat mechanistic theory about long-term cycles into the future. Such a prejudice does not, of course, invalidate the method. In any event, if one is mesmerized by the timing sequence, it is true that the approach could be considered mechanistic. If one considers the number of variables that make up the infrastructure of the timing sequence and the interpretation thereof, application of the long wave pattern of economic activity goes far beyond that which could ever be considered mechanistic and reaches into areas that are beyond the limits of computer technology.

The most common denominator among academics is that we have only three complete cycle reference points to deal with. The purists will say this is hardly significant for statistical purposes. Once again, the existence of only three reference cycles covering the time since the Industrial Revolution may not add credibility to the long wave thesis but it certainly doesn't render the thesis incredible. The three reference points cover approximately 200 years. How many reference points are we going to require before the statisticians are satisfied? I really can't wait for 15,000 years to satisfy the statisticians. Neither can you!

While the record of economic activity prior to the Industrial Revolution may not be as complete as data since the Revolution, meaning we cannot study the infrastructure of the long wave of economic life in the same detail, there is strong evidence to suggest the cycle of deflation and inflation had been taking place in the same manner throughout history. Several economists have studied price histories prior to the Industrial Revolution and it would appear that cyclical continuity of inflation and deflation can be traced back several thousand years. The long-term cycle of interest rates, which forms part of the long-term pattern of economic life, can be traced back 5,000 years. Rogers, in *A History of Agricultural Prices in England*, produces data on wheat prices since 1260 for which it can be shown that fourteen cycles averaging fifty-four years in length have occurred. There is also evidence of a cycle approximately fifty years in length, correlating war and inflation in Rome and Carthage during their period of conflict. No doubt the most detailed demonstration of the shifting forces of inflation and deflation, prosperity and depression, can be seen in the work of Brown and Hopkins who studied price activity between 1271 and 1954.

E. H. Phelps Brown and Sheila Hopkins also refer to fifty- to fifty-two-year cycles of inflation and deflation. The references that were made and the conclusions drawn were independent of the work of the long wave macroeconomic theorists. The work of Brown and Hopkins confirms the works of Rogers, who only studied wheat prices. Once again we can find fourteen reference points of a cycle of inflation and deflation coming full circle. The evidence certainly vindicates the thesis and implies there may be far more than three complete long wave economic cycles involving the same infrastructure that is common to the cycles that have been studied since the Industrial Revolution. Those arguments that rely on the assumption that we have only three cycles to study, making the thesis is statistically insignificant, do not hold water at all. Quite simply, while we do not have 15,000 years of economic symmetry, perfect in every detail, what we do have in our study of long-term economic cycles is a degree of cyclical

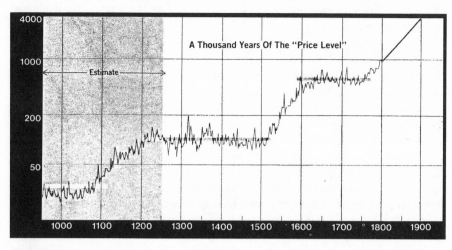

FIGURE 47

continuity that offers a far higher probability of sequential repetitions than anything else that we do have.

Another argument put forth by those who insist "it's all going to be different this time around," is based on the role of government and the manner in which government intervention in economic affairs has increased substantially during the post-war period. Supposedly, government controls and contracyclical policies have been developed to the point where a government is capable of altering or totally eliminating the rhythmic sequence that has prevailed for 200 years and, possibly, 5000. Such an assertion is obviously impossible to prove or disprove since the only test can be after the fact. If we manage to avoid a 1930s-type depression and also avoid a 1920s-type German hyperinflation, then it will have been proven that government has suddenly become more effective following 200 years of failure. So far, the efforts of government are less than encouraging. It is true that the expanded role of government has provided a cushion for the economy during the recessionary periods of the post-war era. But, this is the pattern that we've seen throughout the past 200 years. During the upwave, the economic climate *permits* government to *appear* effective. The post-war era, up until the early 1970s, was the period of the upwave. But we're now in the downwave. As the terminal juncture of the upwave began, the government action that previously was used to blunt the effects of the periodic minor recessions of the upwave, could be seen also to have prevented a correction of the excesses that were built into the recovery phase of the post-war era. As a result, when the downwave began, productivity had suffered and price inflation had become far more entrenched in the system than before. In addition to a profligate monetary policy, other factors, such as wage indexing, pension plans and the like, have acted to prevent the rate of price inflation from coming down during periods when business has been contracting.

As we continue to move through the 1980s, the components of the long-term economic pattern of behavior can be seen to have developed in the same manner as they have throughout history. We've completed the upwave in the traditional manner, involving a superinflationary blow-off which government was powerless to prevent. Following the inflationary surge came the normal recession that follows the inflationary peak and that is traditionally the worst recession since the upwave began. In continuation of the sequence of long-term economic activity, a secondary prosperity emerged following the deep 1973–1975 recession. That secondary prosperity has also ended, leading to a recession far worse than the post-peak inflation recession. If it is assumed that government is going to be able to make a fundamental alteration in the long-term cycle of economic activity, it should be recognized there is very little to warrant such an assumption. About all we have is a few months of economic improvement that looks like nothing more than the result of inventory adjustments. In the meantime, we have seen the rate of inflation come thundering down all over the world, a phenomenon totally inconsistent with the pattern of the upwave and the precedents upon which econometricians base their forecasts. While governments have made every effort to blunt the forces of deflation that have been raging through the world's economy since the fourth quarter of 1979, claiming credit for bringing down the rate of inflation while taking measures that would have ordinarily fueled inflation, the deflationary forces of the downwave have thwarted every effort to stimulate recovery. It would certainly be imprudent to conclude from the experience of Keynesian stabilization techniques over the past thirty years, that the government has suddenly acquired the ability to prolong prosperity and avoid depression in a totally changed environment. So far, there should be little doubt that governments around the world have proven to be powerless in the wake of the long-term economic trends. Government interference in its objective to provide full employment and redistribution of wealth is likely to have succeeded in accentuating the normal distortions which are created over the thirty-year period, making the prospects of a depression more likely than would have been the case with less government.

One of the few arguments against my current prognosis that has a shred of credibility deals with the nature of the secondary prosperity which is currently in the course of disintegration. The secondary prosperity that we recently experienced has indeed differed from previous secondary prosperities markedly. One of the characteristics of the plateau period, or secondary prosperity, is the shift in the government budget position. A large deficit is usually expected at the end of the upwave. During the recession that follows the end of the upwave and the secondary prosperity that follows the recession, the government moves into surplus. Between 1973 and 1979, this condition should have been met within the normal development of the long-term cycle. This condition was not met. The experience during the most recent plateau period has therefore been different from that of other corresponding periods in the long wave economic cycle. The United States has run a record deficit and it would appear that this deficit is likely to increase.

On the one hand, the implications are that there are no limits to the amount of fiat money that can be pushed into an economy and thus avert the ravages of depression. On the other hand, the implications are far more menacing. What lies ahead could make the depressions of the previous downwaves look like eras of prosperity. In order to produce the secondary prosperity that followed the 1973–1975 recession, record budget deficits around the world were called for. Monetary stimulation, on a truly massive scale, unprecedented in anything other than hyperinflationary economies, was necessary to counteract the deflationary forces that were a legacy of the post-war era, but were repeatedly blunted by government Keynesian policies. Essentially, the long period of prosperity that began in the post-war era was carried to levels which are beyond the capabilities of existing technological achievements and national productivity. In an effort to divert the normal corrective mechanism within the economy, government provided fiscal and monetary stimulation, resulting in a price boom that started in the 1960s and continued through the 1970s, stretching to limits that would not have been economically viable during a period of stability. A recession is supposed to have a cleansing effect, alleviating uneconomic excesses and serving to correct pockets of disequilibrium that take place at the mature stages of economic development. Once the excesses are corrected, the economy has a strong base from which renewed growth can take place.

During the upwave that began after World War II, the recession was prevented from fulfilling its normal function, cut short through the introduction of monetary stimuli before the natural economic forces had a chance to complete their work. Each recovery phase since World War II began with a greater number of businesses employing human and physical resources for progressively uneconomic functions. Three men were employed to do what one man could do. Double the resources were employed for performing the task that half the resources could have performed. The burden for the productive elements of the economy became increasingly more acute as uneconomic functions tended to drain the world economy of its resources which meant that even more stimulation was required to keep the productive elements efficient and the unproductive sectors afloat when both showed signs of faltering. Throughout the various phases of expansion and contraction between 1947 and 1973, each phase of expansion required more profligate spending than the one before to produce an even lower level of growth. Each recession required more government support to prevent the system from sinking into the abyss. During each recovery the problems for the unproductive countries, individuals and white-elephant industries increased in scope and numbers, rendering the situation more and more intractable. In the process, a large chunk of the steel industry was lost. A reasonable chunk of the British banking system was lost. Deindustrialization has been taking place at an accelerating rate. Manufacturing industries have been shrinking rapidly. The process continues.

The 1973–1975 recession occurred at a time when the global debt mountain, if liquidated, would have caused the greatest implosion of money in the history of Western civilization. The unbelievable debt mountain that governments, individuals and corporations have accumulated throughout the post-war period not only had to be serviced, but had to be supported at ever increasing costs with interest rates rising to levels that hadn't been seen since the days of the Roman Empire. The high cost of servicing global debt has acted as a drag against economic improvement. The lifeblood of business and of a nation is capital. At the moment, capital is being used to service debt rather than as a factor used to generate profits.

Of course, if the authorities had failed to stimulate the economy through the introduction of more monetary excesses on top of existing monetary excesses in order to keep the game going, we would have already had a 1930s-type depression and a series of self-feeding bankruptcies and concurrent debt liquidation that ran out of control. As the secondary prosperity of 1975 began, there was certainly little scope for any government to move into surplus, in turn leaving us with the most unstable of all secondary prosperities in the 200-year-record of the long wave economic pattern.

The longer governments continue to fight the deflationary forces that are currently working through the system, refusing to permit the global economy to correct the excesses of thirty years of profligate spending and debt accumulation, the greater will be the quantity of monetary and fiscal stimulation needed to offset the cumulative effects of these deflationary forces, and the greater will be the tendency for price inflation to escalate during each period of pseudoeconomic improvement. The result will lead to successively higher interest rates and successively higher inflation until such time as a hyperinflation level is reached that becomes unsustainable.

Now you may say, "Ah, Beckman, you've admitted it! The depression in the downwave can be averted. Governments can continue to stimulate the economy and we may not get a depression after all. We may get hyperinflation but isn't that a helluva lot better than a depression? We've learned to live with inflation. It wasn't so bad after all!"

THE ALTERNATIVE SCENARIO

It is my contention that the evidence presented to support my conclusion is overwhelming. The deflationary aspects of the downwave are perfectly in place. The infrastructure of the long wave cycle of economic continuity has proceeded in precisely the same manner as has been taking place since the beginning of the Industrial Revolution. As we proceed with the decade of the 1980s the probability of a scenario similar to what was experienced during the 1930s and previous periods of cyclical depression is exceptionally high. If I were asked to put a number on it, I would say there is a 90 percent chance that the next three years will be a live-action replay of the depression of the 1930s.

But, when it comes to dealing with probabilities, although the odds may be 100 to 1 in your favor . . . there is always that damn *1*. What might conditions be like if that *1* materilizes? What would be the alternative to the downwave? There can only be one alternative and that alternative would lead to hyperinflation. In the unlikely event that financial markets are able to tolerate further expansion, governments may continue to debase and inflate their currencies, using Keynesian reflationary techniques to blunt the forces of deflation, and disguise the elements of economic deterioration while providing the illusion of economic improvement. All of this would be taking place on top of an existing debt mountain and an economy that is stretched far beyond its means. The object, of course, would be to postpone the day of reckoning for as long as possible, accepting the inflationary consequences and hoping a miracle will occur to make all of the badness go away before the situation degenerates into chaos. When companies are headed for bankruptcies, if they're big enough, the government will bail them out. If unemployment gets higher and the government has to increase transfer payments, they'll print the money to accomplish this task.

The structural differences between the U.S. economy now and the nature of the U.S. economy during the early stages of previous downwaves, is significant. The level of wages is far less flexible now than in the 1930s, for example. During the 1920–1922 recession, wages fell sharply. During the depression of the 1930s they fell even more. Cuts in salaries were commonplace. This is not true of the economy today. The only significant change in the salary structure has been a slowdown in the rate of growth. The effect of the current equation is that we can probably expect to see a much higher level of unemployment for any given degree of deflation and therefore a heightened level of social tension. This is likely to be particularly true of urban areas where unemployment is highly concentrated and the threshold level of social pain is already extremely low. History is replete with examples of massive state interference when the political discomfort of deflation and unemployment threaten the ruling party.

During the early stages of previous downwaves there was little government intervention. The intervention did not come until the more pronounced stages. One of the main explanations for the deep recession that follows the peak inflation is in the decline of government expenditure. Recently, both the U.K. and the U.S. governments have been increasing their expenditure on automatic stabilizers and the military.

The economy and the financial system are now in an extreme state of overextension, while the ravages of the previous inflation have created extraordinary disequilibrium in capital and other markets, and have thus destroyed the balance of relative prices, wages, final goods and credit. Each phase of expansion requires accelerating amounts of money and credit to support the expansion. Any deceleration of money and credit at this time would send the economy back into a relapse which at this stage would send us headlong into a depression involving a massive debt liquidation and subsequent collapse of the financial system. This scenario is certainly recognized by the authorities. The precedent of state interference will not suddenly be thrown out of the window. Shortly after President Reagan took office he stated, "We will not fight inflation on the backs of the unemployed." The secretary of the treasury later stated that we could not have another depression because the Federal Reserve would never let the money supply contract to the same extent it did in 1929–1933.

The alternative scenario to that suggested by the continuity of the long wave pattern of economic activity would therefore be a relapse into recession in early 1984 involving a sharp rise in unemployment and a financial crisis as corporate difficulties and problems of Third World borrowers feed back into a banking system that is severely overstretched. The amount of money and credit now needed to reverse such a relapse would stagger the imagination and sow the seeds for a runaway hyperinflation. We certainly cannot blithely assume that the authorities, faced with a relapse into depression during a presidential election year, would do anything other than what they have done before when deflationary symptoms began to surface —acceleration of government spending programs and more deficits. While many governments have paid lip service to curbing inflation, it is most unlikely that the politically inspired desire to create fiat money has suffered any meaningful setback. Should unemployment start to soar and bankruptcies start to soar, the tough anti-inflation talk could dissipate very quickly.

Another aspect of the current downwave that differs from previous downwaves is the fact that several years ago governments removed any vestige of external impediments that could blunt inflationary forces through a regression to floating exchange rates. The current system has created an engine for inflation which is unprecedented in anything other than the hyperinflations of individual countries in the past. Countries no longer lose significant reserves when they have a payment deficit. In a world of floating exchange rates, instead of a run on the gold reserves of a country, the country simply lets the exchange rate drop. At the early stages of previous downwaves, the fall in the reserves had a tendency to reduce the domestic money supply and act as an automatic mechanism in controlling the fuel for inflation. This automatic mechanism is no longer available. Countries with massive deficits are free to increase their deficits and actually expand their money supply when it should be contracting. During previous downwaves, most countries were on some form of fixed exchange rate. Import excesses had to be paid for out of reserves.

Economically, we are in uncharted waters. We have abandoned the mechanisms originally designed to protect us. It is probable that the subsequent result could be the worst depression since the beginning of the Industrial Revolution. At the same time, we have created a locomotive that could drive us into a hyperinflation that could rival the horrifying inflation that overtook the German people in the 1920s.

THE NIGHTMARE OF INFLATION . . . YOU MAY HAVE TO SELL YOUR EARS!

The German monetary inflation that extended from 1918 through 1923 is a particularly fertile field for the study of inflation in its most grotesque form. The documentation of that period is probably superior to anything ever attempted along those lines to that time. The Statistical Bureau of the Reich and the various economic publications poured forth a volume of data that left very little to be desired in a study of the worst inflation the world has ever known. This was indeed no ordinary phenomenon. The six years encompassed one of the world's most violent economic dislocations, taking place as a result of the German authorities' resistance to the post-peak inflation recession of 1920–1922, in the same manner as the U.S. authorities have been resisting the recessionary forces of contemporary history.

Just before World War I, the German mark, the British shilling, the French franc and the Italian lira, were all worth about the same. The exchange rate was about four to five to the dollar. Ten years later, it would have been possible to exchange one shilling, one franc or one lira for up to 1 trillion marks, provided you wanted marks. Most were unwilling to accept marks in return for anything. The market died. It was worth one million-millionth of its pre-World War I self.

Before World War I the industrialized world lived under a gold standard, enjoying price stability and stable exchange rates. Germany was an industrial power that ranked high among the trading nations. The country was extremely prosperous and abided by the monetary rules laid down by the Bank Law of 1875. The Central Bank was the Reichsbank, which issued the currency. One-third of the currency was backed by gold reserves, the other two-thirds was backed by commercial paper of persons or businesses of proven solvency. The amount of bills taken by the bank was in proportion to the level of economic activity. The amount of currency in circulation was therefore also governed by the level of economic activity.

The outbreak of war placed the German economy in a critical position. The blockade imposed by the Allies all but slaughtered the international trade that Germany had so depended on for its prosperity. When war fever reached its peak in July 1914, a substantial exodus began from Germany, and certain sections of the German public began to panic, starting a run on the Reichsbank to convert their money into gold, as they were entitled to do at the time. Within a short time, the gold reserves were drained of 100 million marks. As a consequence, wartime legislation was passed abolishing currency convertibility into gold. Germany went off the gold standard. The door to inflation was opened.

Since international trade with Germany had come to a standstill, the country had no other way than borrowing to finance the war. The government approved credit of 5 billion marks. At the same time, three-month government Treasury bills were to be substituted for commercial paper to serve as a backing for bank notes. The Central Bank was authorized to take up and discount unlimited amounts of Treasury bills, which, unlike commercial paper, did not represent the underlying security of a solvent borrower. Treasury bills were merely government obligations which were sold to the Central Bank by the government allowing it to create money at will. With currency issued on the strength of Treasury bills and loan-bank credits, the inflation of the currency began. In just two weeks, the amount of money in circulation rose by 2 billion marks.

Germany's total expenditure during World War I amounted to the colossal sum of 164 billion marks. The cost of the war was 147 billion marks. The country had a total income of 121 billion marks. There was a gap of 43 billion marks covered by Treasury bills. The unfunded indebtedness of the Reich was 50 billion marks. By the end of 1918 the amount of money in circulation had reached the sum of 35 billion marks, about five times the level before the war. The profligate issue of currency resulted in a fall in the value of the mark of 50 percent between 1914 and 1918. By 1919 the mark halved again. Prices inside Germany had roughly doubled.

On November 11, 1918, Germany signed the armistice in the forest of Compiegne at a time when the economy was gutted. A large portion of German industry was destroyed during the war. There were about 6 million war casualties, while the mortality rate of the civil population had risen considerably. Productivity had diminished and the reserves of food and raw materials were depleted. In addition, there were the conditions of the armistice. Apart from the surrender of huge quantities of war materials, the Germans were also obliged to deliver 5,000 railway engines, 150,000 railway wagons and 5,000 trucks. The social and economic dislocations that accompanied the transition of a defeated nation from a military economy to a peacetime economy contributed to the overall chaotic state of affairs.

Germany needed money and needed it badly. Money was needed to buy food and raw materials from abroad. The demobilization of the armed forces was a costly business and so was the unemployment caused by the return of the soldiers and redeployment of industry. War victims had to be cared for and pensions had to be paid. The government could have resorted to the use of tight fiscal measures to finance a slow and painful recovery. Instead it decided upon what was perceived as a quicker method: the bulk of government expenditure would continue to be covered by borrowing, deficit spending and printing currency. Between November 1918 and July 1919, the deficit increased by a further 50 percent. The issue of currency marched in step. Internal prices advanced by 42 percent. Beginning in July

1919, the mark began to fall rapidly. By February 1920, prices advanced by 42 percent. Beginning July 1919, the mark began to fall rapidly. By February 1920, the exchange rate against the dollar reached 100 marks, nearly twenty-five times its pre-war parity. The Cost of Living Index published by the German Statistical Office showed a rise of 8.47 times the pre-war level. By mid-1920, conditions began to stabilize a bit. The mark began to hold its own in foreign exchange markets following the deep devaluation, but business conditions were far from buoyant. Wartime price controls continued long after the war ended and even when the controls were relaxed, firms were not able to boost prices to levels which were sufficient to compensate for rising costs. During 1920, net profits of 1,485 German companies averaged only about one-quarter the level of pre-war earnings, adjusted for monetary depreciation but not adjusted for inventory profits.

In 1920 the world plunged into recession. It was to be the worst recession since the depression of the 1890s. Global inflation had peaked in 1920 and the traditional post-peak inflation got underway. The timing couldn't have been worse for Germany, still engaged in a desperate struggle to restore industry to its former glory. Most of the industrialized world remained on a gold standard and therefore acquiesced to the deflationary and restrictive disciplines a gold standard imposed. Germany decided to move in the other direction, attempting to blunt the forces of global recession through more monetary and fiscal stimulation.

The recession took its toll on Germany's export markets. Between May and December 1920, exports fell by 40 percent while unemployment climbed from 1.9 percent in March 1920 to 6 percent by July 1920. From June 1921 through November 1921, the mark began to fall again, picking up momentum in the descent. During that period the mark lost about three-quarters of its value against the dollar. The dollar rate rose to 270 marks. This was a precursor of worse to come . . . far worse.

During desperate times, politicians become desperate. The year 1921 was a desperate one. The German war reparation payments were due for negotiation. At a conference held in Paris the Allies decided Germany was to pay the reparations in annual amounts of between 2 and 6 billion gold marks per year, spread over a period of forty-two years. Controls were to be set up to safeguard the payments. It was at that time that the British criticized Germany for its fiscal policies, stating that the financial burden that was to be born by the German people was ridiculously low in comparison to that of the people of the victorious Allies.

The Allies' reparation demands were rejected by the German government. The Allies replied to the German rejection by applying trade sanctions against Germany, and proceeded to occupy three major German cities —Düsseldorf, Duisburg and Ruhrort—in the Rhine–Ruhr area.

On May 5, 1921, David Lloyd George handed over to the German ambassador what was to become known as the "London Ultimatum." The

total sum of reparation was decided at 132 billion gold marks. This was to
be paid in regular installments of 2 billion gold marks. To be added to the
payment would be a sum equivalent to 26 percent of Germany's exports.
A down payment of one billion gold marks was to be made before the end
of August. In the case of nonacceptance by the German government, the
occupation of the Ruhr was threatened.

The German government in office resigned, refusing to accept the
ultimatum. A new government was quickly formed and the ultimatum was
accepted. The down payment of one billion gold marks due in August was
made as stipulated. The German authorities had great difficulty in arrang-
ing the acquisition of foreign currency needed for the payment. The problems were further aggravated when one of the international loans contracted by the Reichsbank—270 million gold marks from a Dutch banking
consortium—had to be repaid at short notice. Foreign currency, ordinarily
earned by trade transactions, was not available. The only way the German
authorities were able to purchase the foreign currency needed to pay the
Dutch was through the sale of paper marks on the foreign exchange market. The paper marks were duly issued through the creation and discount
of Treasury bills!

The transaction triggered a wave of speculation against the mark. The
situation was made worse still on October 20th, when the Council of the
League of Nations decided that the Upper Silesia region of Germany should
be partitioned and its richest industrial area given to Poland. The ensuing
gloom and despondency in Germany reached panic dimensions. The decision of the League of Nations was the kind of psychological shock that led
to a flight of capital out of marks and out of Germany. On November 29,
1921, the mark plunged again. The mark fell to 300 to the dollar during
November 1921. On November 15th, a further 500 million gold marks were
due under the London Ultimatum. The sum was paid but under protest.
Following the payment, the mark improved, since it was deemed that speculation was overdone. For about three months the mark was stable at a
dollar rate of around 200. In March 1922 the mark resumed its downward
trend, falling to 270 to the dollar in June. The currency in circulation rose
by a further 50 percent between February 1922 and June 1922. The Cost
of Living Index rose from twenty-four to forty-one during the corresponding period. Between June 1913 and June 1922 prices had increased by
forty-one times.

For reasons related to the economy rather than the potential infation-
ary impetus, the mark continued to collapse throughout 1922. In addition
to the scarcity of money, it was widely noticed that the earnings stated by
German industrial companies, although declining, were still too high and
considered totally unrealistic if inflation were to be taken into account.
Although the authorities attempted to tighten money, inflation continued
to rise. The continued rise in the rate of inflation meant that whatever
increase in domestic earnings there might be was being swallowed by the
depreciation of the currency. The dividends that were being paid out by

companies represented nothing more than a depletion of capital rather than a distribution of earnings when the growth in the rate of inflation is factored into the result.

Efforts to control inflation by tightening money sporadically proved utterly futile. The amount that was gained in controlling inflation was offset by the hardships and political pressures that were caused. By mid-1922 the German authorities had completely abandoned any attempt to control inflation through tight monetary policies and gave in to the demands for easy money—and higher inflation. The Reichsbank began to supply credit directly to industries, and in copious amounts, deliberately encouraging the greater use of commercial paper, which the bank, as promised, readily discounted, putting more currency into circulation as they discounted the paper. During the course of 1922, the amount of commercial paper discounted by the Reichsbank rose from 1 billion to no less than 422.2 billion marks in value. Commercial paper joined the Treasury bills in their role as engines for the creation of more and more paper money.

In June 1922 the mark was in free-fall. Between June and December 1922 the mark had fallen from 300 to the dollar to 8,000 to the dollar. German inflation entered a new phase. It now became clear, even to the most casual observer, that the mark was galloping downhill into an abyss. German industrialists had, by then, accumulated enough experience in dealing with a falling currency and rising inflation, that they ruthlessly increased prices in response to every fall in the exchange rate, anticipating a rise in costs. Confidence in the mark totally disappeared and was replaced by a widespread obsession with beating inflation by using it. Industrialists played the game by speculating on further falls in the mark, thus inducing further falls. Speculating on the fall in the mark became the best game in town, circa the autumn of 1922. There were wild spending sprees emanating from the ill-gotten gains of a falling currency. If the mark was dying, the Germans thought they might as well have a bit of fun before the funeral. The terminal stage was far less rewarding than many had expected.

Between June and December 1922 the Cost of Living Index in Germany shot up from 41 to 685. The prices of goods and services increased in Germany by more than 1500 percent in those six months. The currency circulation surpassed 1 billion marks, and so did the German deficit. But, it should be noted that up until the early part of 1923, printing of money to keep the economy moving had its beneficial side effects as it was intended to do. During the summer of 1922 there was full employment in Germany. The rate of unemployment was under 1 percent from April to September 1922, rising only slowly to reach 2.8 percent by the end of the year. German industries, especially those in the export trade, were booming during a period when other countries were suffering the ravages of the 1920–1922 recession. In the fall of 1922, the working week of British coal miners was reduced to a mere two days. German miners were actually working overtime. Of course they had to, given the disastrous fall in real wages as inflation galloped ahead. Yet, the 1500 percent rise in the Cost of Living Index in 1922 was nothing compared to what followed in 1923.

As the fateful year of 1923 began, a dramatic development preceded the commencement of a new and more terrifying phase of inflation than the world had ever seen, which was to terminate in the complete and irreversible collapse of the mark. After twelve months of nervous fluctuation, the mark plunged again in 1923, gathering momentum, dragging social misery, penury and political turmoil in its wake. The German currency at last went over the cliff edge of sanity to which it had, as it were, clung for many months with slipping fingertips. It has been said that capital markets can do anything they like any time they like, without reservation. The annihilation of the German mark proves it beyond any doubt.

The straw that broke the camel's back was a consignment of 125,000 telegraph poles, in addition to a quantity of coal, that were part of the London Ultimatum. These deliveries were to be made to the French in late 1922. Germany failed to execute the delivery. French and Belgian troops then marched into the Ruhr and occupied the region under the sanction that was part of the ultimatum. The result was a public uprising and civil war in Germany. There were arrests, bloodshed and loss of life. Once again the internal strife had to be financed. This was the coup de grace for the mark.

At the beginning of January 1923, the mark was trading at 18,000 to the dollar. By September 1923, the mark was trading at 100 million to the dollar, and still falling. The German government's official reaction to the occupation was "passive resistance." The government ceased all reparation payments of any kind and ordered a general stoppage of work for civil servants and railway workers. In addition, a complete cessation of any activities whatsoever that could conceivably benefit the occupying powers was ordered.

Although Germany's passive resistance to the occupation of the Ruhr prevented the occupying forces from restoring production to any meaningful degree, the price Germany had to pay was a high one. Not only did Germany lose the wealth-generating productive resources of the Ruhr when she could least afford to, but the country also had to provide for the unemployed and refugees who had lost their livelihood because of the passive resistance. On top of that, there was the damage caused to the rest of the nation by general unemployment, disruption, dislocation and administrative difficulties. For example, the German railways depended on coal from the Ruhr to remain operative. Without coal from the Ruhr, food and supplies could not be delivered to the other regions. Germany was obliged to purchase coal from Britain in order to maintain essential services. This meant the purchase of additional foreign currency, to the detriment of the mark.

The Germans had only one method for coping with the situation: the printing press. Notes in circulation increased from 1 billion marks at the end of 1922 to 92.8 trillion by November 15, 1923. By the end of the year the sum was a staggering 496.5 trillion marks. On November 15, 1923,

Germany's floating debt stood at 189 trillion marks. Three percent of Germany's expenditure was covered by taxes and other income. The other 9 percent came from the printing press.

Inflation reached such proportions that certain employees were being paid their wages two and three times a day so they could keep up with the rise in prices. Emergency notes were being issued by towns and cities throughout Germany. These were known as *Notgeld* and they were issued in huge quantities. The total number of *Notgeld* issues is fantastic. It has been recorded that 3,500 cities issued a total of almost 50,000 different notes between 1914 and 1922. Eventually, 30,000 people and over eighty private houses were employed in keeping up with the increased demand for paper money. Many of the earlier German issues of notes were overprinted, some of them twice on the same note.

FIGURE 48   20 MILLION REICHSBANKNOTE

The year 1923 was one of galloping inflation of such a degree that madness gripped Germany's financial authorities and economic disaster overwhelmed millions of people. Under these circumstances, conditions of life became grotesque and unbearable. The inflation was so preposterous that the story has tended to be passed off more as an historical curiosity than as the culmination of a chain of economic, social and political circumstances of permanent significance. As money was dying of the feverish inflationary disease, so was reason and common sense among the people. Printing presses all over the nation disgorged mountains of pieces of paper called "money" which were rushed by rail and road to desperately waiting crowds who hoped to get hold of it in time to buy the necessities of life before inflation had made the money worthless. Yet, however quickly the people grabbed the packets of marks that were thrown down to them, however swiftly they ran to do their shopping, more often than not they were too late, as the prices of the goods they needed jumped again while they were on the way to the market.

In the markets of Berlin, the price of potatoes, eggs and butter were changed six times a day. Grocers refused to part with their goods in exchange for paper money. Barter trade widely replaced transactions involving paper marks. The year 1923 brought catastrophe to the German bourgeoisie, as well as hunger and disease, destitution and sometimes death to an even wider public. Once the gold jewelry had gone, people had to offer their furniture and personal belongings in order to obtain their daily bread. Many had nothing to offer, and there was widespread undernourishment and near starvation. The angry and desperate masses became unruly and there was rioting in the streets throughout Germany. The inflation turned the country into a gigantic national madhouse with the inmates dancing a St. Vitus's Dance of the billions . . . and it all took a mere eighteen months to develop from the time Germany abandoned its "tight money" policy in 1922 to bailout ailing industries and keep consumption rolling.

In 1923 the value of the German mark was a national preoccupation, but who could comprehend a figure followed by a dozen ciphers? In October 1923 it was noted in the British Embassy in Berlin that the number of marks to the pound equaled the number of yards to the sun. Dr. Schact, Germany's National Currency commissioner, explained that at the end of the Great War one could, theoretically, have bought 500 million eggs for the same price as one egg five years later. As the mark reached its trough, and became exchangeable for gold marks, the sum of paper marks needed to buy one gold mark was precisely equal to the quantity of square millimeters in a square kilometer. It is far from certain that such calculations helped anyone understand what was actually taking place at the time but the figures may help focus on the enormity of the problem.

While the jobless, the homeless, the relief lines and the soup kitchens may appear individually synonymous with depression, it is actually difficult to describe the extent of the problems associated with the German hyperinflation. This was a difficulty noted by Lloyd George, who, writing in 1932, said that words such as "disaster," "ruin," and "catastrophe" had ceased to rouse any genuine apprehension anymore, so widespread was the use of these descriptive terms. During the German hyperinflation, the meaning of disaster itself was devalued along with the mark.

"Inflation finished the process of moral decay which the war had started," Erna von Pustau told Pearl Buck. "It was a slow process over a decade or more; so slow that really it smelled of slow death . . . in-between there were times when the mark seemed to stop devaluing, and each time we people got a bit more hopeful. People would say 'The worst seems over now.' In such a time Mother sold her tenanted houses. It looked as though she had made a good business deal, for she got twice as much cash as she had paid. But the furniture she bought . . . had gone up five times in price and . . . the worst was not over. Soon inflation started again with new vigor, and swallowed up bit by bit the savings accounts of Mother and millions of others."

William Guttman and Patricia Meehan, in their book *The Great Infla-*

tion, have a heartbreaking story to tell. " 'A friend of mine was in charge of the office that had to deal with the giving of salaries, pensions and special grants to the police of the whole district around Frankfurt,' recalls Dorothy Henkel. 'This was at the time when the bank notes were showing as many as twelve noughts. She struggled with her task very bravely. One case which came her way was the widow of a policeman who had died leaving four children. She had been awarded three months of her late husband's salary. My friend worked out the sum with great care, checked it and double-checked it and sent the papers on as required to Wiesbaden. There, they were checked again, rubber-stamped and sent back to Frankfurt. By the time all of this was done and the money was finally paid out to the widow, the amount she received would only have paid for three boxes of matches.' "

It may be difficult to fathom the extent to which extreme inflation can ravage society. Probably the best way to demonstrate what was actually happening is through the price history of the period itself. The following table makes the point far better than reams of descriptive literature ever could. During the three months from August 1923 through October 1923, prices were moving hour by hour, at a rate that often took a year and more to accomplish in normal times.

ITEM QUANTITY	PRE-WAR PRICE	PRICE IN SUMMER 1923	PRICE IN NOVEMBER 1923
1 kg rye bread	29 pfennig	1,200 marks (early summer)	428 billion marks
1 egg	8 pfennig	5,000 marks	80 billion marks
1 kg butter	2:70 marks	26,000 marks (June)	6 trillion marks
1 kg beef	1:75 marks	18,800 marks (June)	5.6 trillion marks

A pair of shoes that cost 12 marks in 1913 cost over a million marks in the summer of 1923. By November 1923 the price was 32 trillion marks. The price of a newspaper in November 1923 was 200 billion marks. The price of one match was 900 million marks. Life in the city was complicated even more by the introduction of the "multiplier" which had to be used to adjust the price mechanisms for the spiraling rate of inflation as and when required. An extended mathematical knowledge was needed just to keep body and soul together. Each morning the newspapers would publish a list of prices for public services. One billion involves nine zeroes. The number of digits on a price tag became so unwieldy that these multipliers had to be used. Every trade and each class of goods within that trade had a different index or multiplier. A purchase of the most ordinary items in a shop required several minutes of calculations to determine the exact price. When the price was calculated it then took several more minutes to count up the bundles of notes with denominations of thousands, millions and billions needed to execute the purchase.

SERVICE	PRICE IN MARKS
Tramway fare	50,000
Tramway monthly season ticket for one line	4 million
for all lines	12 million
Taxi-autos: multiply ordinary fare by	600,000
Horse cabs: multiply ordinary fare by	400,000
Bookshops: multiply ordinary price by	300,000
Public baths: multiply ordinary price by	115,000
Medical attendance: multiply ordinary price by	80,000

Prices were moving up so rapidly that salaries, even though they were disbursed two and three times a day, could no longer be readily adjusted by the use of index numbers or multipliers. Workmen who had been receiving 405 million marks a day on October 1, 1923 (about the equivalent of $1.75) and 6.5 billion marks a day by October 20, 1923, suddenly found their pay envelopes swollen with paper notes representing a mere 4 cents in terms of the exchange rate. Business had become virtually impossible. People spent their waking hours with dazzling numbers spinning around in their heads. The publication of the exchange rate twice daily set the human calculating machines in motion in an effort to determine how much money they would receive in their wage packets and how much they could buy with it before prices went up again. Price calculations were multiplied by multipliers then divided by the divisors until people shook with hysteria before going out of their minds.

The brother of William Guttman, coauthor of *The Great Inflation*, worked at the University Psychiatric Clinic in Munich. How the borderline between madness and reality was blurred is illustrated in his story:

When a new patient was brought in, the doctors started their investigation with a simple test to find out whether the patient was an obvious mental case or whether, at least on the face of it, he was normal. They would ask him a few elementary questions such as, how old are you, how many children have you got, what is the height of the Zugspitze? And the answers could be, I'm 25 million years old, have 1,000 or 15,000 children, etc.

The chronic instability of living in a world where money was dying drove the nation to temporary insanity. For some it was permanent. Values and perspectives among the people were twisted and distorted beyond recognition. It was a moral insanity more than anything else. There was a diminishing ability to distinguish the difference between right and wrong. There was a callous and almost paranoid disregard for the rights of one's fellow man in a society where materialism had reached its most horrifying extreme. "An age of Bedlam of unprecedented dimensions," and "a kind of lunacy gripping the people," were two of the phrases used to describe the collective madness of the German inflation by its chroniclers.

Stefan Zweig, in his memoirs, *The World of Yesterday*, describes his horror when witnessing the spectacle of Berlin gripped by the hideous inflation. According to his account, palaces of vulgar and coarse amusement mushroomed in the center of the city. Male prostitutes would parade along the Kurfürstendamm, to a witches' sabbath. He likened the dances of homosexuals of both sexes to orgies transcending those of decadent Rome. The average sixteen-year-old girl in Berlin would have been insulted by the suggestion that she might still be a virgin.

Hans Furstenberg describes in his memoirs the revulsion he felt when seeing the demonstrations of nauseating perversity along the streets of the city center; the flagrant display of nude shows and nightclub spectaculars that flaunted every conceivable form of human and animal sexual degradation.

In the dimly lit and not so dimly lit areas of the city's parks, trying to avoid stumbling over fornicating bodies was like running an obstacle course. One morning a young student was found dead, his hands and legs bound to a tree while semen dripped from his anus like water from a leaky tap. It was later discovered that he had been raped by a band of fourteen male homosexuals.

Berlin was dancing on a smoldering tinderbox loaded with explosives, leading a life of unprecedented apathy without giving the slightest thought to what the next day would bring for fear it might be worse than the day before. Prices could double again, or maybe jump by a thousandfold. Nobody really knew. The money you spent on a bottle of champagne in the evening might only buy a matchstick by morning. The country was experiencing complete and total political upheaval and financial disarray. Any individual, regardless of his walk of life, could be pushed into penury within hours.

People who could afford it, for as long as they could afford to, used whatever means available to escape the recognition of their possible fate. Gambling became excessive and widespread. The number of illegal gambling dens spread like an epidemic, attracting customers in search of diversions and eager to get rid of money that was literally becoming "not worth the paper it was printed on." Drug-taking became extraordinarily fashionable. With the demand for drugs came a vast army of peddlers and pushers who supplied confirmed addicts and those who were being trained to become addicts. Cocaine became a symbol of the age as a delinquent population, who, out of a sense of frustration or the desire to discover a new and more lasting form of escape, plumbed the depths of human depravity.

Human values fell in diametric proportion to the rise in the rate of inflation. Crime of every variety was rampant. The statistics of the time speak for themselves. The number of criminal convictions in Germany rose from 562,000 in 1913 to 826,000 in 1923. The largest gain in the number of convictions was in the area of theft, rising from 115,000 in 1913 to 365,000 by 1923.

Stealing and pilfering proliferated on an unimaginable scale among the middle classes. Apart from the comparatively honorable motive of desperate poverty, the lack of inhibitions among the people made the stealing of anything a normal and acceptable way of life. Not a copper pipe or a brass armature or a sheet of lead on the roofs of buildings was safe. They vanished overnight. Gasoline rose to a fantastic price on the black market. No car was safe unless there was someone to keep an eye on it to prevent the gas from being siphoned out of the tank. Railway carriages were not safe from the passengers. Invariably, they were stripped of their curtains and leather windowstraps. Young boys would wander the street, unscrewing metal doorknobs and metal number plates from doors wherever they could be found. This stolen property would ultimately find its way into the system of exchange and barter. It was easier to buy food with a piece of metal that could be melted down for scrap or a piece of leather that could be used to repair a shoe than with paper money.

Life for the majority of the German population during the inflation years was a matter of animal, sordid, grinding poverty. The standards of well-being declined precipitously. Mortality in general rose quickly. The incidence of stomach disorders and of scurvy grew alarmingly. Typhoid and skin diseases had become frequent because of a lack of hygiene in the handling of food. There was an increase in the number of pneumonia and rheumatic complaints, since many simply could not afford to buy fuel and warm clothing as inflation took prices out of the reach of an increasingly larger portion of the population. Children suffered especially. Infant mortality increased along with cases of rickets and tuberculosis. Most school children were severely underweight.

Food was expensive and hard to come by. There were many shortages. Food virtually disappeared from the shops. Farmers simply were unwilling to sell their produce for paper money. Any supplies of food that managed to get through had to bypass the obstacle of millions of hungry, desperate people. There was a scarcity of potatoes because of the danger of transport. Goods had to be transported after sundown, disguised under canvas and tarpaulin. Any visible food being transported during the daytime would surely have been subject to hijacking.

Between 1913 and 1923 the consumption of beef fell by 50 percent. The consumption of pork fell by even more. The consumption of horse meat remained relatively constant. The eating of dogs was practiced. Dog meat was the only meat item that showed a rise in consumption levels. In the third quarter of 1921, 1,090 dogs were slaughtered for human consumption in Germany. In the third quarter of 1922, 3,678 dogs were slaughtered for the same purpose. In the corresponding quarter of 1923, 6,430 dogs were slaughtered and found their way to the dinner tables of the German people.

One particular landlady was noted for her ability to keep her boarders regularly supplied with meat at the evening meal. She said she had a secret supplier in Münsterberg. Every Thursday she would travel to the city, where she was able to buy as much meat as she wanted and at an especially reasonable price. Münsterberg was the city where the mass-murderer Denke conducted his operations in 1923.

During the depression of the 1930s, hunger and poverty led to the rediscovery of brotherly love. People knew they needed each other. They helped each other. This was certainly not the case during the great inflation in Germany during the 1920s. Callousness was unparalleled. People would humiliate each other without the slightest hesitation. There is the macabre and disgusting incident told by the daughter of a once wealthy landowner in Germany. The local parson demanded as payment for the Father's funeral service one of the last remnants of the vanquished family's fortune . . . a few silver spoons.

Thousands of gallons of milk went unsold because farmers refused to take paper money. Milk was another item in short supply due to hoarding. People couldn't obtain milk in the ordinary way unless they had a certificate to prove there was a baby in the family. A young mother tells of her experience when moving to Berlin: As a visitor to the city, the first thing she did was register with the local authorities so she could get milk for her baby. The woman in charge of disbursing the milk dismissed the young woman's request in a rude and abrupt manner. "We haven't any milk for you." "But, I have a small baby and I'm entitled to it," pleaded the young mother. "Why do you bring babies into the world . . . drown it!" was the heinous reply.

No doubt the next chapter in the story of the German hyperinflation is the worst of all. By November 1923, Adolf Hitler believed his hour had struck. The German currency was utterly worthless. The purchasing power of incomes and salaries was reduced to zero. The lifesavings of the middle classes and the working classes were totally wiped out. The faith of the German people in the economic structure of German society was obliterated.

"What good were the standards and practices of such a society," says William L. Shirer in *The Rise and Fall of the Third Reich*. "A society which encouraged savings and investment and solemnly promised a safe return from them and then defaulted? Was this not a fraud upon the people?"

We live in a world where, if you borrow money, you have to pay it back. But in the case of Germany following World War I, paying back what they owed would have meant immediate hardship for the people. The politicians, who wished to spare the people any hardship and to remain in power, decided they didn't want to pay what they owed in goods and services, so they printed paper money and built up a staggering debt. The inflation could have been halted by balancing the budget but, politically, such a move would have been unfavorable. Adequate taxation could have mitigated the soaring inflation and debasement of the currency. But the new government was afraid of being ousted from office if it imposed adequate taxation. Above all, the politicians wanted to keep their jobs. Instead of drastically raising taxes for those who could afford to pay, the German government actually reduced taxes in 1921.

Aided and abetted by foreign bankers, industrialists and landlords, who stood to gain enormously through foreknowledge of government policy while the masses of German people were financially and morally bankrupted, the government sat idly by while the market tumbled and inflation soared. The State was freed of its public debts and managed to wriggle out of paying full value for its war debts. The destruction of the currency enabled the bankers and industrialists to wipe out their indebtedness by repaying their obligations in worthless German paper money.

It took the German people many years to discover what had actually taken place. They never imagined how profitable their demise had been to the industrialists and bankers, the Army and the State. All the people were aware of was that large bank accounts couldn't even buy a spindly bunch of carrots, a half pound of potatoes, a few ounces of sugar or a pound of flour to make bread. They knew the hunger that gnawed at them daily. Such times were ideal for a man called Adolf Hitler:

> The Government calmly goes on printing scraps of paper because if it stopped that would be the end of the Government. Because, once the printing presses stopped . . . and that is a prerequisite for the stabilization of the mark . . . the swindle would at once be brought to light . . . Believe me, our misery will increase. The scoundrel will get by. The reason: because the State itself has become the biggest swindler and crook. A robbers' state! . . . if the horrified people notice that they can starve on billions, they must arrive at this conclusion: we will no longer submit to a State which is built on the swindling idea of the majority. We want a dictatorship.
>
> —ADOLF HITLER,
> *Mein Kampf*

We have been programmed to fear a depression as if it were some form of bubonic plague. Inflation is perceived to be preferable. As I have shown you, there are far worse alternatives than the depression of the 1930s or the depression that I envisage for the 1980s. Have politicians learned anything from the macabre events that surrounded the German inflation? Is this an isolated case out of the history books that can never happen again? Can we comfortably believe the Federal Reserve can solve our problems by printing more money, bailing out the banks and lame duck companies?

For those who think the fiat money route is the way to go, the Brazilian economy provides a perfect object lesson. Not too long ago Brazil was being hoisted to the top of the flagpole as a country that had learned to live with inflation. Those who advocate an easy money policy point toward Brazil as an economy that seems to survive an inflation rate of 127 percent. Survival, of course, is qualitative. Brazil is currently a bankrupt nation that owes $105 billion. Earlier in 1983 there was rioting in the streets of São Paulo because the Brazilians refused to accept the austerity measures the government wished to impose in order to return the country to stability. The government acquiesced to the demands of the people, fearing a revolution. The result was the near default on a $400 million bridging facility that was due in May but not paid until mid-July. Many bankers fear that Brazil will ultimately default. How are the Brazilian people coping with inflation?

CORNEA FOR SALE . . . PLEASE CALL WORKING DAYS

This ad appeared in a local newspaper in Rio de Janeiro, the capital city, where the wealthy lavish millions of dollars on plastic surgery while the poor and destitute try to make ends meet by selling their kidneys, corneas and blood. You can get about $35,000 for a nice fresh cornea. Kidneys are more abundant and go at a much lower price. If you're a Brazilian you'll only get about $15,000 for one of your kidneys. At the moment, the going rate for blood has hit rock bottom. There are more donors than there are people who need a blood transfusion. Two bucks and a bowl of soup is about the most you're going to get for one pint of Brazilian blood that patients in the hospital pay $45 for. Another reason for the low price of blood is that disease and infection are widespread in Brazil. Special costly measures have to be taken for purification of the plasma.

Extraction of a living person's cornea will cause blindness in one eye for life. People donating corneas usually do so by signing permission for extraction to take place after death. During the summer of 1981 the Brazilian Red Cross sponsored a national campaign to solicit cornea donations for transplants. Squeezed by 100 percent inflation at the time, along with galloping unemployment, many individuals began to place their corneas and kidneys on sale for immediate delivery by advertising their organs in local newspapers.

"The economic situation is critical . . . three years ago I lived better than I do now on half my salary," said one Brazilian who offered a cornea through the papers. He has to support a wife and child on the money he earns working at Rio de Janeiro International Airport. He figured out that if he can get his asking price for the cornea, that will give him enough money to pay for his young son's education. He will also be able to secure his own future as one of the partially handicapped who can claim government subsistence. He feels the loss of the sight in one eye for the rest of his life is a reasonable price to pay for ensuring his son's education along with his own personal survival. What he doesn't know is what the cost of that education will be when the time comes. With inflation now 27 percent higher than it was when he offered his cornea for sale, his partial blindness may buy nothing more than a pencil when the time comes to pay for his son's education.

Many offers to sell organs with the promise of immediate availability appear in the classified columns of the Brazilian newspapers under the "medicine and health" columns. Offers for the sale of kidneys and corneas are usually accompanied by such phrases as "financial problems," "best offer," "urgent" and "good health," "perfect vision" and "young." These offers to sell organs are merely an extension of the long-standing controversy over the still generally legal practice of the poor selling their blood to supplement their income during this period of intractable inflation. About 75 percent of the blood used in Brazilian hospitals is supplied through commercial blood banks, usually located in the impoverished outskirts of the major cities. Regular blood donors are usually the unemployed, sick and undernourished. In 1980 a documentary film was made on the business of trading in blood. An incident was recreated involving an unemployed laborer living in Rio who died of anemia after selling his blood repeatedly in order to feed his family. In spite of the film, the commercial blood banks in Brazil continue to do a booming trade with some estimates of the traffic running at 2,500 gallons of blood a day.

In the suburban slum of Madureira, a blood bank called the Natal Blood Bank faces the railroad station which is used by thousands of commuters to go to work each day. The Natal Blood Bank is one of the many hundreds of commercial blood enterprises. Another commercial blood bank is located across the street from the downtown bus terminal in Madureira where thousands more poor and starving working-class commuters must embark for their daily bread. It is not uncommon for a large number of these working-class commuters to sell their blood at the commercial blood banks in order to raise the money to pay for the train fare, which is the equivalent of 10 cents.

One commercial blood bank was accused of coercing samba dancers into selling their blood in order to pay for their costumes just before the renowned annual carnival in Rio. The owner of the blood bank denied the allegations on the grounds that, "A donation of blood wouldn't even cover the cost of a pair of shoes."

As as American sitting in your comfy condo or watching the paint dry on the ceiling of your office, you may harbor the illusion that Americans would never find themselves in a position where they might have to stoop to those levels. "If Uncle Sam is going to print money, he knows how to make it work," you may say. Oh, yeah!

Darlene Vanderpool, living in California, was willing to sell one of her kidneys just to get the price of the first square meal she and her husband would have eaten in a week. After seven days with nothing to eat but a can of tomato soup, and no prospects of any money for at least another week, Mrs. Vanderpool attempted to sell one of her kidneys through a classified ad in the newspaper. "There are so many people without kidneys, I thought surely I could sell one," she explained. "Of course, I've been sick a lot myself and I don't know how much one of mine will be worth." Fortunately, or unfortunately, depending on how you look at it, Mrs. Vanderpool's efforts failed. The newspaper was unwilling to accept the ad offering her kidney. California state law bars the sale of human organs from live donors. As inflation rampaged in America there were large numbers of people selling their organs through the American newspapers before the law was passed.

Right now, governments around the world are faced with the same choice the German government was faced with in the 1920s. A few figures will tell you about the size of the problem. As of mid-1983, sovereign debt amounts to $700 billion, most of which will never be repaid. Total dollar debt, including all deposits in banks in both domestic and Eurodollar markets, is at least $10 trillion, probably more. The biggest debtor of all, our federal government, is now borrowing at the rate of about $150 billion a year, a la Germany, circa 1920s. A total of $1.15 trillion must be raised each year by all those debtors, most of them illiquid, just to avoid default and the collapse of the international banking system. Any additional debt to expand inventories, buy additional plant and equipment, or hire more workers, generally promoting artificial recovery, will swell the demand for money even more.

The notion that the Federal Reserve can make us all better off by intervening in money markets, bailing out lame duck companies and printing money to foster financial economic recovery is the same notion the German people were led to harbor before the nightmare inflation. Central Bank intervention in money markets has proven itself to be the most persuasive, dangerous, destructive and mischievous of all intentions, primarily because the irreparable damage that is caused doesn't reveal itself for quite some time. The Federal Reserve intervenes by buying paper assets in the same way as the Reichsbank bought Treasury bills. These paper assets are mostly newly printed government securities. So far we have about $145 billion worth. The government buys these paper assets by simply printing pieces of paper that you keep in your pocket in the form of Federal Reserve notes. Sound familiar?

The downwave has come and the message is, it is time to pay the piper. The mountain of debt that has been accumulated through the upwave must now be repaid. It can be repaid in one of two ways. Payment can be made in worthless paper currency which is debased and expanded by government. Or, it can be repaid through the liquidation of assets that have been accumulated but never earned. Given the horrendous level of current debt exposure and the amount of money that will be needed to fund that debt, the first method will produce the kind of nightmare inflation experienced by Germany during the 1920s, the second will produce a 1930s type depression.

Throughout history we have seen the manner in which inflation has debilitated and destroyed the moral fiber of nations and their people. An inflationary economy is the economy of deceit and illusion that John Maynard Keynes said, "Not one man in a hundred thousand can protect himself against." The horrors and strife that have bedeviled people during periods of high and chronic inflation render the hardships of recession and depression insignificant by comparison. There are no alternatives to our current plight. If we're lucky, very, very lucky, the fantasy that began in the summer of 1982 will stumble and fail before the end of the year, after which, the forces of the market will continue to operate, leading us into a global depression from which the world will emerge, healthier and stronger with a brave new face.

To face the future requires courage. Courage means acting when you're afraid to act. There is no courage until you're frightened. But it is very difficult for any politician in a partisan, take it easy, consumer society, to explain to people the perils we all face. History does indeed repeat itself when men and women who have become apathetic and easygoing refuse to learn the lessons of the past. But, those who face what may be perceived as future adversity, decisively, courageously and firmly, are the least likely to encounter that adversity.

BEYOND THE DOWNWAVE

Basically, I'm an optimist. I believe America and the rest of Western industrialized society will turn its back on the inflationary route and through progressive disinflation and then deflation, the coming depression will run its course. The most painful part of the experience will probably be between 1984 and 1986. The economy may then bump along for a few years but what follows can be forecast with a reasonable degree of certainty. The decade of the 1990s is likely to offer a boom just like the post-war boom but the benefits to mankind will overshadow anything in history.

I hope I have made it clear that depression is the more or less inexorable outcome of the post-war expansion. Depression is inherent in the nature of the expansion, in particular of the exceptional growth of debt on which the expansion was built. It *follows* from the resulting rise in real interest rates, the growth in budget deficits across the globe, the overexpansion of productive capacity and the general decline in corporate profitability. The effect of the depression will be to purge these imbalances, and in due course to set the scene for an upwave of expansion which will follow in just the same inexorable way.

What has history to tell us? It was probably not until 1931 that it began to dawn on most people that the sharp recession that had been suffered to that date was the start of something very different from the standard business cycle contraction, attended, as some others had been, by a financial panic. By 1933, the attitude of the public was almost universally defeatist. The growth era of the 1920s was nothing more than a nostalgic memory. "Everyone we talked to, in the schools, in the universities, would have little vision of what this great country and its resources could do," reminisced David Kennedy, then in 1933 at the Fed in Washington, later treasury secretary under Nixon. Both he and Raymond Moley, Truman's right-hand man, are quite clear that despite all the New Deal programs, there was no full recovery from the Depression till 1940: "The war got us out of it, not the New Deal policies."

The statistics confirm this. National income did not pass the magic $100 million mark it had topped in 1929 until 1941. So the apparently universal gloom seems to have been quite justified and to have been shared in some degree by members of the administration. Yet, for the practical purposes that concern us, it was entirely the wrong attitude. By some yardsticks, the worst of the Depression was over by 1932. Further improvement was evident in 1933. By 1935 the inexorable deflationary forces had completed their work. In 1933, the slump in corporate earnings was reversed, moving into a sustained uptrend. By the middle of the decade both commodity and consumer prices were heading up. In retrospect, we can see that the purge of the economy between 1929 and 1933 was so drastic that the conditions for the ensuing upwave had already been laid in four (admittedly not very short) years.

The experience of the 1930s probably provides as good a framework as can be hoped for, when it comes to planning for the future. We shall all need a working plan for the next few years, and in mid-1983 it seems as if it should look something like this. Sometime between now and mid-1985, a recession will begin which will escalate into a worse business slump than that of 1979–1982. It will be accompanied by a severe financial panic, and it may be such a deep slump that it takes a decade to catch up to the levels of prosperity that obtained prior to it.

I have tried to explain the economic background of the downwave to show you how to recognize that component of the downwave characterized by deep depression. The downwave will not move in a straight line. There will be many periods during the downwave when it will appear that an economic recovery is about to take place. Such recoveries will be shallow and brief. Most of all, these recoveries will be treacherously deceptive. Businessmen will equate periods of mild economic improvement to the type of prosperity that followed during the upwave. They will think the world is getting back to the way it used to be. They will be wrong. Long-term plans will be made that will be woefully inappropriate.

The kind of business enterprises that prospered during the upwave will no longer be viable during the downwave. Property development and investment are probably the most notable example. I have focused on the type of business that should be resilient in the downwave and possibly profitable during the coming decade. I have concentrated on investments that will help you protect and hopefully enhance your capital during the dramatic changes in the economic, social and cultural environment that you will have to become accustomed to.

The downwave will produce many fortune-making opportunities. People who sell short, buy put options, buy bonds on margin, sell naked calls and such will be able to amass and compound profits beyond their wildest dreams of avarice. Yet, I have purposely avoided any elaboration of these high-risk strategies. The reason is that most people will not be able to handle the risks associated with these professional strategies. The majority who attempt these grandstand speculative plays will lose money when the most important objective during the downwave will be to preserve your savings above all, in both nominal and purchasing power terms. It would be very unwise to try to get rich quickly during the downwave. Adopt an attitude of contentment in nurturing your savings. Try to get rich slowly . . . and there's a good chance you will. The depression will run its course and then you will be presented with the most rewarding business opportunities of your lifetime. Needless to say, if you dissipate your capital before these opportunities present themselves you will not be in a position to take advantage of them.

The view of the future for most people is an exceptionally shortsighted one. The average businessman and investor becomes euphoric when the economy is booming, believing the boom will never end. He then becomes somber, introspective and negative during a crisis, assuming crisis conditions are a permanent way of life. Successful planning is based on the premise that man will continue in the future to make the same mistakes he made in the past. While circumstances change, the predictability of human behavior is one of the most reliable constants in our economic environment. If people were to accept the inexorability of booms and depressions we would have neither. It is the lack of preparation for change, the anti-change mechanism which is part of the human psyche, that ensures booms and depressions will continue for as long as there are emotional development lags in our technological development.

There should be little doubt that man has a tendency to see the future as a continuation of the present moment while he is desirous of living in a state of permanent financial orgasm. People seem to forget, ignore or dismiss the inescapable truth that the whole cycle of growth and contraction must be perceived in order to gain a realistic view of the coming evolution. Like the panics and crashes that have punctuated history, the Great Depression of the 1930s, the 1973–1975 crisis and the depression that is now approaching did not signify the end of economic growth in our industrialized society, as many people will soon think. We are merely coming to the terminal juncture of one particular economic period. Scientific discoveries, technical progress and the ensuing improvement in global living conditions have certainly not reached the pinnacle of man's achievement. A glorious twenty-first century lies beyond the downwave. Humanity will continue its evolution undisturbed for the three decades to follow.

People tend to look around at the current pace of technological development and conclude that it rules out any chance of a traditional depression. If ever that could have been true, it should have been true in the 1930s. The bulk of all the major inventions that were to power the post-war expansion were in place well before 1930. The automobile from 1887; the airplane from 1903; the automatic telephone exchange from 1891; radio from 1905 and radio telephone from 1906; the vacuum cleaner and washing machine from 1907; the tape recorder from 1899; the punched card from 1884; even the rocket from 1929. But all that did not stop the world economy from wandering ten years in the wilderness.

That is point number one. There is a gap between the invention and its exploitation to the point where it makes a significant impact on economic growth that is wholly unpredictable. Point number two is that forecasters have a very bad record indeed at forecasting how inventions will be modified and applied. From the floppy wood and cloth invention of the brothers Wright in 1903 to the metal jumbo jet of the 1970s capable of carrying 300 people is a conceptual gap that practically no one can bridge. It is a commonplace that forecasting institutes have barely ever succeeded in predicting a single major technological innovation. But the misconception lies in ever thinking it would be likely they should.

So as we look into the future, we might as well do so in the spirit of a game. It is fun to do. It can also stretch the mind. We might as well be aware at the start that the significant events of the coming upwave will be intrinsically highly improbable from our present starting point. That is the way life is on earth. When there are an almost infinite number of improbable things that can happen, and a few apparently probable things, most of what happens is improbable. This seems to be a statistical truth. For purposes of simplicity, the rules of the game call for the plain future tense —no conditionals.

There will be a great consumer boom during the next upwave, but it will happen in the developing world—in China, the Pacific, Nigeria, South America, etc. The share of the advanced countries in this boom will be by way of industrial colonialization. Not only will the capital for this industrialization come from abroad, it will be owned by foreigners. The Soviet Union will in due course join in this exchange. Both America and the Soviet Union will develop infallible defenses against nuclear attack (based on lasers, perhaps) that will end the arms race, warm the cold war, allow the Soviets to devote more resources to its consumers, loosen its autocratic regime and progressively mingle capitalism with its brand of collectivism.

Employment in the OECO countries will not begin to rise until around the end of the century. By then the manufacturing sector's share of the workforce will be in single figures in the United States. Many will be working in the developing world, of course. By then the work week will have fallen below twenty-five hours. Inflation will be between one and minus one percent, after a bout of deflation in the latter 1980s. Interest rates will vary around 4 percent.

The electric car will revolutionize urban transport. This will have been made possible by the use of microprocessors in the control of the electricity offtake from batteries, rather than any revolutionary advance in battery techniques. The improved offtake will treble battery energy conversion in relation to today's forklift truck. (The electric car will first be mass-produced in Britain, partly because the domestic automobile lobby in the United Kingdom is so feeble). The long-distance automobile will be a modular unit to be added to the urban vehicle and stacked at convenient suburban points.

The use of nitrates will be progressively abandoned in agriculture, to be replaced by nitrogen-fixing algae. Totally new crops will be bioengineered. These and proteins from carbohydrates will supplant current livestock feeds, particularly corn. There will be no food shortage. Also, there will be no energy shortage, as microprocessor controls continue to improve utilization factors.

A great many jobs will be created by the digitalization of all knowledge and information. Individual knowledge will become exclusively the knowledge of where to look for information. Translation will be the job of computers. Computer hardware will split in two between the portable and the fixed. The former will continue to be based on silicon chips but the latter will have superconductive processors of the Josephson junction kind. Lewis Branscom of IBM has gone on record as speculating that the ultimate "picoprocessor" might be patterned on the DNA molecule that controls heredity.

Far from developing in a human direction, the computer and robot will develop in parallel with humans. Two of the weaknesses of the human brain are 1) the very poor ability to think laterally and 2) the inability to monitor more than about seven variable factors of a situation at any one time, according to psychologists. The "artificial intelligence" of computers needs suffer from neither defect and will be developed in the area of invention and discovery. Machines will in fact take over the donkey work of technological innovation. Humans will be freer to pursue the frontiers of understanding, in particular the powers of the unconscious mind, and the relationship of chemistry to life and to mind. The wealth of the human unconscious mind is our answer to the "superintelligent" machine so feared by many and usually incarnated in an improbable human robot form.

What is the human unconscious capable of? Hypnosis has given us some answers. Dr. Lyall Watson (Lifetide) recounts an experiment in which a group of students were shown into a room full of paraphernalia of one sort or another under instruction to memorize whatever they could in a few minutes. "Before and after" hypnosis tests showed a staggering improvement in observation and memory performance. In one case, however, the difference was small. The experimenter pressed on and a chance question revealed an astonishing result. Under hypnosis, the subject was able to recall with faultless memory the entire contents of the front page of *The Times* of London. The object had been so far distant that even to read the print was totally beyond his, or anyone else's, capability in the conscious state.

Teleaccess to digitized libraries—which will effectively be a vast encyclopedia of information, discovery and theory, old and new—will produce amazing dividends in synergy and the avoidance of duplicated thinking. It will bring mankind closer to the distant dream of Teilhard de Chardin of one single mind for all humankind. Such an encyclopedia in the field of medicine has been online since 1971 at the U.S. National Library of Medicine under the name of the Medical Literature Analytical and Retrieval System or MEDLARS.

In the field of chemical psychiatry, we are tantalizingly close to a breakthrough point in identifying the chemical basis of memory malfunctions, and various paranoias and phobias. A chemical called vasopressin appears to have been able to provide dramatic and lasting improvements in memory function—even restoring memory to total amnesiacs. Scientists seem to have isolated the chemical responsible for fear of the dark—hence called scotophobin. The chemistry of physical pain and pleasure is becoming clearer. The breakthroughs may come at any time to be exploited during the upwave.

Nowhere has progress been more sensational than in the field of genetic chemistry and so-called bioengineering. Just around the corner seem to lie cures for cancer, for all known viral diseases; indeed, the ability to construct practically any of the building blocks of life. The progress in microprocessing seems almost to guarantee that most of this will be achieved this century. For the pooling of knowledge and the teleaccess to knowledge afforded by digitalization multiply manyfold the chances of breakthrough. Indeed it may, as has been suggested, be computers that make the breakthrough if professional jealousy permits.

In short, we can already see all the technology in place to power the next upwave, even without the much greater bulk that is unforeseeable. The tools are already there for solving any foreseeable shortage of energy or materials that might otherwise be thought to threaten material expansion. If you want, you can go along with visionaries like F. M. Esfandiary, an author who has taught at the New School for Social Research in New York and the University of California at Los Angeles. He sees mankind at the brink of "the age of immortality."

"Anyone alive in twenty years will be alive in 200 years, and if you're alive in 200 years, you'll be around forever," he told *The New York Times* in 1979. He sees us immortals developing into "telehumans . . . whose brains and bodies are at all times connected to other brains, systems and technologies for the sake of instant, direct communication, bypassing the walls, inhibitions and fears that have separated us through the eons." I'm sure he meant it to be taken literally, but taken in the metaphorical sense,

it is just such a development that can be envisioned with the teledigitaliza-
tion of knowledge in the next few decades, rather than centuries.

With a home computer that can be linked by telephone into digitalized
libraries and encyclopedias, along with other home computers and the
computers of various service organizations running the gamut from newspapers to tax lawyers in a constant online two-way feed, we would not be
entirely unlike Esfandiary's "telehumans."

The telephone needed a network before it was any use to the consumer,
but it couldn't have a network until it won its consumers. The television
suffered from a similar chicken and egg problem. It needed a big program
choice to acquire mass consumers, yet it needed mass consumers to justify
the big program choice. In both cases too, the breakthrough in unit price
depended on mass production while mass consumption depended on a
breakthrough in unit price. Unlike either of these, and many other consumer products, the home computer appears to have achieved a mass
market without the mass of users knowing just what they would use it for.
They are learning through possession of the device rather than the other
way round. The trick was to use computer games to give the mass appeal.
And the clincher was the courageous decision among certain pioneering
manufacturers to price the product at tens rather than hundreds of dollars
and trust that the mass market would follow.

It did, and with the learning comes the opening up of new horizons,
quite different applications for different people. And with the multiplication
and crossfeeding of the new horizons in the years ahead will come many
of the threads of growth for the next upwave of which we now simply
cannot conceive.

The next upwave is not possible without the purge of a depression. But
the purge of a depression will make the next upwave inevitable. Probably
before the end of this decade there will be a once in a lifetime opportunity
for exploiting the upwave at the turn of the century as the mind-boggling
technological achievements slowly begin to come into view.

In the meantime, you must come to grips with the behavior pattern
implicit in the remainder of the downwave. If what I have written has
helped you to understand what has happened to the world over the past few
decades, what is happening now, what is likely to happen in the future and
why it is going to happen, then my research and correlations will have
served their purpose. If you feel the possibilities that have been outlined
are as inescapable as I do, then it is likely that you will be able to pick up
the threads where I have left off, developing your own solutions to your
own personal circumstances as the downwave unfolds.

You should now be ready to experience financial, social and economic
conditions unlike anything you have ever known. The world as you have
understood it for the past three decades is about to be turned upside down
. . . or perhaps right side up!

Bibliography

ALIBER, ROBERT Z. *The International Money Game.* New York: Macmillan, 1973.

APPEL, GERALD. *99 Ways to Make Money in a Depression.* New Rochelle, NY: Arlington House, 1976.

BELL, DANIEL. *The Coming of Post-Industrial Society.* New York: Basic Books, Inc., 1973.

BELLINI, JAMES. *Rule Britannia: A Progress Report for Doomsday 1986.* London: Jonathan Cape, 1981.

BERESINER, YASHA, and NARBETH, COLIN C. *The Story of Paper Money.* Newton Abbot, U.K.: David & Charles, 1973.

BLADON, ASHBY. *How to Cope with the Developing Financial Crisis.* New York: McGraw-Hill, 1980.

BRANSON, NOREEN, and HEINEMAN, MARGOT. *Britain in the Nineteen Thirties.* St. Albans, U.K.: Panther Books Ltd., 1973.

BRETZ, W.G. *Juncture Recognition in the Stock Market.* New York: Vantage Press, 1972.

BROWNE, HARRY, and COXON, TERRY. *Inflation-Proofing Your Investments.* New York: William Morrow & Co., Inc., 1981.

BURNS, ARTHUR F. *The Business Cycle in a Changing World.* New York: National Bureau of Economic Research, 1969.

BURTON, THEODORE E. *Financial Crises and Periods of Industrial and Commercial Depression.* New York: Fraser Publishing Co., 1966.

CARDIFF, GRAY EMERSON, and ENGLISH, JOHN WESLEY. *The Coming Real Estate Crash.* New Rochelle, NY: Arlington House, 1979.

CASEY, DOUGLAS R. *Crisis Investing.* New York: Harper & Row, Stratford Press, 1979.

――――. *Strategic Investing.* New York, Simon & Schuster, 1982.

COGAN, L. PETER. *The Rhythmic Cycles of Optimism and Pessimism.* New York: William-Frederick Press, 1969.

COSLOW, SAMSON. *Super Yields.* New Jersey: The Hirsch Organization, Inc., 1975.

DARST, DAVID M. *The Complete Bond Book.* New York: McGraw-Hill, 1975.

――――. *The Handbook of the Bond and Money Markets.* New York: McGraw-Hill, 1981.

DEWEY, EDWARD R. *Cycles: Selected Writings.* Pittsburgh: Foundation for the Study of Cycles, Inc., 1970.

――――, and DAKIN, EDWIN F. *Cycles: The Science of Prediction.* New York: Henry Holt & Co., 1947.

――――, and MANDINO, OG. *Cycles: The Mysterious Forces That Trigger Events.* New York: Hawthorn Books, Inc., 1971.

DINES, JAMES. *How the Average Investor Can Use Technical Analysis for Stock Profits.* New York: Dines Chart Corporation, 1972.

DONOGHUE, WILLIAM E. with TILLING, THOMAS. *Complete Money Market Guide.* New York: Harper & Row, 1981.

DUIJN, JACOB J. VAN. *The Long Wave in Economic Life.* London: George Allen & Unwin, 1983.

FERGUSSON, ADAM. *When Money Dies.* London: William Kimber & Co. Ltd., 1975.

GALBRAITH, JOHN KENNETH. *The Great Crash, 1929.* Cambridge, MA: The Riverside Press, 1954.

GARRETT, GARET, and ROTHBARD, MURRAY N. *The Great Depression and New Deal Monetary Policy.* San Francisco: Cato Institute, 1980.

GAUQUELIN, MICHEL. *Cosmic Influences on Human Behavior.* London: Garnstone Press, 1973.

GRUBEL, HERBERT G. *The International Monetary System.* Harmondsworth, U.K.: Penguin Books Ltd., 1969.

GUTTMAN, WILLIAM, and MEEHAN, PATRICIA. *The Great Inflation.* Farnborough, U.K.: Saxon House, 1975.

HACKER, ANDREW. *U/S: A Statistical Portrait of the American People.* New York: The Viking Press and Penguin Books, 1983.

HOLT, THOMAS J. *How to Survive and Grow Rich in the Tough Times Ahead.* New York: Rawson, Wade Publishers, Inc., 1981.

HOPPE, DONALD J. *How to Invest in Gold Stocks and Avoid the Pitfalls.* New Rochelle, NY: Arlington House, 1972.

HUFF, DARRELL. *Cycles in Your Life.* New York: W.W. Norton & Co., Inc., 1964.

HUNTINGTON, ELLSWORTH. *Mainsprings of Civilization.* New York: John Wiley & Sons, Inc., 1945.

KAHN, HERMAN. *The Coming Boom.* London: Hutchinson & Co., 1983.

KATZ, HOWARD S. *The Warmongers.* New York: Books in Focus, Inc., 1979.

KINDLEBERGER, CHARLES P. *The World in Depression 1929–1939.* London: The Penguin Press, Allen Lane, 1973.

LUNDBERG, FERDINAND. *The Rich and the Super Rich.* London: Thomas Nelson & Sons Ltd., 1969.

MACKAY, CHARLES, LL.D. *Extraordinary Popular Delusions and the Madness of Crowds.* London: George Harrap & Co. Ltd., 1956.

MADSEN, AXEL. *Private Power*. London: Sphere Books Ltd., Abacus, 1981.

MCMASTER, R. E., JR. *Cycles of War: The Next Six Years*. U.S.: Timberline Trust, 1981.

MERRITT, GILES. *World Out of Work*. London: William Collins, Sons & Co. Ltd., 1982.

MILWARD, ALAN S. and SAUL, S. B. *The Development of the Economies of Continental Europe 1850–1914*. London: George Allen & Unwin Ltd., 1977.

MYERS, C. V. *The Coming Deflation: Its Dangers and Opportunities*. New Rochelle, NY: Arlington House, 1977.

PARIS, ALEXANDER P. *The Coming Credit Collapse: An Update for the 1980s*. Westport, CT: Arlington House, 1980.

PHILLIPS, CABELL. *From the Crash to the Blitz 1929–1939*. New York: Macmillan, 1969.

PICK, CHRISTOPHER, ed. *What's What in the 1980s*. London: Europa Publications Ltd., 1982.

PIGOU, A.C. *Industrial Fluctuations*. London: Macmillan & Co., 1927.

PRING, MARTIN J. *How to Forecast Interest Rates*. New York: McGraw-Hill, 1981.

———. *International Investing Made Easy*. New York: McGraw-Hill, 1981.

QUIGLEY, CARROLL. *Tragedy and Hope: A History of the World in Our Time*. New York: Macmillan, 1966.

REID, MARGARET. *The Secondary Banking Crisis, 1973–75*. London: The Macmillan Press Ltd., 1982.

REZNECK, SAMUEL. *Business Depressions and Financial Panics*. New York: Greenwood Publishing Corp., 1968.

ROLFE, SIDNEY E. and BURTLE, JAMES L. *The Great Wheel: The World Monetary System*. New York: The New York Times Book Co., Quadrangle, 1973.

ROSTOW, W. W. *The World Economy*. London: The Macmillan Press Ltd., 1978.

ROTHBARD, MURRAY N. *America's Great Depression*. Kansas City: Sheed & Ward Inc., 1963.

RUFF, HOWARD J. *How to Prosper During the Coming Bad Years*. New York: The New York Times Book Co., 1979.

SCHULTZ, HARRY D. *Panics and Crashes and How You Can Make Money Out of Them*. New Rochelle, NY: Arlington House, 1972.

SCHUMPETER, JOSEPH A. *Business Cycles*. New York: McGraw Hill, 1939.

———. *History of Economic Development*. London: George Allen & Unwin Ltd., 1954.

———. *The Theory of Economic Development*. Cambridge, MA: Harvard University Press, 1934.

SHILLING, A. GARY, and SOKOLOFF, KIRIL. *Is Inflation Ending? Are You Ready?* New York: McGraw-Hill, 1983.

SHUMAN, JAMES B., and ROSENAU, DAVID. *The Kondratieff Wave*. New York: World Publishing, 1972.

SKOUSEN, MARK. *Complete Guide to Financial Privacy*. Alexandria, VA: Alexandria House, 1979.

SMITH, ADAM. *Paper Money*. New York: Summit Books, 1981.

SPENGLER, OSWALD. *The Decline of the West*. London: George Allen & Unwin Ltd., 1926.

STEIGER, BRAD. *The Roadmap of Time*. New Jersey: Prentice-Hall, Inc., 1972.

STEVENSON, JOHN, and COOK, CHRIS. *The Slump: Society and Politics During the Depression.* Quartet Books Ltd., 1979.

STOCKBRIDGE, FRANK PARKER. *Hedging Against Inflation.* New York: Barron's Publishing Co., 1939.

STOKEN, DICK A. *Cycles: What They Are, What They Mean, How to Profit By Them.* New York: McGraw-Hill, 1978.

SUTTON, ANTONY C. *Energy: The Created Crisis.* New York: Books in Focus, Inc., 1979.

TERKEL, STUDS. *Hard Times: An Oral History of the Depression.* New York: Random House, Pantheon Books, 1970.

THOMAS, GORDON, and MORGAN-WITTS, MAX. *The Day the Bubble Burst.* London: Hamish Hamilton, 1979.

The Timetable of Technology. London: Michael Joseph Ltd., A Marshall Edition, 1982.

TINBERGEN, JAN, and POLAK, J. J. *The Dynamics of Business Cycles.* Chicago: University of Chicago Press, 1950.

TOFFLER, ALVIN. *The Eco-Spasm Report.* New York: Bantam Books, Inc., 1975.

———. *The Third Wave.* London: William Collins, Sons & Co. Ltd., 1980.

WANNISKI, JUDE. *The Way the World Works.* New York: Basic Books, Inc., 1978.

WARREN, GEORGE F., PH. D., and PEARSON, FRANK A., PH. D. *Prices.* New York: John Wiley & Sons, Inc., 1933.

WILSHER, PETER. *The Pound in Your Pocket 1870–1970.* London: Cassell & Co., 1970.

WINSLOW, SUSAN. *Brother, Can You Spare a Dime? America from the Wall Street Crash to Pearl Harbor.* New York: Paddington Press Ltd., 1979.

SELECTED PAPERS AND ARTICLES

BANKS, STEPHEN J. "The Great Inflation." *The Financial Analysts Journal,* May–June 1977, pp. 43–55.

BECKMAN, ROBERT C. "Bricks Without Straw: The Coming Property Crash." *Penthouse,* June 1982, pp. 34–40, 96–98.

———. "Global Bankruptcy." *The Crown Agents Quarterly Review,* Spring 1979.

CETRON, MARVIN J., and CLAYTON, AUDREY. "Turbulence and Tranquility: The Outlook for 26 Nations." *The Futurist,* December 1981, pp. 50–55.

———, and O'TOOLE, THOMAS. "Careers with a Future: Where the Jobs Will Be in the 1990s." *The Futurist,* June 1982, pp. 11–19.

CORNISH, EDWARD. "The Great Depression of the 1980s: How It Might Begin." *The Futurist,* June 1980, pp. 29–34.

DEBENHAM TEWSON & CHINNOCKS, CHARTERED SURVEYORS. "Money into Property 1970–1980." August 1981.

FORRESTER, JAY W. "Changing Economic Patterns." *Technology Review,* August–September 1978, pp. 47–53.

———. "A Near View of Business Cycle Dynamics." *The Journal of Portfolio Management,* Autumn 1976.

FRANCOEUR, ROBERT T. "The Sexual Revolution: Will Hard Times Turn Back the Clock?" *The Futurist,* April 1980, pp. 3–12.

GARVY, GEORGE. "Kondratieff Theory of Long Cycles." *The Review of Economic Statistics* 25 (#4).

HAMIL, RALPH. "Is the Wave of the Future a Kondratieff?" *The Futurist*, October 1979, pp. 381–384.

"Housing: A Crash in '84." *Land & Liberty*, November-December 1982, pp. 110–111.

KAISER, RONALD W. "The Kondratieff Cycle." *The Financial Analysts Journal*, May–June 1979, pp. 57–66.

KITCHIN, JOSEPH. "Cycles and Trends in Economic Factors." *The Review of Economic Statistics* 7 (#4).

KONDRATIEFF, N. D. "The Long Wave of Economic Life." *The Review of Economic Statistics* 17 (#6).

———. "Die Langen Wellender Konjunktur." *Archiv für Sozialwissenschaft und Sozialpolitik*, 1926.

"Kondratieff and the Super Cycle: Deflation or Run-Away Inflation." *The Bank Credit Analyst*, June 1978.

"The Kondratieff Cycle." *The Bank Credit Analyst*, May 1973, pp. 27–35.

"Long Swings I—Kondratieff Invents History." *City Bank Monthly Economic Letter*, January 1978.

"Long Swings II—Kuznets Explains History." *City Bank Monthly Economic Letter*, February 1978.

MADRON, THOMAS WILLIAM. "Political Parties in the 1980s." *The Futurist*, December 1979, pp. 465–475.

MICHAELS, JANE W., BALDWIN, W., and MINARD, LAWRENCE. "Echoes from a Siberian Prison Camp." *Forbes*, November 9, 1981, pp. 164–176.

PETERS, TED. "The Future of Religion in a Post-Industrial Society." *The Futurist*, October 1980, pp. 21–25.

SPEILER, JOSEPH. "The Possible Crash of 1980 and How to Make the Most of It." *Quest*, October 1979, pp. 25–35.

STOKEN, DICK. "What the Long Term Cycle Tells Us About the 1980s: The Kondratieff Cycle and Its Effects on Social Psychology." *The Futurist*, February 1980, pp. 14–19.

VINCENT, HELEN D. "The Correlation of Cultural Cycles with Business." *The Society for the Investigation of Recurring Events*, June 1980.

Index